The Price of Prescription Medicine

Examining Costs, Competition, and Reform in the U.S. Drug Market

snova
New York

Business Issues, Competition and Entrepreneurship Series

Sustainable Business Strategies for Startups and SMEs
Sandeep Poddar, PhD, Biswajit Paul, PhD and Amiya Bhaumik, PhD
ISBN: 979-8-89530-819-6
eBook ISBN: 979-8-89530-875-2

Digital Engagement and Optimization – Systematic Reviews on Social Media, SEO, and Business Strategy
Bonginkosi A. Thango, PhD and Lerato Matshaka, PhD
eBook ISBN: 979-8-89530-736-6

Business Sustainability: Strategies, Practices and Global Implications
Aidin Salamzadeh, PhD
ISBN: 979-8-89530-689-5
eBook ISBN: 979-8-89530-785-4

Entrepreneurship and Innovation Management in the Context of the Knowledge Economy and Digitalization
Yusuf Esmer, PhD and Oğuzhan Aytar, PhD
ISBN: 979-8-89530-744-1
eBook ISBN: 979-8-89530-843-1

Golf and Geopolitics: The PGA–LIV Deal and Saudi Arabia's Influence
Colin Baker (Editor)
ISBN: 979-8-89530-581-2
eBook ISBN: 979-8-89530-594-2

More information about this series can be found at
https://novapublishers.com/product-category/series/business-issues-competition-and-entrepreneurship/

Cornelius Lowery
Editor

The Price of Prescription Medicine

Examining Costs, Competition, and Reform in the U.S. Drug Market

snova
New York

Library of Congress Cataloging-in-Publication Data

ISBN: 979-8-90134-014-1 (Hardcover)
ISBN: 979-8-90134-045-5 (eBook)

Published by Nova Science Publishers, Inc. † New York

Contents

Preface

The United States has the largest prescription drug market in the world, yet Americans pay significantly higher prices for medication than most other nations. These exorbitant costs mean that millions struggle to afford essential prescriptions—despite their availability. Shockingly, one in four patients receives a prescription from their doctor only to find that the price is beyond their reach.

The financial burden of prescription drug costs extends beyond individuals; it strains taxpayers and seniors, driving up expenses for Medicare and Medicaid. Meanwhile, as Americans face prohibitive drug prices, pharmaceutical companies continue to reap immense profits. In 2022 alone, the ten largest pharmaceutical firms in the U.S. amassed over $110 billion in earnings—flourishing while many patients struggle to access the medicine they need.

This book examines the systemic forces shaping prescription drug pricing in the United States, exploring transparency, competition, and policy solutions aimed at ensuring fairness and affordability in the marketplace.

Chapter 1

Why Does the United States Pay, by Far, the Highest Prices in the World for Prescription Drugs?*

Committee on Health, Education, Labor, and Pensions

Thursday, February 8, 2024

U.S. Senate, Committee on Health, Education, Labor, and Pensions, Washington, DC.

The Committee met, pursuant to notice, at 10 a.m., in room 430, Dirksen Senate Office Building, Hon. Bernard Sanders, Chairman of the Committee, presiding.

Present: Senators Sanders [presiding], Murray, Casey, Baldwin, Murphy, Kaine, Hassan, Smith, Luja`n, Hickenlooper, Markey, Cassidy, Paul, Collins, Braun, Marshall, Romney, and Tuberville.

---

* This is an edited, reformatted and augmented version of Hearing of the Committee on Health, Education, Labor, and Pensions, United States Senate, One Hundred Eighteenth Congress Second Session on Examining the Cost of Prescription Drugs, Publication No. S. HRG. 118–320, dated February 8, 2024.

In: The Price of Prescription Medicine
Editor: Cornelius Lowery
ISBN: 979-8-90134-014-1

Opening Statement of Senator Sanders

The CHAIR. The Senate Committee on Health, Education, Labor, and Pensions will come to order. Today is a busy day. As we all know, a very important vote is going to be taking place and Republicans Democrats will be meeting in their caucuses. So, people are going to be coming in and out.

I also think that this hearing is important enough that we extend the time for questioning from the usual 5 minutes to 7 minutes, if that is okay with folks. Let me begin by welcoming the CEOs of Bristol-Myers Squibb, Chris—Chris Boerner. We thank you for being here. CEO of Merck, Robert Davis. We thank you for being here. And the CEO of Johnson & Johnson, Joaquin Duato, for being with us this morning, thanks very much.

There is a lot of discussion in our Nation about how divided our people are on many issues, and that is absolutely true. But on one of the most important issues facing our Country, the American people, whether they are Democrats, Republicans, Independents, Conservative, Progressive, could not be more united, and that is the need to substantially lower the outrageous price of prescription drugs in this country.

According to a recent poll, 82 percent of Americans say the cost of prescription drugs is too high and 73 percent say that the Government is not doing enough to regulate drug prices. As a Nation, we spend almost twice as much per capita on health care as do people of any other country—$13,000 for every man, woman, and child.

One of the reasons that we spend so much is the high cost of prescription drugs in our Country. The outrageous cost of prescription drugs in America means that one out of four of our people go to the doctor, get a prescription, and they cannot afford to fill that prescription. How many die as a result of that, how many suffer unnecessarily, nobody knows. But my guess is it is in the millions, and I have talked to many of them in Vermont and around the country.

Meanwhile, our insurance premiums are much higher than they should be, and hospital costs are soaring because of the high cost of prescription drugs. Further, the cost of prescription drugs in this country is putting an enormous burden on taxpayers and seniors by raising the cost of Medicare and Medicaid. Medicare alone spends at least $135 billion a year on prescription drugs.

This is not only a personal issue. It is an issue of the Federal budget. Meanwhile, as we pay by far the highest prices in the world for prescription drugs, 10 of the top pharmaceutical companies in America made over $110 billion in profits in 2022. They are doing phenomenally well while Americans cannot afford the cost of the medicine they need and the CEOs in general receive exorbitant compensation packages.

This morning, we are going to hear a lot from our CEO panelists about how high prices are not their fault, and that the PBMs are forcing Americans to pay much higher prices than they should be paying.

But let us be clear, in 2022, Johnson & Johnson made nearly $18 billion in profit, paid its CEO over $27 million in compensation, and spent over $17 billion on stock buybacks and dividends. That same year, Merck made $14.5 billion in profits, handed out over $7 billion in dividends in their—to their stockholders, and paid its CEO over $52 million in compensation.

Bristol-Myers Squibb made $8 billion in profits last year, while recently spending over $12 billion on stock buybacks and dividends and giving its CEO over $41 million in compensation. Now, why did a majority of Members of this Committee invite these three pharmaceutical CEOs to testify today?

The answer is pretty simple. Mr. Boerner, we will want you to explain to the American people why Bristol-Myers Squibb charges patients in our Country $7,100 a year for ELIQUIS, when that same exact product can be purchased for just $900 in Canada and $650 in France.

Mr. Duato, we are going to ask you why Johnson & Johnson charges Americans with arthritis $79,000 for STELARA, when that same exact product can be purchased for just $20,000 in Canada and just $12,000 in France. Mr. Davis, please tell us later why Merck—why Merck charges Americans with cancer $191,000 a year for KEYTRUDA, when that same product can be purchased for $112,000 in Canada and $91,000 in France.

Let's be clear, Johnson & Johnson, Merck, and Bristol-Myers Squibb are not just charging higher prices in the United States compared to other countries. They are also charging Americans much higher prices today than they did in the past even accounting for inflation.

From 2004 to 2008, the median price of innovative new drugs sold by these three companies was just $14,000, inflation accounted. From 2019 to 2023, where we are today, the median price of new drugs sold by these three companies was $238,000.

In other words, Americans are forced to pay higher and higher prices for the drugs they need to survive. And let's be clear, the overwhelming beneficiary of these high drug prices is the pharmaceutical industry.

How do we know that? Well, that is precisely what they tell their investors. According to their own shareholder reports, Bristol- Myers Squibb made $34 billion selling the blood thinner ELIQUIS in the United States, compared to just $22 billion in the rest of the world combined. Make their money in the United States.

In other words, the U.S. accounts for nearly two-thirds of all global sales of ELIQUIS. Not a single dollar of this revenue is going to PBMs. 100 percent of it is going through Bristol-Myers Squibb. Johnson & Johnson has reported to its shareholders that it made over $30 billion in revenue selling the arthritis drug STELARA in the United States since 2016, more than twice as much as the rest of the world combined.

Nothing to do with PBMs. Merck has reported to its shareholders that it made $43.4 billion selling the cancer drug KEYTRUDA in the United States, compared to $30 billion in the rest of the world combined.

Now, our CEO panelists from the drug companies will tell us this morning how much it costs to develop new drugs and how often the research that they undertake for new cures is not successful. And they are right. We appreciate that.

But what they have not told us in their written testimony is that 14 major pharmaceutical companies, including Johnson & Johnson and Merck, spent $87 billion more on stock buybacks and dividends over recent 10 year period than what they spent on research and development—more on stock buybacks and dividends than in research and development.

In fact, Bristol-Myers Squibb spent 3.2 billion more on stock buybacks and dividends in 2022 that it spent on research and development. Johnson & Johnson spent $46 billion more on stock buybacks and dividends than it spent on research and development since 2012.

In other words, these companies are spending more to enrich their own stockholders and CEOs than they are in finding new cures and new treatments. Now, the average American who hears all of this is asking a very simple question, how does all of this happen? What is going on? How could your companies charge us, in some cases, ten times more than they charge Canadians, people around the world for the same drug?

How did they get away with this when so many of our people cannot afford the high prices of the drugs that they need? How can it be uniquely among industrialized countries that these companies, not just these companies but the pharmaceutical industry in general, can raise prices any time they want to any level they want—want to raise double prices, do it any way they want. How do they get away with all of that?

Here, in my view, is the answer. The U.S. Government does not regulate drug companies. With very few exceptions, the drug companies regulate the U.S. Government. That is the sad state of affairs in a corrupt political system.

Over the past 25 years, the pharmaceutical industry, not just these companies, the entire industry, spent over $8.5 billion on lobbying and more than $745 million on campaign contributions.

Let me be fair here. I don't want to misspeak. They are bipartisan. They give to Republicans. They give to Democrats. I am especially impressed by the Pfizer drug company—Pfizer is not here this morning contributing $1 million to the Republican Party in Kentucky to expand its headquarters named after Republican leader Mitch McConnell.

But again, it is not just Republicans. It is Democrats as well. Unbelievable, this is an astounding fact. Last year, drug companies had over 1,800 well-paid lobbyist here in D.C. to make sure that Congress did their bidding. There are 535 Members of Congress and 1,800 well paid lobbyists, over three for every Member of Congress.

If you want to know why you are paying the highest prices in the world, America, that is why. Now, here is some good news in the midst of all that. We are beginning, beginning to take on the greed of the pharmaceutical industry.

As a result of the Inflation Reduction Act passed several years ago, Medicare for the first time ever is beginning to do what every major country on Earth does and what the Veterans Administration has been doing for over 30 years, and that is to negotiate the lower prices of drugs, including JANUVIA, STELARA, and ELIQUIS.

Let me conclude by saying this, I am proud of what this Committee up to this point has accomplished. Last year, as you will all remember, the CEO of Moderna committed during a HELP Committee hearing that his company would make certain that no one in America would have to pay for their vaccine out-of-pocket.

We appreciated that. In a separate health Committee hearing last May, the CEO of Eli Lilly committed that his company would not raise prices on existing insulin products after having, in fact, lowered them.

But let's be clear, much more needs to be done. I look forward to hearing from our CEO panelists this morning as to how they are going to go forward to substantially lower the cost of prescription drugs in this country.

Senator Cassidy, you are now recognized for your opening state- ment.

Opening Statement of Senator Cassidy

Senator CASSIDY. Thank you. Thank you, Chair Sanders. Let's just be clear, everybody on this panel cares about the high cost of prescription drugs and wants to work on real solutions to address this.

But it is also clear that this hearing is not about finding legislative solutions. It is kind of following a formula. Republicans—we publicly attack private—I don't but others, publicly attack private citizens for being successful under capitalism. We grossly over- simplify our problem and blame corporations.

We demand CEOs come before the Committee for public verbal stoning. We reject the offer to send top executives with subject matter expertise and responsibility regarding issues at hand, and threaten a subpoena when CEOs are suspicious that they won't get a fair shake. Hold the hearing, get sound bites, then pick another set of CEOs for a show trial, but we don't pass meaningful legislation.

That sounds familiar. That has been the hearing of Starbucks founder Howard Schultz, Moderna CEO Stephane Bancel, and now this hearing with the same formula. I would have gladly joined the Chair in explore exploring solutions to address the high cost of prescription drugs. I am a doc. I worked in a public hospital for the uninsured for 25 years. I did my best to get care to those who otherwise would not have received.

I am aware of this. I am also aware of the perverse incentives. The kind of like, my gosh, it shouldn't be high, but it is high. Bad actors game the system and we need solutions that benefit patients and improve access. But the majority was not interested in working with this side of the dais to hold a serious hearing to inform serious legislation.

They didn't seek Republican input. The goal was to haul you guys in, decry capitalism, and blame these corporations for the high cost of drug prices. Now, by the way, of course, drug companies play a role, and hopefully we will get answers today to legitimate questions about how drugs are priced.

But the problem is far greater and more complex than individual companies or even a set of companies within an ecosystem, which is incredibly complex. Why do Americans pay more for certain drugs than patients in other countries? To understand, we need to have a serious effort to navigate the network of perverse incentives throughout the health care system.

I lived in it for 25 years. I am very kind of aware of it. Taking a substantial look at insurance benefit design, price transparency, regulatory barriers, intellectual property barriers, the perverse effect Government discount programs have upon prices charged to commercial patients, etcetera.

One example, just to say again a little bit of complexity here. The 340B drug program resulted in a $54 billion in drug discounts in 2022, but we actually don't know if those discounts lowered prices for the patient who bought the drug.

There are reports that patients paid cash when the intermediary took the full price, even though 340B should have lowered it. That is a serious investigation being conducted by this side of the dais that the other side of the dais was not interested in participating in. That is an understanding of an ecosystem.

I understand there is no one more eloquent than Chair Sanders on Medicare for all, and we can cherry pick examples of how other countries are doing something better. I can cherry pick the opposite. Canada is struggling—just to show you that there is a complexity here. Let me just take an example. Canada is struggling with specialty care.

In May of last year, the Canadian government began to send 4,800 Canadians from British Columbia to Washington State to ''ensure people have faster access to life saving radiation treatment.'' They can afford their system because we are right next door.

Relatedly to this hearing into that, Alison Decliso, a Canadian woman paid for her own treatment in the United States after the provincial health authority in British Columbia denied her access to life saving chemotherapy.

Canada had a lower cost drug, SOLO. They didn't carry the chemotherapy, so she paid for it out of pocket in the United States so she could have lifesaving chemotherapy. The United States is not perfect, but if we cherry pick from other countries, we have to do a more thorough investigation to see, is there a balance there?

Now let's return to prescriptions. Canadians pay less than we do. Let's figure out why. But let's also point out the public health insurance in Canada only covers 21 percent of newly developed drugs.

Now, maybe that is a tradeoff, but I can tell you, you tell an American that they can't have access to a lifesaving court—a life-saving drug, they are going to see you in court. They are going to sue, and they are going to say, I want that access.

The UK only covers 48 percent of newly available drugs. Americans just would not tolerate that. It is fair to say that Ms. Decliso, all those radiation treatment patients, are those not getting the newly developed lifesaving drugs as quickly might die in those countries that don't have access to the same treatments as do we in the U.S.

These are serious questions. One more time, I am a doc. I am aware of this, but we need to fully consider all these issues and then maybe bring you in at the end, but we will bring you in with a context which is complete as opposed to isolated. As I said at the start, it would be best if this were a genuine exercise.

I am so willing to do the work on this, as are my colleagues. We have shown that willingness on work on PBM reforms and generic drugs. And even though the Chair and I got off to a rocky start, we did some pretty good work on that, Mr. Chair. I think we got some good bipartisan legislation.

This Committee, I agree with you, can accomplish that. But I don't want the Committee to devolve into a CEO whack a mole, ends up with no serious legislation as a result. Further proof of what I consider the unserious and cynical nature of this hearing is that the minority asked the Chair to have a witness on the panel that could actually explore some of these issues side by side these CEOs.

That was turned down. We wanted an academic expert in drug pricing who could provide unbiased and substantial input to the issues at hand. Our witness was not allowed. He will be on the next, but the way this works is this get all the publicity and the next one gets crickets.

We have not had that opportunity. And I will also point out we didn't split the majority of minority witnesses into different panels during several hearings, which promoted kind of labor union issues. I can think of no reason to not allow our witness to be here now except perhaps ruining the optics.

As I said at our last markup, what ends up being hollow messaging gives D.C. a bad reputation. Folks want real answers. They want relief from high prices. It is in part what we are going to hear today, but it will be separated from a context that would have made it a lot more productive.

If you are telling voters you are going to do something when you know at the get go you have no legislative solution which emerges, and that is why folks don't trust.

If we are just looking for a social media clip, then I suppose we have accomplished something, but let's make a difference for the people whom we represent—for those patients in hospitals who I once treated who otherwise would not have access to care.

We have the ability to craft meaningful legislation. Let's do it. With that, I yield.

The CHAIR. Thank you, Senator Cassidy. Our first witness will be Joaquin Duato, Chairman and CEO of Johnson & Johnson. Mr. Duato has served as Johnson & Johnson's Chairman since 2023, and Chief Executive Officer since 2022. Mr. Duato, thanks very much for being with us.

Statement of Joaquin Duato, Chief Executive Officer, Johnson & Johnson, New Brunswick, NJ

Mr. DUATO. Chairman Sanders, Ranking Member Cassidy, and Members of the Committee, thank you for the opportunity to be here today.

Johnson & Johnson has collaborated with this Committee over several decades to advance health care solutions for patients, including on diversity in clinical trials, nursing and health care workforce, pandemic preparation, mental health, and regulatory pathways for novel cell and gene therapies.

I applaud this Committee for your commitment to such critical priorities. I have been with J&J for more than 35 years and have held roles in Europe and in the U.S. I understand the global challenges and complexities of health care innovation and delivery, and today I look forward to discussing our approach to pricing and the work we do to advance health care for all Americans.

Fundamentally, our decisionmaking is guided by the values set forth on our credo, which states that our first responsibility is to the patients. Our drug pricing decisions reflect our commitment to bringing forward innovative medicines for patients today and for patients tomorrow.

First, our prices are based on the value our medicines bring to patients, the healthcare system, and society. We take into consideration that our medicines improve patient's quality of life and show revival rates, while often reducing health care costs. And for context, in 2022, the average net price of our medicines declined for the sixth year in a row by 3.5 percentage points.

Over those 6 years, prices have declined by almost 20 percent, and the real inflation adjusted price decline was more than 40 percent. Second, we price our medicines to support patient access.

In 2022 alone, we paid $39 billion in rebate discounts and fees, almost 60 percent of the average list price of our drugs, with the intent that patients benefit from these substantial cost savings. We also support patient affordability and access by funding patient assistance programs.

In 2022, these programs helped more than 1 billion—1 million underinsured patients. And we donated $3.8 billion in free medicines, another support, to help patients with no insurance.

Finally, we price our medicines to meet our commitment to innovate and develop different novel medicines for patients. The investment required to do so is massive. The average cost of bringing a drug through clinical trials in our industry is more than $2 billion.

However, more than 90 percent of the drugs that enter clinical trials do not make it to patients. Consequently, our R&D investment is enormous and totally—totals near $78 billion since 2016.

Despite the tremendous investment required to bring drugs to patients, drug costs in the U.S. have not increased significantly as a percentage of total overall health care costs. In fact, the largest spending in the U.S. is about 14 percent of health care spending, slightly below the average for the rest of the world.

While total U.S. health care spending is higher than other developed nations, this spending allows American patients to receive cutting edge health care earlier than any other country in the world.

However, the burdensome co-pay obligations imposed in the U.S. are hard for patients to meet and undermine access and health equity. Remarkably, the GAO found that patient co-pay obligations often exceed payer costs for their drugs. This means that patients sometimes pay more for their medicines than their insurers.

Clearly, this part of the system is not working as intended. We support proposals to reconcile this inequity and to ensure patient access. As outlined in my testimony, Congress should stop middlemen from taking for themselves the assistance that pharmaceutical companies intend for patients.

Finally, it is essential that we reject the price caps and controls that exist in other countries which stunt innovation. Our nation's robust biopharmaceutical industry was created by policy choices that prioritized earlier patient access to breakthrough medicines and incentivized investment in medical innovation.

Thank you for the bipartisan efforts of this Committee and for the opportunity to engage in today's discussion. I look forward to your questions.

[The prepared statement of Mr. Duato follows.]

Prepared Statement of Joaquin Duato

Chairman Sanders, Ranking Member Cassidy, and Senators of the Committee, I am the Chief Executive Officer of Johnson & Johnson and the Chairman of the Board of Directors, positions I assumed in January 2022 and 2023. I joined Johnson & Johnson in 1989, and for the first 13 years of my tenure, I held various executive positions with the company in Europe. Over my thirty-five years with the company, I have held roles in both our Innovative Medicine sector and MedTech sector. As I have practiced and witnessed throughout my career, Johnson & Johnson's decisionmaking is guided by the values set forth in Our Credo, first adopted in 1943, which states that our first responsibility is to the patients, doctors, nurses, parents, and all others who use our products and services. This responsibility extends to both the patients who need our innovative medicines today to treat some of the most challenging and life-threatening diseases, and to the patients of tomorrow, who need us to continue to research cures and treatments for the unmet medical needs that they will face in the future.

Johnson & Johnson has collaborated with this Committee over several decades to advance the important work of pursuing novel healthcare solutions that benefit patients. Our engagement with the Committee has contributed to the efforts to address the mental health crisis, modernize the biopharmaceutical and medical technology regulatory pathways, provide critical access to affordable medicines and medical technologies, examine frameworks for use of artificial intelligence in health, enhance diversity in clinical trials, ensure pandemic preparedness, and support frontline healthcare workers and their daily challenges. I have long admired this Committee's ability to find common ground and deliver solutions for patients. Having held roles in the United States and Europe, and as a dual citizen of the United States and Spain, I understand well the global challenges and complexities of healthcare innovation and delivery.

I am grateful for the opportunity to discuss these issues, and Our Credo values that shape Johnson & Johnson's approach to pricing for our innovative medicines. I look forward to sharing with you our perspectives on how we may collaborate to improve access to and affordability of medicines for all Americans, while continuing to bring to patients the life-changing and lifesaving medicines that are the hallmark of American healthcare.

Introduction

Johnson & Johnson's drug pricing decisions integrate our commitment to bringing innovative therapies to the patients who need them today, and our dedication to continuous research, innovation, and development of the next generation of medicines across dozens of diseases for the patients of tomorrow.

In furtherance of those objectives, we price our therapies, first and foremost, based on the value that our therapies bring to patients, the healthcare system, and society. Johnson & Johnson focuses on developing transformational therapies that address challenging and complex unmet medical needs. Our drugs improve patients' quality of life and survival rates, while also reducing overall healthcare costs, for example, through fewer surgeries and hospital admissions. The pricing of our medicines reflects these important life-saving, life-enhancing, and financial benefits.

Second, we price our medicines to further our commitment to patient access. To that end, Johnson & Johnson pays significant rebates, discounts, and fees to pharmacy benefit managers (PBMs), payors, and other ''middlemen'' in the healthcare system. It is our intent in making those concessions that patients benefit from these cost savings, not these intermediaries. To foster an open dialog regarding the appropriate recipients of these savings—PBMs, payors, or patients—we started publishing information about our pricing 6 years ago in our annual Transparency Report, available online for all to review. As detailed in the most recent issue, the average net price of our medicines declined for the sixth year in a row, and cumulatively by almost 20 percent over that period. During that same timeframe, consumer prices rose by more than 20 percent, which equates to a decline in the real, inflation-adjusted pricing for our drugs of more than 40 percent. The decline in our average net price is due in large part to the increased amounts paid to these middlemen. In 2022 alone, our average net price declined by 3.5 percent, attributable to our payment of $39 billion in rebates, discounts, and fees to others in the healthcare system— constituting almost 60 percent of the average list price of our drugs.

In addition to these price reductions, Johnson & Johnson furthers patient access by funding patient assistance programs designed to help manage copay obligations and provide free medicines to underinsured patients. As the Transparency Report details, in 2022, these patient assistance programs helped more than one million underinsured patients access Johnson & Johnson therapies their doctors prescribed. We also donated $3.8 billion in free products and other financial support through independent programs and foundations to help uninsured patients obtain the therapies they need.

Third, we price our products to allow us to meet our commitment to innovate and develop new and novel medicines for the patients of today and tomorrow. To do so, we must price our existing medicines at levels sufficient to cover the investment required to pursue the development of broad portfolios of new drug candidates. The requisite investment is massive, as the average cost of bringing a drug candidate through clinical trials to patients is $2.6 billion over 10 years, across the industry. Moreover, we must pursue numerous drug candidates on parallel tracks because, across the industry, approximately 90 percent of the drugs that enter clinical trials (and 92 percent of cancer drugs) fail before they can make it to market. Even after a drug is approved and reaches patients, only around 20 percent to 30 percent of new drugs recoup the significant investments necessary to bring them to market. Consequently, Johnson & Johnson's pharmaceutical research and development spending is enormous, with an investment of $77.7 billion since 2016, $11.6 billion in 2022, and $12 billion in 2023. To our knowledge, this is one of the largest annual investments in research and development made among any of our biopharmaceutical industry peers. Accordingly, we must price our drugs both to recover funds for the investments made and to allow us to continue these efforts—including investments in promising drug candidates that ultimately fail and therefore generate no revenue.

Despite the tremendous investment required to sustain the flow of new medicines, drug costs in the United States have not increased appreciably as a percentage of overall healthcare costs in over a decade. Moreover, the level of drug costs as a percentage of total healthcare spending in the United States is about 14 percent, slightly below the average for other major markets. In some instances, the prices of drugs in the United States are higher than in other countries—and so are the costs of other healthcare services in the United States. This spending allows patients in the United States to receive cutting-edge healthcare as compared to patients elsewhere in the world, including obtaining markedly earlier and broader access to breakthrough innovative medicines.

Conversely, there is one notable attribute of the U.S. healthcare system that differentiates it from other countries in a way that is detrimental to patients. The United States healthcare system alone imposes onerous copayment obligations on patients, which are becoming harder for patients to meet and are undermining access and health equity. There is broad agreement among experts and policymakers that the copayment obligations imposed by both government programs and private insurers is a primary reason for patients' failure to complete prescribed courses of drug therapy, even with regard to cancer and other life-threatening diseases. Remarkably, as the Government Accountability Office found when analyzing the most highly rebated Part D drugs, patients' copay obligations often exceed payors' net costs for those drugs because rebates and other incentives paid by manufacturers to payors are not passed on directly to patients. The diversion of those price reductions from patients to middlemen is one reason that copayment obligations are neither an equitable nor effective means for controlling drug prices. We support the following proposals that have been advanced to address this inequity and to ensure patients receive the full course of drugs prescribed by their physicians.

First, we agree that patient copayment obligations should be reduced. The imposition of lower caps on out-of-pocket costs for Medicare patients under the Inflation Reduction Act (IRA) is a good first step. But access problems remain across multiple markets. Policymakers should closely monitor the effect of these changes to ensure they improve patient access in practice and, in addition, consider ways to reduce cost sharing in the commercial market.

Second, Congress or the Centers for Medicare & Medicaid Services (CMS) should stop payors, PBMs, and their agents from taking for themselves the copayment assistance that Johnson & Johnson and other companies intend for patients by eliminating the economic incentive to do so. As 19 Senators recognized in a recent letter to CMS, certain payors and PBMs have been capturing for themselves the benefits of copay assistance by excluding the patient assistance payments when assessing whether patients have met the copayment caps imposed by law. The economic effect of these programs—with benign-sounding names like ''accumulators,'' ''maximizers,'' and ''alternative funding programs''—is to divert the patient assistance from patients to payors. These programs should be barred, and patients should be allowed to receive the intended benefits of the assistance.

Third, Congress should require that PBMs and payors pass on to patients the rebates and other concessions they demand that manufacturers pay. Overall, in 2022, almost 60 percent of the list price of our medicines went to rebates, discounts, and fees, in many cases as a result of the financial demands of payors and others in the healthcare system. While the amount of these concessions is significant and increasing each year, studies show that the majority of these amounts is retained by these intermediaries and not passed along to patients. No other healthcare system tolerates the diversion of discounts intended for patients to these middlemen.

Fourth, Johnson & Johnson supports pending legislation—such as the Pharmacy Benefit Manager Reform Act passed by this Committee last year—designed to address certain PBM practices that distort the healthcare delivery system by ensuring transparency to the payors that utilize PBM services. This legislation, especially if expanded to require delinking of PBM fees from list prices, would be an important step toward aligning incentives for lower net costs and improved patient access.

Finally, it is essential that the United States reject the price caps and controls that exist in other countries and serve to stunt innovation and deprive patients of life-saving medicines. Our nation's robust biopharmaceutical industry was created and fostered by deliberate policy choices that prioritized and incentivized investment in medical innovation in exchange for a period of patent and regulatory exclusivity that enables innovators to price at levels required to recoup their investments and reinvest in the future. As reflected in the Constitution, this nation's founders recognized as a fundamental tenet, and a cornerstone of a free and capitalistic economy, that the award of exclusivity promotes progress. We can only make the significant research and development investments we do because U.S. policy has respected manufacturers' patent rights and afforded periods of market exclusivity for innovations. Those exclusivity periods are limited and often curtailed because they run from the date of invention, not from the date of market entry, which can be years thereafter. Moreover, as part of the laudable social bargain, upon expiry of patent and regulatory exclusivities, generic drug and biosimilar manufacturers are legally authorized to rely upon and leverage the innovator's investment in safety and efficacy studies to bring competitive drugs to the market. That social bargain is one reason that—over time and on average—drug costs in the United States are only 14 percent of total healthcare costs, which is below the average for other major markets. We support policies that encourage other countries to do more to foster innovation, rather than misguided approaches that would result in the United States doing less. This is critical not only to the health of the United States, but also to our Nation's financial and national security.

The remainder of my testimony contains additional details regarding each of these important subjects.

Investment in Innovation Leads to Treatments and Cures

For more than a century, Johnson & Johnson has created breakthrough scientific innovations that address some of the nation's most important medical needs. We are proud of our proven history of pharmaceutical innovation. Since 2016, our total investments in pharmaceutical research and development have reached $77.7 billion. In 2022 alone, Johnson & Johnson committed $11.6 billion to the discovery and development of medicines. In 2023, we invested $12 billion in pharmaceutical research and development (and $15.1 billion in research and development across the company).

Since 2016, our investment in the next generation of transformative medicines resulted in eight new drugs approved by the Food and Drug Administration (FDA) and an additional fifty-two approvals for expanded indications or new product formulations. Johnson & Johnson may achieve eight more significant approvals by the FDA in 2024. These medicines, if approved, will offer treatments for serious diseases, including multiple myeloma and lung cancer. Johnson & Johnson has an additional 11 significant FDA regulatory submissions that are planned for later this year. In addition, we expect to obtain important data this year from eight Phase III trials and three Phase II trials, which will inform the clinical and regulatory strategy for these significant programs in our pipeline. These figures do not include our entire clinical development portfolio, nor the substantial investment in drug discovery, including internally, in incubator settings and in stand-alone companies.

These significant investments by Johnson & Johnson—and other innovators in the biopharmaceutical industry—have had dramatic effects on the lives of Americans: people live longer and achieve a better quality of life. From 1990 to 2015, biopharmaceutical drugs accounted for at least an estimated 35 percent of the increase in U.S. life expectancy. Over that same period, pharmaceuticals accounted for 76 percent of the mortality reduction achieved for HIV, 60 percent of mortality reduction in cerebrovascular disease, 60 percent of mortality reduction in malignant breast tumors, 52 percent of mortality reduction in ischemic heart disease, and 27 percent of mortality reduction in colon, rectal, and related cancers.

The industry continues to invest in new and life-changing medicines. Across the healthcare sector, the biopharmaceutical industry's spending on research and development accounts for 75 percent of all U.S. investment in medical and health research and development. The biopharmaceutical industry has a robust pipeline of more than 8,000 medicines in clinical development, including more than 800 treatments and cures for diseases that disproportionately affect minority communities.

The medicines that the Committee has identified, and that we are discussing today, are illustrative of the benefits that Johnson & Johnson's investment in medical innovation brings to patients and their providers, and I would like to address each one briefly.

Stelara. Stelara is an innovative treatment for certain chronic and debilitating immune-related diseases. Stelara is approved for the treatment of adult patients with moderate to severe plaque psoriasis, active psoriatic arthritis, moderately to severely active Crohn's disease, and moderately to severely active ulcerative colitis, as well as the treatment of pediatric patients ages 6 years and older with moderate to severe plaque psoriasis and active psoriatic arthritis. These debilitating diseases can cause inflammation, ulcers, pain, bleeding, and serious complications in the intestines; painful itching, burning, and scaling of the skin; and painful swollen and tender joints. Patients living with Crohn's disease and ulcerative colitis are at increased risk for hospitalization and surgery, which both carry risks for patients and cost burdens for the healthcare system.

Stelara was the first significant therapeutic advancement over the prior generation of treatments, TNF-inhibitors. Stelara can have a significant positive impact on patients. For Crohn's disease, a majority of patients were in remission 1 year after responding to the initial treatment with Stelara.

Xarelto. Xarelto is a type of blood thinner called a direct oral anticoagulant that helps patients facing conditions that put them at risk of blood clots, which can lead to thrombotic events such as heart attacks, strokes, and pulmonary embolisms. Initially invented by Bayer in Germany, Johnson & Johnson partnered with Bayer to bring the medication to patients in the United States.

Xarelto is a therapeutic advancement over other blood thinners, such as warfarin. Xarelto's benefits include fewer food and drug interactions, easier standardized dosing, and the elimination of invasive and costly blood tests required with some other therapies. Medical treatment guidelines provide that direct oral anticoagulants, including Xarelto, are preferable to warfarin for certain serious conditions such as nonvalvular atrial fibrillation and venous thromboembolism. Moreover, in about half of its FDA-approved indications, Xarelto is the only approved direct oral anticoagulant.

Imbruvica. Imbruvica is a once-daily oral therapy for the treatment of chronic lymphocytic leukemia and other blood cancers, including small lymphocytic lymphoma and Waldenstrom's macroglobulinemia. It has helped evolve the standard of care for adult patients living with B-cell malignancies, who until about a decade ago had poor prognoses and had to rely largely on chemotherapy and chemoimmunotherapy as the main treatment options available. Imbruvica is the only medicine in its class that has demonstrated a statistically significant overall survival benefit in first-line chronic lymphocytic leukemia and an established safety profile gained through clinical studies, long term follow up, and safety monitoring.

Symtuza. Symtuza is the first complete, darunavir-based single-tablet regimen for the treatment of HIV in adults and children who weigh at least 40kg. Developed by Johnson & Johnson, in collaboration with Gilead Sciences, Inc., Symtuza combines the proven high barrier to resistance of darunavir with a formulation designed for improved tolerability and the convenience of a single-tablet regimen. Symtuza offers an important treatment option for patients. Symtuza has been studied and used in patients who have never been on medications to treat HIV, as well as in those patients who have previously been well controlled on HIV medications and are not known to have any viral resistance to the components of Symtuza.

Pharmaceutical Pricing and Access to Johnson & Johnson Medicines

Johnson & Johnson's approach to pharmaceutical pricing balances our commitment to bring innovative therapies to the patients who need them today, and our dedication to continuous research, innovation, and development of the next generation of medicines across dozens of diseases. We strive to understand and address the serious health problems of today and create the potential medicines of tomorrow.

In setting the prices of its drugs, Johnson & Johnson follows three guiding principles:

1) Value to patients, the healthcare system, and society. In setting drug prices, a primary consideration is the value that the drug brings to patients, the healthcare system, and society as a whole. For patients, these considerations can include improvements in health, an extended lifespan, and an improved quality of life—such as the ability to take a pill rather than travel to a health center for an infusion, or conversely, to take a long-acting, twice-yearly injection rather than a daily pill. For the healthcare system, pharmaceutical innovations can

significantly reduce other costs, such as surgeries and hospital admissions.

2) Affordable access to medicines. Our approach to drug pricing reflects our commitment to making our innovations available to patients who need them. First, we negotiate with insurance companies—and the pharmacy benefit managers they engage to negotiate on their behalves—to encourage insurance plans to cover our medicines. These entities are gatekeepers to patients. We work with these companies to demonstrate the value that our products bring to their policyholders, and we engage in negotiations on discounts and rebates that reduce the costs for our drugs. Second, we seek to ensure that a patient's financial situation is not a barrier to access through a variety of programs and approaches that promote patient access. For example, Johnson & Johnson's Janssen CarePath patient support program provides options for underinsured patients with commercial or private health insurance through solutions like copay assistance and medications free of charge.
3) Investing in future cures and treatments. As demonstrated by our robust pipeline, Johnson & Johnson is dedicated to bringing the next generation of treatments and cures to patients. Drug development is costly and uncertain. Our approach to pricing therefore must include the ability to invest in innovation for the patients of tomorrow. Developing a new medicine requires, on average, a $2.6 billion investment over 10 years. Pharmaceutical pricing must allow for and fund research into potential innovations that ultimately fail. In fact, most promising drugs do not succeed, whether due to unacceptable side effects, limited efficacy, or other factors. Across the industry, approximately 90 percent of candidate medicines that show sufficient promise to warrant a Phase I clinical trial do not eventually result in a new FDA approval. This reality means that the revenue from only about 10 percent of all drugs investigated for therapeutic potential in clinical trials must fund the research and development of all failed drug candidates and the research and development of all innovative treatments and cures of tomorrow. Even more, only around 20 percent to 30 percent of new drugs recoup the significant investments needed to bring them through approval and to patients.

With this understanding of the framework for Johnson & Johnson drug pricing, it is essential to consider the significant and substantial rebates, discounts, and fees that reduce Johnson & Johnson's revenue and result in a much lower effective price of our medicines than may seem apparent from the list price of our drugs. Because pricing trends and the extent of the diversion of discounts and patient assistance away from patients are, unfortunately, hidden from the public by our Country's byzantine drug pricing system, Johnson & Johnson has committed to transparency in its drug pricing and has issued a transparency report every year since 2016.

In Johnson & Johnson's most recent Transparency Report, issued in mid–2023, the company reported that the actual price of its medicines had declined for the sixth year in a row. In 2022, the average net price of Johnson & Johnson's medicines declined 3.5 percent.

There is a striking gap between the list price of medicines—often misleadingly cited in the media and by some in Congress—and the actual amount that Johnson & Johnson receives for its medicines. In 2022, Johnson & Johnson recorded $39 billion in rebates, discounts, and fees to commercial insurers, government programs, and others in the healthcare system. Overall, in 2022, Johnson & Johnson received well under half of the list price of its medicines—almost 60 percent of the list price instead went to rebates, discounts, and fees, in many cases as a result of the financial demands of payors and others in the healthcare system.

These middlemen also put financial pressure on patients, as insurance companies have continued to impose higher deductibles, higher copays, and higher coinsurance requirements—even for patients who thought they were well insured. Nearly a quarter of Americans are now considered underinsured, meaning that they are open to significant financial risk from a healthcare necessity or find that the care they need is financially out of reach because of the requirements imposed by their insurance provider. Since 2014, commercially insured patients with deductibles have experienced a 50 percent increase in out-of-pocket costs for brand medications due to these tactics.

Johnson & Johnson has sought to address these challenges to access with a variety of robust patient assistance programs. For example, Johnson & Johnson's Janssen CarePath Program is a patient assistance program that supports eligible patients on commercial, employer sponsored, or government insurance, regardless of income. Patients with commercial insurance can apply to the program, which includes a number of solutions such as copay assistance and free product. In 2022, more than one million patients were helped with support provided by Johnson & Johnson's Janssen CarePath Program. Also in 2022, we donated $3.8 billion in free product and other financial support to the Johnson & Johnson Patient Assistance Foundation and other independent programs.

Commercial insurers and PBMs have responded to these programs with a variety of tactics designed to thwart manufacturers' patient assistance programs. For example, they impose prior authorization requirements and cost sharing models to control or restrict a patient's ability to access a medicine prescribed by a doctor. They impose exclusion lists that prevent a patient from accessing a prescribed medicine, given these are lists of products determined in the sole discretion of an insurer not to be covered. Exclusion lists have grown nearly 1000 percent since 2014 and now include more than 1,350 drugs.

PBMs' newest tactics are designed simply to divert manufacturers' patient assistance funds to their own pockets. These tactics have opaque names like ''accumulators,'' ''maximizers,'' and ''alternative funding programs,'' but they share a common purpose of undermining manufacturers' access programs. As one example, PBMs improperly inflate patients' copay amounts to astronomical amounts and then seek ''support'' from the assistance programs for this inflated copay. The patients quicky exhaust the available support, and the assistance programs' funds are effectively diverted to the PBMs. Johnson & Johnson brought suit against a company leading this practice in 2022.

The medications we are addressing today exemplify our approach to pricing, the downward trajectory of our prices due to discounts and rebates, and our commitment to patient access. Stelara, for example, has experienced a declining price in six of the last 7 years, once rebates and discounts are included. From 2017 to 2023, the average yearly price decline for Stelara was 5.9 percent. Xarelto similarly experienced a declining price in six of the 7 years between 2017 and 2023.

Each of these medicines also exemplifies the support that Johnson & Johnson provides in our patient assistance programs. Under the benefits provided by Johnson & Johnson's Janssen CarePath Program, eligible patients can pay as little as $5 for each dose of Stelara, $10 per fill of Xarelto, $0 per prescription of Imbruvica, and$0 per prescription of Symtuza.

U.S. Policy Supports and Fosters Innovation

The robust biopharmaceutical industry in the United States—currently the world's leading investor in innovation and developer of breakthrough treatments and cures—did not occur by accident. Instead, it was intentionally created and fostered by the policy choices of this Committee, Congress more broadly, and the many generations of policymakers that preceded those of us here today. Through thoughtful policy choices reflected in bipartisan legislation, in many cases emanating from this Committee, the United States created a medical innovation environment that is unique in the world.

For example, in the 1990's, Congress enacted the Prescription Drug User Fee Act to ensure that the FDA had the resources needed to remain the world's leading drug review agency. The law provided the FDA with a new funding stream to ensure that the FDA could hire and train the staff needed to review drug applications with predictable timeframes. For many new drugs treating serious medical conditions, the statute and associated funding allow the FDA to perform priority review. Patients and their families who were waiting for help and hope in the face of difficult and worrying diagnoses were the great beneficiaries of these policies. This Committee has advanced reauthorizations of the program every 5 years since 1992, including most recently in 2022, to help ensure that critical new, safe, and effective medicines reach American patients as quickly as possible.

Moreover, when the country has confronted challenges in healthcare, it has repeatedly looked for ways to spur private sector research, development, investment, and innovation. For example, when faced with concerns that diseases affecting smaller patient populations were not receiving sufficient attention in medical research, Congress enacted the Orphan Drug Act, which provided incentives such as market exclusivity and reduced taxes to spur investment in research and development. According to the National Organization for Rare Diseases, since the passage of the law, more than 7,000 rare diseases have been identified and more than 1,100 orphan indications for treatments have obtained FDA approval. Similarly, when families and pediatricians identified a need for more pediatric research, this Committee advanced the Best Pharmaceuticals for Children Act, which created an incentive of additional marketing exclusivity to innovators that voluntarily complete pediatric clinical studies. When Congress found that federally funded research grants were producing promising early stage research, but this research was not being developed into products that benefited the public, Congress enacted the Bayh-Dole Act, creating a path for private sector pharmaceutical companies to make the significant investments required to transform this early stage research into new medicines with the knowledge that privately developed intellectual property would be protected.

More recently, when the Nation and the world faced the threat of a global pandemic, Congress's actions supported the development of multiple Covid–

19 vaccines in an unprecedented timeframe. It is no coincidence that the three leading vaccines developed most swiftly—Pfizer, Moderna, and Johnson & Johnson—were ultimately developed by U.S. companies. That result would not have been possible if the United States had made different policy choices along the way that stifled biopharmaceutical companies' investments in researching and developing innovative treatments and cures.

Against this backdrop, the country again faces policy choices, particularly in light of the Inflation Reduction Act. Unfortunately, that statute diverges from the decades of U.S. policies that helped create the robust biopharmaceutical industry that the Nation and its patients have come to expect. Instead of adhering to those principles and ensuring that companies that invest and succeed in discovering and developing innovative new treatments that benefit patients receive appropriate and time-limited protections for their innovations, the IRA forces Johnson & Johnson and other manufacturers to provide innovative, patent-protected inventions to the government on pricing terms that, by law, must be significantly below market-based prices. As a result, the IRA's pricing provisions will constrain medical innovation, limit patient access and choice, and negatively affect the overall quality of patient care. For that reason, last summer, Johnson & Johnson filed a lawsuit challenging the constitutionality of the statute, as did every other manufacturer with a drug subject to the IRA's pricing provisions. We recognize that not everyone agrees with our decision to challenge the law. That is their right, just as it is our right to challenge in court a law that we believe violates the Constitution, upends decades of U.S. policies that have made the United States the center of medical innovation, and will inflict long-lasting damage to the American people by discouraging investment in future innovations.

The unique strengths of the U.S. biopharmaceutical industry, driven by decades of U.S. policies specifically designed to foster the growth of that industry in order to support patients, are also the reason that comparisons between U.S. drug prices and prices abroad are particularly inapt. The United States is unique in the world in the policy choices it has made to spur innovation and invention. Although it is true that there are certain disadvantages associated with these policy choices, including that the United States pays a disproportionate share of the costs of such innovation, the upsides far outweigh the downsides.

Americans access new medicines years earlier than other nations, including other wealthy nations, and sometimes have access to medicines that are never available at all in other countries. One study found that patients in

Europe wait 2 years longer, on average, for new cancer treatments than patients in the United States. Fully 85 percent of new medicines are available in the United States, more than any other country. New medicines launch first and fastest, on average, in the United States compared to other G20 countries. Where Germany, France, and the United Kingdom, on average, face delays between 11 and 20 months to access new medicines, new drugs are available in the United States within 4 months of global launch, on average.

Finally, much of the debate about drug pricing outside the United States uses deceptively selected figures that do not reflect the true nature of drug pricing in the United States and abroad. For example, some critics ignore that about 90 percent of prescriptions in the United States are filled with generic drugs and biosimilars that are often cheaper in the United States than abroad. Lower cost generic drugs and biosimilars are enabled by the research and development of innovative drugs, and as a result of this framework, the United States spends roughly the same share of healthcare spending on medicines as other countries, on average. Additionally, some critics compare U.S. list prices of drugs—which do not reflect the discounts and rebates provided to middlemen—to the prices charged abroad.

Johnson & Johnson supports solutions to address affordability and access to our innovative therapies. Imposing arbitrary price constraints on U.S. drug manufacturers, however, will harm innovation and deprive American patients of life-saving and life-extending therapies.

On behalf of the dedicated Johnson & Johnson employees around the world who work tirelessly to bring innovative medicines to patients in need, thank you for the opportunity to engage in today's discussion. I look forward to your questions and comments.

The CHAIR. Thank you very much, Mr. Duato. Our next witness will be Robert Davis, Chairman and CEO of Merck.

Mr. Davis has served as Merck's Chairman since December 2022 and CEO since 2021. Thank you very much, Mr. Davis, for being here.

Statement of Robert Davis, Chief Executive Officer, Merck, Rahway, NJ

Mr. DAVIS. Chairman Sanders, Ranking Member Cassidy, and Members of the Committee, thank you for the opportunity to be here with you today.

As the CEO of Merck, I am here to offer concrete policy suggestions to address the barriers American patients may encounter as they attempt to access our medicines and the current pricing system, while also ensuring Merck may discover and develop the next generation of lifesaving medicines and vaccines.

Based in Rockaway, New Jersey, our company is one of the world's most advanced, research intensive biopharmaceutical companies—an organization at the forefront of providing innovative health solutions that advance the prevention and treatment of disease in people and animals.

I have worked in the health care industry for the entirety of my 34 year career. I joined Merck 10 years ago in large measure because the company was on the precipice of its first approval for KEYTRUDA, a revolutionary oncology treatment.

At the time, people close to me were battling cancer, and unfortunately, they were not able to benefit from this amazing discovery. Following that first approval, Merck has demonstrated the efficacy of KEYTRUDA in 39 indications and reached nearly 2 million patients, with many of the most widespread cancers afflicting Americans.

The impact of KEYTRUDA and other recent advances is difficult to overstate. With a recent American Cancer Society report finding that cancer mortality in the United States has fallen 33 percent from 1991 to 2021, representing an estimated 4 million Americans whose deaths have been averted, and our work continues as we advanced KEYTRUDA into even more tumor types and earlier stages of cancer.

Remarkable progress like this does not come cheaply. For KEYTRUDA alone, between 2011 and 2023, Merck has invested $46 billion in development, and we expect to invest another $18 billion into the 2030's.

Oncology is just one of Merck's many areas of discovery. Right now, we have nearly 20,000 researchers seeking breakthrough treatments for immune disorders, infectious diseases, Alzheimer's, and other ailments threatening the health of millions of people.

To advance this critical work, we have invested more than $159 billion in R&D since 2010, including $30 billion in 2023 alone, and have invested more than $10 billion in capital in the form of both investments in manufacturing and R&D over the last 5 years in the United States, creating more jobs for Americans.

We do not hesitate to make these investments because they are necessary to further Merck's mission to serve patients. At the same time, many Americans are struggling to afford health care, including prescription medicines, and we are eager to find solutions to these access and affordability challenges.

That is why we supported changes to the Medicare Part D program to create an out-of-pocket cap that allow beneficiaries to pay their cost over time. We have also publicly disclosed our U.S. pri ing data, including the average rebates and discounts we provide.

In addition, we offer coupons and support a patient assistance program for those who cannot afford the medications they need. In the past 5 years, this program has helped nearly 800,000 patients to obtain Merck products free of charge, with an estimated value of $7.8 billion.

But the reality is that Merck's efforts alone are far from sufficient. They do not and cannot address the underlying systemic and structural issues underpinning our system. As more power and control has been concentrated into the ever smaller number of vertically consolidated players, their negotiating strength has increased dramatically.

In contracting with them, Merck continues to experience increasing pressure to provide even larger discounts, and the gap between list and net price continues to grow. And patients are not benefiting from the steep discounts we provide.

These problems could be addressed if other actors' revenue streams were de-linked from list prices, thereby removing incentives for the system to favor high list prices. This would also ensure that less value in the system flows to these middlemen who do not create these medicines, who do not discover, or develop, or manufacture them.

In addition, the substantial savings provided by Merck and other manufacturers should be required to be passed through to patients to lower their out-of-pocket costs. We firmly believe that reforms like these will create a drug pricing system that incentivizes the discovery of new and important medicines, while at the same time ensuring patients can afford those lifesaving medicines and innovations.

Future treatment breakthroughs hinge on what we do now. We must hold on to a U.S. pharmaceutical market that is free, competitive, and predictable. One that encourages and rewards investment, one that drives the American economy and creates jobs, and one that continues to deliver innovation and new treatment discoveries.

I am here today to pledge our support and cooperation in these efforts. Thank you for your time and your consideration of these important perspectives.

[The prepared statement of Mr. Davis follows.]

Prepared Statement of Robert Davis

Chairman Sanders, Ranking Member Cassidy, and Members of the Committee, thank you for the opportunity to be here with you today.

As the CEO of Merck, I am here to share the steps we are taking to ensure that American patients can afford our medicines, explain the barriers to our efforts that we encounter in the current pricing and access system, and offer concrete policy suggestions to both address these barriers and ensure our Country continues to have the world's best climate for pharmaceutical innovation, so that Merck may discover and develop our next generation of lifesaving medicines and vaccines.

On behalf of everyone at Merck, I want to thank you for your interest in working to ensure that safe and effective medicines are broadly accessible to all Americans who need them. As people who go to work each day to help protect and improve the health of others, my Merck colleagues and I share your desire to make today's medicines more widely available—even as we work to discover tomorrow's best treatments.

At Merck, our mission is to use the power of leading-edge science to save and improve lives around the world. We develop and bring forward breakthrough medicines and vaccines and then make those treatments available to patients in the United States and worldwide. Based in Rahway, New Jersey, our company is one of the world's most advanced research-intensive biopharmaceutical companies, an organization at the forefront of providing innovative health solutions that advance the prevention and treatment of disease in people and animals.

With a focus on scientific discovery, our company exists to help solve the world's toughest medical challenges. Indeed, we have a long history of taking on urgent health needs, stretching back more than 130 years to Merck's founding in 1891. Over the decades, Merck has developed essential childhood vaccines; introduced the first protease inhibitor, which helped transform AIDS from a death sentence to a chronic disease; and developed the first statin, markedly reducing the negative health impacts of high cholesterol.

Merck's Groundbreaking Work on the Treatment and Prevention of Cancer

Today, our journey of discovery continues. I have worked in the health care industry for the entirety of my 34-year career. I joined Merck 10 years ago in large measure because the company was on the precipice of its first approval for Keytruda, a novel programmed death receptor–1 (PD–1) inhibitor that had shown effectiveness in preventing cancer cells from suppressing the immune system. At the time, people close to me were battling cancer, and, unfortunately, they did not live long enough to benefit from this amazing discovery.

Following that first approval, Merck has demonstrated the efficacy of Keytruda in 39 indications, in 17 tumor types and 2 tumor-agnostic indications, and reached nearly 2 million patients battling many of the most widespread cancers afflicting Americans: non-small cell lung cancer, melanoma, head and neck cancer, and renal cell carcinoma. The impact of Keytruda and other recent treatment advances is difficult to overstate, with a recent American Cancer Society report finding that cancer mortality in the United States has fallen 33 percent from 1991 to 2021, representing an estimated 4 million Americans whose deaths have been averted.[1] And our work continues, as we advance Keytruda into even more tumor types and earlier stages of cancer.

Merck's breakthrough contributions in vaccine development have also played a critical role in the prevention of cancer. Our product Gardasil is the first-ever vaccine to guard against the human papillomavirus (HPV) that is the leading cause of nearly all cases of cervical cancer, which is the fourth most common cancer among women globally. A study of real world evidence published in the New England Journal of Medicine looking at Swedish girls and women between 10 and 30 years of age found a substantially reduced risk of invasive cervical cancer among those who had been fully vaccinated with Gardasil.[2] The American Cancer Society report found similar transformative public health outcomes in the United States, with a 65 percent decrease in cervical cancer rates in women in their early 20's, following the widespread adoption of HPV vaccines in the United States.[3]

These remarkable advances, and the others we are making in our many other oncology programs, have not come cheaply. Taking just Keytruda as an example, between 2011, when our focused Keytruda research program began, and 2023, Merck has invested $30 billion in our own internal clinical

---

[1] Siegel RL, Giaquinto AN, Jemal A. Cancer statistics, 2024. CA: A Cancer J Clin. https://doi.org/10.3322/caac.21820. Published Jan. 17, 2024. Accessed Feb. 3, 2024.

[2] Lei J, Ploner A, Elfstrom E, et al. HPV Vaccination and the Risk of Invasive Cervical Cancer. N Engl J Med 2020; 383:1340–1348. DOI: 10.1056/NENMoa1917338.

[3] Siegel RL, Miller KD, Wagle NS, et al. Cancer statistics, 2023. CA: A Cancer J Clin. https://doi.org/10.3322/caac.21763. Published Jan. 12, 2023. Accessed Feb. 3, 2024.

development efforts, $14 billion in research collaborations and acquisitions to further the study of Keytruda with other compounds, and $2 billion in capital expenditures to scale up our processes and facilities to manufacture the drug in large quantities. And we expect to invest another $18 billion in Keytruda clinical studies into the 2030's. This is likely now the largest and costliest pharmaceutical research and development program ever undertaken. Over 2,200 clinical trials have been publicly disclosed to study Keytruda alone and in conjunction with other compounds in pursuit of new lifesaving and life-extending applications for this revolutionary medicine.

Merck's Substantial Investments Across Our Research and Manufacturing Efforts

Oncology is just one of Merck's many intense areas of discovery and development. Right now, we have nearly 20,000 researchers seeking breakthrough treatments for immune disorders, infectious diseases, Alzheimer's, cardiometabolic disease, and other ailments threatening the health of millions of people. To advance their critical work, we have invested more than $159 billion in research and development since 2010, including $30 billion in 2023 alone.

In support of these and other efforts, we are also making infrastructure investments, many of which are here in the United States. In fact, over the past 5 years, Merck has made capital investments across the United States totaling more than $10 billion, increasing our domestic capacity for R&D and manufacturing while creating hundreds of new jobs in our U.S. operations. For example, we've invested $3.6 billion in our Pennsylvania facilities since 2018, with plans to invest another $700 million this year. And in the past 5 years, we have invested $1.4 billion in our manufacturing facility in Elkton, Virginia—about 2 hours from here—to increase domestic production capacity for our Gardasil HPV vaccine.

We do not hesitate to make these investments because they are necessary to further Merck's mission: to serve patients—and not just the patients of today, but those who will need the new treatments and cures we have yet to discover. But we know that many Americans are struggling to afford health care, including prescription medicines, despite the best efforts of leaders in government, industry, academia, and the nonprofit community. Even though medicine costs are growing at the slowest rate in years, thanks in part to market competition, patients are too often being asked to pay more out-of-pocket for their medicines. And for some, that burden is simply too much to bear. As has often been observed, a lifesaving drug is not effective if the patient who needs that drug cannot afford it.

Thus, I am here today to share our perspective about the structural elements in our Country's complex system of pricing, distribution, and insurance that have impeded Merck's efforts to bring our medicines to the American patients who need them. And I would humbly ask for your help and partnership in addressing these obstacles.

Merck's Efforts to Address Patient Access Challenges

Merck has worked hard to help patients overcome access and affordability challenges. That work continues. We believe our company and our industry have a duty to act responsibly in our pricing practices and contribute to affordability solutions. That is why we supported changes to the Medicare Part D program to create an out-of-pocket cap and allow beneficiaries to pay their costs over time. And we have a history and heritage of responsible pricing. We are also committed to transparency in our pricing practices. Merck publicly discloses U.S. pricing data, including the average rebates and discounts we provide across our U.S. product portfolio to payers such as insurance companies, pharmacy benefit managers (PBMs), and the government.

We also have programs designed to help patients who cannot afford their medicines. To reduce patient out-of-pocket costs at the pharmacy counter, we provide coupons and other co-pay assistance for our products. Last year the value of this aid totaled $130 million. And through our support of a separate charitable organization that administers our patient assistance program, we provide free medicines to Americans of limited means who do not have insurance coverage or have some other hardship and cannot otherwise obtain their prescribed medications. In the past 5 years, this program has helped nearly 800,000 patients to obtain Merck medicines or vaccines free of charge, with an estimated value of $7.8 billion.

Structural Challenges and Merck's Suggested Improvements for the U.S. System

But the reality is that Merck's efforts alone are far from sufficient. They do not and cannot address the underlying systemic and structural issues underpinning our system, which do not allow patients to benefit from the substantial discounts that manufacturers are providing on the medications they sell.

As more power and control has been consolidated into an ever-smaller number of vertically consolidated players, their negotiating strength has increased dramatically. In Merck's efforts to contract with them, we continue to experience increasing pressure to provide even larger discounts, and the gap between list and net price continues to grow. But patients are not benefiting from the discounts being negotiated by PBMs. Instead, their insurers often base their cost-sharing on the list price, even when PBMs and insurance companies are paying a heavily discounted fraction of that price.

Our diabetes treatment Januvia is a great example of this phenomenon. Today, the weighted average net price for Januvia represents a 90 percent discount off its list price; with the price of Januvia being 33 percent lower than its price when we launched it in 2006. This is, in part, a result of significant discounts and rebates in a highly competitive market over the years. But these discounts and rebates are not being passed along to patients in a way that reduces their out-of-pocket costs.

Simply reducing our list prices is not a solution because patients often experience reduced access to their drugs when they are either not included on or are dropped from PBM and plan formularies. For example, in 2016, Merck introduced our Hepatitis C medicine, Zepatier, at a list price 42 percent below that of the standard of care at the time. Yet, we had difficulty getting plans and PBMs to add the product to their formularies. The situation did not improve in July 2018, when we further reduced the list price by 60 percent and found no increased uptake. More recent efforts by other manufacturers to offer products with lower lists prices have resulted in similarly poor PBM and plan coverage compared to their high list price competitors. Thus, lower list prices can result in reduced access for patients.

Rather than passing the steep savings they obtain through to patients to lower their out-of-pocket costs at the pharmacy counter, we understand that insurance plans retain them to cover overhead costs and reduce insurance premiums for all their insureds. When they do this, rather than reducing medicine costs for those that need them, it means sick people end up effectively subsidizing healthy people. This dynamic is contrary to the basic idea of insurance, which should use the premiums of healthy people to help fund the care of those who are struggling. This is yet another way in which our current system is fundamentally flawed.

From 2010 through 2023, Merck's annual average net price increase across our U.S. portfolio has been in the low-to mid-single digits. In 2017, our average net price actually declined nearly 2 percent. In 2022, the average discount for our medicines and vaccines was 40 percent off the list price. This money is flowing in part to middlemen, not to the innovative manufacturers that would reinvest that money to find tomorrow's cures. And, by and large, patients did not receive the financial benefits of these substantial discounts. Instead, their out-of-pocket costs continue to rise.

Though the issues I have described are complex and impossible for one company— or even the pharmaceutical industry collectively—to address, legislative solutions may not be difficult to implement. If Congress were to require that other actors' revenue streams be delinked from the list price of a medicine, it would remove incentives for the system to favor high list prices. This would also ensure that less of the value in the system flows to these middlemen, who did not discover, develop, or produce the medicines for which they contract.

Another critically important fix is to require that the substantial savings provided by Merck and other manufacturers be passed through to patients to lower their out- of-pocket costs at the pharmacy counter, rather than allowing insurance plans to re tain them. Reforms like these are necessary and will help provide long-term solutions for patients' out-of-pocket costs and ensure they can take advantage of the full breadth of innovative medicines available to keep them healthy and alleviate their suffering.

We firmly believe that it is possible to have a drug pricing system that incentivizes the discovery of new and important medicines and at the same time ensures patients can afford those lifesaving innovations. But reform of our current system is desperately needed to ensure that patients in the United States continue to have the greatest access, to the best medicines, faster than anywhere else in the world. I would encourage you to support legislative or administrative remedies that would address these systemic problems.

Fostering Innovation Alongside Patient Access Solutions

These are exciting times in the biopharmaceutical industry and the wider world of health care. Decades of research investment are producing discoveries of increasing promise and impact. Life-threatening diseases like cancer are being conquered. Patients are living longer, healthier lives, even with serious conditions.

But let me be very clear: today's investments drive tomorrow's discoveries of breakthrough treatments. If we disrupt an ecosystem that incentivizes robust investments in research, we put at risk not only the foundation of American leadership in pharmaceutical development but also the health and lives of countless people who would have benefited from future discoveries.

We do not have to go down that path. In fact, we have examples of efforts that are already working. For instance, the Medicare Part D program facilitates actual negotiation, effectively holding down costs and broadening patient access without threatening to injure or destroy the innovation ecosystem that fosters future treatment breakthroughs.

The most important positive contributions Merck makes in the world—impacting economies, health care systems, and the well-being of countless patients and their families—are pharmaceutical innovations that save and improve lives. Achieving such innovations requires us to invest billions of dollars a year in the often unsung work of thousands of brilliant researchers sitting at lab benches and striving, with all they have, to create transformative breakthroughs.

The odds are stacked against these scientists, but they keep trying, and we keep investing. Even with all the advantages of modern technology, discoveries are few and far between. And, even among those discoveries that spark clinical trials, nine out of ten compounds will fail.

Of course, our Country needs to contain health care costs and reduce out-of-pocket costs to patients. And Merck is committed to being part of the solution. But we must pursue greater affordability and accessibility for medicines—and health care more broadly—in ways that preserve and strengthen our innovation ecosystem across academia, smaller biotech firms, larger pharmaceutical companies, government agencies, insurers, providers, and other stakeholders.

Ultimately, I believe we need to work together across these stakeholders to overcome the access and affordability challenges faced by today's patients without damaging our ability to innovate and discover new treatments for tomorrow's patients. Future treatment breakthroughs hinge on what we do now. We must hold onto a U.S. pharmaceutical market that is free, competitive, and predictable, one that encourages and rewards investment, one that drives the American economy and creates jobs, and one that continues to deliver innovation and new treatment discoveries.

I am here today to pledge our support and cooperation in this effort and other measures to help Americans live longer, healthier lives with improved access to effective and affordable drug treatments, and in ways that protect incentives for future innovation.

Thank you for your time and your consideration of these perspectives, and thank you again for the opportunity to share them with you today.

[Summary Statement of Robert Davis]

Summary

Merck's mission is to use the power of leading-edge science to save and improve lives around the world.

Merck conducts groundbreaking work to treat and prevent cancer.

Keytruda treats cancer in 39 indications, including 17 tumor types and 2 tumor-agnostic indications.

- Since 2011, Merck has invested: $30 billion in internal clinical development; $14 billion in research collaborations and acquisitions; $2 billion in capital expenditures for Keytruda alone.
- We expect to invest another $18 billion in clinical studies into the 2030's.

Merck has made substantial investments across our research and manufacturing efforts.

Merck is making infrastructure investments in the United States. In the past 5 years we invested:

- $3.6 billion in Pennsylvania, with an additional $700 million expected this year.
- $1.4 billion in Elkton, Virginia.

- More than $10 billion total across the United States, creating hundreds of new jobs.

Merck works to address patient access challenges.

We have a duty to act responsibly in pricing practices and contribute to affordability solutions. We:

- Supported changes to the Medicare Part D program to create an out-of- pocket cap and to allow beneficiaries to pay their costs over time.
- Publicly disclose U.S. pricing data, including the average rebates and discounts we provide.
- Provide coupons and other co-pay assistance for our products, totaling $130 million last year.
- Created a patient assistance program providing nearly 800,000 people with an estimated value of $7.8 billion.

Structural challenges increase prices for patients.

The savings Merck provides to PBMs and insurers are not passed on to patients.

- Payors retain the savings to cover overhead and reduce insurance premiums for their insured.
- Sick people end up effectively subsidizing the healthy, contrary to the basic idea of insurance.
- When list prices are reduced, medicines are dropped from formularies, limiting patient access.

Merck has a history of cost reductions.

- From 2010 through 2023, Merck's annual average net price increase across our U.S. portfolio has been in the low-to mid-single digits.
- In 2017, our average net price actually declined nearly 2 percent.
- In 2022, the average discount for our medicines and vaccines was 40 percent off the list price.
- Unfortunately, middlemen absorbed some of the benefits from this price reduction—benefits that should have gone to patients.

Merck urges Congress to consider the following solutions:

- Require that other actors' revenue streams be delinked from the list price of a medicine, which would reduce incentives for the system to favor high list prices.
- Require that substantial savings provided by Merck and other manufactures be passed through to patients to lower their out-of-pocket costs at the pharmacy counter, rather than allowing insurance plans to retain them.

The CHAIR. Thank you very much, Mr. Davis. Our third witness will be Chris Boerner, CEO, Bristol-Myers Squibb. Dr. Boerner has served as CEO of Bristol-Myers Squibb since November 2023. Thanks for being here, Mr. Boerner.

Statement of Chris Boerner, Chief Executive Officer, Bristol Myers Squibb, Princeton, NJ

Mr. BOERNER. Chairman Sanders, Ranking Member Cassidy, and Members of the Committee, thank you for having me here today. I am proud to be representing Bristol-Myers Squibb, an American company that is committed to transforming patients' lives through science.

I have spent more than 20 years in this industry, the majority in smaller, science driven biotechnology companies. I joined BMS because we have a similar focus on driving leading edge scientific innovation, and our scale allows us to bring more medicines to more patients faster.

To help illustrate the type of work that we have been doing for more than 150 years at BMS, let me provide two illustrations of how our innovative medicines have helped patients and provided tangible benefits to society. Our work in HIV/AIDS transformed this disease from a death sentence into a chronic condition.

Similarly, our pioneering immuno-oncology treatments, OPDIVO and YERVOY, harness the body's immune system to fight cancer and have contributed significantly to improved outcomes across a number of tumors, including metastatic melanoma, where the combination of these two medicines has changed the median life expectancy from less than 9 months to over 6 years. I am proud that our record of innovation continues today.

We have invested more than $65 billion in research and development over the past decade. This has resulted in truly novel and transformational medicines, like Camzyos in cardiovascular disease, our cell therapy platform in cancer, and we are working toward bringing to patients the first medicine for the treatment of schizophrenia in 30 years.

These medicines are but a few examples of the innovation that results from an American health care system that not only accounts for the majority of new medicines launched each year, but also one that delivers those medicines to U.S. patients faster than anywhere else in the world. This isn't by chance.

The United States has built a health care system that prioritizes patient and physician choice, as well as the broad and rapid availability of cutting-edge medicines. This is in stark contrast to many systems outside of the United States, which while they may deliver lower prices, carry an often-overlooked tradeoff, that patients often wait longer for new medicines that are sometimes never approved or reimbursed.

For example, Canadian patients have access to approximately half of the medicines available in the United States, and patients in other countries face a similar reality. Despite its benefits, we know our American system is far from perfect.

Patients bear the brunt of a complex U.S. system that results in increasing health care costs and a lack of affordability. We have to make the system work better for them. After all, innovation that does not make it to patients is no innovation at all.

While prescription medicines account for a relatively small portion of overall health care spending, we believe we have an important role to play in prioritizing the development of medicines that will bring savings to the health care system, and as an industry, we should set a higher bar for doing just that.

Similarly, we have a role to play in addressing affordability and stand ready to partner with Congress and others to address this issue for patients in a holistic manner. But in developing those solutions, we should not abandon our system for one that denies U.S. patients the broad and rapid access to vital medicines that they appreciate today.

We support policies that lower patient out-of-pocket costs without ultimately harming innovation. The need to strike this balance should not be abstract. I expect many of us in this room have lost a loved one to cancer or another devastating disease.

In my case, it was one of my best friends and it happened as he awaited a medicine that I believe could have saved his life. This is an almost daily reminder to me that making patients wait for weeks, months, or years can be the difference between life and death.

Thank you again for having me here today. On behalf of BMS and the more than 30,000 employees who share my passion for delivering new medicines for patients, I look forward to answering your questions.

[The prepared statement of Mr. Boerner follows.]

Prepared Statement of Chris Boerner

Chairman Sanders, Ranking Member Cassidy, and Members of the Committee, thank you for the opportunity to testify today on behalf of Bristol Myers Squibb (''BMS''). I appreciate the chance to speak about BMS's groundbreaking work and efforts to enhance access to our innovative medicines for patients. I am proud to testify on behalf of a company that is committed to transforming patients' lives through science.

At BMS, our mission is to discover, develop, and deliver medicines that help patients prevail over serious diseases. Our record of innovation has changed the outlook for countless patients. Groundbreaking BMS therapies helped transform HIV/ AIDS from a death sentence into a chronic condition. Today, our medicines allow people with heart disease, cancer, diabetes, and autoimmune disorders to live longer and healthier lives.

We are not content, however, to rest on our more than 150-year legacy of scientific innovation and are dedicated to developing the next generation of breakthroughs. We are pushing the boundaries of science to treat debilitating diseases, such as cancer, Alzheimer's, and multiple sclerosis, where unmet needs remain. As we look ahead, we are focused on introducing novel treatments in areas we know best: oncology, hematology, immunology, cardiovascular disease, and neuroscience.

We are also focused on increasing access to our medicines. Patients in the United States get new medicines sooner than any other country in the world. That's a significant benefit. But we recognize that patients must be able to afford our medicines to achieve the clinical outcomes those medicines bring. BMS has long worked to enhance access to our innovative medicines for patients, while maintaining an environment that enables investments in cutting-edge science to deliver life-changing treatments, and we remain committed to working with Congress to do so.

Our commitment reaches beyond our medicines. BMS supports programs, initiatives, and organizations that improve health, broaden research opportunities, bolster STEM education, and bring essential human services to our communities. We also promote health equity and strive to increase access to life-saving medicines for populations disproportionately affected by serious diseases. From 2020 to 2023, BMS provided more than $118 million in grants and donations to non-profit organizations and independent medical educational partners for more than 750 health equity projects.

Having spent more than two decades in the biopharmaceutical industry, I joined BMS 9 years ago because of its dedication to improving the lives of patients. I became CEO in November 2023 and am honored to be leading this great company through its next chapter.

During my tenure, I have developed a deep admiration and respect for the over 30,000 dedicated BMS employees in the United States and around the world who harness their intellect, expertise, hard work, and passion on behalf of the patients we serve. From our scientists in the lab, to our manufacturing teams in our facilities, to our patient outreach teams in the field, I am proud to work alongside my BMS colleagues, who are dedicated to creating and delivering life-changing medicines to patients in need.

BMS's Emphasis on Expanding Patient Access

The United States has built a healthcare system that prioritizes the important role of patient choice and broad, rapid availability of cutting-edge medicines. Patients and their physicians in this country have access to more unique medicines than in any other country. This access is critically important because different medicines can have different side effects or safety profiles, different mechanisms of action, and different efficacies at stages of disease, such that the leading or most obvious therapy may not be the most appropriate. By providing physicians in the United States with more options, we give them the ability to choose the best treatment for their patients and offer potentially better outcomes.

Despite the many benefits of the United States system, we acknowledge that patient affordability is a significant issue. It is also one of the least understood. The United States has a unique and complex healthcare landscape, replete with conflicting pressures and perverse incentives driving the system. Many of these factors exert strong influence on patient access and the price patients actually pay for their medicines.

Manufacturers give significant rebates, discounts, and payments to intermediaries between us and patients in the pharmaceutical supply chain.

BMS has provided these intermediaries with over $96 billion dollars of rebates, price concessions, and other discounts and fees over the last 5 years across our portfolio. But patients are not seeing the financial benefits of the sizable discounts because intermediaries are not required to pass on discounts to patients when they fill their prescriptions at the pharmacy counter.

Additionally, the United States healthcare system has not yet evolved to account for the economic benefits of highly specialized innovative medicines that contribute substantial value to patients and the system. For example, a patient on the right medicine may avoid serious or life-threatening medical interventions. This in turn also provides cost savings to the healthcare system by reducing expensive and high-burden hospital stays and conserving capacity.

We share your concerns about what patients pay for prescription medications, and we appreciate your work to examine this key public policy issue. It is our collective—and critical—— responsibility to ensure that patients receive the medicines they need. BMS invests billions in patient support programs with that objective in mind. Although patient support programs are an imperfect solution to these challenges, I am proud of our efforts to help patients access our medicines. Over the past 5 years, we have spent more than $2.5 billion on copayment assistance for commercially insured patients, helping patients receive medicines such as Eliquis, which treats and prevents blood clots. We broadened our existing patient support programs to help eligible patients in the United States without health insurance due to pandemic-related job loss.

We also contribute to organizations that help support patients in need. For instance, over the last 5 years, BMS donated over $12 billion in free medicines to the Bristol Myers Squibb Patient Assistance Foundation. The Foundation is an independent organization that promotes health equity and improved health outcomes for populations disproportionately affected by serious diseases. It supports community-based programs that promote cancer awareness, screening, and care among highrisk populations. In addition, BMS made cash donations to independent charitable organizations to support patients in the United States.

BMS also supports comprehensive efforts across the continuum of care, including projects to train community health workers and patient navigators to help underserved patients navigate the healthcare system. In March 2023, we announced $10 million in grants to be made that year to 17 United States organizations that address social determinants of health. These grants support organizations striving to improve health in the United States, including through healthcare access and literacy and by integrating social care and healthcare to reduce health disparities.

BMS's Commitment to Bringing More Innovative Medicines to Patients Through Research and Development

We are proud to have a promising pipeline of innovative medicines that will allow us to continue delivering cutting-edge treatments to patients. BMS is investing in leading scientific programs, including in our core areas of oncology, hematology, immunology, cardiovascular disease, and neuroscience. Over the past 10 years, BMS devoted over $65 billion—more than 21 percent of our total revenue—to research and development (''R&D'').[4] In 2022, we conducted more than 460 clinical trials.

In fact, our investment in R&D as a percentage of total revenue consistently ranks among the highest of any large company in any industry globally. In the 2023 EU Industrial Research and Development Investment Scoreboard, BMS ranked 15th for total R&D spending among all companies worldwide.

Our investment in R&D has resulted in vastly improved outcomes for patients. For example, BMS is a pioneer in the field of immuno-oncology through the development of three medicines: Yervoy, Opdivo, and Opdualag. Prior to the development and introduction of immuno-oncology treatments for metastatic melanoma, outcomes were generally quite poor, with a median life expectancy of only 6 to 9 months after diagnosis. Today, thanks to these therapies, survival rates have significantly improved among patients with metastatic melanoma. Long-term follow-up studies have demonstrated a median life expectancy of over 6 years with the combination of Opdivo and Yervoy.

Our investment of over $65 billion in R&D over the past decade is fueling the next wave of new treatments for areas of high unmet need. Our R&D pipeline includes potential treatments across a range of platforms, including those that harness the frontiers of genomics to translate that knowledge into gene therapies, cell therapies, RNA oligonucleotides, and other novel modalities. With our CAR T cell therapies, for example, we can now target cancer with a type of immunotherapy that works with a patient's own immune system by reprogramming their T cells. With a single treatment, CAR T cell

[4] Based on non-GAAP calculations.

therapy has been effective at producing durable responses in patients where other treatment options stopped working. BMS is the only company with two cell therapies approved against two distinct targets, and we are pursuing opportunities to bring them to more patients who may benefit.

Overall, we have more than 45 novel compounds in development, with more than 40 disease areas under study. We are conducting late-stage studies for medications to treat various solid tumors, multiple myeloma, Crohn's disease, lupus, and atrial fibrillation. And we are leveraging our expertise in protein homeostasis, immunology, and inflammation to tackle neurological and neuromuscular diseases with new approaches.

Our R&D efforts are not limited to discovering new compounds. We are constantly researching how we can use existing products to provide additional benefits to more patients through new indications and formulations. We are currently running and partnering with other innovators in more than 15 late-stage studies involving existing products.

Our commitment to innovation and to patients also includes establishing strategic partnerships with other biotechnology leaders and acquiring companies that benefit from our global scale and expertise to bring medicines to patients faster. We offer deep scientific leadership, resources, and abilities to invest in research and development programs and highly developed commercial, manufacturing, and supply chain operations. This global scale and range of expertise enables us to reach the greatest number of patients worldwide. Our recently announced plans to acquire RayzeBio and Karuna Therapeutics demonstrate this commitment. We are excited about the potential of Karuna's KarXT, a late-stage developmental medicine with a novel mechanism of action aimed at schizophrenia and other psychological disorders. If approved, KarXT would represent the first new pharmacological approach to treating schizophrenia in several decades.

R&D is complex and resource-intensive, often lasting 14 years or more for a particular compound. Results are far from guaranteed. In fact, the majority of our R&D efforts do not result in a medicine that we can deliver to patients. For instance, last year we had to discontinue two late-stage clinical trials into which we had invested multiple years and many millions of dollars. One was a phase-three trial that evaluated one of our existing medicines, Opdualag, for treating colorectal cancer. We invested more than $80 million and devoted thousands of hours of employee time to this research, which ultimately failed. In another case, after more than 6 years of research, we had to end a study evaluating a combination of our medicines, Opdivo and Yervoy, for advanced treatment of renal cell carcinoma. We invested over $130 million in that study alone.

Because we pursue a wide range of possibilities on the cutting edge of science, we know that some of our research will not culminate in new treatments. Failures are an inevitable part of the process by which we develop new treatments, and we learn from them along the way. Our successes allow us to try. Those successes are a critical engine in our ability to continue to invest in new medicines, allowing the United States to lead the world in bringing new treatments to patients.

The Disadvantages of International Pricing Systems

Rules and regulations regarding the pricing of medicines vary widely by country. Some countries, such as Canada, the U.K., Germany, France, and Japan, essentially allow the government to set pharmaceutical prices. In effect, governments in those countries make choices for patients—choices that often result in patients having access to fewer innovative medicines, and waiting much longer for new medicines as compared to patients in the United States. These delays can be attributed to a variety of factors, including waiting for the government to complete reimbursement assessments, challenges with subpopulation coverage, or a failure to appropriately value innovation.

In Canada and most European Union countries, the government regulates the pricing of a new medicine at launch through some combination of clinical and economic assessments, price negotiations, and international reference pricing. Prices are often reevaluated and further controlled after a medication has been introduced. Patients pay a significant price for these pricing schemes in the form of delays to access. For example, only about 45 percent of new medicines available globally have been introduced in Canada—compared to 85 percent in the United States. In France, Italy, and Japan, this figure is below 55 percent. The United States launched 94 percent of new cancer medicines from 2012 through 2021, while the same figure for the average OECD country was 49 percent. These figures are startling, reflecting dramatic differences in access to medicines around the world.

Patients outside the United States also often face longer wait times and obstacles before getting the medicines they need. According to a report published last week by the United States Department of Health and Human Services, medicines launch in the United States an average of 1 year before they launch in other major OECD markets. Other studies found that on average, there is an 11-month delay from a medicine's first launch globally to its availability and reimbursement in Germany, a 17-month delay in Japan, a 27-month delay in the U.K., and a staggering 52- month delay in Canada. Patients with multiple myeloma in the U.K. waited 4 years after the United States launch for BMS's medicine, Revlimid—a medicine that significantly improves outcomes. Canadian patients did not gain access to Opdivo and Yervoy for melanoma until more than 3.5 years after patients in the United States. Patients in Spain, Japan, Denmark, Australia, and other countries are still waiting for access to Camzyos, the first new treatment in decades for obstructive hypertrophic cardiomyopathy, which was approved in the United States in 2022.

By contrast, the United States is generally first in the world for launching new medicines, and patients usually benefit from access to new medicines within days of regulatory approval. The United States healthcare system has allowed Americans to have access to more new innovative medicines sooner than any other country.

This access generally translates into better outcomes to save and extend lives. For example, while it is challenging to precisely quantify and compare across different countries the impact of delayed access to anticancer therapy on survival outcomes, there is broad agreement that prompt access to effective treatments is a fundamental necessity, and it yields positive outcomes on patients, healthcare systems, and society in general. These outcomes include: lower mortality and avoidable deaths; gains in quality of life for patients, family members, and caregivers; lower healthcare costs; and avoidance in loss of productive employment for patients and caregivers, ultimately lowering costs to the national economy.

BMS's Value-Focused Pricing Philosophy

We believe the prices of our medicines should reflect their benefit to patients, healthcare providers, payers, and society—both at launch and in future years. Guided by this belief, we price our medicines based on three primary factors, including aligning to the value of scientific innovation, investment into research and development, and our ability to provide rapid and sustainable access for patients, among other considerations. That means we look at longevity gains, clinical outcomes, and quality of life, as well as economic impact and productivity gains generated by a healthy population with more options to treat illnesses. We also consider our ability to sustain our research and development investment and to work with payers to secure access, so patients can have coverage for our medicines when needed.

Our product Eliquis, an oral medicine that inhibits a key blood-clotting protein, provides a good example of our approach to pricing. Over the past few years, Eliquis has become the standard of care for decreasing blood clot formation in patients— it is prescribed millions of times each year, and is the most prescribed branded medicine in Medicare Part D. However, it ranked 540th in Medicare spending per patient in 2021. Eliquis can lower the risk of a stroke and prevent deep vein thrombosis and embolism, and it is commonly used to prevent blood clots following certain surgeries. Because Eliquis can help prevent very serious medical conditions that require hospitalization or other expensive medical treatments, numerous studies have demonstrated that Eliquis provides substantial savings to our healthcare system, such as reduced hospitalization and institutional costs. Without the benefits of Eliquis, many patients would have substantially worse medical outcomes, and the healthcare system would face dramatically higher costs. For every 100,000 patients, we estimate that Eliquis offers patients and healthcare systems a $4.9 billion consumer surplus over older, generic products. This value to patients and to the entire United States healthcare system is reflected in the price of this medicine.

Path Forward

The United States healthcare system prioritizes patient choice and access in a way other healthcare systems do not, but it is far from perfect. The system is mired in complexities and incentives that frustrate our efforts to meet patients' medical needs. These hurdles range from complex rebates, to high copays and deductibles, to Federal rules that restrict our ability to assist patients in Federal healthcare programs. I welcome the opportunity to work with your Committee and others in Congress to resolve these issues in our healthcare system. Ensuring access to medicines involves more than just the companies that discover and develop them—it requires the active engagement of the entire ecosystem of governments, payers, healthcare providers, pharmacies, and hospitals. BMS supports policies that remove barriers and perverse incentives in the system and focus on patient out-of-pocket costs. We believe we can do this without harming innovation. BMS stands ready to work with Congress to address affordability and eliminate barriers in the system that fail to pass discounts and rebates to patients, but this cannot be done in a vacuum. The measures we support include: expanding value-based contracting for which there are regulatory impediments today; incentivizing competition and production of biosimilars and generics to ensure a steady supply in the United States; and passing rebates on to patients at the pharmacy counter to address the incentives in a complex system that drive up list prices.

As BMS continues to strive to enhance patient access, we are also committed to ensuring that we have the resources to fund cutting-edge R&D and to attract the private capital needed to do so. We also believe that policymakers should adopt and defend policies that promote innovation. Government policy should encourage innovators to take big risks and invest substantial sums, by promising a return on those efforts for a reasonable period of time. Such policies are the reason that the United States is a leader globally in medical innovations and developing new therapies. At BMS, we are eager to continue driving these efforts.

Again, I am proud to speak here today on behalf of BMS, where we believe patients in the United States should not be deprived of their choice to access the best, most recent technologies and advancements in medicine. I look forward to answering your questions about how we can meaningfully address healthcare costs and patient access.

The CHAIR. Mr. Boerner, thank you very much. Before I begin the first round of questions, let me remind our witnesses that while the HELP Committee does not swear in our witnesses as a general rule, Federal law at 18 U.S. Code Section 1001 prohibits knowingly and willingly making any fraudulent statement to the Senate regardless of whether a person is under oath.

I would also say, in response to many of your testimonies, we are aware of the many important lifesaving drugs that your companies have produced, and that is extraordinarily important, I think, is all of those drugs mean nothing to anybody who cannot afford it, and that is what we are dealing with today, that millions and millions of our people cannot afford the outrageously high cost of prescription drugs in this country.

Now, my time and the time of all of the Members is limited, so we are going to just—I am going to ask—so my time is limited, so I am going to start by asking all of you a number of questions and I would appreciate it if you could respond with a yes or no answer.

It turns out that a dysfunctional and extraordinarily expensive healthcare system, hundreds of thousands of Americans have gone to GoFundMe in order to raise money to pay for their health care needs and for their prescription drugs.

Let me ask Mr. Davis if I might, have you ever searched on GoFundMe for your cancer drug, KEYTRUDA?

Mr. DAVIS. No, I have not.

The CHAIR. Okay. We have, I and my staff have, and we have found over 500 stories of people trying to raise funds to pay for their cancer treatments.

One of those stories is a woman named Rebecca, a school lunch lady from Nebraska with two kids who died of cancer after setting up a GoFundMe page because she could not afford to pay for KEYTRUDA.

Rebecca had raised $4,000 on her GoFundMe page but said the cost of KEYTRUDA on a cancer treatment was $25,000 for an infusion every 3 weeks. Mr. Davis, and please yes or no, is it true that the list price of KEYTRUDA is $191,000 a year in the United States?

Mr. DAVIS. That is close to being true, yes.

The CHAIR. Thank you. Is it true that same exact drug can be purchased in Canada for $112,000 a year, and $44,000 a year in Japan?

Mr. DAVIS. Generally, yes.

The CHAIR. Mr. Davis, even though the price of KEYTRUDA is one quarter of the price in Japan compared to the United States, does your company, does Merck make a profit selling KEYTRUDA in Japan?

Mr. DAVIS. We do.

The CHAIR. What I understand is you make a profit selling KEYTRUDA in Japan for one quarter of the price that you sell it for in the United States. My question to you is a pretty simple one. Will you commit to lowering the price of KEYTRUDA in the United States to the price of Japan?

Mr. DAVIS. Well, Senator, I think—first, I acknowledge the prices in the United States are higher than they are in many of the countries you said, and not for all drugs, but for many drugs.

That is the reality we face. But I think it is also important to point out that you get access in the United States faster and more than anywhere in the world. We have 39 indications for KEYTRUDA across 17 tumor types in the United States. If you look across Europe, it is in the 20's.

If you look across Japan, it is in that number or a little bit less. So, there is a reason why the prices are different, and we need to be careful because we are also seeing in those markets that they are unwilling to support the innovation and we are very hardly— working hard to try to get them to understand the need to help funding the innovation we have——

The CHAIR. I apologize for cutting you off.

Mr. DAVIS. That is fine.

The CHAIR. There are two other witnesses—but I did want to make this point.

Again, we all appreciate the breakthrough and important drugs that you and other companies have produced that save lives. No debate about that.

But I do want to point out that after all is said and done, and after all the money we spend on the prescription drugs and health care in general, the life expectancy in Japan is 9 years longer than it is in the United States. Senator Cassidy talked about Canada. Life expectancy in Canada is 6 years longer than the United States.

Life expectancy in Portugal is 6 years longer. Life expectancy in the UK is 4 years longer. Let me ask the last question to Mr. Davis, because I understand that you made $52 million in total compensation in 2022.

Will you commit to not accepting a single dollar more in compensation until there is not a single GoFundMe page for KEYTRUDA?

Mr. DAVIS. Well, I can tell you at Merck we are very much sensitive to what is happening with patients. That is why we have very important patient assistance programs.

We commented on the fact that we have over 800,000 patients benefiting where we provide free drug for those who can't afford it, as well as other assistance programs that help with co-pay and other.

We are very committed as a company to doing what we need to do to try to help alleviate the challenges patients face that you are focusing on, and that is my focus as the CEO.

The CHAIR. Thank you. Mr. Boerner with Bristol-Myers Squibb, Carolyn from Florida says that she cannot afford ELIQUIS, and so she will, ''stop taking it, though I need it to prevent the risk of having a stroke.''

Mr. Boerner, again yes and no please, the list price of ELIQUIS is $7,100 a year in the United States. Dr. Melissa Barber, an expert at Yale University, has estimated that it cost just $18 to manufacture a year's supply of ELIQUIS. $7,100 what we pay, $1,800 to manufacture.

Is it true that the same exact drug, ELIQUIS, can be purchased in Canada for $900 a year?

Mr. BOERNER. Senator, that is roughly correct.

The CHAIR. Let me ask you this, even at 13 percent of the cost in the United States, does Bristol-Myers make a profit selling ELIQUIS for $900 a year in Canada?

Mr. BOERNER. Senator, we do make a profit.

The CHAIR. All right. So, you are selling the product for 13 percent of what—in Canada of what we pay in the United States.

Obviously, you sell it there because you make money. So, Mr. Boerner, will you commit today that Bristol-Myers Squibb will reduce the list price of ELIQUIS in the United States to the price that you charge in Canada, where you make a profit?

Mr. BOERNER. Senator, we can't make that commitment primarily because the prices in these two countries have very different systems that prioritize very different things.

In Canada, medicines are generally made less available, and it takes oftentimes considerably longer for those medicines to be available. On average, roughly——

The CHAIR. I apologize—I do apologize. Just life expectancy in Canada is 6 years longer than it is in the United States. Mr. Boerner, your company spent over $12 billion on stock buybacks in 2022. Given that reality, can you tell Carolyn why you can't lower the price of ELIQUIS?

Mr. BOERNER. First, Senator, let me say no patient should have to go through the types of choices that the patient you just described go through. It is our commitment to continue to bring down the price of medicines in the U.S., and I would love the opportunity to bring down the price of ELIQUIS in the U.S.

Our net price, is what we are compensated, have actually over the last 5 years declined. At that same time, the list prices have increased. Why is that? Because of the complexity of this system and the billions of dollars in rebates that we have provided to intermediaries that unfortunately do not go to lowering the price of medicines like the patient you just described.

The CHAIR. Again, I apologize. I want to get very briefly to Mr. Duato, who is with Johnson & Johnson. Mr. Duato, is it true that the list price of STELARA is $79,000 here in the U.S.? Is that roughly right?

Mr. DUATO. It is roughly right, but it is also true that the average discount of STELARA in the U.S. is 70 percent.

The CHAIR. All of that, and we have dealt with PBMs, and we are going to get to that I am sure in—this morning. Is it true that while charging $79,000 in the United States, that the exact same product is sold in Spain for $18,000?

Mr. DUATO. I don't know the price in Spain. I can tell you that the average discount in the U.S. is 70 percent. So, the price that you quote, it is 30 percent of that.

The CHAIR. Okay. Mr. Duato, is it true that it costs less than $15 a year to manufacturers STELARA?

Mr. DUATO. The manufacturing cost is only a component that goes into our pricing. When we price our medicines, we are looking at the value that the medicine brings to the healthcare system. Our ability to continue to invest in research.

We invested $15 billion last year. And also, we look at affordability. The average copay, if they use our copay assistance programs in the U.S., for a patient using STELARA, it is $10 to $15 per month.

The CHAIR. I apologize. I am over my time. I am going to give Senator Cassidy the same time that I had.

Senator CASSIDY. Thank you all. Mr. Duato, the—in 2021, Janssen constructed an exclusionary contract with their PBMs to protect REMICADE, their blockbuster drug, a treatment for ulcerative colitis. Very familiar with it. A wonderful drug. Changed the outcome for people with UC.

But this deal protected REMICADE from competition by new biosimilar, Inflectra, which was launched at a 16 percent lower cost than REMICADE. Now, I understand this is confidential in terms of the settlement with the courts but—and by the way, let me just say this involves a rebate wall.

For the sake of those who are watching, a rebate wall is an anti-competitive tool which can be used to restrict a competitor's entry into a formulary. A manufacturer would offer more significant rebates to a health plan through a PBM for access to the formulary contingent upon the PBM blocking a biosimilar.

Now, we have been discussing the promise of biosimilars to lower the cost in a market oriented, competitive way. So, we are not going to have Government regulation, we have got to have a market situation, and the market would be a biosimilar, but this sort of arrangement blocked the biosimilar from entering.

In the full support of a market-oriented approach, do any of your current contracts employ rebate walls to prevent lower cost biosimilars from formulary access?

Mr. DUATO. We welcome biosimilars and generics. We believe it is an integral part of the system.

As a matter of fact, in the U.S., 90 percent of the prescriptions are biosimilars and generics, and that is one of the reasons pharmaceutical expenses have remained flat or increased single digit during the last years.

We believe that biosimilars and generic foster patient access, and we care deeply about that. And we don't——

Senator CASSIDY. But let me ask because my specific question, do any of your current contracts employ rebate walls?

Mr. DUATO. Our current contracts do not employ any technique to avoid biosimilars and generics to have uptick in the market.

Senator CASSIDY. Okay. Thank you. Now, I think at least two of you, maybe all three of you, are working on gene therapy. I have been concerned that we don't really know how we are going to price those.

I think one of the concerns is that there will not be a market for us to lower the cost of an initial gene therapy, which are incredible. It is amazing the lifetime of benefit that gene therapy can create. But I was speaking to a medical director of Medicaid CMO, and he was telling me that the pharmaceutical costs related to Medicaid is now 35 percent were formerly it was like 25 or 30 percent.

He says this is being driven by gene therapy. And when sickle cell comes widely spread, it is going to—I don't know how it is going to be priced, but my state has a lot of sicklers. I don't know how my state is going to be able to afford giving it to everybody who should have access.

Very concisely, how are we going to show restraint on the price of some of these new gene therapies, which already is driving up Medicaid? So again, 35 percent of Medicaid is now pharmaceutical cost. Mr. Boerner, I will start with you.

Mr. BOERNER. Senator. We actually don't work in gene therapy——

Senator CASSIDY. Oh, then let me go to Davis.

Mr. Davis. Mr. DAVIS. We actually do not work in gene therapy.

Senator CASSIDY. Oh, I thought I saw you at a press release that you all were doing so. You had a vector or something.

Mr. DAVIS. No, we are—well, we are doing some very basic research, but we have nothing in advanced stages.

Senator CASSIDY. Mr. Duato.

Mr. DUATO. We do have a gene therapy served for treating inherited retinal diseases. And we support legislation in order to be able to do value-based contracts in the case of gene therapy. So, we welcome legislation in order to be able to have value-based contracts.

Senator CASSIDY. That is a really—that is good. Value based contract will be important, but it still doesn't address the opening cost. Because of the opening cost of sky high, you still—you see where I am going with that.

Now, what would you give to us who believe in markets, a solution to an opening price that would be so much it would be difficult for society to afford the gene therapy. And I can put in any other drug, but let's just start with gene therapy.

Mr. DUATO. We have to look at the value of these therapies and the fact that gene therapy for inherited retinal diseases may affect only less than 1,000 people in the world. So, we have to understand that.

You can rest assured that if we are fortunate enough to bring the solution that people that have diseases that can lead to blindness, we will sit down and evaluate very thoroughly our pricing in order to make sure that patients, all patients that need this therapy, are able to afford it.

Senator CASSIDY. I think I recall a couple of years ago there was a study that was shown, respected, and you probably know it better than I, that $2 million for gene therapy for ultra-rare diseases was a reasonable sort of—it would cover the cost. It would create the incentive to produce more.

That would be for the ultra-rare, where presumably you wouldn't have the ability to produce more. You know, obviously, the more you produce, you get a little bit extra profit. You know where I am going with that. So, but that shows restraint, if you will, on the behalf of the manufacturer.

Now we want to create incentive, but we want to be able to provide access, and without access, it is as if the drug has never been invented. So, is there any other thoughts you have on how society, if that is ultra-rare, $2 million, presumably.

If it is not ultra-rare, it would be less. How can we have a market oriented approach to this? Because I truly am concerned about the ability of a Medicaid program to be able to afford some of these gene therapies.

Mr. DUATO. We care deeply about our medicines getting to the patients that are need it, especially in these, as you have mentioned, ultra-rare diseases that have therapy can have life changing consequences.

We will always sit down and make sure that the way we price is reflective of the value of the medicine, but also importantly, it enables affordability, and it makes it possible that every patient that needs it in America, can get it.

Senator CASSIDY. Now, the affordability though, we are defining affordability for the patient. So, if Medicaid covers it, it is by definition affordable for the patient, or if the insurance does. But then that doesn't necessarily make it affordable for society. And society has got to pay for it.

Obviously, Medicaid is taking more and more of a state's budget and frankly, more and more the Federal budget. I am not sure there is an answer there but let me just challenge you because we want market-oriented solutions.

We want to create incentives so that good companies like the three of you and others are making these new things. But if my state goes bankrupt paying for a new gene therapy, then my state's—the taxpayer, we all are tough—in a tough shape.

Let me just go to one more thing. There is evidence that pharmaceutical companies will do lifecycle management kind of to prolong the sort of exclusivity of a drug. And some have argued that actually defeats innovation because as opposed to making profit from innovation, you can make profit from lifecycle management. Any thoughts about that, Mr. Boerner?

Mr. BOERNER. Senator, I think lifecycle management, if you think about the extension of new indications for a product, is incredibly important to really being able to deliver additional benefits to patients.

Obviously, the patents associated with any product will dictate when a generic enters. We have been in favor of a robust generic entry primarily because our focus is on innovative products.

But think, for example, in cancer where typically you start the treatment of cancer very late in disease, learn more about how the drug works, show it is safe, but ultimately you can bring that into early stage cancer, where you have the potential to potentially cure patients.

Now, that takes quite a bit of time, but that is an example of a lifecycle management where you are actually showing the true potential of a medicine. I would hate for us to cutoff the opportunity to show those benefits.

At the same time, we should be, as an industry, welcoming of generic competition, because ultimately our focus as a company is to take resources as we get close to generic entry and focus those resources on the next wave of new product innovation, which is where I think we ultimately want to go for patients.

Senator CASSIDY. Mr. Davis, you have got 20 seconds. How would you do it?

Mr. DAVIS. Well, the short answer is, as I look at it, one, we very much support generic drugs and biosimilar drugs. I think it is the core of how our system works. We have a period where we are protected.

We are able to recoup our investment, and then society benefits in perpetuity beyond that. As we look at life cycle management, we always are asking, are we bringing value to the patient? I will give you a live example.

If you look at KEYTRUDA. KEYTRUDA now, as I mentioned, is in 39 indications across 17 tumor types. It is revolutionizing the care of patients facing cancer. The reality of it is still only 30 percent of people show overall response.

As great as it is, patients are still suffering. And what we are doing is investing in combination therapies to be able to extend and go beyond that 30 percent, which means much better benefit and value to the patients that will—that ultimately use those drugs.

Senator CASSIDY. Thank you.

The CHAIR. Senator Murphy.

Senator MURPHY. Thank you very much, Mr. Chairman. Thank you for holding this really important hearing. Mr. Duato, looking at your arthritis drug, and we have talked already a little in this hearing about the difference in price between the United States and other countries.

Annual cost around $80,000 in the United States, $20,000 in Canada, $12,000 in France. Are the prices that you receive from a country like Canada or France, which look to me to be about one quarter of the price that you get from the United States, are those prices covering your costs?

Mr. DUATO. Yes they do. To clarify, Senator, the price in the U.S. is discounted by 70 percent. So, the appropriate comparison would be $25,000 in the case of STELARA, if you are considering that price.

Senator MURPHY. Are the prices you are receiving from these other countries, so let's say France—but I will give you the benefit of your argument. France is still 20—it is still 50 percent of the U.S. cost that you are claiming. Are those countries' prices covering your costs?

Mr. DUATO. They do. The difference is that, for example, in Canada, which was the first country you quoted, STELARA, which is mainly indicated for inflammatory bowel disease, Crohn's disease, and ulcerative colitis, not for arthritis, is not just reimbursed in the public system.

Canadian patients that want to access STELARA, they cannot do it in the public system because 8 years, 8 years later is not yet reimbursed there.

Senator MURPHY. You don't identify any free rider syndrome today in which the United States is paying higher prices, allowing other nations to receive lower prices?

Mr. DUATO. I agree with you that the prices in the U.S. are generally higher for medicines, more aligned than what you are describing, as the rest of the healthcare system prices are.

The percentage of pharmaceutical expenses over the total healthcare expenses in the U.S. is 14 percent, and that is lower than most of the advanced economies. The real difference is that in the U.S., patients get access to therapy, lifesaving therapy years before they do in the countries that you mentioned.

Senator MURPHY. If the United States were to restrict the prices we paid, would that create a different negotiating dynamic in countries that right now, for instance, are paying 50 percent of what the United States pays? Would it allow you in your negotiations to get higher prices from other nations that right now are paying far less than the United States?

Mr. DUATO. We believe that price caps are not the way that innovation is going to be fostered. We have worked with the United States Trade

Department and with U.S. embassies around the world to try to reject the price caps that some countries, as the one you to mentioned, impose.

We welcome the support of the U.S. Government in avoiding that these Governments that are ultimately imposing price caps on those that are not benefiting their patients neither.

Senator MURPHY. What do you say to Americans who look at the way that you allocate revenue and wonder why, in your case for instance, you are spending $6 billion on stock buybacks, $11 billion on dividends, and $14 billion on research and development.

You spend all of your advertising time talking about the research and development spend, but I think most Americans would be pretty surprised, given how much the industry talks about research and development, that you are actually spending more money shelling out money to investors and buying back stock than you are on research and development.

What do you say to folks who look at that and come to the conclusion that you care much more about keeping your investors happy and keeping your executives happy than you do in researching and development the next class of drugs that is going to help regular Americans?

Mr. DUATO. We care deeply about patients, Senator, and we care deeply about being able to discover the next medicines that are going to address major problems like Alzheimer's. What we——

Senator MURPHY. But explain to me how you justify that division of dividends and stock buybacks versus research development. You could just choose instead of using $6 billion to buy back stock to put that into more research and development, but you don't.

Mr. DUATO. Our level of R&D investment in the 2-years that referred to the $6 billion program buyback, which were 2022 and 2023, is six times higher.

In that period, we invested $30 billion in R&D and $6 billion in stock buybacks. So, we spent six times more in developing cures for patients than we did in the stock buyback.

Senator MURPHY. Well, I am looking at 2022 profits and spending by Johnson & Johnson, and it shows me $11 billion in dividends, $6 billion in stock buybacks, $45 million in executive compensation, and $14 billion in research and development.

Can you understand—let me ask a different question, do you understand that one of my constituents in Connecticut would look at those numbers and think that you care more about padding the pockets of the folks that work for you and invest in you than in research and development?

Mr. DUATO. Our priority is investing in R&D. We have spent $77 billion since 2016. And yes, we have to pay dividends because it is the only way that the company can remain operational and sustainable.

Otherwise, if we are not operational and sustainable, we are not able to do—fulfill our mission of developing medicine for patients and making them affordable.

Senator MURPHY. Mr. Boerner, you talked in your testimony about, the United States has a health care system that prioritizes the important role of patient choice.

I just want to present you with the case of one of my constituents and ask you about the choices that she faces. So, I have a constituent who needs ELIQUIS. This is a blood thinner that is critical to her survival.

She has priced the Medicare plan that gets her the best possible price. And that price is $350 a month. The average Social Security benefit in Connecticut is about $1,700 a month. And of course, somebody who is on ELIQUIS is likely on other drugs as well.

Here is her choice. Her choice is to pay the $350 and go without food or pay her rent late, or not take the drug and risk heart attack or stroke. Is that the choice you are talking about when you refer to a health care system that prioritizes the important role of choice?

Mr. BOERNER. Senator, absolutely not. And in fact, I would say on behalf of all of our employees at Bristol-Myers Squibb, that is a choice no patient should have to make.

Senator MURPHY. But she makes it. She makes it because you have chosen to price a drug at a point that is not affordable.

Mr. DUATO. Senator, we have priced ELIQUIS in the U.S., in our in our estimation—in fact, we try to do this for all of our medicines, consistent with the value it brings. And we are very happy with the fact that ELIQUIS is the leading anti-stroke drug——

Senator MURPHY. Why not take—why not—you put $8 billion into stock buybacks. Why not do $4 billion and instead take the rest of the money and bring the price of the drug down?

The CHAIR. I am going to keep people to seven.

Senator Tuberville.

Senator TUBERVILLE. Thank you, Mr. Chairman. Thanks for being here today. It is pretty well known where our Chairman stands on this—his worldwide view. Pretty clear that he believes you guys are setting drug prices and it is all about corporate greed.

I am a true believer of capitalism. I believe that we have the best health care system in the world. Problem is we have got the Federal Government involved in it and it is not implemented the way probably it should be. That being said, I just got a few questions here on a couple of things.

Mr. Davis, can you explain to me something, the Biden administration has two huge priorities, dictate prices of prescription drugs, specifically small molecule drugs, and cure cancer. Can you walk me through how those priorities might be in direct contradiction of each other?

Mr. DAVIS. Well, Senator, I think what you are referring to is what is called the pill penalty——

Senator TUBERVILLE. That is correct.

Mr. DAVIS. Underneath the IRA. And what that does is effectively—it says that at 9 years, post your first approval, your price for your drug will be negotiated, and if it is a small molecule—it is $13, if it is a large.

The issue that raises is that it disfavors small molecule development. And the reality of it is if you look across the majority of cancer treatments, they are still small molecules. And, as Chris pointed out earlier, the development of cancer drugs usually starts in a phase starting at the very, most sickest patient, the last stage of disease, and then you work forward into earlier stages of disease where in fact you can start to maybe talk about cure.

To do those studies in early stage disease, often called adjuvant or neoadjuvant care, and we have nine approvals in that space, those studies can take 7 to 9 years to do so. Obviously if at 9 years I have to significantly reduce the price of that drug to a point that it is potentially at basically no profit, my incentive to do those follow on studies is not there.

That is our worry that if you look at cancer care, you are going to see patients suffer because we can't get to really talking about cure, which is in earlier stages disease. I would also point out you didn't ask about Alzheimer's and neuroscience diseases, but most CNS diseases also require small molecules because large molecules, biologics can't penetrate the blood brain barrier.

We are disincentivizing some of the largest areas of sickness and chronic need in our society through that pill penalty you are referring to.

Senator TUBERVILLE. Thank you. Mr. Boerner, we hear a lot about how health care costs are ridiculous high. I think all of us would agree to that some degree. I want to peel back the onion here a little bit.

Today, we are being led to believe that these costs are due to corporate greed. I want to know if we are going to talk about some additional drivers of health care costs. When the Federal Government dumped trillions into various industries during Covid, we up-ended our markets and drove prices through the roof.

You know, when I talked to health care folks back in Alabama, labor cost is one huge problem. But there are other costs, including supplies and raw materials. What impact are these having on the drug development and how drug cost?

Mr. BOERNER. Certainly, Senator, when we look at the cost bases for us doing what we do as a company, which is to bring forward new medicines for patients, we have to factor in all of those costs.

I will give you an example. In cellular therapy, which is really transforming very late line hematologic diseases. These are very complex medicines. You are taking patient cells, manufacturing them and re-engineering them to really target and hone in on cancer cells, and then you are inject them in the patients. This is really a first generation technology.

Unfortunately, it has very high labor costs because this is one that is very manual. It is a multi-step process to manufacture these products. There are transportation costs, their raw material costs.

All of those factors go into a cost of these first generation medicines. Now we are very focused on trying to innovate to get to a second and third generation quickly so we can bring those costs down, not only because it is important for us to be able to funnel additional research into development, but also so that we can bring ultimately the cost down to patients.

They are absolutely a factor, Senator.

Senator TUBERVILLE. Thank you. Mr. Duato, I am going to ask you this. With your accent and mine, we will probably have a tough time. But I know you are probably aware in 2021, you weren't CEO, I don't think, at that time, but the Biden administration announced a mandate that U.S. troops and personnel must take the Covid vaccine in order to serve in the military. Are you familiar with that?

Mr. DUATO. I am familiar, sir. Thank you.

Senator TUBERVILLE. Are you aware that more than 8,400 troops were kicked out of the military for declining to take the Covid vaccine? These were mostly young, healthy Americans for whom Covid risk was low. Are you aware of that?

Mr. DUATO. No, I was not aware of that, sir.

Senator TUBERVILLE. Thank you. Did you or did anyone at Johnson & Johnson encourage the Biden administration to mandate this Covid vaccine to the military? Are you familiar with that?

Mr. DUATO. We did not, sir.

Senator TUBERVILLE. Okay. How much did Johnson & Johnson benefit financially from the administration's military Covid vaccine mandate? Could you have any kind of guess to that?

Mr. DUATO. Our effort in the Covid vaccine that we collaborated with the Government, it was a time of a global emergency, so we thought that as a healthcare company that cares for patients we needed to collaborate with the U.S. Government on that, was entirely non-for-profit.

Senator TUBERVILLE. Do you think the soldiers who were expelled from the military was a right thing to do, and should they be reinstated?

Mr. DUATO. I was not aware of the situation, sir. I am not aware of these circumstances, so I cannot comment on that.

Senator TUBERVILLE. Thank you. Thank you, Mr. Chairman.

The CHAIR. Thank you, Senator.

Senator Murray.

Senator MURRAY. Thank you very much, Mr. Chairman. And thank you all for being here. We really appreciate it. I think we hear from our constituents constantly, and frighteningly, about the cost of some of the drugs that they take.

This is really an important hearing. And I continue to hear, as many have said, that sky-high drug costs are forcing many people, including in my home, State of Washington, to choose between filling their prescription and paying for other things they need, essentials like groceries or rent, and I often talk to people who are skipping their prescription altogether because they can't afford it and it puts their life at risk.

I really believe that Congress does need to do more here, I have for a long time, and I also think pharmaceutical companies need to do much more to put patients first. And that doesn't mean that private companies can't make a profit, and I think we all have a really sincere appreciation for the cutting edge research that happens at each of your companies.

But when you say you are in the business of saving lives and curing disease, you have to think about putting patients over profits, because, as we all know, lifesaving drugs don't do anyone any good if people can't afford them. So, I want to ask you about affordability. And I have heard the numbers. I was listening in my office.

Mr. Duato, your drug company makes product to treat arthritis, STELARA. It costs $79,000 annually here in the U.S., $12,000 in France. Mr. Davis, your company makes a drug to treat cancer, KEYTRUDA. You have been talking about it. Annually, the cost here is $191,000. $44,000 in Japan.

Mr. Boerner, your company makes a drug, ELIQUIS, to treat the risk of stroke that costs $7,100 in the year, and $770 in Germany. So, I mean, either you think that the same prescription drugs sold around the world work better here in America, or we are getting something more for it.

I mean, I don't think that is the case, but I wanted to ask each one of you, explain to us why it costs more in terms that we can tell our constituents and they understand. And, Mr. Duato, let me talk to you.

Mr. DUATO. We share your concerns about what patients have to pay at the pharmacy counter for medicines. In the case of STELARA that you mentioned, the net price in the U.S. is 70 percent lower than the price that you refer, so it would be $24,000. It is still higher than in France, but it is more aligned than here.

The difference is that patients with inflammatory bowel disease, which is the main indication with STELARA, were able to afford STELARA years earlier than they did in other countries. As a matter of fact, in Canada, after 8 years that STELARA was approved, STELARA is not reimbursed in inflammatory bowel disease, nor in Crohn's disease, or ulcerative colitis.

What are we doing for that? We have strong patient assistance programs. A patient that has commercial insurance pays $10 to $15 a month for STELARA, and if they are not insured or underinsured, we have free medicine program. We distributed $3.9 billion in free drug in 2022.

Senator MURRAY. Mr. Davis.

Mr. DAVIS. If you look at KEYTRUDA and the example you are bringing up between the U.S. and Japan, first of all, like all of us, we are trying to focus on making sure that patients everywhere in the world get access to our medicines. Each market operates differently. Japan is a unique market in that the way they price their drugs, and we have been working hard to get this to change.

I think maybe we have successfully gotten some of it to change. Is that after you initially launched your drug, for every indication that comes afterwards, they treat it as a different drug. And in addition, if a competitor launches a drug, then you also still take a price decrease because of the competitor drug.

We are in a strange situation and one that is a very concerning situation to me in Japan, where in reality we as the most innovative, we have the most indications, we were driving the market fastest, we have by far the lowest discounted price in Japan, and the levels in Japan would not be sustainable to support the $46 billion, $40 billion we spent on KEYTRUDA.

We are working hard to help those markets and we could use Government help there to understand that we need to, across the globe, share in making sure we can invest to support innovation.

Senator MURRAY. What would Congress do that would make a difference to lower prices here?

Mr. DAVIS. I think. Well, on one hand it is a different question on lowering prices here. I think that is a question I am assuming we are going to get to, but this is, how do we focus on what is the really large discrepancy between the list price and the net price, which I believe we need to focus on is the out-of-pocket cost to the patient.

That is really the core. We need to address that. But in addition, we need to continue to work together on—we can work on trying to drive innovation clauses into trade agreements, we have had some success with that, to also help us in those markets outside the United States as well.

Senator MURRAY. Mr. Boerner.

Mr. BOERNER. Senator, there is no doubt that patients are going to pay less for our drug ELIQUIS, or frankly most of our drugs outside of the U.S. than in the U.S. That, unfortunately, comes at a fairly significant cost for those patients outside of the U.S.

In Canada, patients will wait roughly three and a half to 4 years to get access to a medicine that is available in the U.S. You see similar sort of stats in virtually every European country and in Japan. What we can do more in the U.S. to do is try to bring out the pockets down—out-of-pocket costs down.

For ELIQUIS, for example, the average out-of-pocket is roughly $50, $55 in the U.S. Most patients will pay less than $40. However, there are still patients for whom this drug is absolutely not affordable. That is not acceptable.

Medicare, in particular, is a space where we can't provide those types of copay support programs that we do in the commercial setting, so we would love to work with Congress on that. But probably the most important thing, and ELIQUIS is a great example of this that we can do, is try to bring down the list cost of ELIQUIS——

Senator MURRAY. Do you set the list price?

Mr. DUATO. We set the list price, but that lowest price for ELIQUIS is driven up by the incentives of intermediaries. And let me give you an example, order of magnitude. Over the last 5 years, we have, as a company, paid almost $100 billion in rebates and discounts to intermediaries.

The majority of those were on ELIQUIS. And our ability—that is unfortunately what patients pay is a co-pay on that list price. We would love to work with Congress to bring that down.

The CHAIR. Senator Marshall.

Senator MARSHALL. All right. Thank you, Mr. Chairman. Mr. Boerner, I will start with you. Bristol Myers makes this new miracle drug, ELIQUIS, relatively a miracle drug.

When I was in residency treating patients, I was using Coumadin—Heparin and then Coumadin. It might take three or 4 days to get someone heparnized, and then we switch them over to Coumadin.

They might be in the hospital for 10 or 14 days. So, in its own right, ELIQUIS saves money. It saves that length in the hospital and prevents hospitalizations as well. So, I want to point that out.

As we think—talk about rationing care, we have discussed how we are rationing care in foreign countries. But I want you to speak about rationing care in this country. How do PBMs ration care when they take a drug like ELIQUIS and don't allow it on their formulary? Does that ever happen?

Mr. BOERNER. Senator, I am glad you raised that point. We have had absolutely that case happen on multiple drugs. We have had it happen on ELIQUIS. We have had it happen where when we have not been able to reach an agreement with an intermediary on a rebate, that they have taken ELIQUIS off of formulary.

When that happens, those patients no longer have access to ELIQUIS and they have to go on to another branded or in many cases, they may go on to Warfarin, as you say. ELIQUIS is the No. 1 product in the oral anticoagulant space——

Senator MARSHALL. Okay, so I am going to—sorry. So, they have to go back to Warfarin, the Coumadin, the drug that I was using in medical school in the 1980's. A drug with significant complications.

Hassle factor, the patient has to go get blood testing done maybe twice a week as well. But with your drug the miracle, one of the miracle parts of it is that a, they don't bleed into their brains anymore. And two, they don't have to go get their blood testing done once a week as well.

It is a huge amount of innovation. And it is just—it amazes me how much power these PBMs have obtained. Let's go to Mr. Davis next.

I want to talk about de-linking. And you have, at the time, a pretty—a miracle drug of your own to treat diabetes with. And there is a list price. How much of that—what percentage of that list price does typically Merck get at the end of the day?

Mr. DAVIS. Senator, if you look at JANUVIA, which is the drug you were speaking to, the list price is $6,900.

Senator MARSHALL. Per year?

Mr. DAVIS. Per year, for Merck. We recognize $690 on that drug per year.

Senator MARSHALL. Of the list price, you are only getting 10 percent.

Mr. DAVIS. It is a 90 percent discount.

Senator MARSHALL. 90 percent discount. Where does the rest of that money go?

Mr. DAVIS. Into the middlemen. Into the system as a whole.

Senator MARSHALL. If we had the time and the energy and a chalkboard, would you be able to explain to me and show me all the little places that goes?

Mr. DAVIS. I could, but I think you appreciate it is highly complex and so complex that at times even learned people who play in the space can't understand it.

Senator MARSHALL. Well certainly, I can't explain it, and that is my point. Is it is so nontransparent, we don't know where this money is going, but certainly, we know that pharmacy benefit managers are taking $0.50 to $0.75 of that dollar, and you are only getting 10 percent of it.

I would like to know where the rest of it goes. Then I will go back to Mr. Boerner. Similarly, with your drug, with ELIQUIS, what type of—what percent of that list price do you think that you all are taking home?

Mr. BOERNER. Senator, it is a relatively smaller percentage. As I mentioned before, we have paid over the last 5 years about $100 billion in rebates and discounts, and the majority of that go to one product and that is ELIQUIS.

Senator MARSHALL. Okay. Go back to Mr. Davis. Let's talk about, you all have an antiviral drug that has been approved. How many drugs did you go down—when Covid hit, you were trying to develop multiple drugs. How many have made it across the finish line? What did you spend on R&D as you look at those all together?

Mr. DAVIS. Yes, so we—when the COVID situation hit, we drove two—or four key programs, two in vaccines, two in antivirals. Only one of those succeeded, which is the drug LAGEVRIO. The total spend across those four programs is a little over $2.5 billion.

Senator MARSHALL. You spent $2.5 billion. You got one across the finish line, an antiviral. Is that being used in the United States?

Mr. DAVIS. Very little. It has emergency use authorization. It never got to full approval. And so, we are actually seeing it being used much more outside the United States.

Senator MARSHALL. In actuality, you spent $2.5 billion and got nonsignificant market share in the United States despite that. Mr. Duato, I will talk to you for a second.

In my 25 years taking care of patients, we were always able to find a solution for their drugs that they needed, 340B programs, rebates. There is always exceptions to the rules, but what type of efforts has J&J made to work with 340B programs and to help some of these people that need help?

Mr. DUATO. Thank you, sir. We care deeply about patient affordability, but also we care about the sustainability of the rural hospitals and the small hospitals that take care of patients that are underserved.

We believe that the 340B program, it is an important program to support those hospitals and we are fully, fully looking forward to collaborate with them in any way we can to support patient access on those hospitals.

Senator MARSHALL. I am going to point out once again, it is just not rural hospitals, it is our community health centers are taking great advantage of the 340B program as well, trying to make sure that every patient in America has access to primary care—true affordable access to primary care, plus having access to affordable drugs as well.

I might make a couple quick points. The people of Kansas sent me here to save Medicare. To save Medicare, I need a miracle drug to treat Alzheimer's. It seems to me that Americans bear the burden of most of the R&D in this world, and other countries benefit from it.

That impacts the price in many ways as well. Mr. Davis, am I wrong? Why does it feel like to me that Americans are feeling most of the brunt of the R&D cost, or is that not accurate? I don't know.

Mr. DAVIS. Well, I think, Senator, it gets down to, as you look across the globe, different markets and I appreciate what the U.S. does. I think the U.S. favors innovation. It values it. It values access for our patients, fast access, most access. Many markets around the world don't do that.

What they focus on more is their budget and how do they meet those budget needs, and we appreciate the budgetary constraints that everyone faces. But as a result of that, often patients aren't getting access to meds. They don't get them as fast, which we have commented on today, and it is harder to see how you can support the innovation we need to do in that situation.

The CHAIR. Thank you. Senator Baldwin. Senator Casey.

Senator CASEY. Thanks so much, Senator Baldwin, for allowing me to jump ahead. Mr. Chairman, thanks for the hearing. I want to start with a sense of what I hear back home.

When I talk to people in Pennsylvania, and a lot of your companies have a lot of interest in Pennsylvania, I hear over and over again this problem, the cost of prescription drugs, is like a bag of heavy rocks.

It is when been people have been carrying this around their shoulders every day, year after year, and they are tired of it. And they don't believe that any player in this is doing enough.

I think most Pennsylvanians are happy that I could vote for a bill in 2022 that allowed Medicare to negotiate for lower prescription drug costs and that we could cap the cost of insulin $35 bucks a month for Medicare Part D beneficiaries. They are happy that we could cap the out-of-pocket cost.

That will go into effect about a year from now. But they are not happy—they are not satisfied that even Congress is doing enough, House or Senate, or either party. But they are certainly not happy with the level of work that you have put into this. Look, I hear all this talk about rebates and cost reductions you are trying to put in place, but it is not cutting back home.

When I talk to people that see what PBMs are doing, they know that they are not meeting the obligation that they would expect them to. So, there is no question that your companies and big pharmaceutical companies are playing a role in this. You bear a measure of responsibility in this.

I wanted to ask you a couple questions about that. First and foremost, tell me what concrete steps, very specific steps, that each of you are taking and your companies are taking to make sure that we can get these costs down. And even by way of repetition, you may have already said it.

I'm not worried about you repeating yourself, but we need to know specifically what you are doing to lowering costs so that no one, especially someone who needs a lifesaving intervention, a lifesaving treatment, is going to be denied that solely, solely because of cost. And I will start on the left, Mr. Duato, going left to right.

Mr. DUATO. Thank you, Senator Cassidy. We absolutely want to be part of the solution. We understand that co-pay obligations for U.S. patients are burdensome, and it does create health inequities.

What are we doing for that? We have a very extensive patient assistance program that, for commercial patients, enables them to be able to pay low co-pays, $5 to $15 per month. We supported more than 1 million patients in 2022 with our copay assistance programs. If a patient is underinsured or not insured, we provide free drug.

We gave $3.9 billion in free drug in 2022. But I think we can do more, and we can work together in order to lower out-of-pocket costs for patients even in Medicare, as you mentioned, because that is a real need that we are committed, all our employees are committed in order to make sure that our medicines get to the patients that did deserve it.

Senator CASEY. Mr. Davis.

Mr. DAVIS. Well, Senator, very much like J&J, we have tiered levels of patient assistance programs because we want to make sure that patients who need our drugs can access them. If you have insurance but you fall below certain means where you are not able to handle your copay, we will give copay assistance to those patients through a program we run.

If you are someone who doesn't have insurance, is not able to qualify for Government programs, we have a patient assistance program that basically provides the drugs for free. So, we are very much focused on this and making sure that we can do everything we can, and we are investing a lot of money on it.

But something I would like to add, because I think it is important to the discussion. We are focusing on prices today, but we also need to think about innovation as a way to fix the problem. And something we are focusing on as a company is a new technology called micro cyclic peptides that allow us to potentially take what historically has been large molecules difficult to make, expensive drugs difficult to deliver, and we are starting to show the capability to convert those into cheaper, small molecule forms, oral forms.

If we are able to do that, we have one in late stage development now called an oral PCSK9, which is for heart disease. But we are looking to do that for others. We are investing millions, billions behind that effort.

I think we need to also think about how can innovation solve the problem. We need to address the price challenges today. We have to lower out-of-pocket costs. But innovation ultimately is what is going to help us fix this.

Senator CASEY. Sir.

Mr. BOERNER. Senator, maybe I would highlight three things. First, we obviously have a very robust, on the commercial side, copay assistance program that brings out-of-pocket costs down in many cases for certainly our oral oncologists, for example, almost to zero.

They are complex at times, so we are working very hard to make those more universally available. That is step one. Step two, we would like to work with this Congress to find ways in which we could apply the same sort of programs in Medicare. There are some complexities.

We want to make sure we are not diverting from the use of generics, for example, but we think there are potential ways that we could do that, and we would love to explore those opportunities with Congress to bring out-of-pocket costs down for Medicare patients.

The second thing I would say is we are looking at doing more innovative work, innovative contracting work where we can. For example, if our drug works, we get paid. If it doesn't work, we get paid less and, in some cases, maybe even not get paid at all. There are technicalities in the U.S. that prohibit us from doing that more in the U.S.

We want to work to get those removed. The third thing, just building on what Rob was saying, is we do believe that innovation plays a role here. Cellular therapy, while not gene therapy per the previous question, those are expensive therapies.

We have got to bring those costs down, and the way we will do that is we will innovate to the next generation, which hopefully is way less complex than what I described previously.

Senator CASEY. Well, I will be submitting some more follow-up questions for the record. Thank you, Mr. Chairman.

The CHAIR. Thank you. Senator Paul.

Senator PAUL. I am not an apologist for big pharma. In fact, when corporations manipulate Government to their advantage, crony capitalism, I am an unfettered critic. But in defense of capitalism, I am a consistent, unapologetic advocate.

Milton Friedman once wrote that if you want to create a shortage of tomatoes, just pass a law that retailers can't sell tomatoes for more than $0.02. Instantly, you will have a tomato shortage. I might also add that is true of prescription drugs. Virtually every shortage of drugs that we have seen in the last few years involves price controls that drive out production of the drug.

One reason the United States leads in pharmaceutical innovation is because while the U.S. adhere to more—a more market based pricing and rewarded innovators, Europe adopted stringent price controls in the 1980's and 90's. It is not surprising that we lead the world in innovation and Europe does not.

But unfortunately, this Committee in this hearing is not here to celebrate American success. Instead, the majority drags us to conduct a show trial to harangue companies challenging the Inflation Reduction Act price controls in court.

They have simply brought forward people who question their partisan legislation. Ten years ago, the 5-year survival rate for patients diagnosed with advanced lung cancer was 5 percent—terrible. Since Merck introduced the cancer drug KEYTRUDA in 2014, the survival rate has grown nearly fourfold, 5 percent to 20 percent.

We should be celebrating that instead of castigating people and telling them how to run their business, and why are you buying your stock back. I have a friend with a genetic predisposition to cancer. He is alive today because of KEYTRUDA. We should be celebrating that. Johnson & Johnson's REMICADE was the first monoclonal antibody approved for treating chronic conditions like Crohn's disease and rheumatoid arthritis.

Since its approval, Remicade has revolutionized treatments for inflammatory disease, made remission a reality for patients with debilitating conditions, and paved the way for development of other autoimmune treatments. When I began in medicine, virtually all patients with rheumatoid arthritis you could see from a distance had crippling, disfiguring arthritis in their hands.

Now, today, it is rarely seen because of the advances of American companies under an American system that allowed profit to occur. In 1987, Merck pledged to donate the entire stock of its drug, Ivermectin, to those suffering from river blindness. Nearly 37 years later, Ivermectin Donation Program treats 300 million people annually, with over 11 million treatments shipped to endemic countries.

This is charity, my friends, from capitalism. You don't get this under socialism because there is no profit under socialism. They have no money to give. They make extraordinary profits. Do they keep some of their investors? Yes, that is what they are supposed to do. But they also have some left over for charity and you don't get that under socialism.

Because of Merck's donation, seven countries eradicated the transmission of the No. 1 cause of blindness in the world. Pharmaceutical innovation has improved cancer rates, cured hepatitis C, doubled the life span of patients living with cystic fibrosis. It goes on and on.

We have tried price controls in general here. We did in the 1970's under a Republican President, under Nixon. It was a disaster, and it led to lines at the gas pump. It was an ultimate disaster. A study at the University of Chicago, found that 254 fewer drug approvals over the course of 18 years would happen under price controls.

Under communism, they knew this. Socialism, communism, and the economic system of socialism from price—it became a running joke. In Poland during the Soviet era there was a story of the guy who went to the store, he was looking for eggs, and he asked the clerk, is this a store with no eggs? And they said, no, this is a store with no toilet paper. The store with no eggs is across the street.

That is the story of socialism. That is the story of price controls. Scarcity and empty shells are the inevitable result of price controls. Those who understand and appreciate capitalism do not need a show trial to dupe them into forgetting that price controls have never worked and never will.

Let's get back to profitability. I don't think you guys did a very good job on answering this. Did you add into your estimate of whether it is profitable in Canada, whether or not it cost you $2.6 billion on average to develop it? You are talking about manufacturing costs. You are talking about how much it cost to make KEYTRUDA and how much you sell it for, and say you have a profit in Canada.

Do you think it would still be a profit, Mr. Davis, if you added in all the R&D, the $2.6 billion to get it through this system, all— the apparatus of your company and you divided all of that out for profitability, would it still be profitable in most of these other countries?

Mr. DAVIS. I have not done that analysis, but I would say that the profitability would be marginal at best.

Senator PAUL. Do you think you would have as much R&D if the whole world were Canada? Do you think you would be developing dozens of new drugs every year if the whole world were Canada?

Mr. DAVIS. No, I do not.

Senator PAUL. This is what we are arguing against, you know. Sure, you can make it for pennies now, but it didn't start that way. And then people were like, oh, my it costs so much in the beginning. That is capitalism. That is the way it works in capitalism. Joseph Schumpeter talked about this, and he said, this is an old anecdote, but he said, the miracle of capitalism is not the queens have silk stockings, but that factory girls ultimately do.

But in the beginning only the queen has silk stockings. Rich people get stuff in the beginning. Rich people drive the innovation. The first calculators that came out, $300 for adding, subtracting, and dividing machine.

Now they are like pennies or free. But you have to allow the price to be higher in the beginning and the market brings it down as you have more widespread market. That is capitalism. We don't know what the correct price is. There is no moral price. There is no moral amount of profit.

There is no business of any of you all telling them how much stock to buy back. Their job is to make a profit. It is actually against the law for them not to maximize their profit. For you to sit in judgment of how much profit they should make and how they should run their companies, you know nothing of running companies.

You know, nobody up here, maybe some, but almost nobody up here has run big companies, billion-dollar companies and you presume somehow to say you are going to tell these people how to run their company. List price versus net price. List price means absolutely nothing. I charged $1,800 for cataract surgery.

The Government paid me $600. Two-thirds of it, nobody stole that. It disappeared because it never existed. So, if I build $1 million in charges, I really was only building $300,000 because that is what I was getting paid. But because of the confusing nature of the system, the list price is much different than the net.

But to quote list price and then compare it to net price in other countries is completely and profoundly unfair. The list price means absolutely nothing. All of these fallacies need to be addressed before we begin haranguing American CEOs. Thank you.

The CHAIR. Thank you for your questioning. Senator Hassan.

Senator HASSAN. Well, thank you, Mr. Chair.

The CHAIR. Senator Baldwin. I am sorry.

Senator HASSAN. She——

Senator BALDWIN. I yielded to Senator Casey.

Senator HASSAN. I know, but I was next——

The CHAIR. All right. Senator Hassan, go in then Senator Baldwin.

Senator HASSAN. Thank you. So, I just wanted to say, at the outset that the last time I checked, when a buyer and seller negotiate for a price, that is capitalism.

I wanted to talk with all three of our distinguished witnesses today, because one of the things that strikes me that we are struggling with is I think at various times in each one of your statements, you talked about your price reflecting the value of your product. And the thing is, human health and life is priceless.

If that is the metric here, you will always have an excuse for charging increasing prices for these lifesaving drugs. And what we are trying to do here is figure out how you can continue the innovation that Senator Paul just so eloquently spoke about. I would suspect that every Member up here has a family member whose life has been saved by innovative medications are greatly improved.

But at the end of the day, we have to find a way to allow you all to innovate but also to make sure that the market here and the system here works for the very people whose lives you are helping to save.

I want to start with a question to you, Mr. Davis. While families in New Hampshire and across the country struggle to afford these lifesaving medications, pharmaceutical companies are doing everything that they can to keep their prices and their profits sky high. And I know you both talked about that not being the case, but let's just look at one thing here.

One way that companies do this is by filing dozens, even hundreds of frivolous patents that lock in their exclusive right to sell their drug for decades.

By playing games like this with the patent system, companies block low cost alternatives like generics from coming to market. Mr. Davis, the list price for Merck's cancer medication, KEYTRUDA is, as we have talked about, $190,000 per year. Can you tell us how many patents have been filed on this medication?

Mr. DAVIS. I don't have the exact number, but I would focus you on probably the most important patents, which are the composition of matter patents. In addition to that, the formulation and manufacturing patents.

There is one suite of composition of matter patents that we have and those are what allow us to continue to have exclusivity.

Senator HASSAN. Well, I don't think it would surprise you to learn that I do know how many patents you currently have. It is 168. This is what this looks like. Sheet after sheet after sheet.

Patent office records show that not only do you have 168, but half of them relate to the process Merck uses to manufacture the drug, not the way that the drug is used to treat patients. Merck is using patent gimmicks and loopholes to delay other companies from selling lower cost versions of this medication, all while raising the price of KEYTRUDA in the U.S. year after year.

It would be good if Merck would just stop blocking patient access to low cost medications by using the patent system in this way. It is clear that Merck and other pharmaceutical companies, you are not alone, won't stop abusing the patent system to keep their prices high.

It is clear we also need to take action on that. And that is something we can do. Senator Braun and I have a bill called the Medication Affordability and Patent Integrity Act, which would help break up these patent rules. And I would urge my colleagues on both sides of the aisle to support that.

Now, Mr. Duato, in your testimony, you mentioned that Johnson & Johnson provides financial assistance to uninsured patients in the United States. However, the barriers to access these programs are unreasonably high.

For an expensive medication like your company's arthritis drug, STELARA, what does a patient have to do to get assistance from the Johnson & Johnson program?

Mr. DUATO. Thank you. We care deeply about patient access, and we put a lot of work in developing well and wide patient assistance programs. And we have mechanisms for patients to connect with us via—mechanisms like a website called Johnson Care Path, in which patients can access patient assistance. We supported 1.1 million people with patient copay assistance last year.

Senator HASSAN. Well, let me just talk a little bit about that. The initial application, which I have here, is six pages long, and it requires pages of additional documents for income verification.

In the fine print, this document even requires the patient to consent to a credit report check and other financial disclosures. Mr. Duato, everyone on this dais wants you to charge a fair price for your company's medications.

But if someone does need assistance paying for their medication, this process has to be streamlined and easily available to anyone who qualifies. So, I would urge you to look personally at this application.

When somebody is dealing with a serious illness, the last thing they need to do is read the fine print and decide that they have to disclose a credit report, the relevance of which kind of escapes me. Mr. Boerner and Mr. Duato, we could also increase competition by making it easier for generic drugs to get approved.

Mr. Boerner let's turn to the BMS stroke prevention drug ELIQUIS. The list price, as we have talked about, is $7,100 per year. How many generics of this drug could a patient in the United States get at the pharmacy today?

Mr. BOERNER. Senator, in the U.S., there are not yet generics available.

Senator HASSAN. Right. There are zero generic versions of ELIQUIS available to patients, even though the original patents on the medication began to sunset in 2019. Because your company has sued to block two approved generics from the U.S. market until 2028 at the earliest, isn't that right?

Mr. BOERNER. Senator, we have allowed for generic entry in 2028. That is correct.

Senator HASSAN. Right. So, we have two generics ready to go. Your original patent is well past expired, but you still are actively trying to prevent generics from coming to market.

Mr. Duato, the list price of Johnson & Johnson's autoimmune arthritis medication STELARA is nearly $80,000 annually. Similar to ELIQUIS, there are currently zero low cost biosimilar versions of STELARA available to U.S. patients. There are zero biosimilars for STELARA available in the United States today because Johnson & Johnson has also sued to delay the launch of a low cost biosimilar drug.

We need—you know, you have all talked about the need to have speed of access—and Mr. Chairman, I am wrapping right up.

Speed of access getting drugs to market, but then you are actively working to block the less expensive biosimilars and generics to come to market, and that is something we should address. Thank you, Mr. Chair.

The CHAIR. Senator Romney.

Senator ROMNEY. Thank you, Mr. Chairman. And I appreciate these executives taking time away from your responsibilities at your respective companies to be here and to inform us, and in some cases, to get berated by us and give us an opportunity to pontificate on our various topics, which I am about to do.

One is that I fully concur with Mr. Paul or Senator Paul indicated just a moment ago, Rand Paul, and that is that a free enterprise system works marvelously. And I know we keep asking you what are you doing to try and reduce the prices of your products?

The answer is that is not what happens in free enterprise and capitalism. I hope it doesn't come as a shock to my colleagues. In capitalism, if you are running an enterprise where you have a fiduciary responsibility to your owners, you try and get as high a price as you can. That is what you try and do.

You try and make as much profit as you can. That is how free enterprise works. You think Chevrolet sits back and says, gosh, how could we get the price of the Chevrolet down? No, it is like, how high price can I get and maximize the profit for my shareholder? What price does McDonald's charge for a sandwich?

As high a price as they can get. But the amazing thing about free enterprise is that someone figured out that if everybody does that and you have competition among all the players, that somehow the prices come down, and the quality goes up, and the access to the product is broader. It is the marvel, it doesn't seem to make a lot of sense, but it is the marvel of capitalism.

Now, obviously wise companies say, well, you don't just raise prices to the roof and do things that are going to harm your credibility and the trust in the marketplace, and have your employees not want to work there because they are going to figure they are working for bad people. So wise enterprises don't just do all the things I just mentioned.

They also say we are going to do other things and care for the poor and care for people who want to come work in our company. We do those things too. But recognize free enterprise is about enterprises battling each other with higher prices in many cases, and then they get pushed out by people who develop new products and put them out of business. It is how it works.

But let me turn to—and I know, as Senator Paul indicated, there are some who would like price controls. There are some who would like socialized medicine. And it is like, have you seen what that produces? It doesn't produce new drugs. It doesn't produce cures. It sounds great.

We are going to—price controls is just another name for capitalism—excuse me, socialism lite. Our system works, but there are ways to improve it. And I am very concerned that this disparity between list price and what you actually get paid is a problem.

I don't know why it is a problem or what we can do about it, but do you have PBMs and getting prices of discounts like this in other countries that you compete in? Yes, Mr. Boerner, yes.

Mr. BOERNER. Senator, we do not. This is a unique element of the U.S. health care system.

Senator ROMNEY. Is that true for you also, Mr. Davis?

Mr. DAVIS. That is true for us as well.

Senator ROMNEY. Mr. Duato, is that also true?

Mr. DUATO. This is unique. The inequity that exists in the U.S. It is because of that we have higher out-of-pocket costs for patients than anywhere else in the developed world.

Senator ROMNEY. I hope we focus on this. We may not have the right bad guys here, all right. These are the guys developing cures and helping people solve diseases.

But we have something here they don't have in the rest of the world, these PBMs that want higher and higher prices because they get paid based on how high the list price is, because they get a percent of the list price.

I am not sure where all the money goes. Some of it goes back to patients, some goes to the companies if they are self-insured. I don't know where it all goes, but I think that is the issue.

Let me ask each of you, if you were in our shoes knowing what you know, what should we be doing to try and get the cost of products down to our—to the people in the country and to the country at large, to the Government that buys a lot of goods, a lot of drugs—what should we be focused on?

I know that you sell to PBMs, so you got to be careful not to step on their toes too hard because they might punish you. But what advice would you give us? What should we be looking at? Where is the problem in this mess? We will start here, Mr. Boerner.

Mr. BOERNER. Maybe three things I would offer, Senator. First, to the complexity that you just described, No. 1, dealing profits from intermediaries from the list price of the drug, and the rebates rather that are provided. If you could delink that, that would be important.

Alternatively, require that those rebates be passed on to lower out-of-pocket costs for patients. That is No. 1. No. 2, I firmly believe we have the ability to help lower out of patient cost in Medicare if we could provide the same types of copay support that we do on the commercial side to Medicare patients.

That would be a second thing. And the third thing, we have referenced it before, we do innovative contracting outside of the U.S. where we get paid if our product works. There are constraints on our ability to do that in the U.S. I would like to see those removed. That would be very helpful.

Senator ROMNEY. Right. Thank you. Mr. Davis.

Mr. DAVIS. I would say that I—Chris, basically covered all of the things we would also look to do.

Senator ROMNEY. Great. Thank you. Mr. Duato.

Mr. DUATO. Yes. Three things. As Mr. Boerner, I would make sure that the rebates and discounts that we pay to PBMs go back to patients to reduce out-of-pocket costs. I will make sure that as we are trying to do, and I know these Committee is looking into that, would delink the compensation of the PBMs from the list price. And finally, I would sit down to see what we can do to provide, a, patient assistance program for patients in Medicare Part D, but also look to further lower the out-of-pocket costs for patients that the IRA is bringing.

Senator ROMNEY. Thank you. You did mention the fact that the PBMs are largely owned by the insurance companies.

Senators, we think PBMs are going to be lowering our costs as an employer, let's say, and you hire a PBM to lower your cost. But it might lower your cost, but then it is passing on their profit to the insurance company. Is that a problem?

Is the fact that the PBMs are owned by the insurance companies, is that a problem here? Is that something we need to look at as well? Do any of you have any comment on that?

Mr. DUATO. The three PBMs are owned by the three largest insurance companies, and together they control about 80 percent of the market of the prescriptions in the U.S.

Senator ROMNEY. Yes. I am a big believer in free enterprise, as you can tell by my opening comments. At the same time, I am concerned that we have got some structures here that are anti-competitive and make markets less effective, and we probably ought to focus on some of those. Thank you. I appreciate your testimony.

The CHAIR. Thank you. Senator Baldwin.

Senator BALDWIN. Thank you. It has been very interesting to listen to the back and forth.

Senator Romney, your points about support of the free market, but understanding that there are times when there is market failures.

We also have an obligation, I think, to oversee because our Committee with the—along with the Finance Committee, oversee and the need to have good stewardship of Medicare and Medicare dollars.

But the point that Senator Romney just made about basically, I don't know—I can't follow the dollars and it is complex, is a real issue. I want to start just by sharing some of my constituents' struggles.

I have a constituent who literally turns down the heat in the winter, because that is how she is able to afford the prescription drug she needs for her wellness. There are choices that people are making. People are rationing their medication. People are forgoing their medication because of affordability.

I think we need more transparency. And I think we need more transparency to inform the policies that we adopt. I was pleased this last May that this Committee advanced my bipartisan Fair Drug Pricing Act, which I lead with Senator Braun.

Our bill would require basic transparency from your companies at any juncture in which you want to raise the price, list price of a prescription drug by more than a certain amount, a certain percentage.

Asking questions like, what is the cost to manufacture the product? What do you invest in R&D, something we really support? How much are you spending on marketing and advertising? What are you doing in terms of stock buybacks? Is there excessive executive compensation?

I agree that we also have to have that transparency within the PBMs. I remember, under the last President, when we were having our confirmation hearing for the—his Secretary—Secretary Azar, who came out of the pharmaceutical industry, and I shared with him a letter from a constituent who has two diabetic sons who is talking about the costs every month, not just the insulin, but the test strips, etcetera.

I said, what do I tell this, dad about the high cost, which had just by the way, increased significantly. And he just responded, it is complicated. I can't tell my constituent, well we can't address this because it is complicated. I remember, when—this is years ago now when the EpiPen doubled in price overnight, went from $100 basically to $200.

My constituents certainly told me what a burden that was. I asked if you could show me—follow the money, a chart, follow the money. Nobody could. We need additional transparency to inform our policies.

Mr. Duato, the price of STELARA in the U.S. is $79,000 a year. And by the way, in Wisconsin, the median household income is $72,000. Your company has made twice as much selling this arthritis treatment in the U.S. than it did in the rest of the world combined. This is going back to 2016.

Under the Fair Drug Pricing Act, you would need to account for this exceptionally high cost. So, just to look at one component of what I am talking about, how much does Johnson & Johnson spend on marketing and advertising for this particular drug?

Mr. DUATO. Senator, thank you for the question. We publish every year since 6 years ago a report that we call it transparency report, and we explain our pricing practices and we give transparency also to the different intermediaries that play into the model. We disclose our advertising expenses and our R&D expenses.

What I can tell you is that in 2022, which was the last year that our report was published and is available, we spent double in R&D, 110 percent more in R&D that we did in sales and marketing.

Senator BALDWIN. Do you know what that dollar figure is for sales—

Mr. DUATO. I don't have it on my hand, but I will be sure to follow-up with you to bring it to you. But it was double the amount in R&D than we did to spend in sales and marketing.

Senator BALDWIN. Well, let's look at, Mr. Boerner, the price of ELIQUIS is—in the U.S. has increased by $4,000 since its launch. In other countries, the cost of this drug is decreasing. How much did your company spend on R&D last year?

Mr. BOERNER. Our company spent just over $9 billion last year on R&D.

Senator BALDWIN. Then how much did your company spend on stock buybacks, dividends, and executive compensation last year?

Mr. BOERNER. I don't have that exact figure, Senator. But we——

Senator BALDWIN. Does $12.7 billion sound right from the health study?

Mr. BOERNER. That is roughly correct.

Senator BALDWIN. Okay. For the first time, thanks to the Inflation Reduction Act, Medicare will negotiate the price of drugs, including ELIQUIS and STELARA, and this is really welcomed news for families in Wisconsin.

But the truth is, it is really not enough, and my constituents should not be forced to decide if they should turn the heat on in winter or buy the medication they need, all while companies are raking in literally tens of millions of dollars or billions. We have more work to do.

The CHAIR. Thank you. Senator Collins.

Senator COLLINS. Thank you very much, Mr. Chairman. I think all of us could agree that when a doctor prescribes said needed medication, that cost should not be an insurmountable barrier to the patient using it.

Yet for more than half of the adults in my state, according to a survey, it is a barrier. They are worried about affording the cost of prescription drugs. And in the last year, nearly one out of three Maine adults reported skipping a dose of medicine, cutting pills in half, or not filling a prescription because of cost.

I talked to a young woman with type 1 diabetes who, after she aged out of her parents' insurance, started cutting back on her insulin. She ended up in the emergency room and was gravely ill because of that.

She felt she just couldn't afford it and took a very unwise chance. So, this is a huge problem. But another aspect of this discussion is that many new medications represent true breakthroughs, disease modifying therapies, or even cures. And the other part is that literally billions of dollars are invested in developing drugs that end up to not be successful. I think we have to balance all of these concerns.

These new drugs often cost more, but they have the potential to reduce the number of unnecessary hospitalizations that lead to better patient outcomes. They may be worth it for disorders like Alzheimer's.

The breakthrough drugs can help keep patients healthier and active longer, benefiting society as well as their families. For example, I heard of a patient being diagnosed with mild cognitive impairment early enough that the patient was able to benefit from the newly available treatment and actually returned to the workforce.

That is quite an accomplishment. Now, last year, the Chairman criticized this particular company for a list price of $26,500 per year, even after the company, in a really unprecedented fashion, issued a lengthy analysis of the process by which they arrived at the price. Still, sticker shock around list prices and speculative claims that certain therapies will bankrupt the Medicare program have contributed to restrictive coverage policies, patient confusion, and limited uptake.

I would like, Mr. Davis, you to discuss how we can balance the need to have affordable medications without hampering innovation, and how access to the next—what would be the impact on access to the next generation of medications if price controls like those in Europe are implemented? How do you see a solution to the balance between affordability and innovation?

Mr. DAVIS. Yes. Senator, thank you for the question. You know, I would start with at Merck and what are the principles we apply when we think about how we price drugs, because I think it also gets to some of the other questions that have been asked about what stops you from just raising your price.

I can tell you that, as a company, and this goes back to the core of who we are over 130 years and is truly the purpose we live by, and that is we look at several elements. We look at what is the benefit to the patient. But equally we do look at what is the benefit of the cost to the system. We look at access and affordability.

I can tell you, for instance, when we launched KEYTRUDA, we launched at parity to market price, even though we knew we had a better product, in part because we wanted to ensure access.

We look at all of that, and then we look at what does it take to absorb the cost of all the failed drugs. We know 90 percent of all drugs we will bring into the clinic fail. The reality of it is the drugs that make it have to fund that failure. In the case of Merck, it is just interesting, I think, to point out.

Since 2014, the minority of drugs we have launched have actually even returned their cost of R&D. The minority—I am sorry, the majority have not returned their cost of R&D. So, it means that when you do get the rare drug that succeeds, it has to help cover that. So that is what we are facing in the system.

But as we look at how can we fix this, I think we have to get to the out-of-pocket costs and we have to find a way to really drive that down, and then continue to find ways to bring better access through the types of access programs we have all talked about here, whether it is through patient assistance programs, copay assistance, all of the ways we can help the individual person address that affordability challenge, which we all know someone who has faced that, and I don't want to see anyone face that.

Senator COLLINS. NIH provides a lot of assistance in the research that—and sometimes partners with pharmaceutical companies. How is the fact that there has been Federal help, for example, in the development of the Covid vaccines, how does that factor into the pricing?

Mr. DAVIS. Well and obviously, as we look at the system, the ecosystem we live in, it is important to understand that all players are important. So, the role of NIH is important.

But the NIH basically does the basic research, if you will. They provide the lock but they don't have the key. We provide the key. We take that basic research. We sculpt it into a molecule.

We are able to say, now that we know a target of disease to go after, how do we do it? And then we spend our resources in the most expensive part of the development and the riskiest part, which is the clinical development, to ensure safety and efficacy, to bring the drug to market. So, we need all players in the ecosystem——

Senator KAINE. If I could ask you to start to wrap up for Senator Smith—

Mr. DAVIS. Yes. And it is important that we do that. And so, I think as you look in the Covid vaccine situation, we didn't have— we did not receive any Federal funding for what we did. We spent all of our own resources at risk.

We commented, it was $2.5 billion. We did that at risk. But one of the programs we did do, LAGEVRIO, did have some basis from the NIH, and they were compensated for that.

Senator KAINE. On behalf of the Chairman, Senator Smith.

Senator SMITH. Thank you, Mr. Chair. Thanks to all of you for being with us here today. I appreciate it. I am going to start with you, Mr. Davis. Could you tell us how much Merck spends on advertising every year?

Mr. DAVIS. If you look in the United States, our direct to consumer advertising is about $350 million.

Senator SMITH. Then also direct to medical providers?

Mr. DAVIS. I don't have that. I wouldn't know that. We can come back to you on that one.

Senator SMITH. Okay. I think it is approximately $2 billion overall is what I think—is what—worldwide. That is worldwide number. Pardon me for that.

Mr. DAVIS. I don't recognize that number, but we can come back to you.

Senator SMITH. Okay. okay. And so one thing I bet most of us on this panel could agree with is that nobody likes that advertising. Doctors don't like it. Patients don't like it. Apparent—I know that the American Medical Association has called for a ban on direct to consumer advertising.

Could you just address this issue? And I think it is also true that you sued to prevent regulations that would require you to disclose the list prices in that advertising. Could you address that?

Mr. DAVIS. Yes, I am happy to do that, Senator. So, direct consumer advertising serves an important purpose.

There has been studies that have shown that it drives better adherence. It drives patients to understand the use of their medications. And it overall will bring benefits to the health system. I do believe there is a valid educational piece to direct to consumer advertising.

I also believe we need to be full and fair and transparent in helping people understand the cost of drugs. The reason we brought suit, the one you are referring to, was our concern that the specific request that was in that was that you show the list price of the drug.

Our concern, based on all the conversations we have had here this morning, is that can often be very misleading, and in fact, could cause patients not to seek the drug when in reality, take JANUVIA as an example.

If we put on an advertisement that it is $6,900, when in reality, if you take the total in the system, it is $690, I would hate to think someone doesn't show up to get that medicine because they don't understand the price.

What we supported instead, which is what we do today, in all of our directing consumer advertising, we drive you to a site that gives our list price, it gives all of the rebates we provide so that you can see it, and we get further information and education.

We think that is a more effective tool and a more accurate tool to stop the misperceptions that exist. That is why we raised that concern.

Senator SMITH. One of the things that I think is really confusing for patients is to try to figure out what—you know, how much things cost in the health system overall, including in prescription medications.

Let me just ask you, I am going to ask you about this, Dr. Boerner, how much would acute myeloid leukemia patient, how much would that patient pay every month for your drug IDHIFA, the cancer treatment. That if let's say they had a 20 percent coinsurance responsibility.

Mr. BOERNER. Senator, I don't have that exact figure off the top of my head. What I can say is that for most of our world oncologic drugs, we are able on the commercial side to bring copays down to a very low amount and in many cases to zero.

Now, to a point that was raised earlier, we have to do more to make that more widely available and an easier process to actually get into those programs, and we are working on that.

We have been doing that since I became CEO in November, and that is something we are committed to. And again, I would like to be able to provide that same benefit on the Medicare side.

Senator SMITH. But if you have a list price that is—and I get what you all are saying about the list price is just the list price. That isn't necessarily what people pay. But if you have a list price and then you have a co-insurance responsibility that is a percentage of the list price, that could still be quite a significant amount of money. I mean, I think it could be in this case $6,800 a month for this medication.

Mr. BOERNER. Senator, what you are pointing out is absolutely why we believe we have got to also look at ways to bring that list price down.

We have been discussing at length this sort of the complexity the intermediaries play in this system that lead to incentives to drive those list prices up.

But unquestionably, because out-of-pocket costs and co-insurance, for example, are typically tied to that list price, we have to find ways to bring that list price down.

Senator SMITH. Well, I would agree with that. I think that is a really significant issue, particularly as I think some of my colleagues have pointed out that when you get to these patient assistance programs, they are quite confusing and hard to navigate through.

I think that, sometimes that is only available if you have commercial insurance. And if you don't have commercial insurance, then you could really be flat out of luck.

Mr. BOERNER. Senator, that is correct. And in fact, I reference that since I became CEO, one of the things we have done on the commercial side is really begun to look at how many hoops do patients have to go through to get access to these copay support programs?

You know, we have provided $2.5 billion in copay support programs over the last 5 years as a company, provided $12 billion in free product. But we have got to make it easier and more universally available for commercial patients to get access to that.

Again, there are some constraints to us being able to provide those services on the Medicare side. There is some very legitimate concerns to providing those on the Medicare side, because you don't want to obviously be diverting patients from, for example, generic products onto these as a result of the—onto branded products as a result of this, but we would love to work with Members of Congress to find ways to do this constructively.

Senator SMITH. Is it true that the cost of those patient assistance programs, you can then turn around and deduct on your taxes, to lower your tax liability?

Mr. BOERNER. Senator, I don't know the answer to that, but I can follow-up.

Senator SMITH. Okay. I want to get at the question—I just have a minute left and so let me see if I can do this really quickly.

One of the challenges that we have are some pretty—often pretty severe shortages in medications. And I have heard so many stories about this from Minnesota folks who, they have a preferred treatment for a disease and then the drug is not available.

I want to ask you all—I will just, I will cut to the chase on this, Senator Collins and Senator Murkowski and I have a piece of legislation that would require reporting of supply chain disruptions that could lead to shortages in medications, and I would like to know whether you all would support that concept to help people understand where these shortages are and where the route chemicals for their medications are coming from.

Mr. DUATO. We work—excuse me, we work very closely with the drug shortage office at the FDA, and we are constantly doing all efforts to dual source the entire supply chain of our medicines so there is no discontinuation in our supply.

Mr. DAVIS. I am not familiar with the specifics of the bill, but I would say in general, the more we can continue to help understand what are the shortages, we should address that.

But I think we got to get at the fundamental issues of why do we have a shortage in the first place. I can tell you in our example, we make a drug called——

Senator KAINE. Again, you are over time. So, could you take those answers for the record, Senator Smith?

Senator SMITH. I would be happy to, Senator Kaine.

Senator KAINE. Great. On behalf of the Chair, Senator Braun. Senator BRAUN. Thank you. I am going to start with Mr. Davis.

What would your definition of a free market be?

Mr. DAVIS. One where you are able to bring goods, and if those goods bring value and the system sees value in them, you are able to bring those at a value you think is fair and reasonable and negotiate with the other sides, in a world where you have free competition.

Senator BRAUN. So right there you said negotiate. Most free markets are typified by this. And I would like y'all to listen to this because I think the big challenge, if I were in your seat running your companies, is that it is not a free market.

A free market means you have got a lot of choices, you have got vibrant competition, no barriers to entry, and you have got an engaged consumer. Now, do any of those apply to your business?

Mr. DAVIS. I think all of those apply. But I think one thing we need to understand in our—in the way our business functions, for a period of time, we have exclusivity. That is during the patent protection period. Thereafter—and in that period, we must reap a return on the investments we make to fund the R&D we do. Thereafter, drugs are freely available and there is total competition in that space.

Senator BRAUN. But yet you would sue to keep transparency in terms of what the consumer price would be or the list price, or you do things like tweak patents. That doesn't happen anywhere else. And you are not alone there. Hospitals and insurance companies do all this stuff behind closed doors as well.

I would think if I were in your shoes, you have got maybe a few years before—so none of that stuff really applies to you guys as I listed it. You might try to spin it that way, but it is not the case. I fixed it in my own business back in, oh, probably 15, 16 years ago by creating health care consumers, by trying to avoid the system through wellness and prevention, which you don't hear much about.

But when you do need it, it has got to be there where you have got a lot of options. And I understand you are a little different in terms of the R&D that goes into it. Then many years ago, you created a monster called the PBM that now is sucking all kinds of money out of the market.

Why can't you fix that in terms of doing alternative ways that would just smother the market with transparency and get it into a different channel of distribution? You got a guy like Mark Cuban that is trying to start a company, Cost Plus.

You are going to probably need to find things like that or you are going to be appearing more often here, and it is going to be where you are going to be regulated like a utility would be. Because in my opinion, you operate more like an unregulated utility kind of cloak yourselves behind free enterprise, and now it is up to 18, 19 percent of our GDP. Something has got to give.

Senator Sanders talked earlier about things costing 10 percent to 25 percent overseas, and I think I heard the excuse was, well they have price controls. Well, I think I would be smart enough to know that sooner or later that will occur here. It is going to be up to the industry to fix it, and you are probably just 15 to 20 percent of the problem.

You could fix the part that you get the most heat for by maybe trying to get more customers like the business Mark Cuban is putting out there that is based upon transparency. If not, you are going to get all the people that don't own health care businesses finally saying, we are not going to pay through the private side, the insurance system, three to four times what it costs through Government.

I will let you complete the logical chain. You are going to have Government as your business partner. So, why would you persist in a paradigm that looks like you are going to be headed toward what you definitely don't want, and that is doing more business with the Federal Government? Mr. Davis.

Mr. DAVIS. Well, I don't want to speculate on the system as a whole. I think what I focus on is what do we need to do to drive the mission of our company, which is in the near term, bring access and affordability.

Make sure that when we bring affordability, we don't sacrifice access. Often patients lose access when we try to address affordability. And that we fund innovation. And that is—whatever ultimately we come to as a solution, if we can protect those elements, I think we will both help patients of today and we can make——

Senator BRAUN. Have you ever looked at having some other system of distribution, like almost any other manufacturer would have when you make something? You do a pretty good job making the pill.

You completely default on how it gets from where you make it to who uses it. You are putting independent pharmacies out of business because the PBMs and other kind of peculiarities in the industry.

Have you thought about, at least in the place where most people confront the health care system with a prescription, about trying to restructure that, smother it with transparency and options to where people can get their stuff, and then apply that to biologics and the entirety of a spectrum, and don't tweak the patents and try to preserve a broken system.

Mr. DAVIS. Yes. So, we have considered should we look at going direct.

The reality of it is, as a single company, when you have now today three PBMs controlling 80 percent of the lives in this country, the ability to do that takes a portfolio of characteristics that we don't currently have.

I don't believe any one company can do that. That is why we continue to believe we need free market, but we——

Senator BRAUN. I bet if you collectively got together with the other drug companies and encouraged others like a Cost Plus that Mark Cuban has done to where you are going—I think you have got it under your control not to perpetuate a bad situation that was created by you. I mean, you make it.

You don't have to necessarily use PBMs. Why don't you encourage an alternative structure? At least show us that you are wanting to compete. Because all I can tell you is that if you don't take it—take the bull by the horns, do something different, you are going to be like all other countries.

You are going to be dealing with the Federal Government as a regulated entity, and I think we could lose some things. But in the meantime, Senator Sanders pointed it out, it costs a lot more here, the health care outcomes are better there, and pharma, hospitals, and insurance better figure it out before it is too late.

The CHAIR. Senator Hickenlooper.

Senator HICKENLOOPER. First, I will echo what Senator Braun said. Second, I will thank each of you for taking the time. And I know how busy you are, and I appreciate you coming in and answering questions.

You know, I grew up like most of us, I think, looking at our pharmaceutical companies as treasures, as companies that America could be rightfully proud of as innovators. But that is slipping away.

When I am back in Colorado, I hear much—let's just be generous—let's be gracious and say a wider diversity of opinion. According to a recent YouGov survey, more than a third of Americans report that cost has prevented them from filling a prescription they need.

A separate Kaiser Family Foundation poll, this one just from last year, said that 83 percent of Americans rated profits made by pharmaceutical companies as the overwhelming contributing factor to the high cost of prescription drugs.

You have all talked about the R&D, the innovation, which there could be no question about that, but what is the value of these cutting edge drugs and therapies if so many people can't afford them?

I think that widespread belief that Americans feel your companies are too focused on profits, it damages your credibility and I think the culture of your businesses and the culture of your customers.

I want to see how you feel about that in terms of the importance of people believing in your mission again, or believing as strongly that you are good leaders of the mission. Why don't we start with you, Mr. Duato.

Mr. DUATO. Thank you, Senator. I can assure you that the 50,000 employees of Johnson & Johnson in the U.S. wake up every day thinking what they can do for patients, and I can represent proudly that sentiment.

What can we do to address the real inequity that exists in the U.S., which is that seniors and patients that need the medicines the most pay higher out-of-pocket costs. In my view, that is the real problem.

There are other things that are positive in the U.S. healthcare system, like the access to breakthrough, cutting edge treatments earlier than any other country in the world, but it is true, we have a real inequity there.

I think we have to work together in order to address that inequity, and there is multiple ways that we can work on that. One is to make sure that——

Senator HICKENLOOPER. Just give me one, because I want to make sure—I have got a couple more questions.

Mr. DUATO. One is to make sure that the discounts and rebates, we paid $39 billion in 2022, that we pay to the middleman, are passed to the patients, so we can lower the out-of-pocket costs.

Senator HICKENLOOPER. Got it. That is a good one.

Mr. DAVIS. Senator, I appreciate the question. And I can tell you at Merck, we have lived by the statement our founder put out, that medicines are for the patients not for the profits. But so long as we have remember that, the profits follow.

It really says we can both do good and do well for our shareholders together. And there is a balance. And I think what you are talking about is where is the balance? And we are always trying to find that balance.

I am very much focused on it as the CEO of the company, because the legacy of Merck, the pride of our 70,000 employees and what we do matters to me, and a strong belief in the mission of the company.

It is why I came to the company, and it is why I am in this industry. So, we are very committed to that. But I do think the challenge we continue to face is the structural issues in the system that are creating the problem.

Senator HICKENLOOPER. We have heard that. I get it.

Mr. DAVIS. Yes.

Mr. BOERNER. Senator, the challenge that we are facing in this Committee today and what we have been discussing is, how do we ensure affordability today without sacrificing tomorrow's innovation? That is what we were focused on.

We have got to make sure we do what you have heard from all of us, are bringing highly innovative medicines to patients, but we also have to do a better job of ensuring that we are bringing drugs like ELIQUIS to market, which save the health care system money.

For every 100,000 patients on ELIQUIS, we estimate we save the health care system $5 billion. We have got to place a high bar on the medicines we bring to patients and stick by that as an industry.

Senator HICKENLOOPER. All right. Well, and I appreciate that. And I do—health is so precious to people that they will pay almost anything if it is serious, so that in a funny way, sometimes we see increasing costs based on that calculus of how much money we are avoiding, which I think can be a false pathway sometimes.

But certainly, as a user of ELIQUIS and grateful recognizing what the old system was and how better ELIQUIS is, I salute that. The higher cost and the lower cost in other countries, you have all answered that.

I understand there is some price setting there. But I think the solution—I mean, we are paying double. Even when you take out the PBMs and the list price from the net price, we are paying double what Europe or Canada and Australia are paying, and somehow that has got to be a negotiation that the rest of the world probably has to pay more, and you guys are going to have to figure out a way to do that.

I am not saying it is easy, but it is one of those things. I want to—it is one of those things we have to address as a country and as an industry. I want to ask, earlier there is some mention of river blindness, of issues in underserved countries.

I want to see if each of you have a—just a quick example of something where your company has gone in there, obviously we have heard about Merck, but done something in a country like that where it really was philanthropic.

Mr. DUATO. Thank you, thank you. We dedicate billions of dollars every year to treat diseases that do not have an economic counterpart. For example, one of the diseases that we have contributed to its treatment and eradication is intestinal worms.

You know, we donate billions of pills every year in order to treat intestinal worms. We have programs to support frontline health care workers in the developing world that have supported more than a million frontline healthcare workers.

We develop a medicine for multidrug resistant tuberculosis, which is widely used in every single protocol and which we are not enforcing our patents as we speak. So, we have made significant contributions.

Senator HICKENLOOPER. That is impressive, but we most people don't know about that stuff. Mr. Davis.

Mr. DAVIS. Well, you mentioned Dymethazine donation, where we have $4.6 billion. I would add another one we did. You know, recently—and we were very focused on COVID now, we forget about Ebola and the scourge of Ebola that hit in 2014, 2016, in Western Africa.

We actually—and no profit to us, developed an Ebola vaccine. Have distributed that, continue to distribute that drug to address that devastating disease.

Senator HICKENLOOPER. Mr. Boerner.

Mr. BOERNER. Senator, we had as a reference to large presence in HIV, and I am incredibly proud that in the late 90's, our foundation worked with governments and local communities to set up the core infrastructure to deliver HIV medicines to sub-Saharan Africa, focusing on children.

The President of Botswana recently congratulated the—or thanked the BMX Foundation for saving a generation from extinction, his words. We are now leveraging that same infrastructure, partnering with Baylor College of Medicine, to reverse something in childhood cancer——

The CHAIR. Mr. Boerner, thank you. I am sorry. His time has expired. Apologize.

Senator HICKENLOOPER. Anyway, thank you all. And I think those stories need to get out. But we also have to solve this issue of the price disparity.

The CHAIR. Senator Kaine.

Senator KAINE. Thank you. Since I have 7 minutes, I am going to do 2 minutes to celebrate innovation and then 5 minutes to go after the cost question.

On the innovation side, there is an article that came out in the Health Affairs Journal in September 2020, and I would like to put it in the record, Contributions of Public Health, Pharmaceuticals, and other Medical Care to U.S. Life Expectancy Changes, 1990 to 2015.

[The following information can be found on page 110 in Additional Material.]

Senator KAINE. The article looked at the fact that between 1990 and 2015, life expectancy in the U.S. increased by 3.3 years, and the authors of the researchers and authors of the study were able to say 44 percent of that increase was because of public health measures, 35 percent of the increase was attributable to pharmaceutical innovation, and 13 percent of the increase was attributable to other improvements in medical care, with 7 percent unknown.

But the fact that pharmaceuticals led to more than a third of that increase in life expectancy is something that we need to acknowledge as a context to this discussion.

In a Virginia example—Mr. Davis, you will know this example very well. In Elkton, Virginia, there is a plant that produces GARDASIL, which your company developed and began to market in the mid 2000's—2006, 2007.

It is a vaccine against a virus, the HPV virus, that create—that leads to a lot of cancers, especially cervical cancer and other as well. And that has just been revolutionary in terms of cervical cancer.

We were one of the first states to put a vaccine mandate in place for HPV vaccine, and cervical cancer among vaccinated populations has dropped 70 plus percent just in the last 15 years. I mean, it is truly remarkable.

I have been to that plant, and I know how proud people are to work there and believe that they have been at the vanguard of a revolution that has helped so many Americans, but people all around the world. So, that is the good side.

Okay, now we got to get to the reality for the hearing which is, people here still pay too much out of pocket. Together with my colleagues here who voted for the Inflation Reduction Act, we said for a long time that we ought to be negotiating on prescription drug prices and we did it. And it passed by only one vote in the Senate.

Each of us who voted for it, we were the deciding vote. And I know not everybody likes that, but it is working. We put the cap, the out of pocket cost cap on seniors under Medicare.

We did the $35 insulin for seniors on the Medicare. And thank goodness that sent such a strong market signal that many of the companies that were reducing insulin cost to $35 a month said, we will just do it for not just Medicare patients, but others. And they wouldn't have done that had we not taking that step in the IRA.

But there is more that we can do. And I really want to focus on one thing, because I think it is just right before us. This Committee took strong bipartisan action about 9 months ago on this PBM reform bill that is sitting on the floor of the Senate right now.

I don't expect you to be the masters of all the details of that bill, but if we were to pass a meaningful PBM reform bill—and much of the conversation today has been about this weird difference between list prices and actual net prices.

If we were able to pass a meaningful PBM reform bill, what would that do to the cost that American patients are paying out of pocket for pharmaceuticals? Please, and I will ask each of you to address that. Mr. Duato.

Mr. DUATO. Thank you. Thank you, Senator, and thank you for recognizing the value for patients of pharmaceutical innovation.

If we were able to pass meaningful reform, meaning a reform that would delink the revenues of the PBMs and insurance companies from the list price, and that would pass rebates and discounts to the patients, I would anticipate two things. One, it would affect list prices.

Two, it would significantly reduce the out-of-pocket cost for the patients. So, I welcome the bipartisan efforts of this Committee to go through PBM reform. It is a linchpin of lowering the cost for patients.

Senator KAINE. Mr. Davis.

Mr. DAVIS. Yes. You know, I also believe that in the provisions that are in the bill, at least some of the big ones around transparency and also de-linking are definitely steps in the right direction. I think we need them.

There are a lot of what we have all been focusing on in our testimony and in the question and answers, and I do think it will—it can benefit patients if we move in that direction, so I am very supportive of what you are trying to do.

Senator KAINE. Mr. Boerner.

Mr. BOERNER. Senator, if we could do that and we could reduce the significant amount that we are paying in rebates to intermediaries who are not passing those rebates on to lower out-of- pocket costs, speaking on behalf of Bristol-Myers Squibb, we could work almost immediately to begin to bring down list prices, and I would welcome the opportunity to work with this Committee to do that.

Senator KAINE. Well, I know that in conversations with the Chair, the intent is to move on that bill pretty soon, potentially with some other health items as well. And I think that the opportunity is right before us.

That bill passed out of Committee overwhelmingly bipartisan. I think it was an 18 to 3 vote, and that tells us that we would have some amendment on the floor. The de-linking provision was not in the bill.

The Chair and Ranking were supportive of the concept, but at the time we marked it up, the CBO hadn't given us the score, and so we agreed that we would wait on that until we got on the floor. But the CBO has now scored the de-linking bill that Senators Marshall, Capito, Braun, and I, and Tester have co-sponsored, and the CBO says that it would save about $650 million over 10 years.

That is in addition to the savings for patients. So, I know we would try, hopefully on the floor to add that in. My colleagues have all talked about the reality of what they hear from constituents, and I hear the same thing.

I know, I think the complexity of the system and the fact that list price is different than net price, and the fact that we have rebates, ''rebates,'' that never show up in people's pockets. And you have programs to try to assist folks who can't afford medicines, but they have a six page application form, and both a sticker price might scare them off or a six page application might scare them off.

We just have to simplify this and cut out a lot of the middlemen in this instance. I have long said to the Chair that I am very concerned about PBMs because we might fight with you about whether you are researching enough or should your research be more than your stock buybacks.

PBMs aren't doing a single bit of research. They are not producing a single product. And yet, they seem to me to be the ones that are scooping up the most of money that is just sloshing through the system right now, so I hope we can address that soon. Thank you, Mr. Chair.

The CHAIR. Senator Luja`n.

Senator LUJA`N. Thank you, Mr. Chairman. Thank you to everyone who is here today. Biosimilar competition is one way to drive down drug costs for patients and increase access. Would you all agree with that?

Mr. DAVIS. Yes.

Mr. DUATO. Yes.

Mr. BOERNER. Yes.

Senator LUJA`N. I appreciate that. Now, one of the concerns I have is we often see competition stifled in this particular area with biosimilars.

The concern that I have is tactics and delay that lead to entry of the lower cost biosimilar drugs keep patients from often having a choice, but also being able to afford their prescription drugs.

Now, Mr. Davis, yes or no, will you commit to not blocking other drugmakers from entering the market when the primary patent on KEYTRUDA expires?

Mr. DAVIS. Well, Senator, at Merck—and we do believe that biosimilar competition and generic competition is core to the system.

We need the patent protection, and then we need a robust biosimilar and generic market.

I can tell you that, when the composition of matter patents expire on our drug KEYTRUDA, I fully expect, and I will not try to stop a biosimilar IV version of KEYTRUDA coming on to the marketplace.

Senator LUJA`N. Is that a yes?

Mr. DAVIS. That is a yes.

Senator LUJA`N. I appreciate that. Mr. Boerner, yes or no, will you commit to not blocking other drugmakers from entering the market when your primary patent on ELIQUIS expires?

Mr. BOERNER. Senator, we have a number of patents on ELIQUIS, and we have certainly anticipated that when the patents that are most relevant for that product expire, we will have generic competition in this case, not biosimilar, but generic competition, and that would be around 2028.

Senator LUJA`N. When the primary patent expires on ELIQUIS, will you commit to not blocking other drugmakers from entering the market?

Mr. BOERNER. Senator, I don't—I am not a patent attorney, so I am not entirely——

Senator LUJA`N. You are the CEO.

Mr. BOERNER. Senator, I would say that when the most important, the most relevant patents expire on ELIQUIS, we will welcome generic competition.

Senator LUJA`N. Is that a yes or no?

Mr. BOERNER. That is a yes, Senator.

Senator LUJA`N. Mr. Boerner, I have the same question on OPDIVO. Yes or no, will you commit to not blocking other drugmakers from entering the market when your primary patent expires?

Mr. BOERNER. When the most relevant patents for OPDIVO expire, we would fully expect biosimilars to enter the market.

Senator LUJA`N. Your answer is yes when—the words you are using are relevant patents, not the primary patent. Is that the clarification that I can—?

Mr. BOERNER. Yes, Senator. I am just not certain exactly what the most—what you are referring to is the primary patent, but when we—when those patents expire, we welcome generic company.

Senator LUJA`N. First patent, primary, the initial one. The one that was filed when you got this drug done. Look, I am not a lawyer. I am not a CEO. I don't work at all. If I am not using the wrong words, please help me a little bit. You know what I am talking about here.

Mr. BOERNER. Yes. When the composition—generally it is when the composition of matter patent expires.

Senator LUJA`N. That doesn't sound like a yes. I hear what you are saying. I am going to move on. Mr. Duato, we know that J&J entered into settlement agreements to delay the launch of some STELARA biosimilars in 2025.

This will prevent competition in the drug market and Medicare negotiation, the way I read it. Will you commit to lowering the price of STELARA in 2025?

Mr. DUATO. Senator, thank you for the question. I anticipate that the price of STELARA will actually be lower in 2025, as it has been lowering during the past decade. The path of STELARA has been a steady decline in the net prices, and I anticipate that the biosimilars in 2025 will further decrease the price of STELARA.

Senator LUJA`N. Are you answering yes to my question?

Mr. DUATO. Yes.

Senator LUJA`N. I appreciate that. Now, we have heard over and over that Medicare drug pricing negotiations will kill innovation.

Mr. Boerner, I want to get a few things clear. Yes or no, is it BMS's position as stated in its lawsuit against the Health and Human Services that, ''the IRA's real victim is innovation, and in turn, the millions of patients who are counting on the pharmaceutical industry to develop new therapies, will save lives, and improve health and well-being.''

Mr. BOERNER. Senator, we have serious concerns about elements of IRA, specifically the fact that this isn't an actual negotiation. We obviously like some elements of IRA, notably the out-of-pocket costs, but——

Senator LUJA`N. I appreciate that, but do you stand by this statement that was filed in the lawsuit to the United States Health and Human Services Department?

Mr. BOERNER. We have very serious concerns about the implication of IRA——

Senator LUJA`N. Do you stand by this statement?

Mr. BOERNER. Yes, sir.

Senator LUJA`N. Yes or no, is it also true that you said in your Q4 earnings call, ''we see a legacy portfolio of well-established products facing headwinds such as IRA.'' Through this portfolio—''or though this portfolio is declining, it is expected to continue to generate strong cash-flows to enable investment in our future growth drivers.'' Do you stand by that?

Mr. BOERNER. Yes. We actually have a legacy product portfolio that will continue to provide the necessary funds to innovate and bring the next wave of innovation to market, yes, Senator.

Senator LUJA`N. Based on that, can I interpret that cash-flows were generated even though the IRA went to place, and they are sufficient to support new innovations, as was reported to the investors?

Mr. BOERNER. Senator, we don't yet have IRA having been fully implemented negotiation. That process is ongoing. But we are generating cash-flows off of our existing products to fund innovation, sir.

Senator LUJA`N. The statement in the same filing to Health and Human Services, what that case said, this portfolio—though the portfolio is declining, it is expected to continue to generate strong cash-flows to enable investment in our future growth drivers. So, is it generating cash?

Mr. BOERNER. Our legacy portfolio products is continuing to generate cash, yes, sir.

Senator LUJA`N. So even in the face of IRA, you are generating cash?

Mr. BOERNER. Again, Senator, we haven't actually finished negotiation yet on our first drug, which is——

Senator LUJA`N. I will move on. I appreciate that very much. This is one of—look, I grew up on a small farm in Northern New Mexico. When a cow does its business in the barn, there is a pile of stuff I have got to go clean. That is what it is. It is manure. It has other a lot of other languages, but that is what it is.

I don't understand why this is so complex. The people in the room make these darn things so complex when no one understands them. I am beside myself, Mr. Chairman, that when a question was asked, can you break down where the money goes in this particular drug?

The answer is, well, it is complicated. We don't know. I am hoping it is included in the filings for investors that people know where the money—well, I will follow-up with more questions.

I have several, Mr. Chairman, but you all, help me and other laymen across the country and around the world to be able to understand what the heck is going on. You all have some good lawyers.

Maybe 1 day I will go to law school and try to get a gig with one of you. I don't know, but this is just frustrating. Thanks, Mr. Chairman.

The CHAIR. Senator Markey.

Senator MARKEY. Thank you, Mr. Chairman, very much. Research is medicine's field of dreams from which we harvest to the indings to give hope to families that a cure can be found for the disease which has been running through their family's history. That is what it is all about. That is what we all hope for.

That is what I represent in Boston, in Kendall Square, two miles from my house, and I have been for 47 years in Congress trying to help that industry to be able to grow and to be able to get the resources from NIH, all the resources to make the breakthroughs, to give hope to ordinary families, like my father who drove a truck for the Hood Milk Company.

The companies have done great work over the years, but that funding, which I was on the Health Committee in these—in the House for 36.5 years, and I fought very hard for NIH funding, and those NIH dollars delivered results. For example, between 2010 and 2016, every drug approved by the FDA was in some way based on biomedical research funded by the NIH.

My father, the truck driver at the Hood Milk Company one mile from Kendall Square, he paid his taxes to make sure that the funding would go to NIH so that research could be made in order to make the breakthroughs that would help him and help his families.

Merck's former president, and you have already quoted him, Mr. Davis, he said we never try to forget that medicine is for the people—you know, my father—it is not for the profits. And Merck's website states that this philosophy is embraced by their leaders and the employees to this day.

FDA approved the cancer drug KEYTRUDA in 2014, based on NIH research that my father helped to pay for as a truck driver at the Hood Milk Company. And last year, the list price was $191,000 for this cancer drug that helps patients with lung cancer and other cancers, $191,000 a year.

The annual meeting and proxy statement of 2023, says that it brought in $21 billion in revenue for the company, and it was driving key growth for Merck's business. And at the same time, patients are also straining under insurance premiums, struggling to afford this drug, taking on debt, or skipping treatments altogether.

Merck has now filed a 168 patents on this cancer drug, KEYTRUDA. And as we know from this early discussion when we discuss this, we can be talking about primary patents or secondary patents.

What I heard earlier was that the witnesses in general just want all the secondary patents to also be exhausted. Now, to a very large extent, of course, 168 patents then bring at least 168 lawyers into the room.

How do we use this patent in order to thwart another smaller company, hundreds of smaller companies from now making the breakthroughs that advance even further the breakthroughs, innovating, discovering. 168 new patents extend further, using lawyers, you know the time at which there can be a lower price drug made available to people so that they can get the treatment, which they need for lung cancer.

Yes, we believe in competition, and we really believe in competition. In Massachusetts, we believe in Darwinian paranoia inducing competition. But when there is a monopoly on a drug, which is the key drug, there is no competition.

There is no paranoia if 168 patents just extend and extend the ability to have new companies, smaller companies, smarter, new scientists to make the additional breakthroughs. And that is the play. We understand the play.

That is how lawyers get into it, not scientists. You keep the lawyers, keep the smarter new 25 year old out with the new insight just by extending and extending. I do believe in research.

Adam Smith hated monopolies. It was the No. 1 thing he hated the most, monopolies. And so, in this particular instance, my father died from lung cancer. And my father was—drove a truck. So, the list price for KEYTRUDA is more than his entire pension. That is what he got from the Hood Milk Company.

One year of his entire pension would have paid for 1 year, and he died from lung cancer. And I don't think that Judge Merck really intended that, that would be what the result of research, ultimately did.

Mr. Davis, would it have been consistent with Judge Merck's philosophy to take research funded by my father's tax dollars, to invent a lifesaving lung cancer drug, charge him hundreds of thousands of dollars of his hard earned retirement for it, manipulate the market using patent law to block out competition that could have brought in new scientists that could have improved it and lowered the cost, and as a result, the costs are unaffordable.

Then use the income you got from him to brag to your investors about the drug as a key growth area for your business. Do you think that is what Judge Merck intended when he had that high minded philosophy, which he used to describe Merck's——

The CHAIR. In 17 seconds. [Laughter.]

Mr. DAVIS. Are you looking for the answer now?

Senator MARKEY. Yes.

Mr. DAVIS. Okay. Well, I would say, the quote was, medicine is for the patients, not for the profits. But so long as we remember that the profits have always followed.

What he was capturing was if you focus on bringing new medicines to benefit patients today and make sure you have an investment and a return to bring medicines for the future—because we are a biopharmaceutical research company.

Research is who we are. Innovation is the lifeblood of our company. Then we can deliver for the mission to the patients. And I can tell you at Merck, and I am very proud of this, we always put patients at the center, and we always look at ways to do that, and that will continue to be what we do.

I do think actually what we are doing is consistent because it allows us to be sustainable for the long term to deliver for patients into the future.

Senator MARKEY. I just think——

The CHAIR. Thank you.

Senator MARKEY. I just think it has turned into medicine for the shareholders and not medicine for the people like my father.

The CHAIR. Okay. Let me—that is the last line of questioning. So, let me thank our three panelists for being here today, and all the Senators who participated. We are now going to turn to our second panel. Thank you all very much, gentlemen.

Mr. DAVIS. Thank you very much. Mr. BOERNER. Thank you.

The CHAIR. Thank you all very much for being here. We have three very knowledgeable guests, panelists, on prescription drugs and pricing.

Our first witness will be Peter Maybarduk, who is the Director of Access to Medicines Program at Public Citizen.

He is a lawyer who has advocated for stronger price regulation and stronger public health protections in patent law in the U.S. and around the world. Mr. Maybarduk, thanks very much for being with us.

Statement of Peter Maybarduk, J.D., Access to Medicines Director, Public Citizen, Washington, DC

Mr. MAYBARDUK. Chairman Sanders, Ranking Member Cassidy, Members of the Committee, thank you. Public Citizen is a national public interest organization. We have 500,000 members and supporters, and for 50 years we have advocated with success for health and consumer protections.

Drug prices are high because of monopoly power, leading to the rationing of treatment and preventable suffering. 1 in 3 Americans has failed to take medicine as prescribed due to cost. Like Louise Chisholm of Fort Worth, who tells us of Merck's diabetes drug, I need JANUVIA to control my blood sugar, but I can't afford it while on Social Security.

Robert Cherivano of Loveland, Colorado, and his wife both trying to afford J&J XARELTO, why do we have to pay so much? We are 90 and 81 on Social Security. Does anyone care about the elderly? Keith Clyburn, Lafayette, Louisiana, I am paying for ELIQUIS and other pricey meds from BMX. So, what do I do? I ration them so that I can eat and pay rent.

Patients for Affordable Drugs has compiled 34,000 such stories from people struggling to afford their medicine, and that is a tiny fraction, a mere sample of the heartbreaking problems out there.

High prices cost people their health. They can cost lives. They force impossible family budget decisions. We all pay for high prices, whether we are patients or not, whether out of pocket or through higher insurance premiums and wasted tax dollars. Medicare and Medicaid spent nearly $200 billion on prescription drugs last year.

Americans pay the highest prices in the world three times what other countries pay, and that is net prices not list, to the point of the last panel—three times more in net prices, the real prices. We also do the most to support research and development.

The world's largest biomedical research funder is a public funder, the National Institutes of Health, and we should be very proud of it, contributing more than $45 billion a year and laying groundwork for many, if not most, new medicines.

Plus, public support is now indispensable to the late stage development of 1 in 4 drugs also. We the people drive innovation together. So, Americans first pay for the research, then contribute to the development.

Then on top of it, when the drug comes to market pay the highest prices in the world. Other countries broadly negotiate prices to protect their people, but here, pharma has accrued tremendous influence in our politics, spending hundreds of millions a year in lobbying, outranking every other industry.

Now, our Government provides patent protection and exclusivity on medicines. In theory, this should support innovation. But in practice, drug corporations write the rules, extending monopoly power sometimes for decades, blocking competition far longer than this body intends.

Senators, it is not a market in the way that you may believe, respectfully. The corporations testifying here today claim any price relief would compromise their ability to invest in new medicines.

No, that framing erases the millions of Americans rationing treatment. It erases the tens of billions of dollars the tax taxpayers invest in R&D for real health priorities.

It erases the hundreds of billions of dollars the industry spends on self-enrichment. Last year, drugmakers selected for Medicare negotiation spent $10 billion more on stock buybacks, dividends, and executive compensation than they spent on R&D.

J&J and BMX each spent $3 billion more on these self-enriching activities. And over the prior decade, Merck's buybacks and dividends also exceed R&D by $3 billion. J&J spent an impressive $43 billion more on buybacks and dividends than R&D over this period. Of course, drugmakers do not set prices according to R&D costs.

Instead, the price of a patented drug is simply the most that we as a society are willing to pay to care for our sick and loved ones, where monopoly power blocks affordable alternatives, blocks market competition, and we have little choice.

Today, perhaps for the first time, our Country is making progress, challenging high prices and rationing, including through price negotiation, encountering price spikes, and we commend the Committee's attention to this problem. But the problem is getting worse, much worse, and more action is needed.

We should negotiate prices from the moment a drug hits market, not wait a decade as we are today, which cost taxpayers tens of billions of dollars. We support legislation before your Committee to strengthen market competition and transparency and accelerate generic entry. Ultimately, we will have to confront monopoly power.

That is the rotten foundation allowing drug makers to project influence, to game the law, and keep prices high.

Other real challenges, including providing patient assistance and challenging middlemen who take advantage, real problems, but these flow inevitably from the patent monopolies that make it so lucrative and so easy to rip off patients.

We can, we must do better for health, for access to medicines. Thank you for your time. Please count us with you in this fight.

[The prepared statement of Mr. Maybarduk follows.]

Prepared Statement of Peter Maybarduk

Chairman Sanders, Ranking Member Cassidy and Members of the committee,

Thank you for the opportunity to testify today on the high prices Americans pay for prescription drugs. I am Peter Maybarduk, Access to Medicines Director of Public Citizen. Public Citizen is a national public interest organization with more than 500,000 members and supporters. For more than 50 years, we have advocated for stronger health, safety and consumer protections; for corporate and government accountability; and in more recent years, for affordable access to essential medicines and biomedical technologies.

I. The Drug Pricing Crisis at the Hands of the Pharmaceutical Industry

This hearing unfolds against the backdrop of a drug pricing crisis in the United States. The Centers for Disease Control and Prevention's (CDC) data from 2021 shows approximately 9.2 million Americans aged18–64 are unable to take medications as prescribed due to costs.[5] 2023 Kaiser data on all adults shows that three in 10 Americans have not taken their medications as prescribed due to costs, 82 percent of Americans say the cost of prescription drugs is unreasonable, and 73 percent say that the government is not doing enough to regulate drug prices.[6] People with disabilities are three times more likely not to take medications as prescribed due to cost barriers.[7]

Americans also confront the highest drug prices in the world, paying nearly three times more for the same drugs than other countries.[8] For the 20 top-selling drugs worldwide, drug corporations made more than $100 billion from sales to American patients in comparison to $57 billion from all other countries combined in 2020.[9] This pricing disparity is even more egregious considering significant taxpayer funded contributions to drug development. The taxpayer funded National Institutes of Health is the largest public funder of biomedical research in the world, investing nearly $45 billion in U.S. taxpayer dollars.[10] Much of this funding focuses on the foundational research on biological targets for drug action that drug development is based upon.[11] Further, recent estimates suggest that publicly supported research was critical to the late-stage development of one in four drugs.[12]

---

[5] Laryssa Mykyta, and Robin A. Cohen, Centers for Disease Control and Prevention, National Center for Health Statistics, Characteristics of Adults Aged 18-64 Who Did Not Take Medication as Prescribed to Reduce Costs: United States, 2021, NCHS DATA BRIEF NO. 470 (June 2023).

[6] Ashley Kirzinger, Alex Montero, Grace Sparks, Isabelle Valdes, & Liz Hamel, Public Opinion Prescription Drugs and Their Prices, KFF (Aug. 21, 2023), https://www.kff.org/health-costs/ poll-finding/public-opinion-on-prescription-drugs-and-their-prices/.

[7] Id. at 2.

[8] ANDREW W. MULCAHY, DANIEL SCHWAM & SUSAN L. LOVEJOY, RAND, INTERNATIONAL PRESCRIPTION DRUG PRICE COMPARISONS: ESTIMATES USING 2022 DATA (2024),*https://aspe.hhs.gov/sites/default/files/documents/277371265a705c356c968977e87446ae/international-price-comparisons.pdf.*

[9] RICK CLAYPOOL & ZAIN RIZVI, UNITED WE SPEND: FOR 20 TOP-SELLING DRUGS WORLDWIDE, BIG PHARMA REVENUE FROM U.S. SALES COMBINED EXCEEDED REV- ENUE FROM THE REST OF THE WORLD (Sept. 30, 2021).

[10] National Institutes of Health, Serving Society, Direct Economic Contributions, IMPACT OF NIH RESEARCH, *https://www.nih.gov/about-nih/what-we-do/impact-nih-research/serving-society/direct-economic-contributions* (last visited Feb. 1, 2024).

[11] Ekaterina Galkina, Jennifer M. Beierlein, Navleen Surjit Khanuja, and Fred D. Ledley, Contribution of NIH funding to new drug approvals 2010—2016, 115 PNAS 2329 (2017).

[12] Rahul H. Nayak, Jerry Avorn, & Aaron S. Kesselheim, Public sector financial support for late stage discovery of new drugs in the United States: cohort study, 367 BMJ l5766 (2019).

Drug pricing abuses also put an enormous strain on the coffers of public health programs, and consequently our tax dollars. Of the more than $400 billion spent on retail prescription drugs in 2022, almost $135 billion came from Medicare and $45 billion from Medicaid.[13]

Excessive drug prices and self-imposed rationing by American patients are the outgrowth of unregulated pharmaceutical monopoly power over drug prices. Prescription drug corporations receive government-granted patent protection on drug inventions and statutory exclusivities on medicines. In theory, this incentivizes innovation of new medicines, and it is critically important that we support research and development. But in practice, the rules have been written by or with the deep influence of drug corporations, to maximize their ability to extract rents from our healthcare system. Corporations extend their exclusive power over new drugs through an array of anticompetitive tactics to the detriment of American patients.[14] For example, many have abused the patent system to obtain subsequent patents over the same medicine with marginal differences or benefits to retain longer periods of exclusivity, sometimes decades.[15]

Pharmaceutical companies have exploited their monopoly power to accrue tremendous influence in our political system and protect their exceptional profits. The pharmaceutical industry expends hundreds of millions of dollars each year in lobbying efforts to advance its interests, outranking every other industry.[16] When Medicare Part D was established to cover prescription costs for seniors two decades ago, pharmaceutical companies successfully lobbied to deprive the program of the power to negotiate drug prices.[17] Federal law requires private insurers, Medicare, and Medicaid to cover FDA approved drugs, which effectively provides a government mandate

---

[13] NHE Fact, CMS.GOV, *https://www.cms.gov/data-research/statistics-trends-and-reports /national-health-expenditure-data/nhe-fact-sheet* (last visited Feb. 5, 2024).

[14] E.g., Aaron Kesselheim, Jerry Avorn, & Ameet Sarpatwari, The High Cost of Prescription Drugs in the United States: Origins and Prospects for Reform, 316 JAMA NETWORK 858 (2016).

[15] Other tactics they use to maintain their extraordinary pricing power over essential medicines include switching patients from branded medications with patent protection nearing expiry to new drugs with no added clinical benefit and longer patent protection. Drug corporations also pay generic companies to delay their competing products in order to extract more profits.

[16] Inci Sayki, Despite record Federal lobbying spending, the pharmaceutical and health product industry lost their biggest legislative bet in 2022, OPEN SECRETS (Feb. 2, 2023), *https:// www.opensecrets.org/news/2023/02/despite-record-Federal-lobbying-spending-the-pharma- ceutical-and-health-product-industry-lost-their-biggest-legislative-bet-in–2022/.*

[17] Amy Kapczynski, The Political Economy of Market Power in Pharmaceuticals, 48 J. HEALTH POL., POL'Y L. 215, 223 (2023).

to buy companies' monopolized drugs with absent or weak measures to contain costs.[18]

Other countries employ cost-containing measures to protect their residents from drug pricing abuses, which is why the price of prescriptions drugs in the United States is so excessive by comparison.[19] Drug companies have been happy to benefit from a slew of U.S. Government actions and policies that have dramatically increased their profits in recent decades, but they balk at any attempt to implement drug pricing measures that already benefit wide swathes of the world.

Drugmakers' largely unregulated, and government-expanded, pricing power has rewarded them with exceptional profits. To protect these profits, pharma trade groups claim that any measure that could deliver drug pricing relief to Americans will restrict resources to invest in new medicines and help patients in the future.[20] That framing usefully erases the millions of Americans that currently self-ration their medicines and are harmed due to pricing abuses. It also erases the tens of billions of taxpayer dollars invested annually in research and development, and the hundreds of billions the industry spends on self-enrichment.

The Biden administration is making significant progress in addressing our Nation's drug pricing crisis through implementation of Medicare drug price negotiation, inflationary rebates, the cap on out-of-pocket costs for insulin at $35 per month for Medicare enrollees, the caps on annual out-of-pocket expenses for prescription drugs in the catastrophic phase of Medicare Part D that will be set at $2,000 next year, and other provisions of the Inflation Reduction Act. Bipartisan reforms which this Committee has considered and advanced can build on that progress.[21] However, far more is necessary to

---

[18] Id.

[19] Id. at 223; Aaron Kesselheim, Jerry Avorn, & Ameet Sarpatwari, The High Cost of Prescription Drugs in the United States: Origins and Prospects for Reform, 316 JAMA NETWORK 858, 860 (2016).

[20] See PhRMA, States Can Help Patients Pay Less for Their Medicines, STATE POLICIES AND ISSUES, *https://phrma.org/en/States* (last visited Jan. 11, 2023); PhRMA, INFLATION REDUCTION ACT'S UNINTENDED CONSEQUENCES, *https:// phrma.org/inflation-reduction.*

[21] Specifically, Public Citizen supports legislation to promote generic competition and lower drug prices through taking on drug corporation citizen petition abuse and exclusivity ''parking'', clarifying the scope of orphan drug exclusivity, and providing greater transparency for generic applicants. Additionally, Public Citizen has supported bipartisan measures advanced through the Judiciary Committee that address pay-for-delay, product hopping and citizen petition abuses.

provide material relief to all patients facing unbearably high prescription drug prices, including people with private insurance and those without insurance.[22]

To highlight the need for stronger measures to deliver drug pricing relief to millions of Americans, this testimony focuses on the drug pricing abuses of Merck, Johnson & Johnson, and Bristol Myers Squibb. In our view, these corporations have taken advantage of weaknesses in our health system to price gouge Americans and used suspect patenting practices to unfairly extend their monopoly power.

II. Merck, Johnson & Johnson, and Bristol Myers Squibb Engage in Pricing Abuses of Life-Saving Medicines

Merck

Merck takes advantage of its monopoly power to excessively price its blockbuster drug, Keytruda, which treats many different cancer types,[23] and Januvia, a widely used drug to treat diabetes.[24] Additionally, Merck exploits its monopoly protections to price gouge Americans on the federally funded COVID–19 treatment, Lagevrio, that cuts the risk of hospitalization.[25] For Keytruda and Januvia, Merck has been granted patent protection beyond their active ingredient or mechanism, which helps prolong its monopoly control over these drugs by deterring manufacturers from bringing more affordable alternatives to market.

---

[22] Public Citizen also supports legislation to build on the Inflation Reduction Act, through expanding the number of drugs negotiated, who benefits from negotiated prices, and reducing and removing the negotiation delay periods currently mandated. Public Citizen has also supported legislation reducing the biologics exclusivity period to 5 years, in parity with that afforded small molecule drugs, and legislation to require reasonable pricing of federally——funded medical inventions. Public Citizen has repeatedly called on Congress to advance insulin access reform to ensure people without insurance and with private insurance can access affordable insulin. Public Citizen also strongly supports additional solutions to address patent thicketing sug- gested by the Initiative for Medicines, Access and Knowledge (I-MAK). See IMAK, ADDRESSING PATENT THICKETS TO IMPROVE COMPETITION AND LOWER PRESCRIPTION DRUG PRICES: A BLUEPRINT FOR REFORM (2023), *https://www.i-mak.org/wp-content/ uploads/ 2023/12/Addressing-Patent-Thickets-Blueprint—2023.pdf)*.

[23] I-MAK, OVERPATENTED, OVERPRICED: KEYTRUDA'S PATENT WALL 3 (2021).

[24] ASSISTANT SECRETARY FOR HEALTH AND PLANNING, HHS, INFLATION REDUCTION ACT RESEARCH SERIES: JANUVIA: MEDICARE ENROLLEE USE AND SPENDING (Nov. 13, 2023), *https://aspe.hhs.gov/reports/ira-research-series-Medicare-drug-price-negotia- tion-program*.

[25] Sharon Lerner, Merck Sells federally Financed Covid Pill to U.S. for 40 times What It Costs to Make, THE INTERCEPT (Oct. 5, 2021), *https://theintercept.com/2021/10/05/covid-pill-drug-pricing-merck-ridgeback/*.

Keytruda

First, Merck exploits its monopoly protections in Keytruda to price the drug outrageously. The price of Keytruda for just 3 weeks is over $11,000,[26] 22 and some patients may need to adhere to Keytruda for one to 2 years.[27] The extraordinary list price of the drug, amounting to over $190,000 a year, means that insured patients routinely hit their out-of-pocket limits, which can be thousands of dollars every year.[28] In 2023, Merck made $25 billion off of Keytruda according to its latest filing with the Securities Exchange Commission.[29] Of the $18 billion in sales of the drug globally in the first 9 months of 2023, Merck extracted $11 billion in revenue from American patients.[30] Evidence suggests the price of Keytruda is not keyed to its research and development costs. Merck itself did not make the original research and development contributions critical to the drug's discovery: it obtained ownership of the drug, and many others, via a corporate acquisition in 2009 for $41 billion.[31] In just 2 years, Merck has more than made up for those costs with $46 billion in sales for the drug.[32]

Second, Merck appears to be engaging in patenting practices designed to unfairly extend exclusivity over this biologic drug to prevent more affordable biosimilars from coming to market.[33] The Initiative for Medicines, Access and Knowledge (I- MAK) found that 129 patent applications have been filed to cover Keytruda, and 50 percent of these applications were filed after the drug's FDA approval in 2014, cutting against claims that these patent applications furthered innovation incentives for the drug's discovery.[34] Fifty-three patent applications have been granted to date, and the primary patents covering the

---

[26] Cost Info and Financial Help, KEYTRUDA, *https://www.keytruda.com/financial-support/*Feb. 1, 2024).

[27] What Do I Need to Know About My Treatment Schedule?, STARTING KEYTRUDA (last visited Feb. 1, 2024).

[28] Bob Herman, The Keytruda Boom, AXIOS (Oct. 19, 2021), *https://www.axios.com/2021/10/29/keytruda-sales-merck-drug-prices*.

[29] MERCK & CO., INC., FORM 8-K, EXHIBIT 99.1 (Feb. 1, 2024), *https://www.sec.gov/ixviewer/ix.html'doc=/Archives/edgar/data/0000310158/000110465924009109/tm244517dl— 8k.htm*.

[30] MERCK & CO., INC., FORM 10-Q FOR THE QUARTERLY PERIOD ENDED SEPTEMBER 30, 2023, at 29, *https://www.sec.gov/ixviewer/ix.html'doc—/Archives/edgar.*

[31] I-MAK, OVERPATENTED, OVERPRICED: KEYTRUDA'S PATENT WALL 3 (2021).

[32] MERCK & CO., INC., FORM 8-K, EXHIBIT 99.1 (Feb. 1, 2024), *https://www.sec.gov/ixviewer/ix.html'doc=/Archives/edgar/data/0000310158/000110465924009109/tm244517dl— 8k.htm*.

[33] I-MAK, OVERPATENTED, OVERPRICED: KEYTRUDA'S PATENT WALL 5–6 (2021).

[34] Id. at 1.

antibody that's considered the main component of the drug were filed in 2008 and will expire in 2028.[35]

The other patents protect, among other things, methods of producing the drug and its use to treat different cancer types.[36] But method of production patents are more critical to biologics like Keytruda than small molecule drugs because the techniques for producing these drugs are more challenging.[37] As such, it's more difficult for manufacturers to work around these patents to create more affordable biosimilar alternatives.[38] Additionally, once the mechanism of action is known for a biologic in addressing one condition, testing its use for other similar indications becomes obvious.[39] Therefore, obtaining multiple patents for different clinical indications for these drugs appears problematic. The secondary patents on Keytruda grant an additional 8 years of Merck's monopolistic pricing power over the drug, and as a consequence of this exclusivity, it is estimated that Americans will spend $137 billion on Keytruda.[40]

In sum, Merck appears to be unfairly extending its exclusivity over Keytruda, which will cost American patients billions in the coming years, in light of the filing pattern of patent applications on Keytruda particularly after its FDA approval, and the granted patent protection to deter biosimilar competitors after the expiry of primary patents.

Januvia

Merck's pricing of Januvia, which treats diabetes, also exemplifies the pricing abuses rampant to the pharmaceutical industry. Merck charges Americans as much as $6,900 per year for Januvia, while the same drug can be purchased for $900 in Canada and $200 in France.[41] Medicare Part D spent more than $4 billion on just this one drug between June 2022 and May 2023,[42]

---

[35] Id.

[36] Id. at 3.

[37] Id.

[38] Id.

[39] Id.

[40] Id. at 4.

[41] Bernie Sanders: U.S. Senator for Vermont, PREPARED REMARKS: Sanders Ahead of Vote to Subpoena CEOs to Testify on Outrageously High Prices of Prescription Drugs in America, PRESS RELEASES (Jan. 25, 2024), *https://www.sanders.senate.gov/press-releases/prepared-remarks-sanders-ahead-of-vote-to-subpoena-ceos-to-testify-on-outrageously* high-prices-of-prescrip- tion-drugs-in-america/.

[42] The White House, FACT SHEET: Biden-.Harris Administration Announces First Ten Drugs Selected for Medicare Price Negotiation, BRIEFING ROOM: STATEMENTS & RELEASES (Aug. 29, 2023), *https://www.whitehouse.gov/briefing-room/statements-*

and the drug has been selected by CMS for the first round of Medicare price negotiation. The drug on average costs Medicare nearly $5,000 annually per enrollee, with out-of-pocket costs amounting to more than $500 each year for enrollees who do not receive the low-income subsidy.[43] On Januvia, and the related product Janumet, Merck made $4.5 billion and $3.4 billion in 2022 and 2023, respectively.[44]

Merck has managed to extend its monopoly pricing power over Januvia through unfair patenting practices. Januvia was first approved by the FDA in 2006,[45] and the original patent covering Januvia's active ingredient, filed in 2002, expired in 2023.[46] Americans already should have access to lower cost generics. Indeed, Merck lost exclusivity for the drug in 2023 in Europe.[47] However, according to the FDA's Orange Book, one patent set to expire in 2027 stands in the way of low-cost generics for American patients.[48] That patent covers a specific salt form of the active ingredient created from a reaction with phosphoric acid.[49] According to Merck, innovating patents after the filing of the primary patent ''enhance[s] the benefits and convenience of treatments for patients.''[50]

The validity of the patent and Merck's argument that these secondary patents, at least for Januvia, benefit patients are belied by the litigation surrounding this patent. Although a district court ultimately upheld the patent based on technical legal rules, it noted that the earlier patent claimed salt forms of Januvia's active ingredient, and most egregiously, the earlier patent

---

releases/2023/08/29/fact-sheet-biden-harris-administration-announces-first-ten-drugs-selected-for-Medicare- price-negotiation/.

[43] Id.

[44] MERCK & CO., INC., FORM 8-K, EXHIBIT 99.1 (Feb. 1, 2024), *https://www.sec.gov/ixviewer/ix.html'doc=/Archives/edgar/data/0000310158/000110465924009109/tm24 4517d1— 8k.htm.*

[45] Merck Sharp & Dohme, LLC v. Mylan Pharm., No. 1:19CV101 4–5 (N.D.W. Va. Sep. 21, 2022); HIGHLIGHTS OF PRESCRIBING INFORMATION, *https://www.accessdata.fda.gov/drugsatfda—docs/label/2012/021995s019lbl.pdf* (last visited Jan. 29, 2024).

[46] Merck Sharp & Dohme, LLC v. Mylan Pharm., No. 1:19CV101 16–17 (N.D.W. Va. Sep. 21, 2022); U.S. Patent No. U.S. 6,699,871 Claim 17.

[47] MERCK & CO., INC., FORM 10-K, at 27 (Feb. 24 2023), *https://www.sec.GOV/ixviewer/ix.html'doc=/Archives/edgar/data/310158/000162828023005061/mrk–20221231.htm.*

[48] Product Details for NDA 021995, ORANGE BOOK: APPROVED DRUG PRODUCTS WITH THERAPEUTIC EQUIVALENCE EVALUATIONS, *https://www.accessdata.fda.gov/scripts/cder/ob/results—product.cfm'Appl—Type=N&Appl—No=021995#23300* (last visited Feb. 2, 2024).

[49] Merck Sharp & Dohme, LLC v. Mylan Pharm., No. 1:19CV101 12–13, 77 (N.D.W. Va. Sep. 21, 2022).

[50] Andrew Seidman, How Merck extended its monopoly on a blockbuster diabetes drug, PHILADELPHIA INQUIRER (Dec. 20, 2023), *https://www.inquirer.com/business/merck-pat- ent-januvia-Medicare-price-negotiations–20231220.html.*

disclosed that a salt could be formed using phosphoric acid and even lists it as one of eight preferred acids for creating such salts.[51] The second patent simply covers the salt form product formed by a reaction of phosphoric acid with the active ingredient.[52] 48 In essence, Merck was able to extend its monopolistic pricing power over Januvia by claiming something it had basically previously disclosed, and what many would consider an obvious variation of the active ingredient. Further, Merck's claim that there is some corollary benefit to patients that arises from its salt patent is contradicted by the record: to reject the generic manufacturer's challenge to the patent's validity, the district court found that the active ingredient by itself was fine and did not need to be reacted with a salt.[53]

Lagevrio

A 5-day-course of Lagevrio, which cuts the risk of hospitalization from COVID– 19, costs $17.74 to produce, but Merck charged the Federal Government $712, or over 40 times more, for the drug in 2021.[54] The government had contracted with Merck to supply 1.7 million courses of treatment at this price for a total of $1.2 billion.[55] The pricing of Lagevrio was particularly egregious because the Federal Government invested an estimated $29–35 million in the development of the drug.[56] In 2023, Merck's sales of the drug brought in $1.4 billion, but in the previous year, Merck made nearly $6 billion off of the treatment.[57]

In sum, Merck has been engaging in excessive pricing abuses with respect to Keytruda, Januvia, and Lagevrio, which bring in billions every year for the

---

[51] Merck Sharp & Dohme, LLC v. Mylan Pharm., No. 1:19CV101 73, 76–77 (N.D.W. Va. Sep. 21, 2022).

[52] 48 Id. at 12–13, 77.

[53] 49 Id. at 85. The district court's reasoning may have been flawed, as it noted earlier that Merck had been motivated to find a salt form of the compound because it proved unsuitable for making pharmaceutical tablets and was unstable. Id. at 7. Even if this were true, this should have provided the motivation for a person to arrive at this salt version of the active ingredient, rendering the patent claim obvious and invalid.

[54] 50 Sharon Lerner, Merck Sells federally Financed Covid Pill to U.S. for 40 times What It Costs to Make, THE INTERCEPT (Oct. 5, 2021), https://theintercept.com/2021/10/05/covid-pill-drug-pricing-merck-ridgeback/.

[55] Id.

[56] Id; Luis Gil Abinader, U.S. government rights in patents on Molnupiravir, based upon funding of R&D at Emory University, KNOWLEDGE ECOLOGY INTERNATIONAL BLOG (Oct. 4, 2021), https://www.keionline.org/36648.

[57] MERCK & CO., INC., FORM 8-K, EXHIBIT 99.1 (Feb. 1, 2024), https://www.sec.gov/ixviewer/ix.html'doc=/Archives/edgar/data/0000310158/000110465924009109/tm244517d1— 8k.htm.

company. Additionally, it has sought to extend its monopolistic pricing power over Keytruda and Januvia using patenting practices we should deem unfair.

Johnson & Johnson

Like Merck, Johnson & Johnson benefits from monopoly protections to price gouge American patients on vital medicines. These drugs include (1) Stelara, which helps treat psoriasis, psoriatic arthritis, Crohn's disease, and ulcerative colitis;[58] (2) Xarelto, which prevents and treats blood clots and reduces health risks for patients with coronary or peripheral heart disease, and is licensed for sale in the U.S. from Bayer AG;[59] and (3) Darzalex, which treats multiple myeloma.[60] Imbruvica is another possible example of Johnson & Johnson's drug pricing abuses. Johnson & Johnson commercializes Imbruvica, which treats blood cancers,[61] outside the United States and has co-exclusive rights with AbbVie to commercialize the drug in the United States, though AbbVie states it is ''the principal in the end-customer product sales.''[62] The companies share profits and losses equally from the commercialization of the drug.[63] Even if Johnson & Johnson does not ultimately control the prices of drugs in the United States, it profits equally from the abuses of its commercial partner.

58 ASSISTANT SECRETARY FOR HEALTH AND PLANNING, HHS, INFLATION REDUCTION ACT RESEARCH SERIES: STELARA: MEDICARE ENROLLEE USE AND SPENDING (Nov. 13, 2023), https://aspe.hhs.gov/reports/ira-research-series-Medicare-drug-price-negotiation-program.

59 ASSISTANT SECRETARY FOR HEALTH AND PLANNING, HHS, INFLATION REDUCTION ACT RESEARCH SERIES: XARELTO: MEDICARE ENROLLEE USE AND SPENDING (Nov. 13, 2023), https://aspe.hhs.gov/reports/ira-research-series-Medicare-drug-price-negotiation-program; BAYER ANNUAL REPORT 2022 97 (2023), https://www.bayer.com/en/investors/integrated-annual-reports.

60 DAVID RIND, FOLUSO AGBOOLA, DMITRIY NIKTIN, AVERY MCKENNA, EMILY NHAN, MATT SEIDNER, & STEVEN D. PEARSON, INSTITUTE FOR CLINICAL AND ECONOMIC REVIEW, UNSUPPORTED PRICE INCREASE REPORT: UNSUPPORTED PRICE INCREASES OCCURRING IN 2022 10 (Dec. 11, 2023), UPI—2023—Report—121123.pdf (icer.org).

61 ASSISTANT SECRETARY FOR HEALTH AND PLANNING, HHS, INFLATION REDUCTION ACT RESEARCH SERIES: IMBRUVICA: MEDICARE ENROLLEE USE AND SPENDING (Nov. 13, 2023), https://aspe.hhs.gov/reports/ira-research-series-Medicare-drug-price-negotiation-program.

62 ABBVIE INC., FORM 10-K FOR THE FISCAL YEAR ENDED DECEMBER 31, 2022, at 66–67, https://www.sec.gov/ixviewer/ix.html—doc—/Archives/edgar/.

63 Id.

Johnson & Johnson also benefits from unfair patenting practices extending exclusivity over Xarelto and Imbruvica, which will incur billions in costs to U.S. patients.

Stelara

Johnson & Johnson prices Stelara exorbitantly in comparison to other high-income markets. The drug is priced at $79,000 in the United States when it can be purchased for a fifth of the price in the United Kingdom.[64] Even considering rebates, the price of Stelara is between 28 percent–81 percent lower in Canada, Switzerland, Germany, Australia, the United Kingdom, France, and Australia.[65] 61 In 2023, Johnson & Johnson made nearly $11 billion in sales from the drug, almost $7 billion of which came from U.S. patients.[66]

The drug has been selected for the first round of Medicare price negotiation, and between June 2022 and May 2023, Medicare Part D spent over $2.6 billion on the drug. Further, Stelara had incurred over $4,000 in out-of-pocket costs annually for enrollees who did not receive the low-income subsidy.

There is reason to believe that Johnson & Johnson has engaged in unfair patenting practices to maintain its monopoly power over Stelara. Hagens Berman filed a class action lawsuit on Dec. 7, 2023 for health benefit providers on the basis that Johnson & Johnson illegally delayed the entry of biosimilar competitors to Stelara.[67] Their complaint alleges that Johnson & Johnson defrauded the Patent and Trademark Office by intentionally misleading the

---

[64] Bernie Sanders: U.S. Senator for Vermont, PREPARED REMARKS: Sanders Ahead of Vote to Subpoena CEOs to Testify on Outrageously High Prices of Prescription Drugs in America, PRESS RELEASES (Jan. 25, 2024), *https://www.sanders.senate.gov/press-releases/prepared-remarks-sanders-ahead-of-vote-to-subpoena-ceos-to-testify-on-outrageousl—high-prices-of-prescrip- tion-drugs-in-america/*; The White House, FACT SHEET: Biden-.Harris Administration Announces First Ten Drugs Selected for Medicare Price Negotiation, BRIEFING ROOM: STATEMENTS & RELEASES (Aug. 29, 2023), *https://www.whitehouse.gov/briefing-room/statements- releases/2023 /08/29/fact-sheet-biden-harris-administration-announces-first-ten-drugs-selected-for-Medicare-price-negotiation/*.

[65] Evan D. Gumas, Paige Huffman, Irene Papanicolas, & Reginald D. Williams II, How Prices for the First 10 Drugs Up for U.S. Medicare Price Negotiations Compare Internationally, Controlling Health Care Costs, THE COMMOWEALTH FUND (Jan. 4, 2024), *https://www.commonwealthfund.org/publications/2024/jan/how-prices-first—10-drugs-Medicare-negotiations-compare-internationally*.

[66] JOHNSON & JOHNSON, FORM 8-K, EXHIBIT 99.2 (Jan. 23, 2024), *https://www.sec.gov/ixviewer/ix.html'doc—/Archives/edgar*.

[67] Stelara Antitrust, HAGENS BERMAN, https://www.hbsslaw.com/cases/stelara-antitrust (last visited Feb. 4, 2024).

examiner on the patentability of a subject patent in Stelara, purchased a manufacturer that had patents in the methods of producing biosimilar alternatives to Stelara, and used these fraudulently and unlawfully obtained patents to delay alternatives that would have been more affordable to patients.[68]

Darzalex

In 2022, the Institute for Clinical and Economic Review found that Johnson & Johnson's 6.8 percent price hike of Darzalex was unsupported by new clinical evidence, increasing spending by an estimated $248 million in the United States.[69] In 2023, Johnson & Johnson made nearly $10 billion on the drug, of which more than $5 billion derived from the U.S. market.[70]

Xarelto

Johnson & Johnson prices Xarelto at $542 for a 30-day supply, which is nearly $7,000 a year in the United States.[71] Even considering rebates, Xarelto is two to four times more expensive in the United States compared to Canada, Switzerland, Germany, Australia, the United Kingdom, in Canada, Switzerland, Germany, Australia, the United Kingdom, France, and Australia[72] Xarelto has been selected for the first round of Medicare price negotiation, and between June 2022 and May 2023, Medicare Part D spent over $6 billion on Xarelto, with over $600 in out-of-pocket costs per year for enrollees who did not receive the low-income subsidy.[73]

---

[68] Id.

[69] DAVID RIND, FOLUSO AGBOOLA, DMITRIY NIKTIN, AVERY MCKENNA, EMILY NHAN, MATT SEIDNER, & STEVEN D. PEARSON, INSTITUTE FOR CLINICAL AND ECONOMIC REVIEW, UNSUPPORTED PRICE INCREASE REPORT: UNSUPPORTED PRICE INCREASES OCCURRING IN 2022 10 (Dec. 11, 2023), UPI—2023—Report—121123.pdf (icer.org).

[70] Id.

[71] HOW MUCH SHOULD I EXPECT TO PAY FOR XARELTO? *https://www.xarelto-us.com/cost* (last visited Feb. 3, 2024).

[72] Evan D. Gumas, Paige Huffman, Irene Papanicolas, & Reginald D. Williams II, How Prices for the First 10 Drugs Up for U.S. Medicare Price Negotiations Compare Internationally, Controlling Health Care Costs, THE COMMOWEALTH FUND (Jan. 4, 2024), *https://www.commonwealthfund.org/publications/2024/jan/how-prices-first—10-drugs-Medicare-negotiations-compare-internationally*.

[73] The White House, FACT SHEET: Biden-.Harris Administration Announces First Ten Drugs Selected for Medicare Price Negotiation, BRIEFING ROOM: STATEMENTS & RELEASES (Aug. 29, 2023), *https://www.whitehouse.gov/briefing-room/statements-releases/2023/ 08/29/fact-sheet-biden-harris-administration-announces-first-ten-drugs-selected-for-Medicare- price-negotiation/*.

Johnson & Johnson benefits from the unfair patenting practices of another company to prolong its exclusive authority to price and sell Xarelto in the United States. Johnson & Johnson licenses Xarelto from Bayer AG, a German company that owns the patents in the drug.[74] Johnson & Johnson received FDA approval for Xarelto in 2011,[75] and the patent protection for two of three patents listed for the drug in the Orange Book expire in 2025.[76] But the protection of a third patent covering the 10 mg, 15 mg, and 20-mg tablets of the drug expires in 2034.[77] Bayer AG describes that the patents covering the active ingredient of Xarelto in the U.S. expire in 2025.[78] Thus, the secondary patent expiring in 2034 for the drug prolongs Johnson & Johnson's monopolistic pricing power over these Xarelto tablets by almost a decade in excess of the protection afforded by the primary patents. This secondary patent appears to be a significant barrier to generic entry, as Johnson & Johnson and Bayer are relying solely on this patent's claims in lawsuits seeking to prevent at least three, and likely more, manufacturers from selling generics of the 10, 15 and 20-mg doses of Xarelto.[79]

While the earlier patents cover the active ingredient, its combination with other substances to form the drug, the process of preparing the drug, a solid oral version of the drug, and its use for preventing or treating cardiovascular issues, the primary marginal benefit claimed by the later-expiring patent appears to be its protection over a once-daily tablet version of the drug.[80] Bayer itself states in its annual corporate statements that the patent covering 10, 15, and 20-mg once-daily tablets in Europe is set to expire in 2026.[81] If

---

74 BAYER ANNUAL REPORT 2022 65 (2023), *https://www.bayer.com/sites/default/files/2023—02/Bayer-Annual-Report—2022.pdf.*

75 Xarelto (rivaroxaban) 10 mg immediate release Tablets, DRUG APPROVAL PACKAGE, *https://www.accessdata.fda.gov/drugsatfda—docs/nda/2011/022406Orig1s000TOC.cfm* (last visited Jan. 29, 2024).

76 Product Details for NDA 022406, Orange Book: Approved Drug Products with Therapeutic Equivalence Evaluations, *https://www.accessdata.fda.gov/scripts/cder/ob /results—product.cfm'Appl—Type=N&Appl—No—022406* (last visited Jan. 29, 2024).

77 Id.

78 Bayer Annual Report 2022 65 (2023), *https://www.bayer.com/sites/default/files/2023—02/Bayer-Annual-Report—2022.pdf.*

79 JOhnson & Johnson, Form 10-K For The Fiscal Year Ended January 1, 2023, at 91–92, *https://www.sec.gov/ixviewer/ix.html'doc=/Archives/edgar/*. The patent's claims are likely barring the entry of even more generic manufacturers according to a more recent SEC filing. See Johnson & Johnson, Form 10-Q For the Quarterly Period Ended October 1, 2023, at 35, *https://www.sec.gov/ixviewer/ix.html'doc=/Archives/edgar/.*

80 Compare U.S. Patent No. U.S. 9,539,218 with U.S. 7,157,456 & U.S. 9.415,053.

81 BAYER ANNUAL REPORT 2022 65 (2023), *https://www.bayer.com/sites/default/files/2023—02/Bayer-Annual-Report—2022.pdf.*

this patent survives litigation in the U.S., it will likely be another instance in which Americans are uniquely deprived of more affordable generic medications.

Imbruvica

Imbruvica was priced at over $180,000 in 2021, nearly double its launch price in 2013.[82] The net price of the drug is higher than in Switzerland, Germany, the United Kingdom, France, Canada, Japan, and Australia.[83] Excluding Switzerland, Imbruvica is priced two to four times more in the U.S. compared to these high-income nations.[84] In 2023, Johnson & Johnson made $3.26 billion in sales from the drug, with over $1 billion coming from U.S. patients.[85] Additionally, the drug has been selected for the first round of Medicare price negotiation, and Medicare Part D spent over 2.6 billion on the drug between June 2022 and May 2023.[86] Imbruvica exacted the highest financial toll on Medicare enrollees of the drugs selected for Medicare price negotiation, with an average annual out-of-pocket cost of $6,497 per enrollee who did not receive the low-income subsidy.[87] The price of Imbruvica is even more unreasonable in light of the preclinical research support from government and nonprofit sources that led to the drug's development and FDA approval, as described by Knowledge Ecology International.[88]

Like Xarelto, Johnson & Johnson profits from patent abuses on Imbruvica committed by its collaborator, AbbVie. There is a massive patent thicket depriving U.S. patients of more affordable alternatives of the drug, with 88 patents granted to date.[89] The House Oversight & Reform Committee reported

---

[82] U.S. House Of Representatives' Committee On Oversight & Reform, Staff Report: Drug Pricing Investigation: Abbvie—Humira And Imbruvica 3 (May 2021).

[83] Id.

[84] Id.

[85] Johnson & Johnson, FORM 8-K, EXHIBIT 99.2 (Jan. 23, 2024), *https://www.sec.gov/ixviewer/ix.html'doc=/Archives/edgar/*.

[86] The White House, FACT SHEET: Biden-.Harris Administration Announces First Ten Drugs Selected for Medicare Price Negotiation, BRIEFING ROOM: STATEMENTS & RELEASES (Aug. 29, 2023), *https://www.whitehouse.gov/briefing-room/statements-releases/2023/08/29/fact-sheet-biden-harris-administration-announces-first-ten-drugs-selected-for-Medicare- price-negotiation/*.

[87] Assistant Secretary for Planning And Evaluation, Office Of Health Policy, Department Of Health And Human Services, Inflation Reduction Act Research Series—Medicare Enrollees' Use And Out-Of-Pocket Expenditures For Drugs Selected For Negotiation Under The Medicare Drug Price Negotiation Program 5 (Aug. 29, 2023), *https://aspe.hhs.gov/sites/default/files/documents/*.

[88] Arianna Schouten, Notes on The Preclinical Development of Imbruvica (Ibrutinib) (2023), *https://www.keionline.org/wp-content/uploads/KEI-BN—2023—4.pdf*.

[89] I-MAK, Overpatented, Overpriced: Imbruvica's Patent Wall 2 (July 2020).

that the initial patent in Imbruvica's active ingredient was filed in 2006 and was expected to expire in 2026.[90] Citing I-MAK, the Committee detailed how a ''drip——feed'' patent strategy was employed to prolong monopoly power over Imbruvica.[91] Under this strategy, multiple additional patents were filed covering aspects of Imbruvica that had already been disclosed in earlier patents but with more pecificity.[92] The sheer number of patents providing protection on the drug is designed to discourage generic competition against the drug. Even then, the Committee reports that nearly a dozen generic manufacturers sought FDA approval of generics, but most entered confidential agreements to delay generic entry until 2032, 6 years after the primary patent was expected to expire.[93]

In sum, Johnson & Johnson price gouges American patients on several critical medicines. Moreover, the unregulated drug pricing power of the company will be unfairly extended by abuses of the United States' patent system.

Bristol Myers Squibb

Bristol Myers Squibb, like Merck and Johnson & Johnson, has engaged in pricing abuses of several drugs to the detriment of American patients, including Breyanzi, a cell therapy for B-cell lymphoma; Pomalyst, which is used to treat multiple myeloma;[94] and Revlimid, which treats the same.[95] This is also true of (1) Abecma, a cell therapy for treating multiple myeloma, that BMS licensed from the company, 2seventy bio, and for which BMS shares profits and losses equally with its commercial partner, and (2) Eliquis, which is a small molecule drug used to prevent and treat blood clots, that BMS developed with Pfizer.[96] Profits and losses are largely shared equally by the

---

[90] Id.

[91] 87 U.S. House Of Representatives' Committee on Oversight & Reform, Staff Report: Drug Pricing Investigation: Abbvie—Humira And Imbruvica 36 (May 2021).

[92] Id.

[93] Id. at 37.

[94] Bristol-Myers Squibb, Form 10-K For The Fiscal Year Ended December 31, 2022, at 2, *https://www.sec.gov/ixviewer/ix.html'doc/Archives/edgar*.

[95] Id. at 3.

[96] Assistant Secretary for Health And Planning, Hhs, Inflation Reduction Act Research Series: Eliquis: Medicare Enrollee Use And Spending (Nov. 13, 2023), *https://aspe.hhs.gov/reports/ira-research-series-Medicare-drug-price-negotiation-program*; Bristol-Myers Squibb, Form 10-K For The Fiscal Year Ended December 31, 2022, At 77. *https://www.sec.gov/ixviewer/ix.html-doc/Archives/edgar*.

companies on a global scale, but BMS ''is the principal in the end customer product sales in the U.S., significant countries in Europe, as well as Canada, Australia, China, Japan and South Korea.''[97]

Eliquis

Bristol Myers Squibb abuses its monopoly protections to charge Americans over $7,000 for Eliquis while pricing the same drug for just $900 in Canada and just $650 in France.[98] Even with rebates, the price of Eliquis is between 35–70 percent lower in the high-income nations of Switzerland, Germany, the United Kingdom, France, Canada, Japan, and Australia.[99] Eliquis was selected for the first round of Medicare price negotiation. Between June 2022 and May 2023, Eliquis was the top spend among the 10 drugs selected for price negotiation, costing Medicare Part D over $16 billion.[100] Medicare enrollees who did not receive the low-income subsidy paid over $600 in annual out-of-pocket costs just for this one drug.[101]

Bristol Myers Squibb has sought to extend its monopoly protections over Eliquis using unjust patenting practices. Although generics received FDA approval in 2019,[102] none will come to market until 2026, with some

---

[97] Id.

[98] Bernie Sanders: U.S. Senator for Vermont, PREPARED REMARKS: Sanders Ahead of Vote to Subpoena CEOs to Testify on Outrageously High Prices of Prescription Drugs in America, PRESS RELEASES (Jan. 25, 2024), *https://www.sanders.senate.gov/press-releases/prepared-remarks-sanders-ahead-of-vote-to-subpoena-ceos-to-testify-on-outrageously—high-prices-of-prescription-drugs-in-america/.*

[99] Evan D. Gumas, Paige Huffman, Irene Papanicolas, & Reginald D. Williams II, How Prices for the First 10 Drugs Up for U.S. Medicare Price Negotiations Compare Internationally, Controlling Health Care Costs, THE COMMOWEALTH FUND (Jan. 4, 2024), *https://www.commonwealthfund.org/publications/2024/jan/how-prices-first—10-drugs-Medicare-nego- tiations-compare-internationally.*

[100] The White House, FACT SHEET: Biden-.Harris Administration Announces First Ten Drugs Selected for Medicare Price Negotiation, BRIEFING ROOM: STATEMENTS & RELEASES (Aug. 29, 2023), *https://www.whitehouse.gov/briefing-room/statements-releases/2023/08/29/fact-sheet-biden-harris-administration-announces-first-ten-drugs-selected-for-Medicare- price-negotiation/.*

[101] ASSISTANT SECRETARY FOR PLANNING AND EVALUATION, OFFICE OF HEALTH POLICY, DEPARTMENT OF HEALTH AND HUMAN SERVICES, INFLATION REDUCTION ACT RESEARCH SERIES—MEDICARE ENROLLEES' USE AND OUT-OF-POCKET EXPENDITURES FOR DRUGS SELECTED FOR NEGOTIATION UNDER THE MEDICARE DRUG PRICE NEGOTIATION PROGRAM 5 (Aug. 29, 2023), *https://aspe.hhs.gov/sites/default/files/ documents/9a34d00483a47aee03703bfc565ffee9/ASPE-IRA-Drug-Negotiation-Fact-Sheet—09-13-2023.pdf.*

[102] FDA approves first generics of Eliquis, NEWS RELEASE (Dec. 23, 2019), *https://www.fda.gov/news-events/press-announcements/fda-approves-first-generics-eliquis.*

alternatives prohibited until 2031 due to patent litigation and settlements.[103] The company's patent for the active ingredient of Eliquis was filed in September 2002, and was set to expire in February 2023.[104] But BMS received an extension of its patent term until November 2026 using a Federal law that can provide extensions for time lost in the premarket government approval process.[105]

On top of its extension on the primary patent, BMS and Pfizer obtained a patent on a pharmaceutical composition with a particular crystalline form of the active ingredient that expires in 2031.[106] In patent litigation, a generic manufacturer argued the claim was obvious because someone would have been motivated to develop the same claim based on what was known at the time. While American courts upheld the patent claim based on a finding that there was no need that would have motivated someone else to pursue this invention, the UK courts invalided the patent.[107] That court argued that it would have been obvious because someone in the field would have arrived at the invention, and if the court believed BMS's argument that there really was no need that would have driven the obvious invention, then the patent would have been invalid for lack of utility.[108] Ultimately, the patent appears to have marginal value given that it was not addressed to a particular issue at the time, but the consequences of 5 years of additional monopoly power over the drug

---

[103] The Bristol-Myers Squibb-Pfizer Alliance is pleased with the U.S. District Court decision to uphold both the composition of matter (COM) patent (U.S. 6,967, 208) and formulation patent (U.S. 9,326,945) covering Eliquis, PRESS RELEASE (Aug. 5, 2020), *https://news.bms.com/news/details/2020/The-Bristol-Myers-Squibb-Pfizer-Alliance-is-pleased-with-the-U.S.-District- Court-decision-to-uphold-both-the-composition-of-matter-COM-patent-U.S.*

[104] U.S. Patent No. U.S. 6,967,208.

[105] Applications for patent term extension and patent terms extended under 35 U.S.C. 156, UNITED STATES PATENT & TRADEMARK OFFICE, *https://www.uspto.gov /patents/laws/patent-term-extension/patent-terms-extended-under—35-usc-156* (last visited Feb. 5, 2024); Patent and Exclusivity for: N202155, ORANGE BOOK: APPROVED DRUG PRODUCTS WITH THERAPEUTIC EQUIVALENCE EVALUATIONS, *https://www.accessdata.fda.gov/scripts/cder/ob/patent—info.cfm'Product—No—001&Appl—No=202155&Appl—type—N* (last visited Feb. 5, 2024).

[106] U.S Patent No. 9,326,945.

[107] Compare Bristol Myers Squibb Co. v. Aurobindo Pharma U.S. Inc., 477 F. Supp. 3d 306, 356 (D. Del. 2020) with Sandoz Limited & Teva Pharmaceutical Industries Limited v. Bristol Myers-Squibb Holdings Ireland Unlimited Company & Pfizer Inc., [2022] EWHC 1831 (Pat) (Mead, J.) at 48.

[108] Compare Bristol Myers Squibb Co. v. Aurobindo Pharma U.S. Inc., 477 F. Supp. 3d 306, 356 (D. Del. 2020) with Sandoz Limited & Teva Pharmaceutical Industries Limited v. Bristol Myers-Squibb Holdings Ireland Unlimited Company & Pfizer Inc., [2022] EWHC 1831 (Pat) (Mead, J.) at 48.

will be enormous. American patients will continue to face hundreds of dollars in out- of-pocket costs and the coffers of public programs will be stretched in the absence of lower cost generics.

Abecma & Breyanzi

The list prices of Bristol Myers Squibb's cell therapies, Abecma and Breyanzi, were $419,500 and $410,300 before BMS hiked the price of Abecma by almost $38,000 and Breyanzi by almost $37,000 in 2023; these spikes were among the nine highest list price increases of that year.[109] The therapies reached a combined $836 million in sales in 2023, with nearly 80 percent of the sales deriving from American patients.[110]

Pomalyst & Revlimid

In 2022, Bristol Myers Squibb hiked the price of its drugs for treating multiple myeloma. It hiked the wholesale acquisition price of Pomalyst by over $4,000, increasing its price to $94,845 for 100 capsules. The company also hiked the price of Revlimid by over $3,500, increasing its price for 100 capsules to $83,322.[111] These price hikes were among the nine highest for 2022 in terms of total dollar amount. In 2023, Revlimid made BMS over $6 billion in sales, of which over $5 billion was earned from the U.S. market.[112] That same year, Pomalyst's sales were $3.4 billion, of which $2.36 billion was earned from U.S. patients.[113]

Thus, Bristol Myers Squibb's pricing practices are yet another example of how drug corporations price gouge American patients. Further, Bristol Myers

---

[109] ASSISTANT SECRETARY FOR PLANNING AND EVALUATION, OFFICE OF HEALTH POLICY, HHS, ISSUE BRIEF: CHANGES IN THE LIST PRICES OF PRESCRIPTION DRUGS, 2017–2023 (Oct. 6, 2023), aspe-drug-price-tracking-brief.pdf (hhs.gov). Due to the opacity of drug pricing, it is difficult to discern the financial burden of this drug on the average patient. Accord- ing to one source from 2021, a single dose of Abecma cost $419,500. See Eric Sagonowsky, Bris- tol's new myeloma CAR-T needs a hefty discount to be cost-effective, watchdogs say while endorsing GSK's Blenrep, FIERCE PHARMA (Apr. 7, 2021), *https://www.fiercepharma.com/ pharma/bristol-s-new-myeloma-car-t-needs-a-big-discount-to-be-cost-effective-watchdogs-say-while*.

[110] BRISTOL MYERS SQUIBB, FORM 8-K, EXHIBIT 99.1 (Feb. 2, 2024), *https://www.sec.gov/ixviewer/ix.html'doc=/Archives/edgar*.

[111] ASSISTANT SECRETARY FOR PLANNING AND EVALUATION, OFFICE OF HEALTH POLICY, HHS, ISSUE BRIEF: PRICE INCREASES FOR PRESCRIPTION DRUGS, 2016–2022, 2017–2023 (Sept. 30, 2023), Price Increases for Prescription Drugs, 2016–2022 (hhs.gov). Due to the lack of drug pricing transparency, it is difficult to determine the price for end users of the drug.

[112] BRISTOL MYERS SQUIBB, FORM 8-K, EXHIBIT 99.1 (Feb. 2, 2024), *https:// www.sec.gov/ixviewer/ix.html'doc=/Archives/edgar/*.

[113] Id.

Squibb engages in patenting practices of marginal value that appear to be widespread in the pharmaceutical industry to extend monopoly control over drug prices and unfairly deprive U.S. patients of lower cost generics.

III. These Companies Spend Billions on Self-Enriching Activities, Often in Excess of Research and Development Expenses

All three companies have alleged that the Medicare price negotiation provisions of the Inflation Reduction Act would detract from the innovation of new life-saving medicines and sued to invalidate these measures.[114] But there is a wealth of evidence that contradicts claims that drug price regulation will impact the innovation of new medicines. First, experts, and even the Congressional Budget Office, conclude there is no connection between a drug's research and development cost and its future price.[115] Rather, the current price of drugs reflects the maximum that companies believe healthcare payers will pay for monopolized drugs with few if any adequate therapeutic alternatives.[116] More specifically, the Congressional Budget Office found that only 13 fewer drugs out of 1,300 (1 percent) would come to market over the

[114] Complaint, Janssen Pharmaceutical Inc. v. Beccera et al., No. 3:23-cv–03818, para. 40. (D. N.J. July 18, 2023); The Inflation Reduction Act's Negative Impact on Patient-Focused Innovation, Value and Access, MERCK: COMPANY STATEMENT (June 6, 2023), *https:// www.merck.com/news/the-inflation-reduction-acts-negative-impact-on-patient-focused-innova- tion-value-and-access/*; Impact of the inflation reduction act on innovative medicines for patients, BRISTOL MYERS SQUIBB (June 16, 2023), *https://www.bms.com/impact-of-the-inflation-reduction-act-on-innovative-medicines-for-patients.html*; Kevin Dunleavy, Johnson & Johnson becomes 4th drugmaker to file suit against IRA's drug price negotiations, FIERCE PHARMA (July 18, 2023), *https://www.fiercepharma.com/pharma/johnson-johnson-becomes— 4th-big-pharma-file-suit-against-ira-drug-price-negotiations*.

[115] CONGRESSIONAL BUDGET OFFICE, RESEARCH AND DEVELOPMENT IN THE PHARMACEUTICAL INDUSTRY (Aug. 2021) (''In CBO's assessment, current R&D spending does not influence the future prices of the drugs that result from that spending.''); Aaron Kesselheim, Jerry Avorn, & Ameet Sarpatwari, The High Cost of Prescription Drugs in the United States: Origins and Prospects for Reform, 316 JAMA NETWORK 858 (2016); Vinay Prasad, Kevin De Jesus, Sham Mailankody, The high price of anticancer drugs: origins, implica- tions, barriers, solutions, 14 NAT. REV. CLIN. ONC. 381 (2016).

[116] Aaron Kesselheim, Jerry Avorn, & Ameet Sarpatwari, The High Cost of Prescription Drugs in the United States: Origins and Prospects for Reform, 316 JAMA NETWORK 858 (2016).

next 30 years as a result of the Inflation Reduction Act.[117] Second, compared to the rest of the globe, the United States is an outlier that does little to protect its residents from the unfair pricing power of drug companies,[118] and bringing American policy into alignment with those of other countries, including other high-income peers, will not destroy the incentive to innovate new medicines. Finally, drug corporations spend in excess on executive compensation, share buybacks, and dividends which enrich their shareholders, cutting against the industry's mistaken impression that it is strapped for resources to research and develop new medicines.[119] For example, in just 2022, the manufacturers of the drugs selected for Medicare price negotiation spent $10 billion more on these self-enriching activities than research and development.[120] Stock buybacks enrich investors by reducing the number of outstanding shares in a company. The fewer shares there are in investors' hands, the more each share is worth. When a company buys back and cancels 10 percent of its shares, that makes each share still held by an investor or insider rise in value, as it represents a greater claim on the company's earnings. Spending money this way allows companies to enrich shareholders silently, as well as the executives often paid in stock.[121] Stock buybacks are particularly problematic as they have historically increased stock value without raising taxable income, can provide a mistaken impression about the economic health of a company, and detract from more worthwhile investments in a company's own workers and productive capacity, such as research and development efforts. Dividends are another way of returning cash to investors. Each fiscal quarter, publicly traded

---

[117] CONGRESSIONAL BUDGET OFFICE, ESTIMATED BUDGETARY EFFECTS OF PUBLIC LAW 117–169 (Sept. 7, 2022), *https://www.cbo.gov/system/files/2022—909/PL117—169— 9—7—22.pdf.*

[118] Amy Kapczynski, The Political Economy of Market Power in Pharmaceuticals, 48 J. HEALTH POL., POL'Y & L. 215 (2023); S. Vincent Rajkumar, The high cost of prescription drugs: causes and solutions, 10 BLOOD & CANCER J. 381 (2020).

[119] Amy Kapczynski, The Political Economy of Market Power in Pharmaceuticals, 48 J. HEALTH POL., POL'Y & L. 215, 230 (2023) (citing Aaron Kesselheim & Jeffrey Avorn, Letting the Government Negotiate Drug Prices Won't Hurt Innovation, WASH. POST (Sept. 27, 2021), *https://www.washingtonpost.com/outlook/2021/09/22/drug-pricing-negotiation-biden-bill/)*; U.S. HOUSE OF REPRESENTATIVES' COMMITTEE ON OVERSIGHT & REFORM, DRUG PRICING INVESTIGATION: INDUSTRY SPENDING ON BUYBACKS, DIVIDENDS, & EXECUTIVE COMPENSATION (July 2021).

[120] JISHIAN RAVINTHIRAN, PUBLIC CITIZEN & PROTECT OUR CARE, PROFITS OVER PATIENTS: SPENDING ON SELF-ENRICHMENT EXCEEDS RESEARCH AND DEVELOPMENT COSTS FOR MANY MANUFACTURERS OF IRA DRUGS (Jan. 18, 2024).

[121] PUBLIC CITIZEN, BAILOUT WATCH, FRIENDS OF THE EARTH, BIG OIL'S WARTIME BONUS 2 (2022).

companies typically issue fixed dividends to shareholders that rise when business is good and shrink or get suspended when business is bad.[122]

Looking at these self-enriching activities, Johnson & Johnson spent nearly $12 billion on dividends to shareholders, over $6 billion on stock buybacks, and $45 million on executive compensation in just the year 2022. In total, Johnson & Johnson spent nearly $18 billion on these self-enriching activities compared to $15 billion on research and development.[123] Similarly, Bristol Myers Squibb spent over $8 billion on stock buybacks, nearly $5 billion on dividends, and 48 million on executive compensation.[124] The company spent approximately $3 billion more on these self-enriching activities compared to research and development in 2022.[125] If we examine these spending patterns from 2012–2021, Johnson & Johnson spent $43 billion more on stock buybacks and dividends than research and development.[126] Similarly, Merck's spending on stock buybacks and dividends over this period exceeded its research and development costs by $3 billion.[127]

In sum, the spending patterns of all three companies belies their impression to the public that their profits are re-invested in research and development capacities; instead, they reallocate their profits mostly to the benefit of their shareholders and executives. As such, there is no necessary relationship between providing drug pricing relief for millions and harming resources for innovating new medicines.

Conclusion

Supermajorities of Americans want decisive government action to rein in the price gouging tactics of the pharmaceutical industry. And though most drug corporations have been happy to benefit from an array of government policies that have expanded their monopoly power over drugs to the detriment of

---

[122] Id. at 8.

[123] JISHIAN RAVINTHIRAN, PUBLIC CITIZEN & PROTECT OUR CARE, PROFITS OVER PATIENTS: SPENDING ON SELF-ENRICHMENT EXCEEDS RESEARCH AND DEVELOPMENT COSTS FOR MANY MANUFACTURERS OF IRA DRUGS (Jan. 18, 2024).

[124] Id.

[125] Id.

[126] WILLIAM LAZONICK & NER TULUM, INSTITUTE FOR NEW ECONOMIC THINKING, SICK WITH "SHAREHOLDER VALUE": U.S. PHARMA'S FINANCIALIZED BUSINESS MODEL DURING THE PANDEMIC (Dec. 6, 2022).

[127] Id.

patients, many now fiercely resist any efforts to deliver material drug pricing relief to millions of Americans. The drug pricing tactics of Johnson & Johnson, Merck, and Bristol Myers Squibb are representative of the broader exploitative practices endemic to the pharmaceutical industry. They use their monopoly control to price life-saving medicines excessively, and either pursue, or benefit from, additional patents of marginal value to extend their power to exorbitantly price drugs. This profiteering demands greater action from the Biden administration and Congress, which would not tangibly impact the innovation of new life-saving medicines.

[Summary Statement of Peter Maybarduk]

Chairman Sanders, Ranking Member Cassidy and Members of the Committee.

Thank you for the opportunity to testify today on the high prices Americans pay for prescription drugs. Public Citizen is a national public interest organization with more than 500,000 members and supporters. For 50 years, we have advocated for stronger health, safety and consumer protections; for corporate and government accountability; and for affordable access to medicines.

Drug prices are high because of monopoly power, leading to treatment rationing and preventable suffering. Three in 10 Americans have not taken their medications as prescribed due to costs. Americans confront the highest drug prices in the world, paying nearly three times more for the same drugs than other countries. In 2020, for the 20 top-selling drugs worldwide, drug corporations made far more from U.S. sales than sales to all other countries combined ($101 billion to $57 billion). Drug pricing abuses drain the coffers of health programs. Of $400 billion spent on retail prescription drugs in 2022, $135 billion came from Medicare and $45 billion from Medicaid.

This pricing disparity is even more egregious considering taxpayer funded contributions to drug development. The world's largest biomedical research funder is a public funder, the National Institutes of Health, contributing more than $45 billion a year and laying groundwork for many if not most new medicines.

Our government grants patent protection and exclusivities on medicines. In theory, this should support innovation. In practice, drug corporations too often are writing the rules to extract maximum rents from taxpayers. In 2022; the manufacturers of the ten drugs selected for Medicare price negotiation spent $10 billion more on self-enriching activities—stock buybacks, dividends and CEO compensation—than on R&D. Drugmakers do not set prices according to R&D costs. The price of a patented drug is the most that we, as a society, are willing to pay to care for our sick and loved ones, where monopoly power blocks affordable alternatives and we have little choice.

Drugmakers extend their exclusive power over new drugs through anticompetitive tactics. Many have abused the patent system to obtain subsequent patents over the same medicine with marginal differences, sometimes for decades. The pharmaceutical industry has accrued tremendous influence in our political system, outranking every other industry in lobbying spending.

Today, perhaps for the first time, our Country is making progress challenging high prices and treatment rationing, including through price negotiations and countering price spikes, among other measures. We commend the Committee's attention to this problem. Far more is necessary.

Ultimately, we will have to confront monopoly power. That is the foundation allowing drugmakers to project influence, game the law and keep prices high. Other real challenges in medicine pricing and access, including secrecy, cost caps, patient assistance, and middlemen taking advantage, flow inexorably from the lucrative patent monopolies that make it so possible and so easy to rip off taxpayers. Thank you for your time, and please count us with you in the fight.

The CHAIR. Thank you. Our next witness will be Tahir Amin, CEO, Initiative for Medicines Access and Knowledge, a nonprofit organization working to address inequalities in how medicines are developed and distributed. Thanks very much for being with us.

Statement of Tahir Amin, Ll.B., Chief Executive Officer, Initiative for Medicines, Access & Knowledge, New York, NY

Mr. AMIN. Chairman Sanders, Ranking Member Cassidy, and Members of the Committee, it is my honor to be invited here to share with you a root cause of why the U.S. pays by far the highest prices in the world for prescription drugs. That root cause is how the pharmaceutical industry manipulates the patent system to lengthen patent protection and its market monopoly in order to block competition, all while increasing prices.

I qualify as a UK attorney in intellectual property, and I have been in the field for 30 years. I spent my first decade of my legal career practicing as an attorney at international law firms and for multinational companies, including American companies.

Through this work, I learned both the legal and business side of intellectual property and its importance to inventors, investors, and companies. I also learned how to use loopholes to game the system.

These loopholes enabled me to invent intellectual property rights so companies could obtain and maintain a monopoly in the market, while continuing to extract maximum profits. It was the reason why I co-founded IMAK and left the commercial world. America is in a severe drug pricing crisis.

More than one-third of Americans say they are not able to fill a prescription for medication because of its cost. Black Americans are most heavily impacted, as they are more likely to require medication for chronic conditions and earn less.

Now, prescription drug spending on retail and non-retail drugs is poised to grow 63 percent this decade to $917 billion, and branded prescription drugs, which are under patent protection, account for 84 percent of that spending.

These price hikes correspond with a dramatic increase in patenting activity in the pharmaceutical sector. Now, we have analyzed the top 10 selling drugs in the United States, and we have found a total of 1,429 patent applications have been filed as of 2022.

741 patents have been granted on these drugs. On average, that is, more than 140 patent applications filed per drug, and 74 patents granted per drug. That is 66 percent of those patents are filed after the drug is approved by the FDA.

Now, if we look at some of the drugs that are on the discussion today with the companies that were here, KEYTRUDA, Merck's ELIQUIS, STELARA, Johnson & Johnson, also IMBRUVICA, which is AbbVie, Johnson & Johnson.

Between them, there is a combined of 494 patent applications filed on them, of which 235 were granted patents. I just want to dig a little bit deeper into Merck and particularly Senate Luja`n's questioning of whether Merck would sort of allow biosimilar competition once the primary patent expires.

You have to remember, KEYTRUDA actually represents 47 percent of Merck's total pharmaceutical revenue. Now, as of June 2002, we have counted 180 patent applications, of which 78 are granted. They have patent protection at least until 2039, which is in total 37 years of patent protection since they filed their first patent, which is 2002. You are supposed to get a patent for 20 years, remember.

Market and media analysts a current reporting that we should see biosimilar competition in 2028, to Senator Luja`n's question. I put myself on record here today, we will not see biosimilar competition until 2034.

They will litigate the hell out of it, and they will use every cent that they can to kind of not leave $100 billion on the table, which is what those patents are worth to them.

All this talk of R&D and new indications, these patents are already disclosing the earlier patents that should be expiring in 2024. Bristol-Myers Squibb, same problem. Bristol-Myers has actually increased the price of ELIQUIS by 124 percent since its induction in 2012.

That is higher than the general rate of inflation. They have filed more patents here in the United States, 2.4 more times than in Europe. In fact, the patents that the CEO from BMX was talking about, the relevant patents, those were actually invalidated in Europe and that is why we have generic competition in Europe.

But those patents are actually preventing competition here in the United States and it is going to cost us $48 billion in branded ELIQUIS. So, this Committee should recognize that the use of patent thickets to extend the market monopoly period on a product is not a case of a few bad actors, it is endemic.

If you want to get to the heart of the problem, the first and most important thing Congress can do is solve the problem, is raise the bar for what classifies as an invention that deserves a patent. It is an enormous monopoly power that should—in the single hands of a drug maker, and we shouldn't leave it to the market and litigation to resolve these issues.

The patenting activity goes well beyond the time limits in monopoly that the Constitution required. Lawyers, exploit sophisticated legal marketing Jedi tricks that they use under the guise of innovation.

We need to actually not get sidetracked by this innovation talk. Most of these patents are tweaks deliberately for the financialization of profits, and that is what the pharmaceutical industry does today. I have been in the business, and I know what it is about. Thank you.

[The prepared statement of Mr. Amin follows.]

Prepared Statement of Tahir Amin

Chairman Sanders, Ranking Member Cassidy, and Members of the Committee. It is my honor to be invited here to share with you a root cause of why the U.S. pays, by far, the highest prices in the world for prescriptions drugs. That root cause is how the pharmaceutical industry manipulates the patent system to lengthen patent protection and its market monopoly in order to block competition, all while increasing prices.

I. Introduction and Background

My name is Tahir Amin. I am a Founder and Chief Executive Officer of the Initiative for Medicines, Access & Knowledge, also known as I-MAK, a non-profit organization working to address structural inequities in how medicines are developed and distributed. We do not accept funding from branded or generic pharmaceutical companies.

I qualified as a UK attorney and have nearly 30 years of experience in the field of intellectual property. I have experience working with the intellectual property and patent systems of several countries in the world, including the U.S., both at the practice and policy level.

I spent the first decade of my legal career practicing as an attorney at international law firms and multinational companies securing and protecting intellectual property. Many of my clients were American companies, as was one of my employers during this time. Through this work, I learned both the legal and business side of intellectual property and its importance to inventors, investors and companies. I also learned how to use loopholes to game the system. These loopholes enabled me to ''invent'' intellectual property rights so companies could obtain and maintain a monopoly in the market, while continuing to extract maximum profits.

After a decade in private practice seeing how intellectual property rights—and especially patents—are often misused for commercial gain, I co-founded I-MAK to help restore integrity and to the patent system. For the past 15 years, I have worked alongside patients and advocates to remove unmerited patent rights that stand in the way of generic and biosimilar competition and keep life-saving medicines out of reach of the patients who need them.

I speak to you today as someone who has seen both sides of this issue.

II. The Link Between Patents and Drug Prices

America is in a drug pricing crisis. More than one-third of Americans say they have not filled a prescription for medication because of its cost.[128] Black Americans are most heavily impacted as they are more likely to require medication for chronic conditions, such as high blood pressure or diabetes, while having median incomes of nearly $30,000 less than white households.[129]

Prescription drug spending on retail and non-retail drugs is poised to grow 63 percent this decade, reaching $917 billion dollars.[130] This increase is fueled by spending on patent-protected branded drugs. While branded drugs make up just 8 percent of prescriptions versus 92 percent for generics, they account for 84 percent of all drug spending in the U.S.[131] Even after adjusting for general inflation, U.S. prescription drug spending increased by 76 percent from 2000 to 2017.

These price hikes correspond with a dramatic increase in patenting activity in the pharmaceutical sector.

It took 155 years for the USPTO to issue its first five million patents in 1991.[132] It has taken less than one fifth of that time for the USPTO to issue its next 6 million. This would suggest that over half of all inventions in the history of the U.S. patent system occurred in the last 30 years. But have we really become more inventive in the last 30 years, or have we just become better at ''inventing'' patents because our patent system is no longer stringent enough?

A similar picture emerges when we drill down into pharmaceutical patents specifically. The number of pharmaceutical patents granted in the U.S. more than doubled between 2005 (1,580 patents) and 2015 (3,742 patents).[133] But nearly 80 percent of the drugs—products based on small molecules—

---

[128] YouGov, More than one-third of Americans have not filled a prescription because of cost, 10 March 2023, available at *https://today.yougov.com/health/articles/45388-americans-have-not-filled-prescription-price-poll.*

[129] Protect Our Care, How High Drug Prices Hurt Black Americans, July 2021 available at *https://www.protectourcare.org/wp-content/uploads/2021/07/POC-Report-How-High-Drug- Prices-Hurt-Black—Americans—.pdf.*

[130] Charles Roehrig and Ani Turner, Projections of the Non-Retail Prescription Drug Share of National Health Expenditures Report, Altarum, July 2022.

[131] The Use of Medicines in the U.S. 2022, The IQVIA Institute, 21 April 2022.

[132] https://10millionpatents.uspto.gov/.

[133] Report—S&E indicators 2018—NSF—national science foundation. Science & Engineering Indicators 2018 Report. Accessed Oct. 31, 2023. https://www.nsf.gov/statistics/2018/nsb20181/report/sections/invention-knowledge-transfer-and-innovation/invention—united-states-and-comparative-global-trends—uspto-patenting-activity.

associated with new patents during this time were not for new drugs, but for existing ones.[134]

Our analysis for the top 10 selling drugs in the U.S. in 2021 alone revealed[135]:

- A total of 1,429 patent applications have been filed as of 2022;
- 741 patents have been granted on these drugs in total;
- On average, that is more than 140 patent applications filed per drug, and 74 patents granted per drug.
- On average, 66 percent of patents filed on these drugs are after the first approval for marketing by the U.S. Food and Drug Administration (FDA).
- On average 55 percent of the granted patents for these drugs were filed after FDA approval.
- Over four times as many patents were granted on these top 10 selling drugs in 2021 when compared to Europe.
- Keytruda (Merck), Eliquis (Bristol-Myers Squibb (BMS)/Pfizer), Stelara (Johnson & Johnson) and Imbruvica (AbbVie/Johnson & Johnson) were 4 of the top selling drugs in 2021. As of June 2022, these four drugs alone have had at least 494 patent applications filed on them, of which 235 were granted patents.
- Most of the patent applications (305) for these four drugs were filed after FDA approval.

A closer look at some of these best-selling drugs reveals the following.

Keytruda (Merck)

Merck's Keytruda belongs to a class of drugs known as immune checkpoint inhibitors used for cancer immunotherapy. It was first approved in September 2014. At the last count in July 2023, it has received an additional 35 FDA approvals across 16 different types of cancer.

Keytruda is projected to become the best-selling drug ever, taking over AbbVie's Humira. Its worldwide sales are forecasted to be $27.19 billion in

---

[134] R Feldman. May your drug prices be evergreen. Journal of Law and the Biosciences, Volume 5, Issue 3, December 2018, Pages 590—647, https://doi.org/10.1093/jlb/lsy022.

[135] I-MAK, Overpatented, Overpriced, September 2022 available at https://www.i-mak.org/overpatented/ and https://drugpatentbook.i—mak.org/.

2024. In 2023, global sales for Keytruda were $25 billion, with $15 billion in the U.S. alone. Keytruda represented 47 percent of Merck's total pharmaceutical revenue in 2023.

As of June 2022, there are at least 180 patent applications and 78 granted patents covering Keytruda and its various indications. 61 percent of the 180 patent applications were filed after the first FDA approval for Keytruda in 2014.[136]

The first patent filed in relation to Keytruda was 2002. Based on our findings, the latest expiring patent for Keytruda will be in 2039, which will be 11 years after the key patents covering the drug are set expire (2028). In total, Merck currently has 37 years of patent protection for Keytruda (it is worth noting that patents are granted for 20 years for an invention). This protection includes:

Market and media analysts are currently reporting that we could see biosimilar competition for Keytruda when the key patents on the drug expire in 2028 (often referred to as the patent cliff). Given the patent thicket that Merck has accumulated around Keytruda, I think that is wishful thinking. If we have learned any lessons from how AbbVie was able to extend its market monopoly on Humira for an additional 7 years beyond its key patent and generate $102 billion in revenue alone in that period (which included continued price increases) because of its patent thicketing strategy (see Figure below[137]), then we can expect Merck to do the same. Based on an analysis of all Keytruda's patents, after all the patent litigation and settlements are done, we will be fortunate if we see biosimilars for Keytruda enter before 2034—roughly 6 years after the key patents expire. I also predict, as AbbVie did with Humira, that Merck will continue to increase prices for its branded Keytruda during the additional market monopoly period because of its extended patent protection. I do not see Merck leaving some $100 billion plus on the table, they will use whatever patents they have to litigate for every cent of it.

---

[136] 9 *https://drugpatentbook.i-mak.org/*.

[137] I-MAK, Overpatented, Overpriced, September 2022.

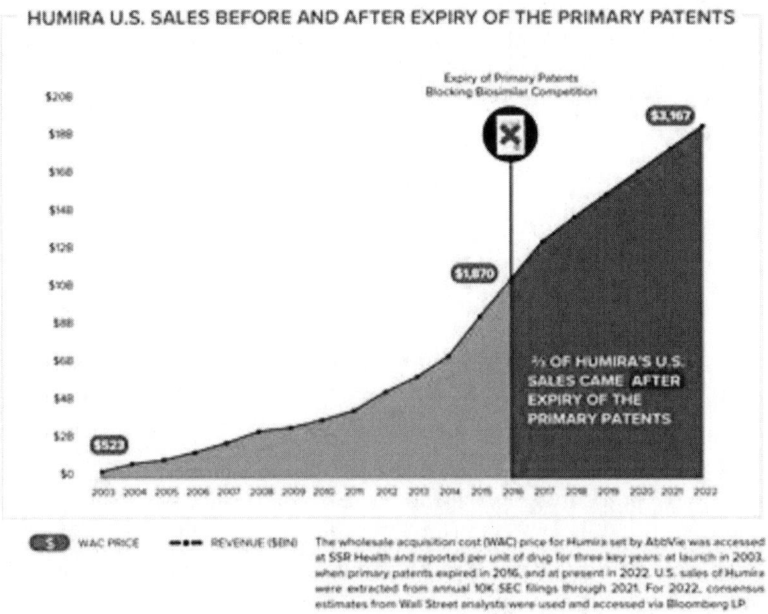

Imbruvica (AbbVie/Johnson & Johnson)

Imbruvica is a drug used to treat a variety of B cell cancers, including leukemia and lymphoma. It was first approved in 2013 and is approved by the FDA for several different indications.

The price of Imbruvica has increased by 108 percent in the U.S. since it was introduced in 2013, compared to a 30 percent general inflation increase in the same period.[138] 11 Imbruvica's list price has increased nearly 32 percent in the U.S. in the past 5 years, from $431 in 2019 to $567 per capsule (70mg).

As of June 2022, AbbVie has filed 195 patent applications, of which 96 have been granted to date. That roughly works out to over one patent filed every month for the last 14 years. Over half of these patent applications were filed after Imbruvica received its first FDA approval. Currently, granted patents for Imbruvica give AbbVie patent protection for 29 years, until 2036—nine additional years beyond its original 20 years of patent protection.

---

[138] 11 Noah Tong, Here are 25 Medicare Part D drugs that have skyrocketed in Price, Fierce Healthcare, 10 August 2023, available at *https://www.fiercehealthcare.com/payers/here-are-25- Medicare-part-d-drugs-have-skyrocketed-price.*

Despite generic companies litigating AbbVie's patents, we have already seen six companies enter into patent settlement agreements. As a result of these agreements, competitors will delay introduction of generic versions of Imbruvica until 2032 and 2033. These 5 additional years of market monopoly because of extended patent protection could help AbbVie and Johnson & Johnson secure over $7 billion dollars in revenue.

Eliquis (Bristol Myers Squibb (BMS)/Pfizer)

Eliquis is an anticoagulant medication used to treat and prevent blood clots.

Sales for Eliquis in the U.S. increased by 10 percent to $8.6 billion in 2023. Eliquis accounts for 27 percent of BMS's sales in the U.S. The price of Eliquis has increased by 124 percent since its introduction in 2012 as compared to 31 percent general inflation increase during the same period.[139] 12 In January this year, the list price for Eliquis increased by 6 percent from the year before. This increase outpaced inflation and the annual price increases of the top 50 best selling drugs.

As of June 2022, BMS/Pfizer have filed at least 43 patent applications for the drug, of which 22 are granted. Sixteen of these patent applications were filed after FDA approval. There are 2.4 times more granted patents in the U.S. than in Europe. Generic versions of Eliquis entered some European countries in 2022 after several patents that would have extended the market monopoly period were found invalid.[140] 13 However, in the U.S. these same patents were held valid after litigation and generic versions are not expected to enter until 2028. As a result of extended patent protection, generic versions will have entered Europe almost 6 years earlier than in the U.S. By our estimate, BMS/Pfizer will make $48 billion in revenue during this extended market monopoly period.[141] 14

---

[139] Ibid.

[140] 13 Amy Sandys, Court of Appeal confirms invalidity of Bristol-Myers Squibb apixaban patent, 9 May 2023, available at *https://www.juve-patent.com/cases/court-of-appeal-confirms-inva- lidity-of-bristol-myers-squibb-apixaban-patent/.*

[141] 14 I-MAK, Overpatented, Overpriced, September 2022.

III. Solutions to the Patent and Drug Pricing Problem

This Committee should recognize that the use of patent thickets to extend the market monopoly period on a product is not a case of a few bad actors. This is an endemic problem across the pharmaceutical industry.

If we want to get to the heart of addressing our National drug pricing crisis, the first and most important thing Congress can do to solve this problem is raise the bar for what gets patented. Over the last 30 years, more and more patents have been sought and granted for things that are not new inventions given what we know in the pharmaceutical sciences today.

For example, no reasonable researcher would call combining two existing drugs or switching dosages novel science by today's standards. And yet, drugmakers regularly get 20 years of patent protection for this commonly practiced knowledge.

In 1962, Senator Estes Kefauver of Tennessee said:

> ''If you want to tweak a drug, and you want to get another patent on it, the modified version has to be significantly better, therapeutically, for patients.''[142]

A patent puts enormous monopoly power into the hands of a single drugmaker. That power should only be granted if the invention is original and materially better than what already exists. We cannot rely on the market and litigation to resolve these problems; they need to be addressed before a patent monopoly is granted in the first place.

Conclusion

The Constitution grants Congress the power to ''promote the progress of science and useful arts by securing for limited times to authors and inventors the exclusive right to their respective writings and discoveries.''

But patenting activity today goes well beyond the time limited monopoly intended by the Constitution. Today's patent system has become less an engine for real invention than a tool for companies and their lawyers to exploit using sophisticated legal and marketing Jedi tricks.

---

[142] *https://www.ncbi.nlm.nih.gov/pmc/articles/PMC4101807/.*

This is not an indictment of the pharmaceutical industry. Drugmakers and their armies of patent lawyers—people like me in my former life—are simply doing what the system incentives them to do, and what they are bound by their shareholders and clients to do.

But it is in Congress's power to end this perversion and restore integrity to the patent system. Instead of incentivising investment in minor modifications for the purposes of extending a patent, we need a system that incentives bold research— breakthroughs that are therapeutically better than existing alternatives and fill a real market need, not low-hanging fruit designed to maximize profits. Congress has the ability to return the patent system to what it was always intended to be: not a vehicle for unprecedented profits, but an engine for inventions that are truly original and unprecedented.

[Summary Statement of Tahir Amin]

A root cause of why the U.S. pays, by far, the highest prices in the world is because of how the pharmaceutical industry manipulates the patent system to lengthen patent protection and its market monopoly.

I. The Link Between Patents and Drug Prices

Keytruda (Merck), Eliquis (Bristol-Myers Squibb (BMS)/Pfizer), Stelara (Johnson & Johnson) and Imbruvica (AbbVie/Johnson & Johnson) were 4 of the top selling drugs in 2021. As of June 2022, these four drugs alone have had at least 494 patent applications filed on them, of which 235 were granted patents. Most of the patent applications (305) for these four drugs were filed after FDA approval.

Keytruda (Merck)

There are at least 180 patent applications and 78 granted patents covering Keytruda and its various indications. 61 percent of the 180 patent applications were filed after the first FDA approval for Keytruda in 2014. Given the patent thicket that Merck has accumulated around Keytruda, we will be fortunate if we see biosimilars for Keytruda enter before 2034—roughly 6 years after the key patents expire (2028). During that extended monopoly period Merck will continue to increase prices and could pocket over $100 billion in sales.

Imbruvica (AbbVie/Johnson & Johnson)

AbbVie has filed 195 patent applications, of which 96 have been granted to date. As a result of patent litigation generic companies have entered settlements and will delay introduction of generic versions of Imbruvica until 2032 and 2033. These 5 additional years of market monopoly because of extended patent protection could help AbbVie and Johnson & Johnson secure over $7 billion dollars in revenue.

Eliquis (Bristol Myers Squibb (BMS)/Pfizer)

BMS/Pfizer have filed at least 43 patent applications for the drug, of which 22 are granted. There are 2.4 times more granted patents in the U.S. than in Europe. Generic versions of Eliquis entered some European countries in 2022 after several patents that would have extended the market monopoly period were found invalid. However, in the U.S. these same patents were held valid. after litigation and generic versions are not expected to enter until 2028. As a result of extended patent protection, generic versions will have entered Europe almost 6 years earlier than in the U.S. BMS/Pfizer could make $48 billion in revenue during this extended market monopoly period.

II. Solutions to the Patent and Drug Pricing Problem

If we want to get to the heart of addressing our National drug pricing crisis, the first and most important thing Congress can do to solve this problem is raise the bar for what classifies as an invention that deserves a patent.

The CHAIR. Thank you very much. Senator Cassidy.

Senator CASSIDY. Pleasure to introduce our witness, Darius Lakdawalla, currently the Quintiles Chair in Pharmaceutical Development Regulatory Innovation at University of Southern California Mann School of Pharmacy and Pharmaceutical Sciences.

He also serves as Director of Research for the USC Schaeffer Center for Health Policy and Economics, a partnership between the Mann School and the USC Price School of Public Policy.

He received his Ph.D. in economics from the University of Chicago as a renowned researcher and thought leader in health economics and health policy, which obviously impacts us today. Thank you, sir.

Statement of Darius Lakdawalla, Ph.D., Director, Research, University of Southern California Schaeffer Center, Los Angeles, CA

Dr. LAKDAWALLA. Thank you. Chairman Sanders, Ranking Member Cassidy, and honorable Members of the Committee, thank you for the opportunity to testify today about drug prices and the assessment of medical technologies.

My name is Darius Lakdawalla. I am an Economist and a Professor at the USC Mann School of Pharmacy and Pharmaceutical Sciences and USC Price School of Public Policy. I am also the Director of Research at the USC Schaeffer Center for Health Policy and Economics. The opinions I offer today are my own and don't represent the views of the University of Southern California or the USC Schaeffer Center.

I would like to start with a story. In December 1984, a young boy from Indiana named Ryan White was diagnosed with AIDS, a result of a transfusion with infected blood. In the immediate wake of his passing in 1990, Congress passed the Ryan White Care Act, ensuring affordable care for HIV/AIDS patients.

The value of this program was fully realized 5 years later, when highly active antiretroviral therapy emerged as a lifesaving treatment for patients with HIV. Today, 9 out of 10 patients receiving care through the Ryan White Program enjoy viral load so low that they are no longer infectious.

Thanks to breakthrough medical innovation and to forward thinking public policy that made innovative HIV therapies affordable to many, HIV positive patients can now expect to live well into their 70's and beyond.

But increasing patient access through bold expansion of affordable care means little when there are no valuable cures or treatments to access, and breakthrough medical therapies provide little value if high cost sharing pushes them out of patients' reach. This is the fundamental tradeoff we are here to address today.

This tradeoff between innovation and affordability has played out in different approaches taken across the globe. There is little doubt that U.S. consumers access newer drugs sooner and more often than their overseas counterparts, and this increased access to the latest treatments matters.

Schaeffer Center research suggests that introducing European style pricing policies would ultimately reduce innovation and cost American consumers just over half a year of life expectancy, about what would be lost if all American surgeons suddenly forgot how to perform heart bypass surgery.

Yet there is no denying the sentiment that U.S. consumers unfairly pay higher drug prices than their peers overseas. The deteriorating accessibility of prescription drugs in recent years threatens to derail the access advantages and health gains American consumers have so far enjoyed and is one component of this growing sentiment.

Even patients with good insurance are struggling to access the therapies their doctors prescribe. Plans frequently employ coinsurance requirements and utilization management tools that severely restrict access. These changes likely harm health, since the link between increasing out-of-pocket costs and worse patient adherence is well-established.

Surprisingly, coverage has deteriorated even while the average manufacturer net prices of brand drugs, the amount manufacturers receive after rebates and discounts, have declined in each of the last 5 years.

Shaeffer research analyzing the flow of money spent on insulin, found that while net prices fell by 31 percent, total expenditures remained nearly constant because intermediaries were pocketing the additional rebates and price concessions instead of passing them on to consumers.

Transparency and pricing throughout the pharmaceutical distribution system would be a major step toward ensuring that drug prices reflect the actual value provided to patients, and don't simply enrich intermediaries.

Rewarding drugs that do provide value promotes investment in the right kind of therapies and ensures good health will be increasingly within the reach of American patients for generations to come. Decades of economic research demonstrate that where innovators predict higher returns, innovative effort and discovery follow.

Outside the U.S., many countries adopt pricing approaches that either fail to measure value to patients or make it hard to predict future returns to innovation. The UK, Australia, and Canada employ relatively transparent and predictable methods that nonetheless rely on quality adjusted life years, which discriminate against vulnerable patients.

On the other hand, France and Germany avoid qualities and focus on rating clinical benefits in a way that often fails to correspond to the eventual price. These tradeoffs also underscore the risks of so-called reference pricing approaches that would tie American prices to those charged by other countries.

In so doing, Americans would be forced to live with the vagaries of pricing systems designed and implemented elsewhere around priorities that may differ from ours. Ultimately, the right policies for American patients need to focus on the affordability of good health.

Affordable and generous health insurance, transparent and predictable pricing, and an emphasis on value to patients provide the ingredients for a better approach that secures the health of American families now and for generations to come. Thank you very much.

[The prepared statement of Dr. Lakdawalla follows:]

Prepared Statement of Darius Lakdawalla

Key Points:

- The challenge for public policy is to sustain the pace of medical innovation while ensuring that valuable new technologies remain affordable and accessible.
- The U.S. is by far the largest market for pharmaceuticals in the world and the engine of global pharmaceutical innovation. Other countries, in effect, free ride off the innovation stimulated by the American market.
- Despite stable or falling net prices paid to prescription drug manufacturers over the past decade, novel medicines lie increasingly beyond the financial reach of American patients.
- Blunt price controls are not the solution to the worsening affordability of prescription drugs or to global free-riding: Schaeffer Center research suggests that introducing European-style pricing policies would reduce Americans' life expectancy.
- Instead, aligning drug prices with the actual value provided to patients stimulates innovation that benefits patients and discourages innovation that does not.

- Legislation to increase drug price transparency, coupled with better information about value, can help payers and consumers spend their money wisely.
- Affordable and generous insurance for prescription drugs ensures that drugs remain within the financial reach of American families.

Chairman Sanders, Ranking Member Cassidy, and Honorable Members of the Committee, thank you for the opportunity to testify today about drug prices and the assessment of medical technologies.

My name is Darius Lakdawalla, and I am an economist, a professor at the USC Mann School of Pharmacy & Pharmaceutical Sciences and USC Price School of Public Policy, and the Director of Research at the USC Schaeffer Center for Health Policy & Economics. By way of background, I have been studying innovation in the health care sector for nearly three decades, I co-wrote the chapter in the *Handbook of Health Economics* on intellectual property and biomedical research, and I co-authored the book *Valuing Health* on modern methods for valuing medical technology. The opinions I offer today are my own and do not represent the views of the University of Southern California or the USC Schaeffer Center.

The Value of Innovation in Global Context

In December 1984, a young boy from Indiana named Ryan White was diagnosed with AIDS, as a result of a transfusion with infected blood. While his doctors gave him just 6 months to live, Ryan outlasted those predictions and lived six more years. In the immediate wake of his untimely passing in 1990, Congress passed the Ryan White Care Act, which has since ensured affordable care for generations of HIV/AIDS patients. While the Act played a critical role in the fight against HIV almost immediately, its full value would not be realized until 5 years after its passage, when highly active antiretroviral therapy (HAART) emerged as a life-saving treatment for patients with HIV. The Ryan White Care Act put effective medical care within reach for many HIV+ patients that would otherwise have gone without it, while medical innovation brought new forms of treatment that changed the lives of patients and their families. Today, *9 out of 10 patients* receiving care through the Ryan White program enjoy viral loads so low that they are no longer infectious. Thanks to breakthrough medical innovation, and to forward-thinking public policy that made it affordable to many, HIV+ patients treated with HAART in a timely fashion can now *expect to live* well into their 70's and beyond.

The case of HIV illustrates a pair of health policy truisms. Increasing patient access through bold expansion of affordable care means little when there are no valuable cures or treatments to access. At the same time, breakthrough medical therapies provide little value if high cost-sharing pushes them out of patients' reach. The challenge for public policy is to sustain the pace of medical innovation while ensuring that valuable new technologies remain affordable and accessible to the patients who need them.

At first blush, it may seem impossible to navigate the narrow straits between affordability and innovation. Medical innovation investment carries high risk that drives up the cost of discovery. Among investigational medicines that undergo human trials, *90 percent will fail to launch.* Pharmaceutical and medical device firms will undertake these costs only if they expect to recoup the cumulative costs of their investments and receive a reasonable rate of return. However, these returns on innovation must ultimately be paid by all Americans, through out-of-pocket payments, health insurance premiums, and taxes. In this respect, therefore, greater rewards for innovators lead to *more innovation* but less affordability. The converse is also true: bluntly lowering prices makes new medicines more affordable for today's patients, but limits innovation for future generations of patients.

This tradeoff between innovation and affordability has played out in the different approaches taken across the globe. There is little doubt that U.S. consumers access newer drugs *sooner and more often* than their overseas counterparts. Academic research shows how this tendency results in more and earlier new drug launches in the U.S., and correspondingly *fewer and later launches* in other countries. Schaeffer Center research suggests that introducing European-style pricing policies would ultimately lower innovation and cost American consumers just over *half a year of life expectancy,* about what would be lost if American surgeons suddenly forgot how to perform heart bypass surgery.[143]

Meanwhile, academic research finds that the American healthcare system *performs better* than its European counterparts in treating disease. For example, American mortality rates from breast, colorectal, and prostate cancer have *fallen faster* than European rates. Indeed, an analysis of cancer care

---

[143] Bypass surgery adds about 1.1 years of life to patients treated with it. The lifetime risk of cardiovascular disease is around 60 percent. Thus, even if every heart disease patient received bypass surgery, it would add just over half a year of life.

across 16 countries found countries where cancer spending has grown more rapidly have also experienced *faster declines* in cancer mortality rates. According to our research, where the U.S. lags is in the prevention of *chronic diseases* like heart disease, hypertension, and diabetes. Faster growth in American obesity appears to have played an outsized role in driving these differences. In short, America's relatively low life expectancy appears to be in spite of, not because of, its healthcare system.

Despite the good news, however, there is no denying the sentiment that U.S. consumers unfairly pay higher drug prices than their peers overseas. On the one hand, we cannot readily observe the actual extent of the difference between U.S. and overseas prices. Too often, price comparisons in the public discussion rely on U.S. list prices, which are easily accessible, but almost never reflect what is truly paid for a drug. While researchers have a rough idea of the *average discount paid in aggregate,* this provides little insight into the actual prices of specific drugs. Economic principles predict that volume will be higher on drugs offering higher discounts. Therefore, applying the average discount to the list price of every individual drug will overstate U.S. prices.

Nonetheless, economic principles *also predict* that U.S. prices probably are higher than prices overseas, even if we do not know by exactly how much. The culprit is the problem of "free-riding." The U.S. is by far the *largest market for pharmaceuticals* in the world. Smaller market countries have rational, self-interested incentives to pay lower prices, knowing that their small size allows them to save money without meaningfully reducing global pharmaceutical innovation. In effect, their lower reimbursements "free-ride" off the American market, which remains the engine of pharmaceutical innovation that benefits patients throughout the world.

Americans have understandably become frustrated by footing so much of the world's bill for innovation. Unfortunately, we have no reliable ways to coerce other countries to act against their own self-interest. And, while it may seem tempting to stop paying higher prices and to join with the free riders, the resulting slowdown in innovation would *harm American patients and their families most of all.* Fortunately, there are actions we can take to ensure that patients benefit from medical advances, today and in the future.

Ensuring Patient Access to Treatments: Net Prices Are Not the Problem

The deteriorating accessibility of prescription drugs in recent years threatens to derail the access advantages and health gains American consumers have so far enjoyed. Even patients with ''good'' insurance are struggling to access the therapies their doctors prescribe. Plans frequently impose co-insurance requirements, where patients pay a share of their drug's list price, exposing them to artificially inflated list prices even when drugs' true costs are much lower. Plans are also restricting access or denying it altogether for an increasing share of drug compounds. Since 2012, the three largest pharmacy benefit managers have excluded a sharply increasing number of drugs from their formularies—last year, each of them excluded from coverage more than 600 products. At the same time, the average manufacturer net prices of brand drugs—the amount manufacturers receive after rebates and discounts—have declined in each of the last 5 years.

If it is getting cheaper to buy these drugs from manufacturers, why are they growing harder for patients to access? Part of the answer can be seen in a 2021 analysis of the flow of money spent on insulin. Between 2014 and 2018, net manufacturer prices for insulin fell by 31 percent, but the total expenditure per unit of insulin remained nearly constant. Growing discounts and concessions offered by manufacturers were not being passed on to patients or taxpayers in the form of lower insulin expenditures. Instead, those savings were being pocketed by intermediaries in the pharmacy distribution system, including pharmacy benefit managers, pharmacies and wholesalers. Pending legislation aimed at increasing transparency in the distribution system will shed more light on the commercial practices that enable PBMs to divert savings like this and provide more insight into where our drug spending is going. Neither third-party payers nor consumers observe the net prices they themselves are paying for individual drugs. Even large self-insured employers may be unable to get simple answers about how much they are paying for a given drug, no matter how widely used. Transparency in pricing would be a major step toward ensuring that drug prices reflect the actual value provided to patients, and don't simply enrich intermediaries.

Some academics and Federal agencies have asserted[144] that price transparency harms consumers, purportedly by providing a means for pharmaceutical firms to cooperate with each other in raising prices. This

[144] See page 362.

argument is specious. In the first place, there are no academic studies showing that pharmaceutical price transparency limits competition; the argument against transparency proceeds primarily by means of a flawed analogy to a 25 year-old study of the Danish ready-mix concrete industry. Moreover, the critique of price transparency rests on the quaint notion that confidential rebates yield vigorous price competition that benefits consumers. On the contrary, our research illustrates how confidential rebates explain why competition among branded drug companies is currently associated with higher-not-lower-list prices for drugs, and correspondingly higher costs for patients paying co-insurance for their medicines.

In addition to hitting American families in the pocketbook, higher out-of-pocket costs for drugs also harm health. The link between increasing out-of-pocket costs and patient adherence is well-established. USC Schaeffer Center research found that higher out-of-pocket burden corresponds with lower patient utilization of insulin, while other studies have found similar relationships between patient costs and adherence in rheumatoid arthritis, breast cancer, and chronic kidney disease. In addition, USC Schaeffer Center research demonstrated in the context of novel oral anticoagulants (NOACs) that prior authorization and step therapy restrictions in Part D plans harmed patient health. Patients in plans with more restrictions were less likely to use NOACs, had worse adherence when they did use NOACs, took longer to fill their initial NOAC prescription, and faced higher risk of mortality/stroke/transient ischemic attack. This research does not imply that every access restriction harms patient health. Rather, it highlights the need to evaluate the risks and benefits of access policies, just as we evaluate the risks and benefits of new medicines.

Sustaining Innovation for American Patients and their Families

Fortunately, reforms that promote patient access do not have to lower medical innovation. Indeed, our research shows that generous prescription drug insurance unlocks affordability and access for patients while still enabling sufficient rewards for innovation. This is not to say, however, that all innovation should be unquestioningly rewarded. The goal is to encourage innovations that benefit patients and their families, and to discourage those that do not. These goals can best be achieved when prices reflect value to patients.

Decades of economic research demonstrate that innovation follows pricing incentives. Where innovators expect higher returns, innovative effort and discovery follow. In contrast, innovators will avoid investing where they expect lower returns. As a result, aligning the price of every drug with the value it brings patients stimulates innovation that benefits patients and discourages innovation that does not. At a minimum, this requires a transparent and predictable approach to price-setting that rewards value. Predictability matters, because innovation investments follow what innovators expect prices will be, often many years in the future. Second, value must be measured in a way that holistically reflects what patients and their families care about. Doing otherwise stimulates the wrong kind of innovation.

Looking outside the U.S., many countries adopt pricing approaches that force a tradeoff between predictability and the holistic measurement of value. The United Kingdom, Australia, and Canada employ relatively transparent systems that set prices based on three kinds of data: the clinical benefits of the new drug, the expected economic benefit of the new drug, and the likely cost impact of the new drug. Even though prices are not determined in a purely formulaic manner, drugs are more likely to be reimbursed when their prices result in sufficient economic benefit, and vice-versa. And, since economic benefit is computed using a known mathematical framework, this approach results in more predictable pricing outcomes.

However, while these countries employ a more predictable approach, they also rely on old-fashioned methods of economic analysis—for instance traditional cost-effectiveness calculations using quality-adjusted life-years (QALYs). While many have correctly observed the ethical challenges posed by the discriminatory nature of QALYs, our research demonstrates that traditional QALYs also get the mathematics and economics of value assessment wrong for patients.

On the other side of the coin are countries like France and Germany, which recognize the pitfalls of traditional economic evaluation of new medicines. For the most part, these countries focus on clinical benefits as the main criterion for reimbursement decisions, rarely if ever attempting to form specific economic estimates of value. While these countries avoid flawed estimates of value, their approach compromises predictability. In contrast to economic evaluation, which is focused on estimating a monetary benefit, clinical evaluation typically considers many dimensions of health improvement without a clear and quantitative method for weighing these different dimensions against each other. For example, one academic study found that only 2 out of the 5 official criteria specified for clinical benefit in

France are statistically associated with the official rating of clinical benefit. Moreover, even if estimated clinical benefits are predictable, their effect on prices may not be. Under the German system, which uses a very specific, albeit complicated, process for measuring clinical benefit, there remains no clear quantitative relationship between measured clinical benefit and negotiated prices.

These tradeoffs also underscore the risks of so-called ''reference pricing'' approaches that tie American prices to those charged by other countries. In so doing, Americans would be forced to live with the vagaries of pricing systems designed and implemented elsewhere, around priorities that may differ from ours. Moreover, academic research finds that bringing reference pricing to the U.S. would likely inflate overseas prices but leave U.S. prices largely unchanged. The net result will be little if any benefit for American families in the short-term, and some degree of harm to long-term medical innovation in the bargain.

Instead, aligning prices with value encourages innovators to invest in areas that patients value. Achieving this outcome requires better information about value, which is ironic because we already have an overload of certain kinds of information about value. Prescription drugs nearly always arrive to market with studies estimating their value, often many of them, and they frequently reach divergent conclusions. Instead of even more studies, payers and consumers need an objective review and translation of the evidence on value. This might not result in a single, incontrovertible estimate of economic value, but even a range of values, when objectively determined, would benefit the people and organizations ultimately footing the bill for prescription drugs. Better information about value, coupled with price transparency, helps ensure payers and consumers spend their money wisely.

While it is yet to be determined what the true impact of the Inflation Reduction Act (IRA) will be on biomedical innovation, there is strong evidence that cuts to Medicare's pharmaceutical spending will reduce discovery of new treatments as well as new uses for existing drugs. But there are ways to mitigate these adverse impacts. Most importantly, it is essential that Maximum Fair Price (MFP) determination hew to the principles of transparency and value to patients. Economic research provides transparent approaches that can be leveraged by CMS, and relying on economics no longer means relying on the old-fashioned QALY. For example, one new value assessment method based on research at the USC Schaeffer Center corrects the QALY's errors by recognizing the long-established principle that goods are more valuable to people who have less of them. Analogously, health improvements are more valuable for people with disabilities, terminal illness, or other severe disease. This approach comports with Federal law by avoiding value assessments that discriminate against vulnerable patients with disabilities or terminal illness.

Finally, Medicare Part D's benefit design also implicitly encourages high list prices. Part D insurers favor high list prices in part because they move patients more rapidly to the catastrophic phase of coverage, where Federal reinsurance payments await. While the IRA's Part D benefit redesign provisions may moderate these reinsurance-related incentives somewhat, other program features (such as an intense focus on premiums) suggest the upward pressure on list prices will continue absent other market changes.

Sustaining Affordable and Valuable Innovation

Ultimately, the right policies need to focus on the affordability of good health, not simply of health care. This is especially true for diseases with few or no treatment options. The least affordable drugs are those that have not yet been discovered. For example, in the days before the discovery of effective vaccines, freedom from the most devastating consequences of COVID–19 could not be bought at any price. To be sure, affordable and generous insurance for prescription drugs remains part of any solution, because today's medicines already put good health within reach for millions of Americans suffering from chronic disease. Making prices transparent and generating actionable information on value will help wring out wasteful spending that fails to benefit patients and their families. Finally, rewarding drugs that do provide value helps sustain innovation and ensures good health will be increasingly within the reach of Americans for generations to come.

[Summary Statement of Darius Lakdawalla]

Ensuring Affordable and Valuable Pharmaceutical Innovation for Patients

Increasing patient access through bold expansion of affordable care means little when there are no valuable cures or treatments to access. At the same time, breakthrough medical therapies provide little value if high cost-sharing pushes them out of patients' reach.

This tradeoff between innovation and affordability has played out in the different approaches taken across the globe. There is little doubt that U.S. consumers access newer drugs sooner and more often than their overseas counterparts. And this increased access to the latest treatments matters. Schaeffer Center research suggests that introducing European-style pricing policies would ultimately reduce innovation and cost American consumers just over half a year of life expectancy, about what would be lost if American surgeons suddenly forgot how to perform heart bypass surgery.[145] Thus, even though other countries likely free-ride off the revenue generated in the American market, importing overseas pricing policies will harm the health of American families.

Nonetheless, the deteriorating accessibility of prescription drugs in recent years still threatens to derail the access advantages and health gains American consumers have so far enjoyed. Even patients with "good" insurance are struggling to access the therapies their doctors prescribe. An increasing number of plans frequently impose co-insurance requirements and exclude drugs from their formularies. These changes in the marketplace likely harm health, since the link between increasing out-of-pocket costs and patient adherence is well-established.

Surprisingly, coverage has deteriorated even while the average manufacturer net prices of brand drugs—the amount manufacturers receive after rebates and discounts—have declined in each of the last 5 years. Transparency in pricing throughout the pharmaceutical distribution system would be a major step toward ensuring that drug prices reflect the actual value provided to patients, and don't simply enrich intermediaries.

Rewarding drugs that do provide value helps sustain innovation and ensures good health will be increasingly within the reach of American patients for generations to come. Decades of economic research demonstrate that innovation follows pricing incentives. Where innovators expect higher returns, innovative effort and discovery follow. As a result, aligning the price of every drug with the value it brings to patients stimulates innovation that benefits patients and discourages innovation that does not.

[145] Bypass surgery adds about *1.1 years of life* to patients treated with it. The lifetime risk of cardiovascular disease is *around 60 percent.* Thus, even if every heart disease patient received bypass surgery, it would add just over half a year of life.

Ultimately, the right policies need to focus on the affordability of good health, not simply of health care. The least affordable drugs are those that have not yet been discovered.

The CHAIR. Let me start the questioning by saying that I have heard some of my Republican colleagues talk about free market capitalism. Mr. Maybarduk, isn't the entire pharmaceutical industry based on Government granted monopoly power?

Mr. Amir, you may want to also speak to that. What does that have to do with free market capitalism if the Government is guaranteeing monopoly for many, many years?

Mr. MAYBARDUK. Well, precisely, Senator. Prices are high because drug makers have monopolies over products we can't just substitute. A patient can't just say, I will take this alternative. The patents block them from having affordable access. That is a monopoly, not a market system.

American taxpayers stand up to the world's largest and most productive funder of biomedical R&D at NIH. And it is we the people that fund the risk—we the people that support the risky early stage research that has led to such significant medical breakthroughs in the areas of mRNA, cancer, heart disease, gene therapy.

The CHAIR. In other words, the Government has played a very active role in the entire process. Mr. Amin, what about free market capitalism and monopolies?

Mr. AMIN. Well, I mean, it is—the Constitution grants Congress the power to promote the progress of science and useful laws, securing for limited times a right to their inventions. What we have now is a system where the patent system is not a limited time.

It is in a monopoly that gets extended, extended, extended. When we think about the free markets and the principles of capitalism, it is interesting Senator Paul mentioned Milton Friedman.

In fact, the neoliberals actually didn't like monopoly power, and they really did actually believe in the free market, but the fact that the intellectual property system, the patents has been corrupted by the modern pharmaceutical system to kind of extend those monopolies, actually goes against the principles of free market.

o, in a sense, they are not living up to the bargain of the free market.

The CHAIR. Okay. Mr. Lakdawalla, what do you think about free market capitalism and Government protection of monopolies?

Mr. MAYBARDUK. Thank you, Chairman. Well, truly free markets exist only on the whiteboard in my classroom at USC, first of all. But it is also true that without patent protection, there would be no innovation. That is a result that has been known in economics for centuries.

The real question is how do we balance patent protection, which induces innovation, against the value of new innovations and being able to broadcast them more widely after the end of a patent? And that tradeoff can be tricky, although in the case of pharmaceuticals, we have a useful instrument which is health insurance, and that allows patients to access drugs at much lower prices than what manufacturers receive even during the patent period.

That is an opportunity for us to expand accessibility even during the patent protection period.

The CHAIR. Thanks very much. My last question for all three of you is I believe you all heard the CEO's testimony in response to questions. What would you say, briefly, about their responses?

Did they in fact, effectively address the issue as to why we pay by far the highest prices in the world for prescription drugs, and why one out of three people can't afford the medicine that doctors prescribe?

Mr. MAYBARDUK. Well, Senator, we heard some wild stuff up here this morning, including a lot of blaming middlemen for the problem of high prices. Look, drug makers' high prices are the whole reason that we have a middleman problem.

It is because we have exceedingly high prices at the outset that there is an attractive market for middlemen to enter. But the fish rots from the head. If you break up the market, if you look at where the revenue is, drug makers capture two-thirds, $323 billion. Pharmacy benefit managers are a small slice, $23 billion.

You can't fix the problem of the pharmaceutical industry by going off middlemen who are just trying to skim off the top. You have to get to the root of the problem, which is the monopoly power.

The CHAIR. Mr. Amin.

Mr. AMIN. I agree with what Peter says, and I would just add that some of the answers that these CEOs gave, for example, the Merck CEO about allowing biosimilar competition in when their primary patent ends, I believe that is not going to happen. I think if you look at all the patents that they have stacked up, they know what their game plan is.

You just have to look at what happened Humira and AbbVie. Similarly, I believe you just look at what is happening with these weight-loss drugs. We are looking at the patents on those now. These are potentially going to become $1 trillion drugs.

The CHAIR. Okay. Dr. Lakdula—Lakdawalla—pardon me for——

Dr. LAKDAWALLA. No problem. I think an important point that maybe is often missed is that net prices of pharmaceuticals have been falling for the past 10 years very consistently. CMS recently released its national health expenditure accounts data, and it confirms this fact as well. We have to reconcile that with rising costs for consumers.

I think intermediaries are actually playing a bigger role than it might appear. About $0.40 of every dollar spent on pharmaceuticals goes to intermediaries. And unlike pharmaceutical firms, they are not engaging in innovation that ultimately improves health.

The CHAIR. Thank you very much. Senator Cassidy.

Senator CASSIDY. Thank you all. Mr. Maybarduk, I think it is made very persuasively—by the way, clearly, patents are part of the free market system, is the way that you protect intellectual property, and you incent creativity.

Now, whether it is being abused is another issue. And you mentioned the patent thickets, which is actually legislation sponsored by John Cornyn to do away with them. So, that is recognized. But I think without protection of intellectual property, we would not have this innovation. Now, why would you—why would you put the time into it?

Let's just make that point. But Mr. Maybarduk, Dr. Lakdawalla makes, I think, a persuasive point that without the profit incentive, you will not get the innovation. Are you disputing that?

Mr. MAYBARDUK. I am not.

Senator CASSIDY. You are just kind of—the degree of the profit taking, if you will. I will point out, by the way, that the three examples you gave seem to be all Medicare patients and there is legislation out there which will cap the out-of-pocket exposure to—for Medicare patients on these expensive drugs. I think it will be $2,000 in June 2025, and the catastrophic portion is going away now.

But Dr. Lakdawalla, that said, somebody is paying. Yes, insurance is making it more affordable. Medicaid is making it more affordable. Medicare is making it more affordable. I could go down, but somebody is paying. In my state, I was recently told that pharmaceutical costs for the Medicaid program are now 35 percent of the total. And so, yes, maybe we could do some value-based purchasing.

That is a lot of money, though. That is a huge program. That is not hospitals and doctors. It is a pharmaceutical cost. So, I think Mr. Mubarak would say, listen, they have got enough profit to innovate. What we are really talking about is more than the profit required to incent. Would you disagree with that?

Dr. LAKDAWALLA. Well, I think the question is really how much—whether we want to decrease profits or not. And we know that whenever you decrease profits, you get less innovation.

The research that we have done gets exactly that question. If you were to reduce prices and profits, what would the net result be? You would certainly save money, but you would also lead to fewer new drug discoveries and——

Senator CASSIDY. Are we at the sweet spot now, or could we do something to make drugs a little bit more affordable to the Medicaid program, for example? Because I am looking at this gene therapy and obviously how they are initially price is only based upon the restraint of the company.

But if you have a compelling gene therapy, they could almost name their price and it is going to be very difficult for a Medicaid program not to cover. So, but this could bankrupt taxpayers. So, thoughts on that?

Dr. LAKDAWALLA. Yes. So, I don't think we are at a spot where lowering prices makes us better off. But for gene therapies, I absolutely agree there is a significant problem. And the issue is that the prices are all paid upfront when there is the most uncertainty about whether the gene therapy is going to work in the long run.

Senator CASSIDY. Now, value-based purchasing could obviously play a role here. But if you do value based purchasing, you still have a—how do you negotiate the upfront cost? I come up with a drug for a gene therapy for sickle cell. I treated a lot of sicklers.

You want to treat them, and you charge $20 million a person. I can't believe they would get that, but you see, the only thing that would stop them from asking that may be the sticker shock. So, how do you negotiate that first out of the gate price?

Because I think that is a kind of a question that is kind of hanging out there. And you are the free market guy, so I would like your opinion. You are the whiteboard guy.

Dr. LAKDAWALLA. On the white board, yes. That is correct. It is actually not the case that you should negotiate the actual price upfront. Instead, a value based price would mean that the price will respond over time. So, imagine a situation where gene therapies were paid for in installments—

Senator CASSIDY. I get that. And believe me, I have written about that in Stat, if you ever wish to dig up something out of Stat behind a paywall. But it still means that if you have got an initial high price, no matter what your value-based purchasing arrangement is, it could still be something which society could not afford. What do you think of the German model? Dr. Baker, I think, came up with that in which there is—you know, you can ask whatever price you want for the first 2 years, but then after that, there is going to be some sort of negotiation based upon real world data.

Dr. LAKDAWALLA. Yes. I think the challenge with the German model is it is actually very hard to predict the outcomes. That if you look at the ratings that the Germans produce of the benefits of drugs, they are not well correlated with negotiated prices.

If I am an innovator trying to figure out what I am going to get paid in Germany, it is really hard. And if you can't predict your returns, then they are not going to work as financial incentives.

Senator CASSIDY. Mr. Amin, have you had a chance to evaluate the bill that is working its way through Judiciary Committee—it might be included in a year end package. It is to its effectiveness in addressing patent thickets. Yes, push your button——

Mr. AMIN. Senator Blumenthal and Cornyn's bill?

Senator CASSIDY. Yes.

Mr. MAYBARDUK. I think it will potentially cap the biologics patents that can be enforced to about 20. I have actually given some technical advice on that bill. I don't think it is going to resolve the problem.

Senator CASSIDY. You don't think it is going to resolve the problem?

Mr. MAYBARDUK. No.

Senator CASSIDY. I see. Okay. Well, thank you all. Very thoughtful.

The CHAIR. All right. Thank you all. Very good discussion. Appreciate you being here. That is the end of our hearing today, and I want to thank all of our witnesses for their participation.

For any Senators who wish to ask additional questions, questions for the record will be due in 10 business days, February 23rd at 5.00 p.m. And finally, I ask unanimous consent to enter into the record three statements from stakeholder groups and experts about the cost of prescription drugs.

[The following information can be found on page 106 in Additional Material.]

The CHAIR. With that, the Committee stands adjourned. Thank you.

Additional Material

Families USA, Washington, DC 20005,
February 8, 2024.

Senator BERNIE SANDERS, Chairman
U.S. Senate Committee on Health, Education, Labor, and Pensions,
Dirksen Senate Office Building,
Washington, DC 20510.

Dear Members of the House of Representatives,

Chairman Sanders and Ranking Member Cassidy, on behalf of Families USA, we want to thank you for holding this important and timely hearing and offer our appreciation for lifting up the reality of high drug costs in the United States. It is well documented that the United States is paying significantly higher prices for prescription drugs compared to peer countries. A recent report from the Assistant Secretary for Planning and Evaluation (ASPE) at the Department of Health and Human Services (HHS) found that in 2022, across all brand name and generic drugs, families in America pay nearly three times as much as 33 Organization for Economic Cooperation and Development (OECD) countries.[146] And this gap is continuing to widen as drug prices in the U.S. continue to skyrocket. This problem can easily be traced directly back to failures in U.S. patent policy that incentivize big drug corporations to keep old drugs on the market and push out healthy competition, as well as these corporations' ability to price gouge year over year with no repercussions.

Congress and the Biden administration have taken meaningful steps to address high drug costs for Americans, importantly through enactment and implementation of the Medicare price negotiation program and inflationary rebates. It is essential that Congress build off this critical progress by taking additional steps to further address this uniquely American failure.

The Impact of High Drug Prices on Families

While high drug prices are a source of seemingly constant policy debate in Washington, DC, for millions of America's families, they are a painful and

---

[146] "Comparing Prescription Drugs in the U.S. and Other Countries: Prices and Availability" *https://aspe.hhs.gov/reports/comparing-prescription-drugs.*

burdensome reality that often impacts their ability to meet basic necessities of life. For example, consumers facing increased drug costs report cutting back on key areas of their budget, such as buying food.[147] For some the choice is even more dire, with research showing that nearly three in ten adults—approximately 80 million people—in our Country have not taken required medicine as prescribed due to its costs.[148] Approximately one in five adults forgo essential medications altogether because they can't afford to fill their prescription in the first place.[149] The impact of being forced to make these decisions has on health is clear: medication nonadherence, such as rationing or skipping needed medication, causes an estimated 125,000 deaths a year.[150]

While people who need high-priced drugs often face the most significant financial pain from high and rising prices, the impact of the skyrocketing cost of drugs is widely felt beyond the pharmacy counter. Approximately 20 percent of health insurance premiums are driven by the rising cost of prescription drugs, which means as drug prices continue to rise so do premiums, deductibles, and other health care costs for all families—even those who are not taking prescription medications.[151]

Big Drug Corporations Abuse U.S. Patent System to Protect Profit and Limit Competition

The business model of big drug companies is rooted in exploitation. They take extreme steps to create a monopoly drug market and then abuse it for profit, including price gouging, protecting drug exclusivity through anticompetitive behavior, and increasing profits on old drugs rather than investing in new and

---

[147] Gill, Lisa L. ''How to Pay Less for Your Meds.'' Consumer Reports. April 5, 2018, *https://www.consumerreports.org/drug-prices/how-to-pay-less-for-your-meds/.*

[148] Kirzinger, Ashley, Lunna Lopes, Bryan Wu, and Mollyann Brodie. ''KFF Health Tracking Poll—February 2019: Prescription Drugs.'' The Henry J. Kaiser Family Foundation. March 01, 2019. *https://www.kff.org/health-costs/poll-finding/kff-health-tracking-poll-february—2019-pre- scription-drugs/.*

[149] ''Americans' Challenges with Health Care Costs'' The Henry J. Kaiser Family Foundation, December 14 2021, *https://www.kff.org/health-costs/issue-brief/americans-challenges-with- health-care-costs/.*

[150] Fred Kleinsinger. ''The Unmet Challenge of Medication Nonadherence'' National Library of Medicine. *https://www.ncbi.nlm.nih.gov/pmc/articles/PMC6045499/.*

[151] Kim Keck, ''Six Ways We're Lowering Drug Prices,'' Blue Cross Blue Shield of America, March 3, 2022, *https://www.bcbs.com/the-health-of-america/articles/six-ways-were-lowering- drug-prices.*

innovative treatments to help our Nation's families.[152] Drug companies regularly deploy a barrage of tactics to extend their exclusivity periods, keep generics off the market, and maintain their market dominance.[153] Common examples include blanketing one drug with multiple and overlapping patents to create a ''patent thicket'' and ''product hopping'' a patent by making minor tweaks to existing drugs that typically confer no additional clinical benefit but allow for extended patent protections. In fact, the 10 top-selling drugs on the market today have been granted an average of 74 patents per drug, with an average of 140 patents filed for each of them.[154]

Once these big drug corporations have blocked other competitors, they are free to raise their drug's price year after year at shocking rates, even long after the drug's release. We see this problem across the drug market: Between July 2021 and July 2022, 1,216 drug products had price increases that were higher than the inflation rate (8.5 percent). Some drug prices increased by more than 500 percent.[155] These prices are not being justified by any additional benefits or effectiveness of that drug. In fact, one study of high-spend drugs showed that seven of the 10 drugs reviewed provided no additional clinical benefit relative to other available drugs.[156]

These abuses only occur because of the loopholes littered throughout the U.S. patent system and are major contributors to the uniquely high drug prices that American families face.

---

[152] 7 Bailey Reavis and Hazel Law, The Reality of Prescription Drug Innovation: Drug Manufacturers Limit Innovation to Protect Patents and Profits (Washington, DC: Families USA, August 2023), *https://familiesusa.org/wp-content/uploads/2023/08/Drug-Companies-Limit-Innova- tion-for-Profit—2.pdf.*

[153] Patricia Kelmar and Abe Scarr, The Cost of Prescription Drug Patent Abuse: How Drug Companies Abuse the Patent System and Demand Inflated Monopoly Prices in America (U.S. PIRG Education Fund, April 2023), *https://pirg.org/edfund/resources/the-cost-of-prescription- drug-patent-abuse/.*

[154] Tahir Amin and David Mitchell, ''Big Pharma's Patent Abuses Are Fueling the Drug Pricing Crisis,'' Time, February 24, 2023, *https://time.com/6257866/big-pharma-patent-abuse-drug- pricing—modifications.*

[155] Bailey Reavis and Hazel Law, The Reality of Prescription Drug Innovation: Drug Manufacturers Limit Innovation to Protect Patents and Profits (Washington, DC: Families USA, August 2023), *https://familiesusa.org/wp-content/uploads/2023/08/Drug-Companies-Limit-Innova- tion-for-Profit—2.pdf.*

[156] Eliot Fishman, Our Broken Drug Pricing and Patent System Diverts Resources Away From Innovation and Into Mergers, Patent Gaming and Price Gouging (Washington, DC: Families USA, August 2021), *https://familiesusa.org/wp-content/uploads/2021/08/RX—2021—209—In- novation-Drug-Pricing-Issue-Brief.pdf.*

Proposed Legislation Could Address Corporate Pricing Abuses

Recently, Congress took important steps to systemically bring down drug prices and rein in the rate of skyrocketing price increases. The Inflation Reduction Act (IRA) of 2022 is landmark legislation that includes several key provisions to address the high prices that are a hallmark of the American experience with prescription medication. The recently passed reforms include giving Medicare the authority to negotiate the price of drugs, as well as penalties (through rebates) for big drug companies that raise the price of their drug higher than the rate of inflation. These are both foundational steps that change the incentives specific to the U.S. market that have led to these high drug costs.

Congress can build on this foundation to further rein in prescription drug costs and make health care more affordable for everyone in two key ways:

1) Extending the reforms in the IRA to apply to the commercial market to better protect all consumers from high and irrational drug costs. This includes allowing the commercial market to adopt Medicare's negotiated rates and extend the inflationary rebate to fight price gouging year over year in the commercial market.
2) Close loopholes that allow companies to create monopoly drug markets and prevent generics from coming to the market in a timely fashion. This includes ending patent abuses like patent thickets and product hopping, simplifying the generic approval process and ending pay for delay policies.

Conclusion

High and rising drug costs are a uniquely American problem and a major factor as to why health care affordability is an American crisis. Drug prices threaten the health and financial security of families and individuals in every state and community. Big drug companies abuse the patent system, delay the entry of generic drugs, and price gouge to support their greed while families and individuals go into medical debt, ration or skip medications, and have to choose between filling their prescription or filling their fridge. Even those not taking prescription drugs are left with difficult financial decisions due to rising insurance premiums, higher deductibles, and stagnant wages—all of which can be tied back to rising drug costs. This cannot be allowed to continue. We appreciate the important work of this Committee to address these concerns and look forward to continuing to work with you to ensure all families can achieve affordable health and health care.

Dear Members of the House of Representatives,

As organizations representing patients and consumers, we write in opposition to H.R. 485, the so-called Protecting Health Care for All Patients Act of 2023. This bill claims to protect people from discrimination but would in fact result in harm to patients if enacted into law.

There is no single factor more important in arriving at an appropriate price for a new drug than the value to patients. It is axiomatic that to stimulate and reward innovative new drug development, we should pay more for high-value drugs and less for low-value drugs. Put another way, we want drugs with high clinical effectiveness against the disease or condition they target and with a low burden of undesirable side effects or toxicities.

Patients in this country—especially those with disabilities—need a reliable system for evaluating the value of a medicine. Comparative Effectiveness Research (CER) can clearly and transparently assess the value of drugs in order to both inform patient decisionmaking and arrive at appropriate prices. Instead of prioritizing legislation that could lower prices, assess value, and improve health, the House Committee on Energy and Commerce advanced a version of H.R. 485 that would impose further limits on CER. If enacted, language referring to ''similar measures'' in the current version of the bill would introduce ambiguity across the health sector that could invite lengthy lawsuits from an industry eager to stop any efforts to constrain its ability to set prices as high as it wants for any drug—regardless of the drug's value. This is not a new fight. Powerful drug companies have fought to block CER for years with the single goal of preventing policymakers and payers from scrutinizing value in order to rein in prices.

If the leaders of this bill truly wish to protect people with disabilities from discrimination, they would instead advance legislation to address our drug price system at its core given that high drug prices disproportionately harm people living with disabilities, chronic conditions, and low-income communities. In fact, a recent study found thatpeople living with disabilities were about three times more likely to ration medications as those without a disability. High drug prices also disproportionately impact people of color. Big drug companies exacerbate health inequities and inflict harm by charging prices as high as the market will bear, untethered from the value of a drug and at the expense of people's lives and livelihoods.

To be clear, we emphatically support measures that protect people with disabilities, the elderly, and those with chronic or terminal illness from analytical tools that are discriminatory. Due to concerns about the use of the Quality Adjusted Life Year (or QALY), we believe its use should be prohibited in Federal programs. But we must also preserve the ability of our Nation to employ other measures that value all lives equally, such as the Equal Value of Life Years Gained (evLYG). Unfortunately, the leaders of the bill have rejected amendments that would ban QALYs while preserving non-discriminatory tools to assess value. So in the interests of patients, consumers, employers, taxpayers, and all Americans who pay for health care and prescription drugs and who need and want high value, innovative treatments, we urge a no vote on H.R. 485 in its current form.

Signed,
ACA Consumer Advocacy AFL–CIO
AFSCME
Alliance for Retired Americans

Center for Popular Democracy Action Citizen Action/Illinois
CT Health Policy Project Communities United Health GAP
Labor Campaign for Single Payer Lower Drug Prices Now MomsRising Oregonizers
Patients For Affordable Drugs Now People's Action
Protect Our Care Public Citizen Salud y Fa`rmacos
Social Security Works Spaces in Action
Unite HERE International Union Universities Allied for Essential Medicines VOCAL-NY

PUBLIC HEALTH

By Jason D. Buxbaum, Michael E. Chernew, A. Mark Fendrick, and David M. Cutler

DOI: 10.1377/
hlthaff.2020.00284
HEALTH AFFAIRS 39,
NO. 9 (2020): 1546–1556

Contributions Of Public Health, Pharmaceuticals, And Other Medical Care To US Life Expectancy Changes, 1990-2015

Jason D. Buxbaum (jasonbuxbaum@g.harvard.edu) is a student in the Program in Health Policy at Harvard University, in Cambridge, Massachusetts.

Michael E. Chernew is the Leonard D. Schaeffer Professor of Health Care Policy and director of the Healthcare Markets and Regulation (HMR) Lab in the Department of Health Care Policy, Harvard Medical School, in Boston, Massachusetts.

A. Mark Fendrick is a professor in the Department of Internal Medicine and director of the Center for Value-Based Insurance Design at the University of Michigan, in Ann Arbor, Michigan.

David M. Cutler is the Otto Eckstein Professor of Applied Economics in the Department of Economics at Harvard University and a research associate at the National Bureau of Economic Research, in Cambridge, Massachusetts.

ABSTRACT **Life expectancy in the US increased 3.3 years between 1990 and 2015, but the drivers of this increase are not well understood. We used vital statistics data and cause-deletion analysis to identify the conditions most responsible for changing life expectancy and quantified how public health, pharmaceuticals, other (nonpharmaceutical) medical care, and other/unknown factors contributed to the improvement. We found that twelve conditions most responsible for changing life expectancy explained 2.9 years of net improvement (85 percent of the total). Ischemic heart disease was the largest positive contributor to life expectancy, and accidental poisoning or drug overdose was the largest negative contributor. Forty-four percent of improved life expectancy was attributable to public health, 35 percent was attributable to pharmaceuticals, 13 percent was attributable to other medical care, and −7 percent was attributable to other/unknown factors. Our findings emphasize the crucial role of public health advances, as well as pharmaceutical innovation, in explaining improving life expectancy.**

Growth in medical spending consistently outpaces overall economic growth in the United States, prompting questions about the extent to which health care expenditures deliver value to justify their cost. If medical advances have contributed substantially to improved survival (life expectancy increased 3.3 years between 1990 and 2015), then growing investment in medical spending might be more palatable. The issue is particularly acute for pharmaceuticals, whose spending growth averaged 2.3 percentage points above growth in the rest of the health sector between 1990 and 2015.[1]

A recent synthesis estimated that a lack of modern medical care is directly responsible for 5–15 percent of premature mortality, with most premature mortality attributable to health-related behavior and social circumstances.[2] However, the impact of medical advances in explaining improving life expectancy over time has received somewhat less attention. One study estimated that half of all health improvements between 1960 and 2000 are due to medical care, although that estimation was extrapolated from a small number of conditions.[3] The difficulty is in part because medical care is difficult to evaluate as a whole. The determinants of health may shift within and across conditions over time, and many once-accepted scientific consensuses are later modified.

Even when one looks at a particular type of care, such as pharmaceuticals, the evidence of health impact is mixed. One recent study estimated that the expansion of cardiovascular medications led to a large reduction in heart disease mortality.[4] At the same time, evidence on the cost-effectiveness of anticancer agents varies greatly.[5,6] Further, excessive use of opioids has led to tens of thousands of deaths annually, contributing to flat or declining life expectancy between 2015 and 2017.

Given the salience of health care value in policy discussions, we sought to quantify the importance of medical care in total, and pharmaceutical treatments specifically, for recent changes in US life expectancy. We focused on 1990–2015 because some data sources used were unavailable for more recent years.

We began with vital statistics data to apportion improvements in mortality to various causes. For each of twelve causes responsible for life expectancy changes of 0.1 years or more, we reviewed the literature on the factors explaining mortality changes. We apportioned survival improvements into public health, pharmaceuticals, other (nonpharmaceutical) medical care, and a residual category comprising other or unknown factors. Aggregated results provide insight into the key drivers of increasing life expectancy between 1990 and 2015.

Study Data And Methods

CALCULATING CHANGES IN LIFE EXPECTANCY

▸ **DATA SOURCE:** Data on mortality by age and cause were obtained from the Centers for Disease Control and Prevention Wide-ranging Online Data for Epidemiologic Research (CDC WONDER) resource for 1990 through 2015. We identified causes using a hybrid of the National Center for Health Statistics' 113-cause-of-death and 39-cause-of-death classification systems. Details on our approach are in online appendix exhibits A1–A3.[7]

Although the 39-cause list is common in analyzing mortality, the level of aggregation is problematic with respect to some key conditions. For example, all accidents not caused by motor vehicles are grouped together. Accordingly, we conducted the analysis described here on both the 39- and 113-cause lists. We used the 39-cause list as our starting point, but we turned to the 113-cause list to avoid obscuring meaningful differences in trends among causes of death in overly broad categories, reduce the size of the "all other deaths" category, and group infant deaths together. Appendix exhibit A2 lists relevant *International Statistical Classification of Diseases and Related Health Problems*, Tenth Revision (ICD-10), codes.[7]

Data were available in *International Classification of Diseases*, Ninth Revision (ICD-9), for 1990–98 and ICD-10 for 1999–2015. ICD-9-to-ICD-10 comparability ratios were used to adjust pre-1999 death rates to form a consistent series and minimize potential bias associated with changes in coding practices (appendix exhibit A3).[7]

▸ **ESTIMATION:** Cause-deletion methods were employed to estimate the relative contribution of each condition to overall improvement in life expectancy at birth. This entailed starting with 1990 mortality rates and estimating sequentially the impact of changes in mortality for each condition on life expectancy at birth, holding other conditions at their 1990 mortality rates. The difference between life expectancy with and without the change for each condition is the life expectancy gain or loss attributable to that cause. For each cause studied in detail, we also examined mortality change in successive five-year intervals.

EXPLAINING LIFE EXPECTANCY CHANGES We sought to apportion mortality changes for each cause of death associated with an increase or decrease in life expectancy of 0.1 years or more into the change attributable to public health, pharmaceuticals, and other medical care. We used multiple approaches because the most preferred method was not always possible (appendix exhibit A1, flowchart B).[7]

Whenever available, statistical models appearing in the peer-reviewed literature were used to explain changing mortality. Literature reviews were conducted to identify models using the union of the following Medical Subject Headings (MeSH) terms: "United States/epidemiology," "mortality/trends," and the condition name. On finding a relevant article, we consulted citations (a technique known as "snowballing") and used reverse citation look-up to identify related studies. We contacted subject-matter experts for guidance when we were unable to identify suitable sources through literature reviews. Some models were identified that did not cover the full period of interest. In these instances, we updated the model if the condition represented a large share of life expectancy change. Otherwise, we used the results available.

In some instances, we were unable to identify suitable existing condition-specific models. In those cases, we relied on alternative approaches to apportion mortality change among factors. These included the creation of new models, published surveys of physician opinion, and literature-informed judgements as to plausibility. Appendix exhibit A1 (flowchart C) depicts our approach in these cases.[7]

Public health was broadly defined as reductions in identifiable risk factors for injury or disease not classified in the three following categories: pharmaceuticals, which included opioids, biologics, and oncology agents among other agents; other (nonpharmaceutical) medical care, which included physician/hospital services such as cancer screenings, diagnostic testing, radiotherapy, and surgery; and a residual category for other/unknown factors. There may be overlaps among factors. For example, public health efforts could lead to more cancer screenings, which could reduce mortality. Our primary analysis looked at the most proximal cause, so benefits would be attributed to medical care, not public health, in the previous example. We performed a sensitivity analysis to vary characterizations in areas with the greatest overlap of potential characterizations: overdoses, cancer screenings, and pregnancy terminations.

Public health improvements accounted for the largest part of mortality improvement overall.

LIMITATIONS This approach had limitations. First, the attribution of responsibility for improved survival to public health, pharmaceuticals, and other medical care was constrained by the availability of literature and the need to impose subjective distinctions. It was also limited in that current knowledge may change over time. Second, the use of cause deletion required assuming that competing causes of death are independent from one another. This implies that the impact from any given cause may be misstated if the cause is strongly correlated with other causes. Third, life expectancy trends vary over time by race, ethnicity, education, geography, and other key dimensions, whereas this analysis is limited to overall trends. Fourth, coding changes over time, including the switch from ICD-9 to ICD-10, could affect findings (appendix exhibit A3).[7] Fifth, we examined life expectancy at birth. Results could differ with related metrics, such as average populationwide mortality rates. Sixth, morbidity changes may be equally important but were not included in our primary analysis. Seventh, the time period of the study predated the coronavirus disease 2019 (COVID-19) pandemic. Accordingly, COVID-19 was not analyzed as a unique cause of death.

Study Results

AGGREGATE CHANGES IN LIFE EXPECTANCY The cause-deletion methodology explained 3.3 years of improvement in life expectancy at birth for the modified list of 113 causes of death (appendix exhibit A4).[7] This corresponds with the observed change in life expectancy between 1990 and 2015. Exhibit 1 shows the contribution of each cause of death to changing life expectancy for the modified list of thirty-nine causes of death. Ischemic heart disease (1.76 years), lung cancer (0.34 years), and stroke (0.33 years) accounted for the greatest shares of improvement. Accidental poisoning or overdose (−0.32 years), dementia excluding Alzheimer disease (−0.19 years), and Alzheimer disease (−0.14 years) accounted for the greatest decrements in life expectancy.

Exhibit 2 shows causes of death that accounted for an increase or decrease in life expectancy of at least 0.1 years. Diseases of the circulatory system, cancers, and trauma (excluding suicide) accounted for 62 percent, 18 percent, and 9 percent of life expectancy improvement, respectively.

Changes in life expectancy were generally continuous across five-year intervals (appendix exhibit A5).[7] Exceptions included ischemic heart disease, for which life expectancy increases slowed after 2005, and HIV, for which gains were concentrated in the 1995–2000 period. The negative impact of accidental poisoning or overdose on life expectancy also increased over time.

EXPLANATIONS FOR CHANGES IN LIFE EXPECTANCY Exhibit 3 attributes life expectancy increases to the impact of public health, pharmaceuticals, other medical care, and other/unexplained factors.

▸ **ISCHEMIC HEART DISEASE:** IMPACT is a validated statistical model that has been used in more than twenty countries to explain changes in death from heart disease over time.[5,6] We updated a 2019 version of the IMPACT model with 1990–2015 US-specific data to explain reductions in ischemic heart disease mortality.[6] Appendix exhibit A6 contains additional details.[7] The IMPACT model estimated that 52 percent of the decrease in mortality was attributable to pharmaceuticals and 7 percent was attributable to other medical care (exhibit 3).

The most important pharmaceutical treatments were care for hypertension and high cholesterol and, to a lesser extent, medications for secondary prevention after myocardial infarction and angina. With respect to other (nonpharmaceutical) medical care, rehabilitation and revascularization were of approximately comparable importance. Another 39 percent of mortality decline was attributed to improved public health not resulting from medications, principally reduced cholesterol and blood pressure. Although smoking decreased, benefits were partially offset by increases in body mass index and diabetes; we characterized these changes as public health. Approximately 2 percent of

EXHIBIT 1

Changes to US life expectancy, by cause of death, 1990–2015

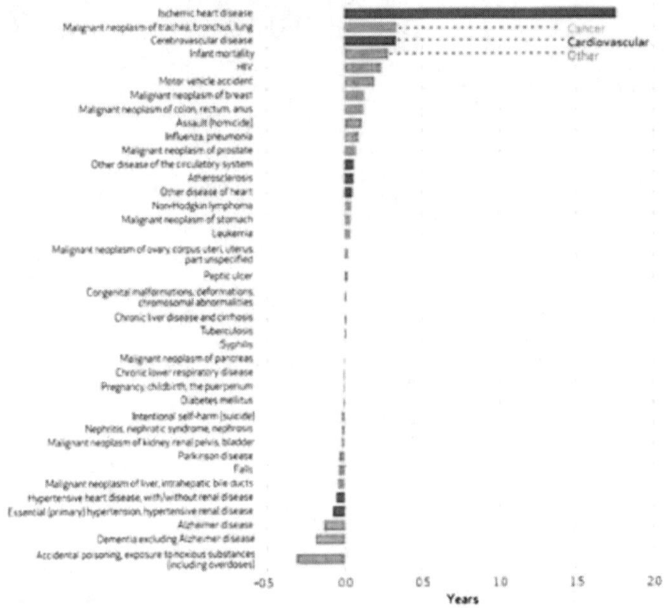

SOURCE Authors' analysis of data from the National Vital Statistics System. **NOTES** Causes of death other than infant mortality exclude deaths for people younger than age one. See online appendix exhibits A1–A4 for further detail (see note 7 in text).

mortality improvement was not explained by the IMPACT model.

▶ **CEREBROVASCULAR DISEASE:** We updated a previously published cerebrovascular disease-specific extension of the IMPACT model to determine the causes of reduced cerebrovascular disease (appendix exhibit A7).[4,7] Sixty percent of reduced mortality was attributable to pharmaceuticals (including antihypertensives, statins, and anticoagulants), and 8 percent of reduced mortality was attributable to other medical care (carotid endarterectomies and rehabilitation). The remaining 32 percent of mortality reduction was attributed to unmodeled public health improvements, such as reduced smoking and hypertension not achieved through medical treatment.

▶ **LUNG, BRONCHUS, AND TRACHEA CANCER:** We did not identify any suitable existing models specific to lung, bronchus, and trachea cancer. We therefore used Surveillance, Epidemiology, and End Results Program data to create a new model (appendix exhibit A8).[7] Age-adjusted lung or bronchus cancer incidence fell 25 percent between 1990 and 2015, whereas mortality decreased 31 percent. Thus, decreasing incidence accounted for 81 percent of the decrease in mortality. Because smoking is the primary risk factor for lung cancer, we attributed 81 percent of reduced mortality to public health.

For these cancers, average five-year survival after diagnosis improved from 13 percent to 18 percent during 1990–2015. Stage migration has likely had only small impacts in lung cancer; screening was recommended only at the end of our study period, and symptomatic lung cancers

EXHIBIT 2

Top contributors to US life expectancy changes, by category, 1990–2015

Categories/causes of death	Years of life expectancy gained or lost	Contribution to overall life expectancy change (%)
Circulatory system		
Ischemic heart disease	1.76	53
Cerebrovascular diseases	0.33	10
Malignant neoplasms		
Malignant neoplasm of trachea, bronchus, lung	0.34	10
Malignant neoplasm of breast	0.13	4
Malignant neoplasm of colon, rectum, anus	0.12	4
Trauma		
Motor vehicle accident	0.19	6
Assault (homicide)	0.11	3
Neurological		
Alzheimer disease	−0.14	−4
Dementia, excluding Alzheimer disease	−0.19	−6
Other		
Infant mortality	0.28	8
HIV/AIDS	0.24	7
Accidental poisoning or overdose	−0.32	−9
Total	2.86	85

SOURCE Authors' analysis of data from the National Vital Statistics System. **NOTES** Limited to causes corresponding with increases or decreases of more than 0.1 years. See online appendix exhibits A1–A5 for further detail (see note 7 in text). Figures may differ from totals in text and table because of rounding.

generally grow rapidly. Further, there was little change in stage distribution of diagnosis; such changes accounted for only 4 percent of mortality reduction. We characterized this improvement as other/unknown.

Meta-analyses suggest a reduction in mortality risk of 13 percent in association with chemotherapy for treatment of non-small-cell lung cancer (roughly 80–90 percent of lung cancers). The share of patients with lung, bronchus, and trachea cancer receiving chemotherapy increased from 28 percent of known patients in 1990 to 40 percent in 2015. Even without accounting for advances in therapeutic effectiveness, increasing chemotherapy use accounted for 5 percent of reduced mortality. We attributed the residual mortality improvement (11 percent) to other nonpharmaceutical medical advances, such as improvements in surgery and radiotherapy.

▸ **BREAST CANCER:** We identified a 2018 Cancer Intervention and Surveillance Network article attributing reduced breast cancer mortality to advances in treatment and screening.[9] The article described findings from six models analyzing contributors to trends in breast cancer incidence and avoided mortality between 1975 and 2012. Averaging across models, 60 percent of improvement was attributable to medications, 31 percent of improvement was attributable to screenings, and 9 percent of improvement was unexplained (see appendix exhibit A9).[7]

▸ **COLORECTAL CANCER:** The Microsimulation Screening Analysis Cancer Intervention and Surveillance Network Colorectal Cancer Model has been used to estimate the source of longevity gains for colorectal cancer.[10,11] The most recent Microsimulation Screening Analysis results are from the period 1990–2000. The models were then used to forecast to 2015 under various scenarios. The "optimistic" scenario matched well with observed trends for the most important contributors to colorectal cancer incidence and mortality (appendix exhibit A10).[7] In this scenario, 27 percent of improved survival was attributable to pharmaceuticals (chemotherapy), 42 percent was attributable to medical care (cancer screening), and 31 percent was attributable to public health (especially decreased smoking).[10,11]

▸ **MOTOR VEHICLE ACCIDENTS:** Two studies in the traffic safety literature can be used to estimate the impact of medical care on motor vehicle accident fatalities. One study modeled traffic fatalities per 100,000 people at the state-year level as a function of automobile characteristics, road characteristics, and the White infant mortality rate for the state-year. The latter served as a proxy for the impact of medical technology.[12] We used this model to estimate the percentage of the time series change in motor vehicle accident fatalities attributable to medical advances (appendix exhibit A11).[7] The estimate suggests that improved medical care accounted for 10 percent of the reduction in motor vehicle traffic fatalities. We attributed the residual 90 percent to public health, such as improvements in vehicle safety.

A second model relates mortality for people in motor vehicle accidents to the receipt of high-level trauma care.[13] The study showed that the relative risk for death was 0.71 for people transported to a Level I or II trauma center compared with people transported to other locations. Using data on the share of people taken to Level I or II trauma centers over time implies that 10 percent of reduced motor vehicle accident fatalities were due to greater access to Level I or II trauma centers (appendix exhibit A11).[7] The alignment of results across models provided additional support for attributing 10 percent of reduced motor vehicle accident fatalities to other medical care and 90 percent to public health.

▸ **HOMICIDE:** We updated the approach used by Anthony Harris and colleagues in 2002 to estimate the contribution of medical care to reduced homicide.[14] These authors proposed that aggravated assaults be viewed as potential homicides where the outcome was not death. Change in the incidence of aggravated assault over time

EXHIBIT 3

Estimated impact of pharmaceuticals, other medical care, and public health on changes in US mortality, by cause of death, 1990–2015

		Contribution to mortality changes (%)				
Categories/ causes of death	**Contribution to mortality reduction (%)**	**Public health**	**Pharmaceuticals**	**Other medical care**	**Other/ unexplained**	**Comments**
CIRCULATORY SYSTEM						
Ischemic heart disease	53	39	52	7	2	Most important pharmaceutical therapies: statins, antihypertensives Most important public health improvements: reductions in cholesterol, hypertension, and smoking
Cerebrovascular disease	10	32	60	8	—	Most important contributors: antihypertensives, statins, warfarin
MALIGNANT NEOPLASMS						
Malignant neoplasms of trachea, bronchus, lung	10	81	5	11	4	Reduced incidence of lung cancer used as proxy for public health factors
Malignant neoplasm of breast	4	—	60	31	9	Figures reflect 1990–2012 "Other medical care" reflects screening
Malignant neoplasm of colon, rectum, anus	4	31	27	42	—	Figures reflect experience (1990–2000) and projection (2000–15) "Other medical care" reflects screening
TRAUMA						
Motor vehicle accident	6	90	—	10	—	White infant mortality rate used as proxy for medical care Confirmatory findings from second model
Homicide	3	91	—	9	—	Aggravated assault rate used as proxy for nonmedical contributors to homicide
NEUROLOGICAL						
Alzheimer disease	−4	—	—	—	100	Possible changes in coding practices
Dementia, excluding Alzheimer disease	−6	—	—	—	100	Possible changes in coding practices
OTHER						
Infant mortality	8	39	21	20	20	See exhibit 4 and appendix exhibit A13[a]
HIV/AIDS	7	—	76	24	—	Figures reflect physician survey Confirmatory evidence from timing of HAART introduction
Accidental poisoning or overdose	−9	4	96	—	—	Includes deaths related to opioid crisis
TOTAL						
All causes	85	44	35	13	−7	

SOURCE Authors' analysis of data from the National Vital Statistics System and sources cited in text. **NOTES** Figures reflect 1990–2015 unless otherwise indicated. Figures may differ from totals in text and table because of rounding. HAART is highly active antiretroviral therapy. [a]See note 7 in text.

may thus be viewed as change in the risk for death from homicide not attributable to changes in the deadliness of the average aggravated assault, reporting patterns, or medical care.

According to federal Uniform Crime Reporting statistics, aggravated assaults fell by 44 percent between 1990 and 2015. During the same period, the homicide rate fell by 48 percent. The additional reduction in homicide deaths of 4 percentage points is 9 percent of the decline in homicides. Thus, we attributed 9 percent of reduced homicide mortality to medical care and the remaining 91 percent to public health. As with motor vehicle accidents, the medical care component was mostly nonpharmaceutical; we recorded it accordingly (exhibit 3).

▸ **ALZHEIMER DISEASE AND DEMENTIAS:** The reasons for underlying apparent increases in recorded mortality from Alzheimer disease and other dementias are unclear, as mortality trends were age adjusted. There are no established modifiable risk factors for Alzheimer disease, and the overall trend across known risk factors for non-Alzheimer dementia did not clearly worsen during 1990–2015 (appendix exhibit A12).[7]

There is generally "a blurred distinction between death with dementia and death from dementia."[15] Vital records-based estimates of changes in dementia mortality may be particularly influenced by changes in disease awareness and place of death that took place between 1990 and 2015.[15] Given the absence of clear medical or public health explanations for the increases in dementia-related mortality, as well as the plausibility of changes in coding practices as the key explanatory factor, we attributed mortality increases to other/unexplained.

▸ **INFANT MORTALITY:** No comprehensive models to explain overall changes in infant mortality were identified. We therefore investigated the factors contributing to improved survival for the five conditions responsible for the greatest reductions in infant mortality between 1990 and 2015 (90 percent of the total; exhibit 4). Appendix exhibit A13 contains details.[7]

Reductions in sudden infant death syndrome accounted for 39 percent of all infant mortality gains. Sudden infant death syndrome–related improvements were attributed to advances in public health, particularly campaigns to prevent stomach sleeping in the 1990s. Reduced mortality from respiratory distress syndrome accounted for 23 percent of gains (exhibit 4). According to data from two neonatal hospital quality improvement collaboratives (appendix exhibits A13.1–A13.3),[7] the use of surfactant and antenatal steroids, both of which markedly reduce the risk for death among low-birthweight babies, increased sharply in the 1990s. We estimated that increasing use of these pharmaceuticals explained 89 percent of the observed respiratory distress syndrome mortality reduction. The large increase in life expectancy resulting from infant mortality reductions in the 1990–94 period is temporally consistent with advances associated with sudden infant death syndrome and respiratory distress syndrome (appendix exhibit A5, panel D).[7]

Fourteen percent of reduced infant mortality was a result of decreases in fatal congenital anomalies of the heart, most likely driven by nonpharmaceutical medical innovations. Eight percent of reduced infant mortality was attributed to reduced death from chromosomal anomalies. We attributed these reductions to increases in selective terminations and categorized them as other/unknown. Finally, 6 percent of reduced infant mortality was a result of reductions in lung-related congenital anomalies. There were important advances in surgery and diagnostic technique over our period of interest, particularly for diaphragmatic hernia repair, which we characterized as other medical care. Appendix exhibit 13.1 provides details and supporting references.[7]

Aggregating, we estimated that 39 percent of reduced infant mortality was attributable to public health, 21 percent to pharmaceuticals, and 20 percent to other medical care (exhibit 4).

▸ **HIV:** The literature review did not identify a suitable model to explain HIV mortality improvement. We therefore relied primarily on expert

EXHIBIT 4

Estimated impact of public health, pharmaceuticals, and other medical care on changes in US infant mortality, by cause of death, 1990–2015

		Contribution to mortality changes (%)				
Causes of death	**Contribution to mortality reduction (%)**	**Public health**	**Pharmaceuticals**	**Other medical care**	**Other/unexplained**	**Comments**
Sudden infant death syndrome	39	100	—	—	—	Spread of safe sleep practices Reductions in cigarette smoking among pregnant women
Respiratory distress syndrome	23	—	89	—	11	Increased use of surfactant and antenatal steroids in preterm births
Congenital anomalies of the heart	14	—	—	100	—	Interventional cardiac procedures and associated technology (for example, miniaturization of tools, increases in NICU access) Improved prenatal diagnosis
Chromosomal anomalies	8	—	—	—	100	Edwards and Patau syndromes are in this category Increases in prenatal screening and selective terminations
Congenital anomalies of the lung	6	—	—	100	—	Increasing use of diaphragmatic hernia repair
Other	10	—	—	—	100	Not investigated
Total		39	21	20	20	

SOURCE Authors' analysis of sources in online appendix exhibit A13 (see note 7 in text).

Our results suggest the importance of minimizing cost-related barriers to key preventive and chronic care services.

opinion, as reported in a survey of sixteen physicians specializing in the treatment of HIV.[16] Surveyed physicians estimated that pharmaceuticals accounted for 76 percent of reduced HIV morbidity and mortality between 1990 and 2015. Nonpharmaceutical medical technologies, such as diagnostic testing, accounted for nearly all the remainder. Responding physicians reported that other factors, including public health, accounted for only 0.3 percent of improvement.

Observed trends support these estimates. Seventy-one percent of the reduction in HIV-related deaths between the peak of the HIV/AIDS epidemic in 1994–95 and 2015 took place in 1996–97 (appendix exhibit A14), when highly active antiretroviral therapy first became widely available.[7,17] Similarly, Frank J. Palella Jr. and colleagues showed that protease inhibitors (an essential element of highly active antiretroviral therapy) reduced mortality by 70 percent for people with low CD4+ cell counts.[17]

The low estimate for net benefit from public health also appears reasonable. Male-to-male sexual contact is the most common mechanism of HIV transmission in the US. Risky sexual practices among men who have sex with men increased between 1992 and 2013.[18] Therefore, although transmissions might have increased faster but for public health efforts, it is unlikely that public health efforts contributed to improvements between 1990 and 2015.

▸ **ACCIDENTAL POISONING OR OVERDOSE:** We used vital statistics data to understand changes in the factors contributing to fatal accidental poisoning or overdose. Ninety-six percent of the increase in poisoning or overdose was attributable to increases in fatal prescription and nonprescription drug use, particularly opioids; the remaining component was attributable to other sources such as alcohol consumption (data not shown). The prescription drug component of opioid deaths is most readily characterized as pharmaceutical. The nonprescription component is somewhat more difficult, as it reflects the use of heroin and fentanyl. Evidence suggests that many people transitioned into these substances after prescription opioids were made more difficult to obtain.[19,20] Thus, we attributed these deaths to pharmaceuticals as well, even if some of the "technology" was related to the ability to supply illegal drugs.

SENSITIVITY ANALYSIS In the sensitivity analysis, we varied the characterization of three contributors to changing mortality: overdoses, cancer screenings, and selective pregnancy terminations for genetic anomalies (appendix exhibit A15).[7] Our overall findings were sensitive to reallocating opioid-related mortality from pharmaceuticals to public health (for example, lack of sufficient Food and Drug Administration and Drug Enforcement Administration oversight). In this alternative scenario, 35 percent of gains were due to public health gains and 44 percent of gains were due to pharmaceutical gains.

Discussion

We studied contributors to life expectancy changes for twelve conditions accounting for 2.9 years of improved life expectancy in the US between 1990 and 2015 (exhibit 2). We found great variation in the key drivers of mortality change across causes. In our primary analysis, 44 percent of improvement was attributable to public health, 13 percent was attributable to nonpharmaceutical medical care, and 35 percent was attributable to pharmaceuticals (exhibit 3). The share of survival deterioration attributed to pharmaceuticals (−9 percent) was outweighed by the share of improvement attributed to pharmaceuticals (44 percent) (based on authors' calculations of unrounded data from exhibit 3). There was also a residual of −7 percent attributable to other/unexplained factors.

In addition to heterogeneity in the drivers of mortality avoidance across conditions, there was heterogeneity in the extent to which improvements were attributable to new technologies versus greater diffusion of existing technologies. For example, the 1990s saw the introduction of highly active antiretroviral therapy and the widespread diffusion of statins, which were crucial to mortality reduction for HIV and ischemic heart disease, respectively. There were also increases in the use of surfactant and antenatal steroids, technologies that reduced infant mortality. However, reductions in life expectancy attributable to opioids underscore the potential for severe harm when technologies diffuse beyond appropriate populations.

We found additional heterogeneity in the pace of mortality reduction over time and across conditions. Paralleling the work of Anne Case and Angus Deaton,[21] we observed a sharp slowdown in 2010–15 in improvement in ischemic heart disease mortality (appendix exhibit A5).[7] This change contrasts with trends for other causes of death, as well as longitudinal trends in heart disease-specific mortality in peer countries.[21] Explaining this slowdown requires further research.

We identified 3 percent of life expectancy gains as resulting from increases in breast and colorectal cancer screening (exhibit 3). The benefits of these screenings have been debated. For example, H. Gilbert Welch and colleagues argue that mammography and colorectal cancer screening have much smaller, if any, effects on overall mortality than on disease-specific mortality.[22] However, the most current reviews suggest reduced overall mortality in conjunction with these two types of screening, although estimates are not statistically significant.[23,24] In addition, the most recent screening modalities have not been fully evaluated (for example, colonoscopy instead of sigmoidoscopy).

Apart from screening, our models found that key gains in other (nonpharmaceutical) medical care included surgical care for adults with ischemic heart disease and stroke and for babies with congenital anomalies. Other nonpharmaceutical interventions were important for people with lung cancer.

Public health improvements accounted for the largest part of mortality improvement overall (44 percent), outranking any other driver analyzed (exhibit 3). This extends previous work suggesting that public health is the dominant determinant of longevity in general.[2] In our work, public health improvements were driven by increased adoption of risk reduction practices known before the 1990s, such as smoking reduction and seatbelt usage, as well as by important "low-tech" breakthroughs, such as awareness of the danger of stomach sleep for infants. Improved traffic safety was also a big contributor to improved health.

Our emphasis on public health and pharmaceuticals as the key drivers of reduced mortality is specific to 1990–2015. Had we studied the 1980s, other (nonpharmaceutical) medical care likely would have been assigned greater responsibility for improved outcomes, given the 250 percent growth in cardiovascular procedures over that decade[25] and the fact that statins only became available in the late 1980s. Had we studied only the years after 2010, our estimate of the net benefit of pharmaceuticals would have been reduced, given the acceleration of the opioid epidemic over this period. Even an analysis of the drivers of life expectancy change during 1990–2015 conducted some years from now might yield revised estimates as knowledge of the impacts of various interventions changes.

If we could translate knowledge from existing public health "wins" to areas with less success, longevity gains could be very large.

Our work sought to explain the reasons for mortality reduction and did not consider differing effects by race, ethnicity, geography, and education. Future work should address this important limitation. Future work should also consider the drivers of morbidity reduction. Global Burden of Disease Study data suggest that disability and mortality moved in tandem during 1990–2015 (appendix exhibit A16).[7] However, the extent to which the drivers of mortality reduction are also drivers of morbidity reduction is unclear, as we did not examine many of the conditions most responsible for reduced disability between 1990 and 2015 (including mental illness and visual impairment).

Policy Implications

Our findings have implications for the ongoing debate regarding the value of health care spending in general, and spending on pharmaceuticals specifically. Although our findings do not speak directly to the value of treating additional people with medications, they do underscore the central role of medications overall in explaining reduced mortality. Policy making on drug pricing should consider the implications of potential legislation across the full spectrum of conditions—both those where the societal return on drug investments is high and those where expected value is more ambiguous.

Our results also suggest the importance of minimizing cost-related barriers to key preventive and chronic care services. For example, coverage expansions through the Affordable Care Act have been associated with increases in early-stage cancer diagnoses[26] as well as increased use of heart disease medication.[27] For the insured, elimination of cost sharing for primary prevention may have led to increases in cancer screenings.[26] Given substantial underuse of high-value care, longevity gains might have been larger if coverage gains had been more complete and if out-of-pocket spending for secondary preventive services had also been reduced. Expanding coverage and advancing value-based insurance design[28] therefore remain important needs.

Conclusion

Our results emphasize the need to build on existing public health successes. In recent decades, smoking has become much less prevalent and driving has become safer. Simultaneously, obesity has increased and opioid-related mortality has soared. It is not clear what most explains this mixed record: the intrinsic nature of the behaviors or the lack of appropriate interventions. If we could translate knowledge from existing public health "wins" to areas with less success, longevity gains could be very large. ■

All authors report grant support from Pharmaceutical Research and Manufacturers of America. Jason Buxbaum reports research support from the Agency for Healthcare Research and Quality (Grant No. T32-HS000055). Buxbaum has received consulting income from the University of Michigan. Michael Chernew is chair of the Medicare Payment Advisory Commission, in Washington, D.C. He has received consulting income from Madelena Consulting. He has received speaking fees from American College of Cardiology, American Medical Association, America's Health Insurance Plans, BCBS of Florida, HealthEdge, Humana, MedAxiom and Washington University. He sits on the Advisory Board for Archway Health, MITRE, Virta Health, and National Institute for Health Care Management. He provides editorial services for Elsevier Inc. and MJH Life Sciences. He has research grants from Arnold Ventures, Agency for Healthcare Research and Quality, Centers for Medicare and Medicaid Services, National Institutes of Health, Blue Cross Blue Shield Association, Health Care Service Corporation, Ballad Health, Peterson Center on HealthCare, Robert Wood Johnson Foundation, and Commonwealth Fund. He reports having equity in Archway Health and V-BID Health. A. Mark Fendrick has received consulting income from AbbVie, Amgen, Centivo, Community Oncology Association, Covered California, EmblemHealth, Exact Sciences, Freedman Health, GRAIL, Harvard University, Health & Wellness Innovations, Health at Scale Technologies, MedZed, Penguin Pay, Risalto, Sempre Health, State of Minnesota, Department of Defense, Virginia Center for Health Innovation, Wellth, and Zansors. He has received research support from the Agency for Healthcare Research and Quality, Arnold Ventures, Gary and Mary West Health Policy Center, National Pharmaceutical Council, Patient-Centered Outcomes Research Institute, Robert Wood Johnson Foundation, State of Michigan, and Centers for Medicare and Medicaid Services. He reports having equity in V-BID Health. David Cutler has received consulting income from the American Economic Association, Colorado Center for Nursing Excellence, *Journal of the American Medical Association*, and the Scientific Advisory Board of F-Prime Capital Partners. He has been retained by counsel for plaintiffs to provide expert services in pending litigation involving opioid pharmaceuticals. The content is solely the responsibility of the authors and does not necessarily represent the official views of the Agency for Healthcare Research and Quality or the Medicare Payment Advisory Commission. The authors gratefully acknowledge the assistance of Kaushik Ghosh and Ken Langa.

NOTES

1 Centers for Medicare and Medicaid Services. National health expenditure data: historical [Internet]. Baltimore (MD): CMS; 2019 Dec 19 [cited 2020 Jul 29]. Available from: https://www.cms.gov/Research-Statistics-Data-and-Systems/Statistics-Trends-and-Reports/NationalHealthExpendData/NationalHealthAccountsHistorical.html

2 Kaplan RM, Milstein A. Contributions of health care to longevity: a review of 4 estimation methods. Ann Fam Med. 2019;17(3):267–72.

3 Cutler DM, Rosen AB, Vijan S. The value of medical spending in the United States, 1960–2000. N Engl J Med. 2006;355(9):920–7.

4 Cutler DM, Ghosh K, Messer KL, Raghunathan TE, Stewart ST, Rosen AB. Explaining the slowdown in medical spending growth among the elderly, 1999–2012. Health Aff (Millwood). 2019;38(2):222–9.

5 Howard DH, Bach PB, Berndt ER, Conti RM. Pricing in the market for anticancer drugs. J Econ Perspect. 2015;29(1):139–62.

6 Howard DH, Chernew ME, Abdelgawad T, Smith GL, Sollano J, Grabowski DC. New anticancer drugs associated with large increases in costs and life expectancy. Health Aff (Millwood). 2016;35(9):1581–7.

7 To access the appendix, click on the Details tab of the article online.

8 Ogata S, Nishimura K, Guzman-Castillo M, Sumita Y, Nakai M, Nakao YM, et al. Explaining the decline in coronary heart disease mortality rates in Japan: contributions of changes in risk factors and evidence-based treatments between 1980 and 2012. Int J Cardiol. 2019;291:183–8.

9 Plevritis SK, Munoz D, Kurian AW, Stout NK, Alagoz O, Near AM, et al. Association of screening and treatment with breast cancer mortality by molecular subtype in US women, 2000–2012. JAMA. 2018;319(2):154–64.

10 Edwards BK, Ward E, Kohler BA, Eheman C, Zauber AG, Anderson RN, et al. Annual report to the nation on the status of cancer, 1975–2006, featuring colorectal cancer trends and impact of interventions (risk factors, screening, and treatment) to reduce future rates. Cancer. 2010;116(3):544–73.

11 Vogelaar I, van Ballegooijen M, Schrag D, Boer R, Winawer SJ, Habbema JD, et al. How much can current interventions reduce colorectal cancer mortality in the U.S.? Mortality projections for scenarios of risk-factor modification, screening, and treatment. Cancer. 2006;107(7):1624–33.

12 Noland RB, Zhou Y. Has the Great Recession and its aftermath reduced traffic fatalities? Accid Anal Prev. 2017;98:130–8.

13 Melton SM Jr, McGwin G, Abernathy JH 3rd, MacLennan P, Cross JM, Rue LW 3rd. Motor vehicle crash–related mortality is associated with prehospital and hospital-based resource availability. J Trauma. 2003;54(2):273–9, discussion 279.

14 Harris AR, Thomas SH, Fisher GA, Hirsch DJ. Murder and medicine: the lethality of criminal assault 1960–1999. Homicide Stud. 2002;6(2):128–66.

15 Ganguli M, Rodriguez EG. Reporting of dementia on death certificates: a community study. J Am Geriatr Soc. 1999;47(7):842–9.

16 Wamble DE, Ciarametaro M, Dubois R. The effect of medical technology innovations on patient outcomes, 1990–2015: results of a physician survey. J Manag Care Spec Pharm. 2019;25(1):66–71.

17 Palella FJ Jr, Delaney KM, Moorman AC, Loveless MO, Fuhrer J, Satten GA, et al. Declining morbidity and mortality among patients with advanced human immunodeficiency virus infection. N Engl J Med. 1998;338(13):853–60.

18 Hess KL, Crepaz N, Rose C, Purcell D, Paz-Bailey G. Trends in sexual behavior among men who have sex with men (MSM) in high-income countries, 1990–2013: a systematic review. AIDS Behav. 2017;21(10):2811–34.

19 Alpert A, Powell D, Pacula RL. Supply-side drug policy in the presence of substitutes: evidence from the introduction of abuse-deterrent opioids. Am Econ J Econ Policy. 2018;10(4):1–35.

20 Evans WN, Lieber EMJ, Power P. How the reformulation of OxyContin ignited the heroin epidemic. Rev Econ Stat. 2018;101(1):1–15.

21 Case A, Deaton A. Mortality and morbidity in the 21st century [Internet]. Washington (DC): Brookings Institution; 2017 Mar 23 [cited 2020 Jul 29]. Available from: https://www.brookings.edu/bpea-articles/mortality-and-morbidity-in-the-21st-century/

22 Welch HG, Schwartz L, Woloshin S. Overdiagnosed: making people sick in the pursuit of health. Boston (MA): Beacon Press; 2011.

23 Jodal HC, Helsingen LM, Anderson JC, Lytvyn L, Vandvik PO, Emilsson L. Colorectal cancer screening with faecal testing, sigmoidoscopy, or colonoscopy: a systematic review and network meta-analysis. BMJ Open. 2019;9(10):e032773.

24 Barbeau P, Stevens A, Beck A, Skidmore B, Arnaout A, Brackstone M, et al. Breast cancer screening: Part A. An evidence report to inform an update of the Canadian Task Force on Preventive Health Care 2011 guideline [Internet]. Ottawa: Ottawa Hospital Research Institute; 2017 [cited 2020 Jul 29]. Available from: https://canadiantaskforce.ca/wp-content/uploads/2019/02/Systematic-Review-Evidence-Report_v2_FINAL.pdf

25 Gillum BS, Graves EJ, Jean L. Trends in hospital utilization: United States, 1988–92. Vital Health Stat 13. 1996;(124):1–71. Table 19.

26 Zhao J, Mao Z, Fedewa SA, Nogueira L, Yabroff KR, Jemal A, et al. The Affordable Care Act and access to care across the cancer control continuum: a review at 10 years. CA Cancer J Clin. 2020;70(3):165–81.

27 Ghosh A, Simon K, Sommers BD. The effect of health insurance on prescription drug use among low-income adults: evidence from recent Medicaid expansions. J Health Econ. 2019;63:64–80.

28 Chernew ME, Rosen AB, Fendrick AM. Value-based insurance design. Health Aff (Millwood). 2007;26(2):w195–203. DOI: 10.1377/hlthaff.26.2.w195.

Melissa Barber, Ph.D. Postdoctoral Fellow
Yale School of Medicine, Yale Law School, and Yale Collaboration for Regulatory Rigor, Integrity, and Transparency (CRRIT) email: melissa.barber@yale.edu https://scholar.harvard.edu/melissabarber

U.S. Senate Committee on Health, Education, Labor & Pensions (HELP) 428 Senate Dirksen Office Building
Washington, DC, 20510
February 5, 2024

Statement for the record for hearing Why Does the United States Pay, by Far, the Highest Prices in the World for Prescription Drugs?

Background:

I thank the Committee for their continued work in seeking to understand and address the problem of high drug prices in the United States.

I am a health economist based at Yale University. I completed my PhD at Harvard University in 2023 have served as a consultant on pharmaceutical issues for the World Health Organization (WHO), Médecins Sans Frontières (MSF), the Global Fund to Fight AIDS, Tuberculosis, and Malaria, and the World Bank. In September 2023 I testified before the House Committee on Energy and Commerce on Legislative Proposals to Prevent and Respond to Generic Drug Shortages. I represent only myself in this submission.

In this statement for the record, I will briefly outline the results of my research on the production costs of pharmaceuticals that the Committee may find useful in their investigation.

Summary of methods used to estimate the cost of production of medicines:

I have worked to develop and refine methods for estimating the cost of production of medicines since 2016. The core costing algorithm was commissioned by WHO for the Fair Pricing Forum in 2017, [1] and has since been expanded and further developed and applied to hundreds of medicines. The costing methods included herein have been extensively peer reviewed in a range of journals (British Medical Journal (BMJ) Global Health, BMJ Open, Journal of Virus Eradication, and The Lancet Oncology) and presented at numerous international conferences (International AIDS Society, European Society for Medical Oncology, and the European Society of Clinical Microbiology and Infectious Diseases). My co-authors and I have published cost estimates for all tablets/capsules and injectable medicines on the WHO Essential Medicines List (where permitted by available data),[2-3] insulin including insulin analogues,[4] HIV medicines and treatments for opportunistic infections,[5,6] direct-acting antivirals for hepatitis C, [7] cancer medicines,[8] and antihypertensive medicines.[9] Our 2018 BMJ Global Health paper was recently included as a reference for cost of production by Novartis researchers, giving us further confidence that our methods, developed in academic contexts, are also regarded as accurate within industry.[10]

Analysis

Sample selection: I include cost of production estimates for drugs (where permitted by available data) covered under Medicare Part D selected for negotiation as part of the Inflation Reduction Act. This sample of drugs was chosen as they were identified by CMS as significant cost drivers in Medicare expenditures, amounting to 20% of total Part D gross covered prescription costs.[11]

Table 1. Estimated cost of production for medicines subject to Medicare negotiation

		Cost (unit)		Cost (annual)	
Drug	Unit	Estimated cost of production	NADAC	Estimated cost of production	NADAC
Eliquis *apixaban*	5mg tablet	$0.02	$9.50	$18	$6935
Entresto *sacubitril / valsartan*	97mg/103mg tablet	$0.16	$11.00	$130	$8030
Farxiga *dapagliflozin*	10mg tablet	$0.04	$18.62	$16	$6796
Fiasp Flextouch *insulin aspart*	3 mL 100unit/mL disposable pen	$1.26	$107.13	$61	$5214
NovoLog FlexPen *insulin aspart*	3 mL 100unit/mL disposable pen	$1.26	$26.85	$61	$1307
Imbruvica *ibrutinib*	140mg capsule	$0.75	N/A	$1091	N/A
Januvia *sitagliptin*	100mg tablet	$0.06	$18.32	$23	$6687
Jardiance *empagliflozin*	10mg tablet	$0.04	$19.53	$16	$7128
Stelara *ustekinumab*	45 mg/0.5 mL in syringe	$2.82	$12,760	$12	$55,293
Xarelto *rivaroxaban*	20mg tablet	$0.03	$17.37	$12	$6340

In the interests of brevity for this submitted statement, I have submitted summary results. The methods are described in detail in the technical appendix and publications linked in the endnotes.

Should Committee members have further inquiries, including questions about cost of production methods and their application, I am available to support as may be helpful.

Melissa Barber

Sincerely, Melissa Barber

Technical Appendix

1) Cost comparison to NADAC prices methodology
    - NADAC costs: National Average Drug Acquisition Cost. Most recent price reported as of 31 Jan 2024.
    - Many drugs have multiple indications. See Table A1 for assumptions about the indications and other considerations used in calculating annual treatment costs. Note: Unit costs are rounded to the second decimal point, but were not rounded in calculating annual costs.

Table A1. Indication and treatment assumptions in calculating annual costs

Drug	Unit	Treatment regimen	Representative indication used for comparison (FDA label)	Notes / assumptions
Eliquis *apixaban*	5mg tablet	5mg x 2 daily	reduce the risk of stroke and systemic embolism in patients with nonvalvular atrial fibrillation	
Entresto *sacubitril / valsartan*	97mg/103mg tablet	97mg/103mg x 2 daily	to reduce the risk of cardiovascular death and hospitalization for heart failure in adult patients with chronic heart failure. Benefits are most clearly evident in patients with left ventricular ejection fraction (LVEF) below normal.	target maintenance dose as recommended in AHA/ACC/HFSA 2022 guidelines
Farxiga *dapagliflozin*	10mg tablet	10mg daily	adjunct to diet and exercise to improve glycemic control in adults with type 2 diabetes mellitus	Typical dose
Fiasp Flextouch *insulin aspart*	3 mL 100unit/mL disposable pen	40 units/day	Improve glycemic control in adults with diabetes mellitus	WHO DDD 40 units/day
NovoLog FlexPen *insulin aspart*	3 mL 100unit/mL disposable pen	40 units/day	Improve glycemic control in adults with diabetes mellitus	WHO DDD 40 units/day
Imbruvica *ibrutinib*	140mg capsule	140mg x 4 daily	Mantle cell lymphoma (MCL) who have received at least one prior therapy	
Januvia *sitagliptin*	100mg tablet	100mg daily	adjunct to diet and exercise to improve glycemic control in adults with type 2 diabetes mellitus	
Jardiance *empagliflozin*	10mg tablet	10mg daily	reduce the risk of cardiovascular death in adults with type 2 diabetes & established cardiovascular disease	
Stelara *ustekinumab*	45 mg/0.5 mL in syringe	45 mg/0.5 mL in syringe every 12 weeks	moderate to severe plaque psoriasis (Ps) who are candidates for phototherapy or systemic therapy.	Maintenance dose, assumed weight <100kg
Xarelto *rivaroxaban*	20mg tablet	20mg daily	reduce risk of stroke and systemic embolism in nonvalvular atrial fibrillation	

2) Cost of production methodology:

The costing algorithm includes costs of materials (active pharmaceutical ingredient, excipients), and formulation costs. This technical appendix briefly summarizes the methodologies of peer- reviewed publications to describe how different parameters were sourced. This summary is not comprehensive. Please see referenced publications and their supplementary appendices for a full description of data source, data cleaning algorithms, and costing considerations.

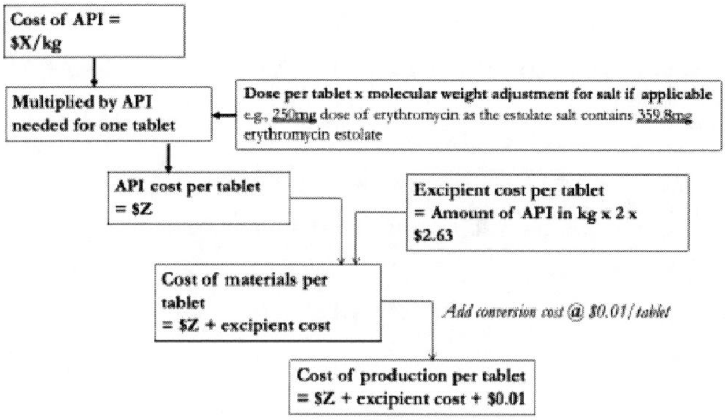

Figure A1. Cost of production algorithm for solid oral dosage formulations.

Algorithm as published in Hill A, Barber MJ, Gotham D. Estimated costs of production and potential prices for the WHO Essential Medicines List. BMJ Global Health 2018; 0: e000571.

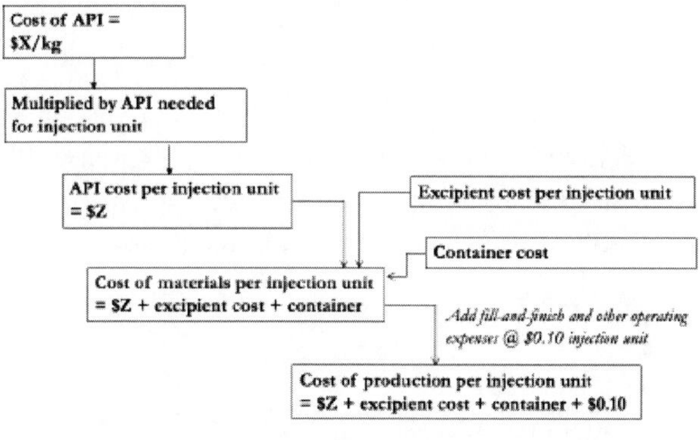

Figure A2. Cost of production algorithm for injectable formulations.

2.1 API cost

The price of active pharmaceutical ingredient (API) is the most important determinant in the cost of a production of a medicine. In order to identify shipments of API, a proprietary export/import database was searched for dates between Jan 2020 and Dec 2023, including import-export shipments from India, the United States, Mexico, Costa Rica, Panama, Bolivia, Brazil, Chile, Colombia, Ecuador, India, Paraguay, Peru, Uruguay, Venezuela, China, India, Indonesia, Pakistan, Sri Lanka, and the Philippines.[a] Data were not available for etanercept.

Data on shipments were manually cleaned to exclude shipments that did not represent genuine API, using criteria developed in peer-reviewed publications (e.g., shipments of working or reference standard, API with impurities, finished product, etc).[b] Outliers were defined as those with values higher than the third quartile plus 1.5 times the interquartile range, or lower than the first quartile minus 1.5 times the interquartile range, and were excluded. Weighted least-squares regression was used to fit linear models, with weights corresponding to shipment volume in kilograms. The outcome (unit cost) was log-transformed to reduce skew in the residuals. The predicted value on 1 December 2023 was used as the assumed average market price for API; we did not extrapolate beyond observed data.

Statistical analyses were performed and visualizations generated in R version 4.2.

Figure A1. Example of API cost data: rivaroxaban

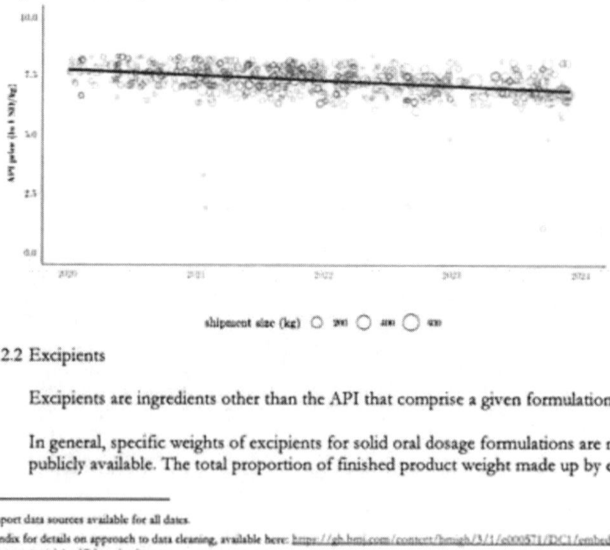

2.2 Excipients

Excipients are ingredients other than the API that comprise a given formulation.

In general, specific weights of excipients for solid oral dosage formulations are not publicly available. The total proportion of finished product weight made up by excipient

[a] Not all import data sources available for all dates.

[b] See Appendix for details on approach to data cleaning, available here: https://gh.bmj.com/content/bmjgh/3/1/e000571/DC1/embed/inline-supplementary-material-1.pdf?download=true

is typically between 20% and 60%.[12] Table A2, below, shows typical costs of excipients used in solid oral formulations, and typical proportion of total finished pharmaceutical product (FPP) weight made up by each excipient.

Table A2. Costs of excipients used in solid oral formulations, and typical proportion of total FPP weight made up by each excipient

Excipient	Typical weight as % of FPP weight		Cost per Kg (USD)	
	Min	Max	Min	Max
Sodium benzoate	1%	3%	$1.62	$2.19
Cellulose or microcrystalline cellulose	10%	60%	$2.00	$3.22
Talc	0.2%	2%	$2.00	$3.57
Sodium starch glycolate	1%	5%	$0.96	$4.93
Crospovidone	2%	5%	$3.03	$3.03
Lactose	5%	40%	$3.03	$3.77
Xylitol	5%	10%	$2.20	$5.75
Calcium phosphate, dibasic	5%	50%	$2.46	$5.70
Carboxymethylcellulose sodium	5%	25%	$3.25	$5.99
Starch, pregelatinised	5%	35%	$2.00	$9.00
Xanthan gum	5%	15%	$5.02	$7.44
Croscarmellose sodium	1%	5%	$6.56	$9.51
Methyl paraben	1%	2%	$11.50	$11.50
Povidone	5%	20%	$8.59	$17.11
Magnesium stearate	0.25%	4%	$4.30	$23.50
Potassium sorbate	0%	2%	$18.00	$37.00
Sodium lauryl sulfate	1%	2%	$36.00	$51.00
Aluminium oxide	0%	5%	N/A	N/A

Excipients composing the major part of FPP weight are in general very cheap – for example, cellulose, lactose, calcium phosphate, carboxymethylcellulose, pregelatinised starch. More expensive excipients, for example potassium sorbate, methyl paraben, and sodium lauryl sulfate, typically account for only a small proportion of the pill weight (< 5%).

Using the data in the table above, and the assumption that excipients make up 50% of the FPP weight for tablets, we have calculated an average excipient cost of $2.63 per kilogram of FPP.

Excipients for injectable formulations were sourced from Niazi (2020) and/or regulatory submissions to FDA or EMA. [13,14]

1.3. Formulation Costs

These are operating expenditures, minus API and excipients, needed to convert raw API into a FPP. Similar algorithms have been used and validated in previous studies.[15]

Multiple sources were consulted in order to inform a choice of assumed conversion cost per tablet/capsule. These are described individually below, summarized, and the final choice of assumed conversion cost is explained.

It is our view that, based on the values suggested by the available analyses, outlined above, the most plausible average conversion cost is between $0.005 and $0.01 for a solid oral dosage formulation. Of all the cost of production analyses identified (Table A3), it is only the Pinheiro et al study from Brazil in 2001 that has a per-unit estimate significantly greater than $0.01. We have set the assumed conversion cost in our generic price estimation algorithm at $0.01/tablet.

Table A3. Per-unit cost component values available from various analyses

Report	Cost components included in estimate	Conversion cost per tablet
LOCOST/JSS (2004)[16]	Conversion cost not including depreciation of capital, distribution, but including quality control (testing) and packaging	$0.0016
Lowest-priced product in UK, South Africa, India (2016)	Cost per unit of lowest-priced solid oral formulation FPP	$0.0011–$0.0043
Chaudhuri et al (2015)[17]	Conversion cost including depreciation of capital and packaging, but not including sales and distribution	$0.0056
	Conversion cost including depreciation of capital and packaging, and including sales and distribution	$0.0105
Discussion by authors with large generic companies (2016)	Conversion cost including packaging, but not sales and distribution	$0.006
McKinsey & Company (2014)[18]	Total production costs, lowest-cost plants (not further specified)	$0.013
Pinheiro et al (2006, data from 2001)[19]	Conversion cost (direct and indirect costs)	$0.057
	Conversion cost (direct and indirect costs) plus operating margin	$0.101

Formulation costs for injectable products are described in Estimation of cost-based prices for injectable medicines in the WHO Essential Medicines

List, Production costs and potential prices for biosimilars of human insulin and insulin analogues, and a publication in press.[3, 4.]

End Notes for Technical Appendix

[1] WHO. At WHO Forum on Medicines, countries and civil society push for greater transparency and fairer prices. WHO. 2019; published online April 13. https://www.who.int/news/item/13-04-2019-at-who-forum-on-medicines-countries-and-civil-society-push-for-greater-transparency-and-fairer-prices.

[2] Hill A, Barber MJ, Gotham D. Estimated costs of production and potential prices for the WHO Essential Medicines List. BMJ Global Health 2018; 0: e000571. https://gh.bmj.com/content/bmjgh/3/1/e000571.full.pdf.

[3] Gotham D, Barber MJ, Hill AM. Estimation of cost-based prices for injectable medicines in the WHO Essential Medicines List. BMJ Open 2019; 9: e027780. https://bmjopen.bmj.com/content/bmjopen/9/9/e027780.full.pdf.

[4] Gotham D, Barber MJ, Hill A. Production costs and potential prices for biosimilars of human insulin and insulin analogues. BMJ Global Health 2018; 3: e000850. https://gh.bmj.com/content/bmjgh/3/5/e000850.full.pdf.

[5] Barber M, Gotham D, Hill A. Cost-based estimated prices for key HIV, HCV, and MDR-TB medicines. Poster presentation at 23rd International AIDS Conference (AIDS 2020: Virtual), 6-10 July 2020.

[6] Barber M, Gotham D, Hill A. Estimated cost-based generic prices for treatments of opportunistic infections. AIDS 2018, Amsterdam. https://www.researchgate.net/publication/326914620_Estimated_cost-based_generic_prices_for_treatments_of_opportunistic_infections.

[7] Barber MJ, Gotham D, Khwairakpam G, Hill A. Price of a hepatitis C cure: Cost of production and current prices for direct-acting antivirals in 50 countries. Journal of Virus Eradication 2020; 6: 100001. https://pubmed.ncbi.nlm.nih.gov/33251019/

[8] Hoen E, Meyer S, Durisch P, et al. Improving affordability of new essential cancer medicines. The Lancet Oncology 2019; 20: 1052–4. https://www. thelancet.com/journals/lanonc/article/PIIS1470-2045(19)30459-0/fulltext.

[9] MSF, Resolve to Save Lives. Under Pressure: Strategies to improve access to medicines to treat high blood pressure in low- and middle-income countries report. 2022 https://msfaccess.org/under-pressure-strategies-improve-access-antihyper tensive-medicines-low-and-middle-income-0.

[10] Siirola E, Debon A, Eggimann F, Snajdrova R. Computer-guided substrate scope exploration of engineered peptide- modifying biocatalysts. (Preprint). Available from: https://www.researchsquare.com/article/rs-3639162/v1.

[11] U.S. Department of Health and Human Services. HHS Selects the First Drugs for Medicare Drug Price Negotiation. 2023; published online August 29. https://www.hhs.gov/about/news/2023/08/29/hhs-selects-the-first-drugs-for-medicare-drug-price-negotiation.html.

[12] Joseph Fortunak, Ngozwana S, Tsige Gebre-Mariam, Tiffany Ellison, Paul Watts, Martins Emeje, et al. Raising the Technological Level: The Scope for API, Excipients, and Biologicals Manufacture in Africa. In: Making Medicines in Africa: the Political Economy of Industrializing for Local Health. 2016.

[14] Niazi S. Handbook of Pharmaceutical Manufacturing Formulations: Sterile Products. Boca Raton, FL: CRC Press, Taylor Francis Group; 2020.

[15] Van de Ven N, Fortunak J, Simmons B, Ford N, Cooke GS, Khoo S, et al. Minimum target prices for production of direct-acting antivirals and associated diagnostics to combat hepatitis C virus. Hepatol Baltim Md. 2015 Apr;61(4):1174– 82; Hill A, Gotham D, Cooke G, Bhagani S, Andrieux-Meyer I, Cohn J, et al. Analysis of minimum target prices for production of entecavir to treat hepatitis B in high- and low-income countries. J Virus Erad. 2015 Apr 1;1(2):103–10; Hill A, Gotham D, Fortunak J, Meldrum J, Erbacher I, Martin M, et al. Target prices for mass production of tyrosine kinase inhibitors for global cancer treatment. BMJ Open. 2016 Jan 27;6(1):e009586; Hill A, Simmons B, Gotham D, Fortunak J. Rapid reductions in prices for generic sofosbuvir and daclatasvir to treat hepatitis C. J Virus Erad. 2016 Jan 1;2(1):28–31; Gotham D, Fortunak J, Pozniak A, Khoo S, Cooke G, Nytko FE, et al. Estimated generic prices for novel treatments for drug-resistant tuberculosis. J Antimicrob Chemother. 2017 Jan 10;dkw522.

[16] LOCOST/JSS. Impoverishing the Poor: Pharmaceuticals and Drug Pricing in India [Internet.. 2004 [cited 2017 Jan 2.. Available from: http://www.jssbilaspur.org/wordpress/wp-content/uploads/2015/10/Impoverishing-the-poor-Pharmaceuticals-and-drug-pricing-in-India.pdf.

[17] Chaudhuri S, West A. Can local producers compete with low-cost imports? A simulation study of pharmaceutical industry in low-income Africa. Innov Dev. 2015 Jan 2;5(1):23–38.

[18] Keeling D, Lösch M, Schrader U. Outlook on pharma operations. McKinsey & Company; 2014.

[19] Pinheiro E, Vasan A, Kim JY, Lee E, Guimier JM, Perriens J. Examining the production costs of antiretroviral drugs: AIDS. 2006 Aug;20(13):1745–52.

[Whereupon, at 1:25 p.m., the hearing was adjourned.]

Chapter 2

Ensuring Fairness and Transparency in the Markets of Prescription Drugs*

Senate Committee on Commerce, Science, and Transportation

Thursday, May 5, 2022

U.S. Senate, Subcommittee on Consumer Protection, Product Safety, and Data Security, Committee on Commerce, Science, and Transportation,

Washington, DC.

The Subcommittee met, pursuant to notice, at 10:10 a.m., in room SR–253, Russell Senate Office Building, Hon. Richard Blumenthal, Chairman of the Subcommittee, presiding.

Present: Senators Blumenthal [presiding], Cantwell, and Blackburn.

Opening Statement of Hon. Richard Blumenthal, U.S. Senator from Connecticut

Senator BLUMENTHAL. The Subcommittee on Consumer Protection, Product Safety, and Data Security will come to order. Welcome to our very distinguished panel and to the Senators who will be joining us. I want to thank

---

* This is an edited, reformatted and augmented version of Hearing Before the Subcommittee on Consumer Protection, Product Safety, and Data Security of the Committee on Commerce, Science, and Transportation United States Senate One Hundred Seventeenth Congress, Second Session, Publication No. S. HRG. 117–836, dated May 5, 2022.

In: The Price of Prescription Medicine
Editor: Cornelius Lowery
ISBN: 979-8-90134-014-1

particularly Senator Blackburn for her collaboration on this topic, and welcome all of you to address the anti-consumer and anti-competitive practices that increase and drive-up health care costs for the American people.

Today we are specifically focused on pharmacy benefit managers, or PBMs, and how the tactics they use impact drug costs and consumer choice. This hearing is really part of a more general discussion on how to lower costs and remove barriers to care for patients, and we will continue to have hearings on that topic. If you ask the average American to tell you what a pharmacy benefit manager does or even what it is, you are probably met with a blank stare, which is understandable.

PBMs have long operated in relative obscurity with little transparency, acting as middlemen between insurer, drug companies, and pharmacies. PBMs exist to manage the drug prescription benefits for 266 million Americans. So even if you have never heard of a PBM, you have almost certainly been impacted by one.

They are hired to hire—they are hired to buy health plans to— by managing the health plans' prescription drug benefit, lower costs to the health plan by exacting rebates from drug companies and managing what drugs will be covered for patients and at what cost. Then they act as the intermediary between the health plan and the pharmacy, reimbursing the pharmacy for the prescription drugs they dispense.

PBMs stated goal is to lower health care costs for consumers through this complex system. The problem is that patients rarely see or feel the benefits. Drug prices continue to rise. Insurance costs continue to eat into incomes. And more and more often, drug—the drugs patients need are not covered by their health care plan at all. In this way, PBMs are part of a broken drugs supply chain that leads to increasing profits for drug companies, increasing profits for PBMs, and increasing drug costs for patients.

PBMs benefit from high prices. They receive rebates and administrative fees from drug companies that are often based on the initial price. It is called the list price of a drug. This means the higher the initial cost of a drug, the higher the profits for the PBM. PBMs will argue that these rebates lower the cost of your insurance, that they largely pass these rebates along to insurers who use them to lower your health care costs.

But truly, we have no idea whether this is accurate, because PBMs shroud this information in secrecy. If these rebates are lowering the cost of health care, that is news to patients. Insurance premiums and deductibles have not gone down. Instead, increasingly, they are eating into Americans' hard earned dollars and savings. PBMs are a significant part of the drug pricing problem, but drug companies shouldn't get a pass.

As Professor Feldman, one of our witnesses here today wrote in her aptly entitled article, and I am quoting here, "driving up prices is a win-win for PBMs and drug companies. Drug companies can charge more for their products, while PBMs increase their slice of the pie." The one who loses out is the patient, because even though that initial price isn't what anyone else in the drug supply chain pays, it oftentimes directly impacts what you pay.

That is because for nearly half of people with commercial insurance and nearly all Medicare beneficiaries, out-of-pocket payments are based on an initial drug price, not the reduced rate. The higher the initial price, the more you pay, and PBMs have a financial incentive to keep that initial price high. PBMs also limit choice. PBMs are the ones who decide which prescription drugs your health plan will cover and which they won't. They determine which drugs will be preferred by your insurance plan, meaning which drugs will cost you more out of pocket and which will cost you less. Increasingly, PBMs have taken to excluding drugs entirely from health plans.

More and more patients who receive a diagnosis are working with their doctors to find a prescription drug that works for them, only to be denied access to it at the pharmacy counter. This happened to April Flowers, a teenager from Texas, whose family told their story to Consumer Reports. She had taken the same medication for her seizures for years when suddenly her family learned at the pharmacy counter that her out-of-pocket costs was now $1,700. Her family made frantic calls to figure out the problem.

What they learned was that her drug was suddenly dropped with no warning. Her drug was no longer covered. They scrambled. They enlisted her doctor. With 2 days of medicine left, April got an exception. The stress, the threat to her health must have been infuriating. April's situation is shockingly common. In fact, in recent years, PBMs' refusal to cover certain drugs has skyrocketed.

Now hundreds of drugs are excluded by the biggest PBMs every year. Certain types of insulin, drugs to treat chronic conditions, and in recent years, cancer drugs are all fair game. A poll cited in the same Consumer Reports article found that more than a third of people with prescription drug coverage said they or someone in their home had dealt with the same issue as April within the last 12 months.

Let's be clear, PBMs are just part of a broken system. It is massively broken. It has left millions of Americans without a way to afford lifesaving medicine like insulin. Drug prices have skyrocketed, and drug companies have made record profits while engaging in anti-competitive tactics that keep cheaper drugs off the market. I pushed for reform, so have many of my colleagues.

The biggest and most important priority we have is to lower the cost of prescription drugs. And that is a health care imperative as people feel the weight of high health care costs. We cannot ignore the power of PBMs and their influence in drug pricing and eroding patient and provider choice. I hope that today's hearing will lead to action. And I turn to the Ranking Member.

Statement of Hon. Marsha Blackburn, U.S. Senator from Tennessee

Senator BLACKBURN. Thank you, Mr. Chairman. And good morning and welcome to all and to our witnesses that are joining us remotely today. We welcome them also. And Chairman Blumenthal, I am so pleased that we are doing this hearing about the issue of the PBMs and the impact that these arrangements have on our consumers.

And when you look at the fact that the PBMs are the middleman and over the past few decades, they have grown, really escalated with Medicare Part D. And initially the purpose was, save money for the employers and the insurance companies, try to keep the costs down. But in those 20 years since the Medicare Part D has been with us, it seems that the role of the PBM has become really quite complicated.

Three PBM middlemen accounted for nearly 80 percent of all the prescription claims in 2020, and that is not lost on us. And one of the reasons we are wanting to look at the market, the size of the market, the inefficiencies that are there—maybe there are ways to create efficiencies and save money for the system and for consumers who seem to be paying an ever higher cost.

We understand and appreciate rebates are a part of this system and are really a part of the payments that are made by the pharmaceutical companies to the—to keep certain drugs in a formulary. And we know that the PBM has a lot of control over what pharmaceutical can actually reach the consumer that is on a specific plan. And we know and are curious about some of the other rebates that are recouped from pharmacists by the PBMs.

And pharmacists tell me that this is done without transparency or accountability by the PBMs. Distorted incentives within the pharmaceutical supply chain have created a dynamic where middlemen involved in distributing and paying for prescription medicines benefit from higher list prices and higher rebates, and the consumer pays more.

Senators Grassley and Wyden published a two-year investigation into the cost of insulin. I know that each of you are familiar with this. And what they noted was how the PBMs really stood in the way of a lot of transparency in this process. They concluded that the PBMs have an ''incentive for manufacturers to keep list prices high.'' And that is a direct quote from them. Now, this is really a 180 from what the purpose of a PBM was to be initially. In recent years, 40 states, including Tennessee, have enacted legislation to curb some PBM practices.

The bill recently passed by the Tennessee General Assembly includes reimbursement transparency and protects patients from being steered to PBM-affiliated pharmacies. This shows you how you have gotten away from a core mission with the PBM when the states jump in and say we are going to protect our citizens.

That is why we need to look at this. You have got onerous audits, claw back provisions, and patients steering into anti-competitive behaviors by PBMs that have caused small pharmacy businesses to struggle to survive. While CMS recently proposed rule to end retroactive DIR fees, which harm independent pharmacies and raise costs for seniors, they unfortunately delayed implementation until 2024.

That is unacceptable. This delay gives PBMs another year to play games that cause seniors to pay higher cost sharing and pharmacies to face huge claw backs. As they say, sunlight is the best disinfectant, and it is time for more transparency about the impact of potentially anti-competitive PBM practices on patients, small pharmacy businesses, and taxpayers.

To this end, I have introduced S. 298, the Pharmacy Benefit Managers Accountability Act. I have done that along with Senator Braun. The bill would require GAO to submit a report to HHS and Congress on PBMs and their role in the pharmaceutical supply chain. I encourage my colleagues to take a look at it and consider co-sponsoring that legislation. I would note that a few months ago the FTC asked for public input on PBMs and their impact on patients, physicians, and businesses.

I am not opposed to this line of inquiry. Last year, I sponsored a bipartisan bill with Senator Blumenthal and Chair Cantwell and others that directed the FTC to report to Congress on anti-competitive practices. But I want to emphasize that this is not a blank check for the FTC. It is not for them to move forward with any type of rulemaking that they want to pursue without the direction of us in Congress, especially given the need for more information and the important role of HHS and the states in this area.

So these are all issues for our discussion today. We look forward to hearing you. Thank you, Mr. Chairman.

Senator BLUMENTHAL. Thanks so much, Senator Blackburn. We have a great panel. Welcome to all of you. I will introduce you and then ask for your statements. David Balto, who is a Principal in the law offices of David Balto. He is an expert on health care competition and regulation, and an antitrust attorney with over 25 years of experience in both the private and public sectors.

Mr. Balto served as a trial attorney in the Department of Justice's Antitrust Division and in several senior level positions at the FTC during the Clinton Administration, including as Policy Direc tor for the Bureau of Competition. Craig Garthwaite, who joins us personally, is the Herman Smith Research Professor and Hospital and Health Services Management, Professor of Strategy and Director of the Program on Health Care at Northwestern University's Kellogg School of Management.

He has a Ph.D. in economics from the University of Maryland and is an expert in health care policy and the biopharmaceutical sector, and I understand is a native of Stanford, or at least has a connection there. Robin Feldman is the Arthur J. Goldberg Distinguished Professor of Law, Albert Abramson Distinguished Professor of Law Chair, and Director of the Center for Innovation at the University of California Hastings. She is an expert in the legal junction of intellectual property, health, and medicine.

Her work illuminates how and why practices often operate to the benefit of the pharmaceutical industry over consumers, and she offers solutions. J.C. Scott, who joins us in person, is the President and CEO of the Pharmaceutical Care Management Association representing America's Pharmacy Benefit Managers. He joined PCMA in the fall of 2018 and before that held roles with Abiomed and the American Council of Life Insurance.

He also has held various staff offices in the House of Representatives. We are going to go in alphabetical order, beginning with David Balto, then Craig Garthwaite, Robin Feldman, and J.C. Scott. Mr. Balto, if you can hear us, the floor is yours.

Statement of David A. Balto, Antitrust Attorney, David A. Balto Law Offices

Mr. BALTO. Thank you. Good morning, Chairman Blumenthal, Ranking Member Blackburn, and other members of the Subcommittee. I am very grateful that you are holding this hearing and that you invited me to speak. There is increasing attention to PBMs, and it is very justifiable.

PBMs are an increasing source of cost increases in the pharmaceutical area, and they are probably the least regulated area, and they have a significant impact on health care costs that is appropriate for attention. And unfortunately, our antitrust and consumer protection enforcers, especially FTC, have given them a green light and consumers have paid dearly for that. In my written testimony, I make four basic points.

First, PBMs are probably one of the least regulated areas of the drug supply chain. There is no Federal enforcement and very little State enforcement, and that has left PBMs free to engage in anti-ompetitive conduct. When you look at the—listen to the complaints of the community pharmacists in your state, what they are subject to in trying to deliver better services to consumers is truly — [technical problems]—tremendous power of PBMs.

Second, the—because of the lack of enforcement, the PBMs have formed a tight oligopoly, as ranking member noted. There are three elements you need for competition to exist in the market. First, you need choice. You need to be able to play competitors off against each other. Now, Mr. Scott is going to tell you there are 70 PBMs. That doesn't matter. Three firms dominate the market. The question of whether a firm has market power is the ability of a customer to say no.

And when a PBM goes to a pharmacist and says, I am going to take all these DIR fees or I am going to force you to reimburse below cost, or when a generic drug company comes to a PBM and says, please put me on the formulary and the PBM says, no, you are not offering me rebates like the branded drug manufacturer receives, that means the PBM has market power. It has the ability to act anti-competitively. What is the result? We have seen PBM profits more than double to over $20 billion a year.

Now, pause for a second. These aren't firms that are producing products. These are firms that are moving information and money and negotiating contracts, and for that, they are taking $28 billion, adding $28 billion of cost into the system. Why should consumers be paying so much for so little? And the reason that happens is because of the lack of competition. Factor two, transparency.

You have to go no further than PBMs imposing — [technical problems]— saying that they don't want any form of transparency in the market. Then third, conflicts of interest. PBMs—the purpose of PBMs is to lower drug prices, but as the ranking member noted, they make more money in rebates when prices go up. So their interest is in seeing prices increase. And that is why you see them deny access or provide inferior access to biosimilars or generic drugs or some competing drugs.

It is basically an auction for shelf space in which they say the highest cost product to the consumers is going to win the auction. And that is why prices are increasing so significantly. In my testimony, I outline how the FTC has really failed at this. And nothing is worse than a decade ago when they made the Faustian bargain to allow two of the three biggest PBMs, Express Scripts and Medco, to merge under the assumption that that increased market power would lead to lower prices for consumers.

Well, they were dead wrong. What is the result? We see sky-rocketing rebates over the past decade. We see more restrictive networks and consumers being denied their pharmacies of choice as there has been a flood of PBM consolidation over those 10 years. One message I want to leave you with is consumers care a lot about their community pharmacy.

The community pharmacist is the health care provider that provides the greatest access to consumers, and that is vital, vital in underserved, rural, and inner city markets. They are the most accessible health care professional. And we saw that during the vaccine crisis over the past several years.

My testimony ends by outlining several amendments to the Federal Trade Commission Act, specifying anti-competitive practices for the Commission to dig its teeth into to prevent—to make this market competitive. And I think at the top of that list has to be the impact on pharmacies and also this rebate system that is leading to skyrocketing drug prices.

Thank you very much for the opportunity to testify. [The prepared statement of Mr. Balto follows:]

Prepared Statement of David A. Balto, Antitrust Attorney, David A. Balto Law Offices

Good morning, Chair Blumenthal, Ranking Member Blackburn, and Members of the subcommittee: I thank you for giving me the opportunity to testify on the con cerns and the need for regulation and accountability in the pharmacy benefit manager (''PBM'') market. My testimony documents the tremendous competitive and consumer protection problems in the PBM market and need for stronger antitrust enforcement, oversight, regulation, and Federal legislation. For years PBMs have existed with scant regulation, and consumers have paid a heavy price in higher costs, less choice and inferior service. Congress and regulators need to reverse this permissive stance toward PBMs to lower prescription drug prices for patients.

My testimony is based on my 30 years of experience as a public interest antitrust attorney and an antitrust enforcer for both the Department of Justice and the Federal Trade Commission (FTC). From 1995 to 2001, I served as the Policy Director of the FTC's Bureau of Competition and the attorney advisor to Chairman Robert Pitofsky. Currently, I work as a public interest antitrust attorney in Washington, DC. I have represented consumer groups, public interest organizations, health plans, unions, employers, retail and specialty community pharmacy associations, and even PBMs on PBM regulatory and competitive issues. I led the consumer opposition to the proposed mergers of Anthem and Cigna and Aetna and Humana and worked with consumer groups to oppose CVS' acquisition of Aetna.

I have testified before Congress on several occasions and before fourteen state legislatures on the need for PBM reform and regulation and served as an expert witness for the State of Maine on its PBM legislation.

My testimony makes the following points:

- PBMs are one of the least regulated sectors of the healthcare system and drug supply chain. There is almost no Federal antitrust enforcement, oversight, or regulation. The lack of antitrust enforcement and regulation has created an environment in which PBMs are free to engage in anticompetitive, deceptive, and fraudulent behavior that harms patients, payors, employers, unions, and pharmacists and significantly increases drug costs.[1]
- Because lax antitrust enforcement allowed the three largest PBMs to become vertically integrated and form a tight oligopoly,[2] the PBM market lacks the essential elements for a competitive market: 1)

---

[1] How PBMs Make Drug Pricing Problem Worse, David Balto, August 31, 2016, The Hill, https://thehill.com/blogs/pundits-blog/healthcare/294025-how-pbms-make-the-drug-price-problem-worse/.

[2] Reforming Biopharmaceutical Pricing at Home and Abroad, The Council of Economic Advisors, White Paper, February 2018, https://trumpwhitehouse.archives.gov/wp-content/uploads/2017/11/CEA-Rx-White-Paper-Final2.pdf.

choice, 2) transparency, and 3) a lack of conflicts of interest. PBMs leverage this lack of competition to further their own interests at the expense of patients, employers, and others in the system.

- The PBM rebate system turns competition on its head with PBMs seeking higher, not lower prices to maximize rebates and profits. In the past decade, PBM profits have increased to $28 billion annually.[3] PBMs are supposed to control costs, but because of the perverse incentives the rebate system creates, they frequently deny access to lower cost drugs including lower cost generics and biosimilars, to maximize rebates available from higher cost drugs.[4] That is why major consumer and patient groups and unions supported the past administration's efforts to eliminate the antikickback safe harbor for PBM rebates.[5]
- Because of their market power and vertical integration these middlemen increasingly stifle competition from this country's most accessible and trusted health care professionals—community pharmacies. PBMs create endless schemes to reduce reimbursement, claw back funds, restrict networks, and effectively force pharmacies to provide drugs below cost. In 2020 alone, PBMs took $9,535,197,775[6] from independent pharmacies who serve Medicare Part D participants. Community pharmacies are crucial for consumers in underserved low income and rural neighborhoods. These unfair and coercive tactics by PBMs result in inferior health care, less choice and higher costs.
- The FTC has failed to protect consumers from unfair, deceptive and egregious conduct in this market. Thus, the Committee should

---

[3] PBM Accountability Project, Understanding the Evolving Business and Revenue Models of PBMs, 2021, https://www.pbmaccountability.org/_files/ugd/b11210_264612f6b98e47b3a850205 4f66bb2a1.pdf?index=true.

[4] Charlie Grant, Hidden Profits in the Prescription Drug Supply Chain, February 24, 2018, Wall Street Journal.

[5] Comments of Consumer Action, Consumer Federation of America, Consumer Reports, NETWORK Lobby for Catholic Social Justice, and Public Research Interest Group PIRG in Support of Department of Health and Human Services Office of Inspector General's (''HHS'') proposed new rules to eliminate the safe harbor for rebates in Medicare Part D plans, April 8, 2019, https://docs.wixstatic.com/ugd/1859d0_c7d2ccf1d47d4f65a8965e9bbaed989d.pdf.

[6] Medicare Program; Contract Year 2023 Policy and Technical Changes to the Medicare Advantage and Medicare Prescription Drug Benefit Programs; Policy and Regulatory Revisions in Response to the COVID–19 Public Health Emergency; Additional Policy and Regulatory Revi sions in Response to the COVID–19 Public Health Emergency, CMS 4192–F, https://public-inspection.federalregister.gov/2022-09375.pdf.

> consider amending the FTC Act to specify unfair acts or practices and unfair methods of competition that PBMs engage in that the FTC should address and provide a clear mandate for strong enforcement. Consumers should no longer be forced to pay billions for the schemes of these middlemen.

For the PBM market to function properly for patients, employers, unions, and other stakeholders, we need strong oversight and regulation as well as greater antitrust and consumer protection enforcement. Any conversation on drug pricing reform must include a discussion on how to rein in PBMs.

The PBM Market Is Broken

Ensuring that patients can afford lifesaving and life-managing prescription drugs is critically important to public health because better use of medicines has been shown to help patients live longer and healthier lives. Unreasonably high out-of-pocket costs for prescription drugs at the pharmacy counter threaten patient access to medicines, as some choose to stop or delay treatment because they cannot afford it.[7]

Undoubtedly, rising prescription drug prices are a serious problem for patients.[8] PBMs were supposed to be a solution to this problem, but a lack of competition, transparency and existing conflicts of interest enable PBMs to game the system and put profits before patient welfare.

PBMs represent themselves as ''honest brokers'' or intermediaries between drug manufacturers, health insurers, plan sponsors, and providers. Although PBMs in principle have great promise in terms of their potential to control prescription drug costs, over time their role has evolved. Now, there is a pattern of self-dealing and anticompetitive behavior. Patients pay higher prices for drugs than they should because PBMs are not fulfilling their cost-

---

[7] Press Release, Kaiser Family Foundation, Poll: Nearly 1 in 4 Americans Taking Prescription Drugs Say It's Difficult to Afford Their Medicines, including Larger Shares Among Those with Health Issues, with Low Incomes and Nearing Medicare Age (Mar. 1, 2019), https://www.kff.org/health-costs/press-release/poll-nearly-1-in-4-americans-taking-prescription-drugs-say-its-difficult-to-afford-medicines-including-larger-shares-with-low-incomes/.

[8] Leigh Purvis and Stephen W. Schondelmeyer, Brand Name Drug Prices Increase More Than Twice As Fast As Inflation in 2018. AARP Public Policy Institute, November 2019, https://press.aarp.org/Brand-Name-Drug-Price-Increases-2018-Rx-Price-Watch?intcmp=AE0POL-TOENG-TOGL.

control function. Consider that two of the three largest PBMs are in the Fortune 10 and all three in the Fortune 15.[9] The Pharmaceutical Care Management Association (''PCMA''), the PBM trade association, frequently says that PBMs are ''the only actors in the pharmaceutical supply chain whose fundamental role is to negotiate lower drug prices for patients,'' but PBMs are not ''fulfilling their primary mission to lower prescription drug costs for consumers and health plan sponsors.''[10] *Instead, consumers are funding profits of more than $28 billion annually for network intermediaries that make no products and provide no health care, but rather basically serve primarily to transfer data and money.*

Let me be clear, the PBM market is broken because it lacks the essential elements for a competitive market, namely: (1) choice, (2) transparency and (3) a lack of conflicts of interest.[11]

First, there is a lack of choice. The PBM industry is a tight oligopoly, which results in reduced consumer choice. According to the Council of Economic Advisors (CEA), three PBMs—CVS Caremark, Optum Rx, and Express Scripts—control over 80 percent of the market, ''which allows them to exercise undue market power against manufacturers and against health plans and beneficiaries.''[12] *Indeed, the three largest PBMs have a higher gross margin than any other players involved in the drug supply chain,*[13] *and in*

---

[9] Fortune Rankings, https://fortune.com/fortune500/2021/search/.

[10] J.C. Scott, FTC's Inquiry of PBMs Won't Lower Prescription Drug Costs, The Hill, April 18, 2022, https://thehill.com/blogs/congress-blog/3272225-ftcs-inquiry-of-pbms-wont-lower-prescription-drug-costs/.

[11] ''Protecting Consumers and Promoting Health Insurance Competition,'' Testimony of David Balto, Before House Judiciary Committee, Subcommittee on Courts and Competition Policy, October 8, 2009, at http://www.dcantitrustlaw.com/assets/content/documents/CAP/protecting% 20consumers.pdf.

[12] CEA White Paper, *supra* note 2. The Top Pharmacy Managers of 2021, the big get even bigger, Drug Channels, April 2022, *https://www.drugchannels.net/2022/04/the-top-pharmacy- benefit-managers-of.html.* I expect the witness from PCMA will note that there are dozens of PBMs. But these firms are not competitors at least from the perspective of competition law and economic policy. Under the antitrust laws, a ''competitor'' in a relevant market is a firm that can constrain prices. *FTC v. Staples, Inc.,* 970 F. Supp. 1066, 1078 (D.D.C. 1997) (''The pricing evidence indicates a low cross-elasticity of demand between consumable office products sold by Staples or Office Depot and those same products sold by other sellers of office supplies. This same evidence indicates that non-superstore sellers of office supplies are not able to effectively constrain the superstores prices, because a significant number of superstore customers do not turn to a non-superstore alternative when faced with higher prices in the one firm markets.'') None of these much smaller PBMs have either the incentive or ability to constrain the anticompetitive conduct of the three dominant PBMs.

[13] Charley Grant, *Hidden Profits in the Prescription Drug Supply Chain,* February 24, 2018, Wall Street Journal, *https://www.wsj.com/articles/hidden-profits-in-the-prescription-*

recent years, more of the increase in spending on brand medicines has gone to payers, including PBMs and health plans, than to drug manufacturers.[14] PBM profits have more than doubled in the past decade. It is hard to see what value these middlemen have added to our healthcare system in return for the skyrocketing profits.[15]

Second, the PBM market lacks transparency. PBM operations are cloaked in secrecy, and they fight efforts to require transparency tooth and nail. There is no better example of their efforts to hide information than ''PBM gag clauses'' which PBMs long used to prevent pharmacists from telling consumers about available lower-cost alternative medications. While Congress finally prohibited PBMs from imposing such clauses for federally funded patients (i.e., Medicare beneficiaries), in many states, PBMs still utilize such clauses to ensure continued receipt of substantial profits on the backs of consumers. *There is simply no pro-consumer reason to deny consumers the necessary information to receive drugs at the lowest cost. None.*

PBMs establish tremendous roadblocks to prevent payors from knowing the amount of rebates they secure. Even sophisticated buyers are unable to secure specific drug by drug rebate information. PBMs prevent payors from being able to audit rebate information. As the Council of Economic Advisors observed, the PBM market lacks transparency as ''[t]he size of manufacturer rebates and the percentage of the rebate passed on to health plans and patients are secret.''[16] Without adequate transparency, plan sponsors cannot determine if the PBMs are fully passing on any savings, or whether their formulary choices really benefit the plan and subscribers.

Legislation requiring transparency or imposing a fiduciary duty might be one solution. Yet PBMs regularly fight against any such legislative proposals. For example, the PBMs fought against a 2014 Department of Labor

---

drug-supply-chain-1519484401#:_™text=Drug%20distributors%20converted%2046 %25%20of,benefit%20 from%20higher%20drug%20prices.

[14] Brownlee A., *The Pharmaceutical Supply Chain,* 2013–2020, Berkeley Research Group, January 2022, *https://www.thinkbrg.com/insihts/publications/pharmaceutical-supply-chain-2013– 2020/;* Van Nuys K, Ribero R, Ryan M., *Estimation of the Share of Net Expenditures on Insulin Captured by U.S. Manufacturers, Wholesalers, Pharmacy Benefit Managers, Pharmacies, and Health Plans from 2014 to 2018,* JAMA Health Forum, 2021, *https://doi.org/10.1001/ jamahealthforum.2021.3409.*

[15] PBM Accountability Project, Understanding the Evolving Business and Revenue Models of PBMs, 2021, *https://www.pbmaccountability.org/_files/ugd/b11210_264612f6b98e 47b3a850205 4f66bb2a1.pdf?index=true.*

[16] CEA White Paper *supra* note 2.

consideration of transparency even though the proposal was supported by HR Policy Association, the AFL–CIO and Consumers Union.[17]

Third, PBMs create and exploit numerous conflicts of interest. PBM rebate schemes create a clear conflict between the PBM and the payor. The payor prefers the lowest cost drug. But to maximize its profits PBMs often prefer the drug with the highest list price. And they often will prevent lower cost drugs such as generics and biosimilars from receiving preferred access on their formularies.

Conflicts of interest also abound because PBMs are vertically integrated with health insurers, mail order operations, specialty pharmacies, and in the case of CVS, the largest retail and specialty pharmacy chain, and the dominant long term care pharmacy. All three PBMs own their own specialty pharmacies, which they favor, discriminating against rival pharmacies. These PBMs steer patients to their own pharmacies as a requirement for patients to access their full prescription benefit. And all three PBMs are owned by or affiliated with the three largest insurance companies—United, Aetna and Cigna. *How can they offer fair contracts to their clients when they have a vested interest in driving traffic to their own pharmacies? Who sets the standards and audits the affiliated pharmacies, and do they have to meet the same standards as the independent pharmacies? Are affiliated pharmacies charged the DIR fees that independent pharmacies pay and have exceeded billions of dollars annually? The fox is guarding the henhouse, and Congress needs to ensure that patients are not paying the price in less choice, inferior service and higher prices.*

---

[17] PCMA Testimony to the ERISA Advisory Council, William J. Kilberg, June 19, 2014 *https://www.dol.gov/sites/dolgov/files/EBSA/about-ebsa/about-us/erisa-advisory-council/2014-pbm-compensation-and-fee-disclosure-kilberg-06–19.pdf;* Consumers Union Testimony, June 12, 2014, *https://www.dol.gov/sites/dolgov/files/EBSA/about-ebsa/about-us/erisa-advisory-council/2014-pbm-compensation-and-fee-disclosure-quincy-06–19.pdf.* I expect that Professor Graithwaite will suggest that that PBM transparency may be harmful because it may lead to collusion. I firmly disagree with that suggestion. First even Professor Graithwaite seems to admit the PBM market may not be competitive. TESTIMONY OF CRAIG L. GARTHWAITE, Ph.D., Before the House Committee on Education and Labor Subcommittee on Health, Employ- ment, Labor, and Pensions On ''Making Health Care More Affordable: Lowering Drug Prices and Increasing Transparency,'' September 26, 2019, at 21, *https://edlabor.house.gov/imo/media/doc/GarthwaiteTestimony0926191.pdf.* Second, although there may be a theoretical argument that excessive transparency can lead to collusion, I think that is rather unlikely in this market. It assumes that buyers will disclose the precise amount of rebates to rival manufacturers. I rep resent payors and based on my experience I doubt that would occur. Moreover, in my 15 years as an antitrust enforcer including working as the FTC Policy Director, I cannot recall a single case where transparency led to the type of collusion the Professor suggests.

A Broken Market Leads to Escalating Drug Costs and Rapidly Increasing PBM Profits

The most significant conflict that leads to escalating drug costs involves PBMs' incentives to maximize the rebates paid by manufacturers to get preferred access on their drug formularies. PBMs were formed to act as honest brokers to negotiate with drug manufacturers for lower prices for payors, but when PBMs share in the rebates that they negotiate, it creates an incentive for them to want higher, not lower, list prices. According to a recent Senate Finance Committee Report, ''PBMs have an incentive for manufacturers to keep list prices high, since the rebates, discounts, and fees PBMs negotiate are based on a percentage of a drug's list price— and PBMs may retain at least a portion of what they negotiate.''[18] PBMs have gone so far as to require additional payments in the event of any reduction in manufacturer list prices.[19]

PBMs' Demand for Rebates Results in Patients Not Having Access to the Most Efficacious and Affordable Medicines that they Need

PBMs base formulary access decisions on the amount of the rebates, which encourages drug manufacturers to focus on offering higher rebates to secure that preferred status. Focusing on rebates gives PBMs incentives to put higher-cost drugs on their formularies, because the rebates are based on a percentage of a drug's list price. In essence, PBMs are making decisions on inclusion of a drug based not on clinical research or evidence-based efficacy and safety, but on which manufacturer offers a higher rebate payment. In pursuit of higher rebates, PBMs routinely deny access to formularies, change drug formularies, or require prior authorization for drugs that may be best for a patient's condition, even in cases where a more affordable medication is available. For example, a PBM often excludes a lower priced generic or biosimilar because the higher priced branded drug offers higher rebates.

As important as cost is the adverse impact on patient health. PBM rebate schemes interfere with doctor-patient relationships, and harm patients' health

[18] Senate Finance Committee. Insulin: Examining the Factors Driving the Rising Cost of a Century Old Drug, 2021, https://www.finance.senate.gov/imo/media/doc/Grassely-Wyden%20 Report%20(FINAL%201).pdf.

[19] Sagonowsky, E., UnitedHealthcare demands drug rebates even if pharma cuts list prices: analyst, February 2019, https://www.fiercepharma.com/pharma/letter-to-pharmas-united health care-seeks-to-protect-drgug-rebates-from-price-reductions.

when they cannot get the drugs they need. PBMs may exclude new innovative drugs that may be less expensive and more effective, in favor of higher rebates.[20] On many occasions PBMs may require patients to go through cumbersome and health-threatening step therapy programs in order to secure the more efficacious drug. As Robin Feldman, a professor at UC Hastings College of Law, puts it, ''the system contains odd and perverse incentives, with the result that higher–priced drugs can receive more favorable health-plan coverage, channeling patients toward more expensive drugs.''[21] Uninsured patients face higher prices and insured patients pay higher coinsurance or pre-deductible out-of-pocket costs when list prices rise.[22]

PBMs use Their Market Dominance to Harm Community Pharmacies

As detailed below, PBMs engage in a long list of egregious, unfair and abusive practices that harm community pharmacies. Community pharmacies simply have no reasonable bargaining power with PBMs who extend contracts on a ''take it or leave it'' basis. You simply have to look no further than pharmacy direct and indirect remuneration fees. As noted above, the PBMs pulled in over $9 billion dollars in these fees in 2022 alone. The foundation for these fees are the inflated price points that were established by PBMs themselves. The fact that these fees skyrocketed from practically nothing to over $9 billion demonstrates the PBMs market dominance. They reap additional fees beyond the $9 billion by way of inflated coinsurance payments by seniors. There is simply no pro-consumer reason to inflate Medicare Part D beneficiaries' coinsurance costs at the point of sale. Never have seniors received a rebate from PBMs for overpayment of their coinsurance.

---

[20] Mariana Socal and Gerard Anderson, Favorable Formulary Placement of Branded Drugs in Medicare Prescription Drug Plans When Generics Are Available, JAMA, March 18, 2018, https://jamanetwork.com/journals/jamainternalmedicine/fullarticle/2728446.

[21] Robin Feldman, Why Prescription Drug Prices Have Skyrocketed? Washington Post, November 26, 2018, https://www.washingtonpost.com/outlook/2018/11/26/why-prescription-drug- prices-have-skyrocketed/.

[22] American Patients First: The Trump Administration Blueprint to Lower Drug Prices and Reduce Out-of-Pocket Costs, U.S. Department of Health and Human Services (''HHS''), May 14, 2018, pg. 17.

Lax Antitrust Enforcement of the PBM Industry Has Led to Widespread Anticompetitive Conduct

The U.S. antitrust agencies have effectively placed PBMs in a regulatory free zone. The Department of Justice Antitrust Division (''DOJ'') and the FTC have failed to take any meaningful enforcement actions, while permitting massive consolidation and anti-consumer practices. In the case of the PBMs' ''gagging'' of pharmacists, preventing them from telling consumers of lower-priced alternatives. The FTC knew about this conduct yet did not act.

As authors from the Institute for Local Self Reliance have observed:

> The FTC was designed to be a forward-thinking agency that would use its investigatory and rule-making authority to stamp out unfair methods of competition and protect the less powerful from fraud and abuse. But the FTC has been quick to dismiss concerns about the impact of concentration on small independent businesses. The agency has presided over an increasingly consolidated economy and has repeatedly embraced vertical integration despite evidence that such industry structures invite self-dealing and inflict harm on small businesses and the communities they serve.[23]

Ten years ago, the FTC faced a critical decision—whether to approve the merger of two of the three largest PBMs—Express Scripts and Medco. Despite the fact the merger violated the Merger Guidelines, and there was strong opposition by employers, unions, pharmacists and consumer groups, and dozens of Congresspersons raising significant competitive concerns, the FTC approved the merger. The Commission statement is illustrative of its misguided views.[24] The Commission suggested that there were ten competitors in the market, yet by this point its list looks more like a list of fossils—a record of firms that have since been acquired or exited the market. The Commission also suggested the concerns of pharmacies were unfounded because they ''negotiate'' contracts with PBMs, but no one with any business sense would

---

[23] Stacey Mitchell and Zach Freed, How the FTC Protected the Market Power of Pharmacy Benefit Managers, February 19, 2021, Pro Market, https://www.promarket.org/2021/02/19/ftc-market-power-pharmacy-benefit-managers/.

[24] Statement of Commission Concerning Proposed Acquisition Medco Health Solutions and Express Scripts, Inc., FTC File No. 111–0210, April 2, 2012, https://www.ftc.gov/sites/default/files/documents/public_statements/statement-commission-concerning-proposed-acquisition-medco-health-solutions-express-scripts-inc./120402expressmedco statement.pdf.

suggest those are anything more than take it or leave it arrangements. The merging parties suggested that the country needed the merger so the merged firm could force down drug prices. The FTC bought into this Faustian bargain, but the real result was skyrocketing prescription drug prices, rebates, and massive profit increases.

The PBMs did secure the market power that the antitrust laws are meant to protect against. Rather than use that market power to effectively lower drug prices they used it to massively increase rebates and rebate schemes. As the following two charts demonstrate, PBMs have taken a majority of any reductions in pharma ceutical drug costs in the form of rebates and fees over the past five years and they are pocketing an increasing portion in profits.

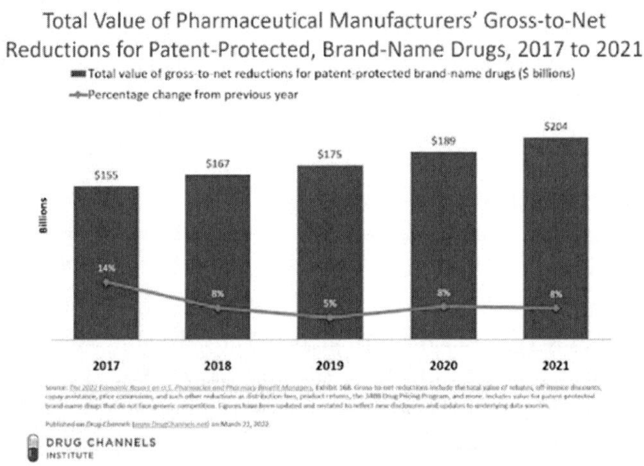

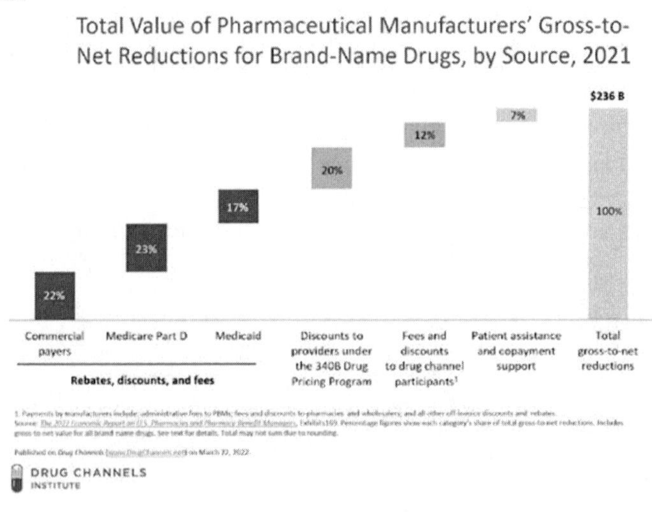

In other words, drug manufacturers are attempting to lower costs through rebates, but an increasing portion of those rebates are being pocketed by the PBMs. They can do that because of the lack of competition, transparency and the conflicts of interest in the system.

Contrast the FTC decision to ‘‘hope’’ creating mega-middlemen would benefit consumers with the DOJ decision five years later to block the Aetna-Humana and Cigna-Anthem mergers. The insurance companies presented many of the same arguments as ESI-Medco—there were lots of competitors, there was little risk of monopsony power because healthcare providers could protect themselves, and the mergers were needed to lower healthcare costs. But the DOJ saw that approving the mergers were a poor bargain for consumers and properly challenged them. Consumers and providers today benefit from competition between the four firms.[25]

Unfortunately, the FTC decision to green light the ESI-Medco merger led to a flood of additional PBM mergers as the major PBMs devoured their smaller rivals and specialty pharmacies. None of these transactions were challenged by the FTC, yet the underlying structural factors were far worse.

The lack of FTC merger enforcement is only the tip of the iceberg of misguided efforts. States have recognized the rampant consumer protection concerns and proposed legislation to regulate PBMs. When states tried to regulate deceptive and anti-consumer conduct of PBMs, the FTC staff sided with the PBMs, suggesting that ‘‘economic theory’’ teaches that PBM-pharmacy and PBM-drug manufacturer relationships result in lower prices and that regulation would harm consumers.[26] For example, the FTC has consistently opposed PBM transparency even though both Republican and Democratic Administrations have been strong advocates for healthcare transparency. In many cases, the FTC staff has relied on an outdated 2005 FTC mail order study, which Commissioner Julie Brill acknowledged was ‘‘antiquated.’’[27] Ultimately, many states rejected the FTC advocacy and adopted state regulations, but the broad statements in the FTC’s own advocacy

[25] Unfortunately, the DOJ allowed CVS to acquire Aetna, Inc. and Cigna, Inc. to acquire Express Scripts, Inc. in 2019.

[26] FTC Press Release, FTC Staff: Mississippi Bill That Would Give State Pharmacy Board Authority Over PBMS Likely Would Increase Prices, March 22, 2011, https://www.ftc.gov/news-events/news/press-releases/2011/03/ftc-staff-mississippi-bill-would-give-state-pharmacy-board-authority-over-pbms-likely-increase.

[27] See Commissioner Brill’s Letter to the ERISA Advisory Council, August 19, 2014, available at https://www.ftc.gov/system/files/documents/public_statements/579031/140819 erisa letter.pdf.

hamper the ability of states or Federal regulators to engage in meaningful PBM regulation.

One of the reasons the FTC advocacy and nonenforcement has missed the mark is that it has focused on the wrong set of consumers—payors rather than patients. With the vertical integration of the three largest PBMs with an insurer, a lowering of cost to the insurer through a sharing of rebates and other revenue does not directly equate to lower prices for patients taking prescription drugs. Under the current system, vulnerable patients are left to pay artificially high prices when their cost sharing is tied to the undiscounted list price of a medicine, rather than the lower net price the PBMs and insurers pay. And uninsured patients are in an even worse predicament. That is why consumer groups and unions supported reform of PBM rebates in the prior Administration.

The lack of enforcement has harmed pharmacies, and this has a direct impact on consumers. I know as a consumer advocate that consumers place tremendous value on their access to community pharmacies. Community pharmacists are consistently ranked as our most trusted health care professionals. And community pharmacies are often the most accessible form of health care services in underserved rural or inner-city markets. Community pharmacies provide essential advice and health care monitoring especially for patients taking specialty drugs. Yet despite receiving hundreds of complaints from community pharmacies for the egregious and deceptive actions by PBMs, the FTC has never brought an enforcement action. Not even one. Just one example of egregious non-enforcement involves the numerous allegations that large PBMs are engaging in predatory pricing activities through the use of retrospective Direct and Indirect Remuneration (''DIR'') and related fees. In practice, these fees depress reimbursement rates to pharmacies. In some cases, PBMs ''claw back'' more than the pharmacy initially received for the prescription, resulting in a net loss to the pharmacy.[28] In fact, PBM claw backs of pharmacy revenue has been increasing each year, causing significant financial strain on these small businesses.[29] The FTC, however, has not prevented PBMs from engaging in these predatory acts. Congress should ask what the basis for these fees is and how they benefit consumers, and why they have increased so dramatically.

---

[28] Markian Hawryluk, The Last Drugstore: Rural America is Losing Its Pharmacies, WASH. POST (Nov. 10, 2021), https://www.washingtonpost.com/business/2021/11/10/drugstore-short-age-rural-america/.

[29] Id.

Moreover, PBMs have engaged in a variety of practices that fundamentally can be defined as theft from the pharmacies, ultimately to the detriment of patients. For example, in 2018, the Ohio State Auditor audited its Medicaid Prescription Drug Program and found that the difference between what independent pharmacies are paid and what PBMs report back to the plans, commonly referred to as the ''spread,'' had been growing. However, this growth in savings failed to translate into lower costs for the state.[30] The Auditor further described that the spreads, which resulted in reimbursement cuts to local providers, actually turned into PBM profits.[31] The Ohio Pharmacist Association explained that ''[b]eing that PBMs also own their own pharmacies, this essentially amounts to one pharmacy company reaching into the pockets of competitors, pulling out cash, and putting it right into their own. Regardless of the intent, this warped incentive has absolutely no place in a fair, competitive marketplace.''[32] Again, the FTC has failed to act despite numerous examples of this type of behavior.

And, because antitrust agencies have allowed PBMs to vertically integrate with insurers, mail order operations, and pharmacies, PBMs have financial incentives, and the necessary market power, to steer patients to their affiliated services.[33] Since PBMs have their own pharmacies (indeed the largest pharmacy chain CVS owns the second largest PBM) PBMs frequently access rival pharmacy patient data and provide it to their pharmacy affiliate in an effort to steer patients away from rivals. Patients may be forced into PBM-owned mail order or 1–800 specialty pharmacy operations that provide an inferior level of service to competing community pharmacies and specialized pharmacies like AIDS Healthcare Foundation pharmacies.[34] Or the PBMs may engage in egregious auditing practices to harm rival pharmacies.

---

[30] See Pharmacy Middlemen Made $223.7 Million From Ohio Medicaid, Kaitlin Schroeder, June 23, 2018, Dayton Daily News, https://www.daytondailynews.com/news/pharmacy-middlemen-made-223-from-ohio-medicaid/JsPLtbs3wfKoBmaGbF9GrK/.

[31] Id.

[32] Ohio Pharmacist Association Press Release, Ohio Auditor releases stunning Medicaid PBM audit report, https://www.ohiopharmacists.org/aws/OPA/pt/sd/news_article/184063/_PARENT/layout_interior_details/false.

[33] Vertical Integration Isn't Great for Health Care Consumers or Purchasers, PURCHASER BUSINESS GROUP ON HEALTH (Aug. 23, 2021) available at https://www.pbgh.org/despite-claims-vertical-integration-isnt-great-for-health-care-consumers-or-purchasers/.

[34] Dr. Michael Wohlfeiler of the AIDS Healthcare Foundation testified in the CVS-Aetna Tunney Act proceeding that the merger could endanger HIV and AIDS patients because the merged firm could steer its ''patients to leave HIV and AIDS specific treatment providers for providers that are unequipped to treat those conditions.'' United States v. CVS Health Corp., 407 F. Supp. 3d 45, 57 (D.D.C. 2019). AHF has created an extraordinarily successful model for delivery of care to HIV/AIDS patients, a one stop shop model in

PBMs ''offer'' independent pharmacies ''take it or leave it'' contracts, where a pharmacy must choose between accepting unfavorable reimbursement terms, or exclusion from the PBM's network (and patient population). In some cases, pharmacies are coerced into agreeing to below-cost reimbursement. This unsustainable choice has forced many pharmacies to close their doors.[35] This has caused what has been characterized as ''pharmacy deserts'' and has disproportionately harmed rural and urban African American and Hispanic populations that now lack pharmacies because PBMs have driven the independents out of business, but these PBMs do not put new pharmacies in these locations and instead they steer patients to mail order or long distance driving.[36] This is a significant problem for these vulnerable patients because no group of healthcare providers is as accessible, service oriented and dedicated as community pharmacies.[37] A community pharmacist is there to serve the patients and make sure they get the right prescription at the lowest cost. That is why consumer and patient groups have consistently supported the advocacy efforts of community pharmacies and their requests for PBM reform. The FTC has heard these concerns but has chosen not to take any action to prevent PBM predatory behavior designed to eliminate pharmacy competition. Patients lose when community pharmacies are handcuffed in the competitive battle.

And, when state legislatures try to pass basic reform laws to protect independent pharmacies and consumers from predatory practices of PBMs, the PBMs, without fail, bring lawsuits to challenge such statutes based on ERISA (the Employee Retirement Income Security Act of 1974) pre-emption. Recently, such PBM reform passed by the State of Arkansas, which guaranteed that Arkansas pharmacists would be reimbursed by PBMs for the dispensing of drugs at least the amount of their wholesale cost, was challenged

---

which AHF functions as a testing, linkage, specialist, health insurer, pharmacy, and price care facility. Patient steering to cookie-cutter models results in fragmentation of care, inferior quality of care, and severance of trusted pro- vider relationships, which is very problematic for vulnerable patients with chronic conditions like HIV.

[35] Markian Hawryluk, The Last Drugstore: Rural America is Losing Its Pharmacies, WASH. POST (Nov. 10, 2021), https://www.washingtonpost.com/business/2021/11/10/drugstore-short- age-rural-america/.

[36] Id., Stacy Mitchell and Charlie Thaxton, The Rebirth of Independent Pharmacies Could Cure Rural Ills, The American Conservative, November 5, 2019, https://www.theamerican conservative.com/articles/the-rebirth-of-independent-pharmacies/.

[37] See, Stacy Mitchell, Small Pharmacies Beat Big Chains at Delivering Vaccines. Don't Look So Shocked, Washington Post, February 5, 2021, https://www.washingtonpost.com/outlook/small-pharmacies-beat-big-chains-at-delivering-vaccines-dont-look-so-shocked/2021/02/05/6bb3 07ec-671b-11eb-886d-5264d4ceb46d□story.html.

by the PCMA. This lawsuit culminated in a unanimous decision by the U.S. Supreme Court that such PBM reform legislation aimed at protecting independent pharmacies in the wake of PBM oppression is not pre-empted by ERISA. See Rutledge v. PCMA, 141 Sp. Ct. 474 (2020). While consumers hold out hope that such state protections could open a fair playing field for pharmacies, PBMs have found ways to circumvent such laws resulting in more invasive pharmacy audits, network exclusions and increased pharmacy terminations.

Legislative Action to Prevent PBM Abuse

We are at a crucial turning point on PBMs. It is increasingly evident that these middlemen are significantly increasing drug costs and reducing access because of clear market failures and a lack of meaningful regulation. We can ill afford middlemen that extract $28 billion in profits or $9 billion in DIR fees and increasingly deny consumers access to the lowest price and most efficacious drugs and the most effective pharmacy services.

This Committee should consider amending the FTC Act to specify certain practices that harm consumers and competition as ''unfair or deceptive acts or practices'' and ''unfair methods of competition.'' Congress established the FTC to use a broad range of powers including enforcement and regulation to prevent and proscribe practices that were harmful to the marketplace. In doing so, Congress established a flexible standard in which it has occasionally proscribed certain practices as an ''unfair or deceptive act or practice.''

This Committee should evaluate what practices should be considered for potential enforcement. Some of the practices that should be considered include:

- Failing to pass on all rebates and clawbacks to payors and patients;
- Basing PBM compensation on the price of a drug;
- Schemes that prevent lower priced drugs from being included on a formulary or being placed in a disadvantageous position;
- Discrimination in reimbursement to pharmacies;
- Forcing pharmacies to dispense below acquisition cost;
- Failing to disclose DIR and other associated fees; and
- Discriminatory practices against community pharmacies.

The FTC should be given broad rule making power to address these practices. In addition, the Commission should be instructed to use its 6b power to study past PBM mergers including the ESI-Medco merger. Congress should use all its powers to insure this is a major priority for the FTC.

Concluding Thoughts

The dominant PBMs play a significant role in driving up prescription drug prices, reducing patient choice of medicines that they need, and lessening competition among pharmacies. Patients care deeply about rising healthcare costs, including out-of-pocket costs for prescription drugs, as well as ensuring they can access the medicines that they need. If PBMs continue to evade FTC scrutiny, they will continue to engage in egregious conduct that is fraudulent, deceptive, and anticompetitive. What health plans and employers should fundamentally be purchasing is the service of an honest broker to secure the lowest prices and best services from both pharmaceutical manufacturers and pharmacies. When PBMs exist in a regulatory- free environment, the result is misaligned incentives and inherent conflicts of interest. Fraud, deception, anticompetitive conduct, higher prices, and reduced choice harms payors, including the government and taxpayers, and, most importantly, patients, who rely on access to lifesaving and life-managing prescription drugs.

I look forward to answering any questions.

Senator BLUMENTHAL. Thank you so much, Mr. Balto. And now, Mr. Garthwaite.

Statement of Craig L. Garthwaite, Ph.D., Professor of Strategy, Herman Smith Research Professor in Hospital and Health Services Management, Director of Program on Healthcare at Kellogg (HCAK), Kellogg School of Management, Northwestern University

Mr. GARTHWAITE. Thank you, Chairman Blumenthal and Ranking Member Blackburn for inviting me today. As we discussed, the high and rising price of pharmaceuticals attracts a deservedly large amount of attention from policymakers, the press, and citizens across the United States.

Many point to these high prices as evidence of a clearly broken market. However, it is not clear that is obviously true. High pharmaceutical prices represent a fundamental tradeoff that sits at the center of the U.S. health care market. New drugs are developed through a risky and expensive process where we ask private firms to provide enormous amounts of capital at risk to fund scientific progress.

Evidence of the progress in this field abounds as we now treat huge numbers of diseases that previously would have been death sentences. In order to generate the incentives to make these investments, we provide innovative firms with time limited periods of market exclusivity where they have the ability to charge higher prices. These higher prices do decrease access to medications today. However, we tradeoff that lack of access today in order to get new drugs in the future. In this way, the system provides access in the future to people who have no treatments available at any price today. And while there are many potential current concerns about our existing pharmaceutical system, a critical point is that the high prices today need to generate sufficient returns to generate new products in the future.

If instead, these firms are captured or dissipated by other people in the pharmaceutical supply chain, our existing system may not provide the optimal incentives. Understanding whether firms are capturing this value requires more context about prices in the pharmaceutical supply chain. In the U.S., there are many prices associated with prescription drugs, as we have talked about already.

Of particular importance in today's hearing is that there is a publicly available list price that is set by the manufacturer. Payers, such as insurers or large employers, then employ pharmacy benefit managers to, among other things, negotiate rebates or discounts from this list price. And that leads us to the focus of the hearing today, these PBMs or pharmacy benefit managers.

As Chairman Blumenthal noted, most Americans have no clue what a PBM is, but they are central to everything about pharmaceutical distribution and insurance in the United States. They take their relatively obscure position in the market, but they control everything about our access to drugs. In return for those activities, PBMs do earn revenue through a variety of means.

A primary concern, then, is whether they capture too much value through those means. And given the high concentration in the market that David Balto spoke about, and increasing amounts of vertical integration, it is logical people should be concerned about a possibility of where the market is providing an efficient outcome. One primary area of concern are these list prices and rebates in the system, which directly cause higher consumer cost sharing payments. Given PBMs often receive their payments as a function of the list price, the pitch—the push for high list prices is seen as abuse by PBMs of the market. But like many things in health care, the reality is likely far more complex.

Plan sponsors, these insurers and these large employers, use the system of rebates and high cost sharing as a way to decrease the premiums for their insurance products. This is done to make the products more competitive and to help them gain share in the market. The result of that is that we are witnessing, through rebates and cost sharing, a reintroduction of the concept of medical underwriting in health insurance that was taken away by the Affordable Care Act.

Through a combination of predictable cost sharing payments and high premiums, individuals with chronic conditions such as diabetes and those with expensive acute conditions such as cancer are paying more for insurance so healthy people can pay less. It is important to note this does not appear to be driven independently by the PBMs. Instead, it is driven by the demands of their clients.

PBMs have long offered contracts to these plan sponsors where rebates were passed along to the customer at the point of sale. Plan sponsors have routinely ignored these contracts in favor of capturing high rebates. That fact should influence policy. If we are worried about high list prices leading to high cost sharing, we should attack that directly through Congressional action.

That said, there are also features of the markets where PBMs do appear to be exploiting a lack of transparency. For example, we are now seeing increasingly administrative fees that are a function of the list price. Those are often not apparent to the plan's sponsor. They do not have insight into the amount of money that is going between the manufacturer of the pharmaceutical and the pharmacy benefit manager.

And given that those fees are a function of the list price, you may be concerned that PBMs are taking advantage of that lack of transparency. In my testimony, I identify ways in which we can try and improve transparency to allow more complete contract negotiations between plan sponsors and PBMs. It should be clear that PBMs do play a valuable role in the market. They are counterpoint to the market power of innovative pharmaceutical firms. It is important we provide them with the tools to negotiate these lower prices.

That said, any compensation they get should reflect their unique contribution to the market. As a closing point, I will agree with what the chairman and the ranking member said, we just lack insight in many ways into the PBM market.

And so, Ranking Member Blackburn, I am heartened to hear that you have a bill to have the GAO look more into this because without more information about how PBMs interact with manufacturers and PBMs interact with the plan sponsors that they are giving rebates to, we simply are not going to be able to develop good policy in this area. Thank you very much.

[The prepared statement of Mr. Garthwaite follows:]

Prepared Statement of Craig L. Garthwaite, Ph.D., Professor of Strategy, Herman Smith Research Professor in Hospital and Health Services Management, Director of Program on Healthcare at Kellogg (HCAK), Kellogg School of Management, Northwestern University

In contrast to other developed countries, the United States relies more heavily on private markets to finance and provide healthcare services. This use of economic markets is not a policy accident and instead reflects an intentional belief that market-based healthcare provides many advantages. A large and diverse country such as the United States has a wide variety of preferences and meaningful differences in the willingness to pay for quality. In this setting, the central planning inherent to regulated prices is unlikely to maximize welfare, and an economic market is the superior method of allocating goods and services. This is even more true once we consider the variety of economic actors necessary for the development of innovative new healthcare products and services. It is hard to imagine what omniscient actor could balance the forces necessary to promote value creating innovations more efficiently than the market.

Therefore, despite many contentions to the contrary, a market-based system remains the best mechanism for providing the appropriate incentives for long term welfare maximization in the U.S. healthcare market. However, relying on the market for the provision of such a vital set of goods and services requires both recognizing that healthcare markets, like any other market, can fail and that all markets require vigilant protection of the structures and institutions necessary to promote robust and vigorous competition.

Concerns about the appropriate role for markets in healthcare are perhaps most frequently discussed in the world of pharmaceuticals. These discussions are motivated by high and rising pharmaceutical prices. While many claim these high prices provide prima facie evidence of a market failure, in reality they are the result of the complex and delicate balancing of incentives that sits at the center of the U.S. healthcare market.

This delicate balance is necessary because market failures at the center of the innovative process for developing new drugs requires some degree of market intervention in the first place. This failure results from that fact that the scientific advancements generated by firms developing innovative pharmaceutical products are essentially a public good, i.e., the knowledge is effectively non-rival and non-excludable.[38] Rational firms realize they will be unlikely to capture a sufficient amount of the value generated by the large, fixed, and sunk investments necessary to bring a product to market. This results in an economic phenomenon known as ''hold up'' whereby firms, absent some form of government intervention, are unwilling to make value creating investments in the first place.

To address this initial market failure, governments offer various forms of intellectual property protection. Through patents or other forms of market exclusivity, governments arm firms with time limited periods of enhanced market power that allow them to capture a larger portion of the value created by their innovative products. During this limited time period, higher prices than would otherwise exist curtail some access to valuable medicines. This reduced access is deliberately traded off for the development of new products in the future.[39] These new products, however, provide access to patients for whom there would otherwise be no available treatments. In this way, policies governing the development of pharmaceutical products involve trading off the static inefficiency of reduced access to products today in order to create the dynamic efficiency of the increased development of new products. To the extent the value created by the new products exceeds the welfare losses resulting from the high prices (and decreased quantity), the granting of these

---

[38] The degree to which this is fully a public good depends on how much information can be gleaned from the actual product, the regulatory filings, and the published research. For exam- ple, small molecule products can be more easily reverse engineered and therefore absent intel- lectual property protections are relatively easier to copy. Biologic products, however, have a more complex production process and therefore copying the technology is easier than making the product *de novo* but harder than for a small molecule product.

[39] In considering this tradeoff it is important to consider the role of health insurance in miti- gating decreased quantity resulting from high prices. To the extent that insurance mitigates some of this quantity decline it is possible that the welfare loss are smaller than would be ex- pected. See D. Lackdawalla and N. Sood, ''Health Insurance as a Two-Part Pricing Contract,'' *Journal of Public* Economics, 2013, 102: 1–12.

periods of market exclusivity is welfare enhancing. This could be true even if the prices today are quite high.

This tradeoff is a source of much of the controversy surrounding prescription drug prices because it involves some number of readily identifiable individuals who are unable to access existing and potentially life-saving medications.[40] Unsurprisingly, this particular form of a lack of access garners large amounts of press and political attention. However, it is critical to remember a perhaps far greater access problem for patients suffering from conditions for which no treatment options exist at all.[41] For these individuals, there is no price at which they can purchase a treatment. These patients will gain access in the future only as a result of the dynamic incentives created by intellectual property protection. As we consider the optimality of policies governing the pharmaceutical market, we must balance the oft-discussed need for access to existing products with the less-discussed lack of access from the absence of effective treatments.

A central parameter of this tradeoff of static and dynamic incentives is the relationship between the elevated prices paid for prescription drugs today and the incentives of innovative firms to develop new products in the future. Economic research has clearly documented a relationship between increased market size and investments in research and development.[42] Therefore, to the extent high prices signal expected economic returns for the providers of the risk-based capital necessary for innovation then the prices could represent a welfare enhancing policy choice. However, if the revenue generated by high drug prices is instead captured by other parts of the value chain there are valid concerns that our current policies are not providing an optimal level of innovation to outweigh the welfare losses from the price related reduced access.

---

[40] Garthwaite, Craig, and Benedic Ippolito. 2019. ''Drug pricing conversations must take the cost of innovation into consideration.'' STAT. January 11.

[41] This is particularly true because the impact of high prices on quantity is far more complicated in a world of widely available health insurance. Those who are insured may not suffer as much decreased access as they would in a market without third party payment. However, those for whom drugs do not exist certainly will not access a treatment at any price.

[42] D. Acemoglu and J. Linn. 2004. ''Market Size in Innovation: Theory and Evidence from the Pharmaceutical Industry,'' *The Quarterly Journal of Economics,* 119(3): 1049–1090; A. Finkelstein, ''Static and Dynamic Effects of Health Policy: Evidence from the Vaccine Industry,'' *Quarterly Journal of Economics,* 119(2): 527–564; Dubois *et al.,* 2015''Market size and pharma- ceutical innovation,'' *RAND Journal of Economics,* 46(4): 844–871; and Dranove, Garthwaite and Hermosilla, 2020. ''Pharmaceutical Profits and the Scientific Novelty of Innovation,'' *NBER Working Paper #27093.*

Determining the optimality of this tradeoff in today's market requires a more careful understanding of the pharmaceutical supply chain. In particular, it is important to understand how various firms capture a share of the value created by innovative pharmaceutical products. provides a broad overview of this supply chain and the flow of funds across firms at its various stages. Perhaps most important for today's hearing is the relationship between manufacturers, payers, and pharmacy benefit mangers (PBM), which is depicted in the figure's upper right corner.

While largely unknown to customers, PBMs are the private firms that effectively manage all aspects of insurance coverage for pharmaceuticals. Despite their relative lack of attention, these firms occupy a central role in nearly every facet of the pharmaceutical distribution and insurance market. At a high level, PBMs sign contracts with plan sponsors (e.g., risk bearing health insurers or employers) to undertake activities such as negotiating drug prices, establishing pharmacy networks, processing pharmaceutical claims, and developing drug formularies.

In return for these activities, PBMs earn revenue through a variety of means. These include, but are not limited to, direct per member per month (PMPM) fees paid by plan sponsors, the ability to keep a negotiated share of the rebate (i.e., the discount from the manufacturer that the PBM is able to negotiate), spread pricing (i.e., the difference between what a PBM is paid by a plan sponsor for a drug and what they pay to the pharmacy to fill the prescription), and various administrative fees from manufacturers.

The primary role of PBMs is to help manage the static inefficiency resulting from high prices. Historically, these firms emerged to implement some degree of managed care and negotiation to the pharmaceutical benefit offered by plan sponsors. In particular, they allowed relatively small insurers to pool together and negotiate as a group against manufacturers.[43] By constructing formularies, PBMs negotiate lower prices and can increase access to products and potentially to insurance overall. Of course, such activities limit revenues to pharmaceutical manufacturers and have been shown to blunt incentives to develop new products.[44] This demonstrates the importance of the role of PBMs in the tradeoff central to drug development.

[43] Z. Brot-Goldberg, C. Che, and B. Handel, "Pharmacy Benefit Managers and Vertical Relationships in Drug Supply: State of Current Research," *NBER Working Paper #29959,* April 2022.

[44] L. Agha, S. Kim, and D. Li, "Insurance Design and Pharmaceutical Innovation," *forthcoming American Economic Review: Insights.*

It is important to note that if the construction of formularies represents the preferences of consumers for access to new products, a reduction in innovative activity is not necessarily a problem. After all, our goal is to maximize welfare not innovation. However, if the reduction of revenues to manufacturers comes instead from PBMs capturing an inappropriately large fraction of spending as profits—there could be concerns about whether the pharmaceutical market is operating in a way that maximizes welfare. In particular, concerns about whether the welfare losses from the lack of access today are sufficiently offset by incentives to develop new products in the future. These concerns are central to today's hearing investigating the PBM market.

Concerns about this possibility stem from features of the existing market. For example, the PBM market is dominated by three large firms—Caremark, Express Scripts and OptumRX. Figure 2 contains the market share of each of these firms in 2021 and shows that these firms comprise approximately 80 percent of all volume in this market. Beyond concentration, there have also been changes in the vertical structure of this industry over time as each of these PBMs is now part of a larger firm that also owns health insurers, specialty pharmacies, and medical providers. The degree of vertical integration can be seen in Figure 3.[45] These concerns are magnified by the relative opacity of the process by which pharmaceutical prices are determined. While none of these market features (i.e., the high concentration, increased vertical integration, or opaque pricing) provide clear evidence of a potential problem they are areas that should be investigated. This is likely why this market has attracted the attention of a variety of regulators and policymakers.

Given these concerns, I will concentrate my testimony today on the relationships between plan sponsors (i.e., third party payers such as insurers and employers), PBMs, and manufacturers. In particular, I will focus on the degree to which features of these relationships may allow PBMs to capture more value than might be appropriate or whether negative features of the market instead reflect the actions and incentives of firms in other parts of the value chain.

A consistent point to consider throughout my testimony is that any analysis of this market is meaningfully hampered by a lack of information about numerous features of the contractual arrangements between the various types of firms. While it is easy to identify potential areas of concern, without more information about the nature of these arrangements it is difficult to truly

[45] In earlier testimony, I discussed the potential benefits and concerns of this vertical integration. This testimony is available at: *https://www.judiciary.senate.gov/download/garthwaite-tes-timony*.

understand the validity of such concerns. Therefore, Congressional action in this area should be initially focused on creating more insight for regulators into these areas. That said, I will also highlight several policy options that exist to more directly confront potentially undesirable features of the current pharmaceutical market without generating unintended consequences.

I. Pricing, Rebates, and Cost Sharing in the U.S. Pharmaceutical Market

In the U.S., there are many prices associated with pharmaceutical products. Of particular importance to today's hearing, pharmaceutical products have a publicly available list price that is set by the manufacturer. Payers then employ PBMs to, among other things, negotiate rebates (i.e., discounts from list prices) on the pharmaceuticals purchased by their enrollees.

PBMs are able to secure the discounts based on their ability to shift customers across competing therapeutic substitutes. For example, if there are two brand-name statin medications that treat high cholesterol, the PBM can place the product from a manufacturer offering a lower net price on a more preferential tier of its formulary, thus lowering the out-of-pocket payments from an individual enrollee when they purchase the drug. This should result in this product selling higher quantity, albeit at a lower price. In extreme cases, a PBM could entirely exclude a product from its formulary if the manufacturer is unwilling to provide a sufficiently low net price (i.e., they are unwilling to pay the PBM a sufficiently large rebate). The use of exclusion lists has grown in recent years. Figure 4 shows the number of products that are excluded by the largest PBMs. It is this ability to credibly threaten to move volume across products that results in larger discounts from the list price.

The increased use of strict formularies and exclusion lists has contributed to a growing spread between the list and the net (i.e., post rebate) price. Figure 5 depicts these prices from 2014—2020 and documents a large spread between the publicly known and often discussed list prices and the actual prices received by manufacturers. This figure demonstrates that any discussion of list prices provides an, at best, incomplete picture of the returns to innovative manufacturers in this market.

The spread between list and net prices has resulted in a large amount of total rebates in the system. Figure 6 shows that in 2016, pharmaceutical manufacturers paid total rebates of approximately $127 billion—an increase of 108 percent ($66 billion) since 2011. The recent rise is larger in both absolute and relative terms than the history of this market. From 2007 to 2011, the total magnitude of these rebates increased only 42 percent, for a total increase of $18 billion.

While the increasing magnitude of rebates in the system is often discussed in a negative light, it is not necessarily a problem. After all, higher rebates could simply reflect more sophisticated or effective bargaining by PBMs. The ultimate question is which parties in the supply chain capture the value of those rebates and what features of the market determines the ability of those firms to capture that amount of value. The split of the rebate between the PBM and the payer is dictated by a contract that is the result of a bilateral negotiation between those firms. The specifics of this contract depends on the relative bargaining power of the two parties. Figure 7 contains estimates of the existing contractual structure in the commercial market with respect to rebates over time based on whether plan sponsors are large or small employers. From 2014–2018, there has been a marked increase in employers with PBM contracts that entitle them to receive 100 percent of the rebates. By that year a majority of both types of employers were using such contracts.

Unsurprisingly, PBMs often point to increasing rebates as evidence of their effectiveness. It is not clear this is accurate. After all, a large rebate can come from a higher list price, a lower net price, or a combination of both. If rebates are only the result of higher list prices then the actual price paid in the market (and the return to manufacturers) has not necessarily changed. It is tempting to think that in that situation the high list prices have little economic effect. However, even in contracts where 100 percent of the rebate flows to the plan sponsor, higher list prices can negatively impact other market participants.

In particular, high list prices can have direct and economically meaningful impacts on consumer out-of-pocket payments. This relationship between cost sharing and list prices results from the desire to maintain the confidentiality of negotiated prices. Such confidentiality provides stronger incentives for larger discounts. For this reason, the size of rebates paid to each PBM is kept strictly confidential, up to and including onerous audit restrictions in the contracts that limit the ability of the payer to monitor the financial activities of the PBM.[46]

To maintain this confidentiality, consumers whose cost sharing for pharmaceutical products is tied to prices (either because of a deductible or percentage based coinsurance) make these cost sharing payments as a function

[46] Weinberg, Neil, and Robert Langreth. 2017. "Inside the 'Scorpion Room' Where Drug Price Secrets Are Guarded." Bloomberg. May 4.

of the list rather than the net price.[47] Thus, any inefficiencies that create incentives for higher list prices (even if those are entirely offset by rebates) affect consumer out of pocket spending.[48] In the presence of liquidity constraints, this cost sharing could meaningfully reduce access to drugs in ways that magnify the static inefficiency of high drug prices. For this reason, high cost-sharing is not simply a financial inconvenience for consumers. Recent evidence has shown that increased cost sharing for consumers results in the decreased use of prescription drugs and increased mortality.[49]

The importance of cost sharing for prescription drugs has grown over time. Consider the evidence in Figure 8, which contains the average annual out of pocket payment for Medicare patients purchasing insulin. According to these data, in 2018 nearly 30 percent of Medicare patients purchasing insulin were paying more than $5,000 per year out of pocket. This is a marked increase from 2010 where less than 5 percent of those customers had that level of cost sharing.

Insulin is not the only place where we see high cost-sharing. Overall, prescription drugs enjoy far less insurance coverage than other parts of healthcare. Figure 9 shows that insured patients are exposed to only 3 percent of their hospital spending. In contrast, patients directly pay 15 percent of their prescription drug spending out of pocket.

Given the negative health and financial effects of high cost-sharing, it is at first puzzling why such high cost-sharing persists in the market. Cost sharing is intended to be a form of utilization management that attempts to overcome the potential moral hazard arising from patients that are fully insured for their pharmaceutical purchases. This moral hazard could occur both through the overconsumption of products where the price exceeds value or more often from purchasing products that have less expensive therapeutic substitutes. Both of these would be negative features of an insurance product that cost sharing was intended to mitigate. The ability to use cost-sharing to move patients across products is a key tool that PBMs use to negotiate lower net prices from manufacturers. However, we increasingly see high cost-sharing on products that are unlikely to be overconsumed (e.g., insulin and oral oncology products) or in areas where there are no therapeutic substitutes.

---

47 This is mainly an issue for consumers enrolled in certain high-deductible health plans, as well as Medicare beneficiaries.

48 While the number of consumers with this type of cost-sharing has grown, it should be noted that customers in the pharmaceutical market are largely shielded from list prices.

49 A. Chandra, E. Flack, and Z. Obermeyer, "The Health Costs of Cost-Sharing," *NBER Working Paper #28439,* February 2021.

This suggests this high cost-sharing serves goals other than simply utilization management.

It is not obvious that cost-sharing at the levels we observe is an independent strategic choice PBMs undertake to maximize their profits. After all, if plan sponsors desired less onerous cost-sharing they certainly could instruct their PBMs to construct such a formulary. In fact, in recent testimony before Senate Finance Committee, Cigna's Chief Clinical Officer noted that formularies which pass rebates along to customers at the point of sale have existed for many years but have failed to gain traction with plan sponsors.[50]

Instead of signing contracts that pass rebates to customers, plan sponsors increasingly demand higher rebates from PBMs—even when those rebates are not associated with lower prices.[51] Such rebates come from surging list prices and contribute to higher cost sharing payments by patients. It appears that this is because the combination of large rebate payments and high cost-sharing for expensive products provides a mechanism for plan sponsors to offer lower premiums to healthy patients and higher expected costs to sick patients requiring expensive medications.

Consider the stylized example in 0 where a consumer in the deductible period pays the full list price of the drug. This customer does not benefit from any of the negotiation efforts of the PBM. Both the PBM and plan sponsor, however, can profit from the consumer's purchase of a prescription drug because these firms still collect a rebate when one of their patients buys a pharmaceutical product. This is true even when the product is entirely paid for by the patient. A similar logic exists when a patient makes a very large cost sharing payment because of coinsurance. Sponsors are then able to use those extra rebate dollars to lower premiums or decrease the cost of employer provided healthcare. In this way, high cost sharing combined with large rebates reintroduces medical underwriting and unwinds the community rating of health insurance premiums.

This stylized example is not simply an academic exercise. In a recent Senate Finance Committee report on insulin pricing, the Eli Lilly CFO for Diabetes noted that PBMs reacted negatively to a potential lower list price product because their customers (i.e., plan sponsors) reported that "such

---

50 https://www.finance.senate.gov/imo/media/doc/Cigna%20ExpressScripts%20Testimony%20of%20Steven%20Miller%20MD.pdf.

51 https://www.finance.senate.gov/imo/media/doc/Grassley-Wyden%20Insulin%20Report%20(FINAL%201).pdf.

adjustment may impair market competitiveness (i.e., rebate levels on lower gross price levels translating to higher plan premiums.''[52]

Understanding these dynamics is important in considering the causal role of PBMs with respect to increasing list prices and rebates. It suggests that much of the furor at PBMs over increasing list prices, rebates, and cost sharing may be aimed at the wrong target. If such contractual features are being dictated by PBM clients (i.e., plan sponsors) than regulators should more carefully consider the incentives of those plan sponsors when constructing policy in this area. Furthermore, as I discuss below, if the concern about high list prices is primarily motivated by the effect on cost sharing there are policies that can be considered which more directly address this cost sharing.

II. Lack of Transparency in Financial Relationships in the Value Chain

While a large portion of plan sponsors have signed contracts that allow them to collect all of the rebates associated with prescription drug purchases by their customers, there are still many contracts where the PBM receives a percentage of the rebate as compensation. In addition, PBMs collect other fees that I discuss below which are also a function of the list price. Some have proposed that this provides a perverse incentive for the PBM to prefer higher list priced products where there is a large rebate compared to even lower prices products with a smaller rebate.

The concern about PBMs being attracted to higher-priced drugs can be best demonstrated by a simple example. Consider a drug that currently has a list price of $100. The manufacturer proposes to the PBM a 20 percent list price increase—resulting in a new list price of $120, which is initially paid by the payer (i.e., employer or fully funded insurer). The manufacturer also proposes to increase the rebate paid to the PBM by $15, resulting in a net price increase of only 5 percent (i.e., the number that is reported in charts such the one shown in Exhibit 6). However, the PBM is only required by its contract to transfer 50 percent of rebates to the payer, meaning it keeps $7.50 of the rebate and the payer gets $7.50. Therefore, the payer spends $12.50 more, with $5 going to the manufacturer and $7.50 for the PBM.

---

52 *https://www.finance.senate.gov/imo/media/doc/Grassley-Wyden%20Insulin%20Report%20(FINAL%201).pdf.*

Ultimately, the unanswered question is whether the $7.50 collected by the PBM in this example represents ''too much'' surplus or instead is the appropriate payment for its negotiating activities. In a well-functioning competitive market, we would expect that if the $7.50 the PBM captures from the example above represents too much of the surplus, the PBM would ultimately face competition from another firm offering a better contract to the payer. Such a contract would propose to decrease the total spending to the payer. However, this requires a market with multiple PBMs actively competing for contracts, a situation that may not exist in the current concentrated PBM market. Price competition between PBMs also may not emerge if the existing firms realize there are large barriers to entry and that incumbent firms would be better off not actively engaging in price wars to gain share.

Strong competition is even less likely to emerge if payers are unaware of the full scope of surplus created by their prescriptions. As discussed above, many large firms hire sophisticated benefit consultants and increasingly demand fully transparent contracts that provide them a complete picture of all ''rebate'' dollars. In theory, this provides information about the surplus created by their prescriptions. That said, there are reasons to be concerned that despite these efforts at disclosure, payers remain unaware of all of the funds (particularly those not labeled as rebates) flowing between the PBM and the manufacturer. For example, in addition to rebates, PBMs also receive various administrative fees and other payments from manufacturers— fees that are often a function of the list price of a drug.

The PBM and the manufacturer determine which of these payments are classified as ''rebates'' (and therefore covered by the price transparency and rebate sharing requirements), and what is instead an ''administrative fee'' (that does not need to be disclosed or shared).[53] These fees are not trivial—for some contracts they can account for 25–30 percent of the money moving between the manufacturer and the PBM.[54] Furthermore, since these fees are often structured as a function of the list price there is little economic distinction between an ''administrative fee'' and a ''rebate.'' Describing this system, the Senate Finance Committee report on insulin pricing said ''[a]lthough Part D plans are required to report rebates to CMS, they are not required to report administrative fees collected and retained by PBMs 'if the fees are for bona

[53] Eickelberg, Henry C. 2015. ''The Prescription Drug Supply Chain 'Black Box': How it Works and Why You Should Care.'' American Health Policy Institute. December.

[54] Dross, David. 2017. ''Will Point-of-Sale Rebates Disrupt the PBM Business?'' Mercer. July 31.

fide services and are at fair market value.' This basic lack of transparency in the Medicare program has been an area of concern to HHS OIG, as has the competing interests that PBMs and manufacturers find themselves in due to the administrative fees being based on the WAC price.''[55] Figure 11 documents the increase in such fees over time in this market.

If we consider the simple example above, the situation for the payer could be even worse if, instead of offering a ''rebate'' of $15, the manufacturer offers a $15 ''administrative fee'' to the PBM. In that case, the payer would bear the full cost (i.e., $20) of the list price increase, and the PBM and manufacturer would split the surplus. Ultimately, manufacturers are agnostic between describing payments to the PBM as ''fees'' or ''rebates''—they simply care about the total amount of money they collect and distribute as a result of these negotiations.[56] Given the existing structure of contracts and cost sharing, other members of the value chain are far less agnostic about the labeling of these fund transfers.

To further complicate matters, sophisticated payers hoping to gather more information about the flow of funds between the PBM and manufacturers that results from their prescriptions often face meaningful restrictions on the ability to audit their PBM-payer contracts.[57] These can include the exclusion of particular auditors that are deemed to hold views that are hostile to PBMs, requirements that audits be held at the headquarters of the PBM, unwillingness to provide contracts with manufacturers, restricted access to claims data, and strict limitations on the number of years that can be audited.[58] While many of these restrictions can be cast as attempts to maintain rebate confidentiality, they also increase the amount of asymmetric information between PBMs and payers about the amount of available surplus. Such information asymmetries can affect the efficiency of bargaining between these two groups.

As a result of these concerns, some have proposed policies where PBMs are not allowed to have contracts in which they are compensated based on the size of the rebate or the list price of a product. While this would certainly eliminate any perverse incentives for large rebates, it would also diminish the

---

[55] https://www.finance.senate.gov/imo/media/doc/Grassley-Wyden%20Insulin%20Report%20(FINAL%201).pdf, page 81.

[56] To the extent manufacturers have preferences about this labeling it is likely related to the intersection with cost sharing discussed above. Note that high cost sharing impacts manufacturer revenue by reducing demand for pharmaceutical products.

[57] Weinberg, Neil, and Robert Langreth. 2017. ''Inside the 'Scorpion Room' Where Drug Price Secrets Are Guarded.'' Bloomberg. May 4.

[58] Advisory Council on Employee Welfare and Pension Benefit Plans. 2014. ''PBM Compensation and Fee Disclosure.'' Report to the United States Secretary of Labor.

incentives for PBMs to push for large discounts. If the primary motivation for such policies is an underlying concern about the competitiveness of the PBM market, eliminating the ability for firms to sign incentive compatible contracts could have meaningful unintended consequences.

In a similar vein, the Department of Health and Human Services previously proposed to instead address this problem by eliminating the safe harbor for rebates in the Medicare program. While this policy has been abandoned, other efforts underway have the same goal of ending confidential rebates based on the price of the drug and shift the market to a series of up-front price discounts and flat fees negotiated between PBMs and manufacturers.[59] This would effectively end the confidentiality of negotiated prices while also not decreasing the amount of surplus captured by PBMs—after all, a PBM with market power can calculate a flat fee as easily as the current percentage based-rebate system.

It is perhaps not surprising that policies from both parties are coalescing on attempting to end rebates. Frustrated by rising drug prices, people are looking for a scapegoat and a system of shrouded prices by large firms fits a convenient narrative. That said, it would be extremely unwise to limit the ability of PBMs to negotiate large discounts. Instead of ending the current system of confidential rebates, I've proposed (along with Fiona Scott Morton) that we move to a system where all payments currently paid between the manufacturer and the PBM flow first to the payer before being split between the payer and the PBM.[60] PBMs and payers would be free to negotiate any split of the rebates, fees, and other funds that are paid by the manufacturer—including contracts that compensate a PBM as a percentage of the savings that they generate. Importantly, under this policy these contracts would emerge from a negotiation between two parties with equal information about the amount of money at stake. There are variety of ways to implement the move to such a system. One possible solution would be for regulators to end the safe harbor for payments between manufacturers and PBMs and instead create a separate safe harbor for payments between manufacturers and payers. I'd note that if the current PBM market is truly competitive, this proposed policy solution should have little effect on the distribution of surplus.

---

[59] U.S. Department of Health and Human Services. 2019. ''Trump Administration Proposes to Lower Drug Costs by Targeting Backdoor Rebates and Encouraging Direct Discounts to Patients.'' January 31.

[60] Garthwaite, Craig, and Fiona Scott Morton. 2017. ''Perverse Market Incentives Encourage High Prescription Drug Prices.'' ProMarket Blog. November 1.

III. Congress Should Address Cost Sharing and Price Negotiations More Directly

While the optimality of the existing PBM market remains unclear, it is becoming apparent that Congress should enact some meaningful reforms in this area. I offer some suggestions for such policies below.

As a starting point, there is a clear case for a reform to Medicare Part D's reinsurance program. Currently, this program blunts the incentives of firms to negotiate price discounts for the most expensive drugs and increases consumer cost sharing. Figure 12 shows the distribution of spending responsibilities under Part D. During the deductible period, the beneficiary is responsible for all the spending. Then, during the initial coverage phase, enrollees are responsible for 25 percent of their drug spending and the plans are responsible for the remaining 75 percent of spending. If individuals spend through the initial coverage period, they find themselves in the coverage gap where they are responsible for 25 percent of spending, the plan is responsible for 5 percent, and manufacturers are required to give a discount of 70 percent. If an individual spends more than the catastrophic coverage threshold (approximately $8,000 in 2019), then the government is responsible for 80 percent of all additional costs, plans are responsible for 15 percent, and beneficiaries are responsible for the final 5 percent. Given the lack of a lifetime limit on out-of-pocket spending by enrollees, this benefit structure is part of the reason why beneficiaries find themselves on the hook for exceptionally high cost-sharing for prescription drugs.

Furthermore, for high priced products the private firms empowered to negotiate on behalf of Medicare are largely shielded by reinsurance from the costs of most price increases—limiting the ability of the market to lower these drug prices. Perhaps more concerning, PBMs operating in both the commercial and the Part D markets may face different incentives for rebates across these different markets and could use the confidential nature of rebates to unnecessarily increase government Part D spending. Initially, reinsurance was not a dominant feature of Part D. This has changed. Figure 13 shows the average national plan bid across Part D firms by its component parts—the direct subsidy from the government, the base premium from the enrollee, and the expected reinsurance payment. These data show that from 2007 to 2018, the reinsurance component of Part D spending has grown from a relatively minor part of the program (25 percent of the plan bid) to the dominant source of payments to firms under Part D (60 percent of the plan bid).

This level of reinsurance shields plans from the costs of the most expensive specialty drugs—a category of products that represents a growing share of overall prescription drug spending. While such a large amount of reinsurance may have been necessary to attract plans to the newly established Part D market, it is highly unlikely this remains true today. Part D is now an established market where firms have sufficient data to make reasonable projections about potential risk. Therefore, I propose that Congress either remove catastrophic reinsurance entirely from Part D (and force plans to pay 100 percent of the cost of these expensive products) or at a minimum switch the cost sharing so that the plan is responsible for 80 percent of the spending above the catastrophic limit and the government is responsible for 20 percent.[61] This would provide the appropriate incentives for firms to strongly negotiate for larger rebates and lower prices within Part D.

Beyond changing the incentives to negotiate prices, it is clear we should find policy solutions to pass along more of the negotiated discounts to consumers. However, it is critical that any policy solution saves the proverbial baby while throwing out the bathwater by maintaining the ability of PBMs to effectively negotiate larger rebates with manufacturers. Therefore, I propose that PBMs be required to base cost-sharing payments on a number that more closely approximates the net price of the product even if it is not the exact net price associated with that purchase. For example, this number could be the average net price across PBMs for that product, the average net price for the therapeutic class, or the minimum price paid in the market, i.e., the Medicaid best price. Assuming PBMs have sufficient ability to modify their formularies, any of these options should still expose the patient to enough of the cost of the product to address moral hazard concerns while not exposing consumers to artificially high prices that unwind the generosity and efficiency of the insurance contract.

Some have complained that policies that pass along rebates to consumers at the point of sale would lead to higher premiums. This fact is almost certainly true. However, this is not necessarily a problem. Our current system of using cost sharing by patients requiring expensive products to lower the premiums paid by healthier patients subverts many popular policy goals regarding the treatment of pre-existing conditions in the health insurance market. In addition, these higher premiums would reflect, in part, a more complete insurance product. It is not immediately clear consumers are fully aware of the

[61] As I discuss below, very large consumer cost sharing (such as the 5 percent of spending that patients must pay under Part D) can decrease the efficiency of insurance.

financial exposure they have to expensive medications, and therefore we should not think that increasing the completeness of insurance in this setting is clearly a negative outcome.

IV. More Information is Needed Before Implementing New Policies Aimed at PBMs

The role of various entities in the supply chain is clearly complicated. Pharmaceuticals move through a relatively lengthy supply chain inhabited by private firms with differing incentives, information, and market power. Given their central role in both negotiating prices and establishing formularies, it is tempting to blame PBMs for every negative feature of the system we observe. And it is possible that such blame may ultimately be valid. However, it is also apparent that we simply lack the information necessary to determine the degree to which these aspects of the market are actually caused by the independent motivations of PBMs to maximize profits versus how much they reflect the incentives of other firms in the value chain. For example, as mentioned above PBMs have offered contracts where rebates are passed along to customers at the point of sale and plans sponsors have largely avoided those plans. This suggests a more complicated story is necessary to explain the current market dynamics.

Given the uncertainty in this area, it is incumbent on policymakers and regulators to gather more information before attempting to develop and implement solutions. Certainly, the recent Senate Finance Committee investigation into insulin pricing shed some important light on the relationships between PBMs and manufacturers. In that document we learned more about the role of administrative fees and the views of PBMs about the motivations of their customers, i.e., the plan sponsors. However, that report fell short on investigating the relationship between PBMs and plan sponsors. More information about those contracts and whether the actions of PBMs vary based on the contractual relationship with the plan sponsor would be useful for understanding the degree to which potentially undesirable features of the market are the result of the structure of the PBM market or other features of the supply chain.

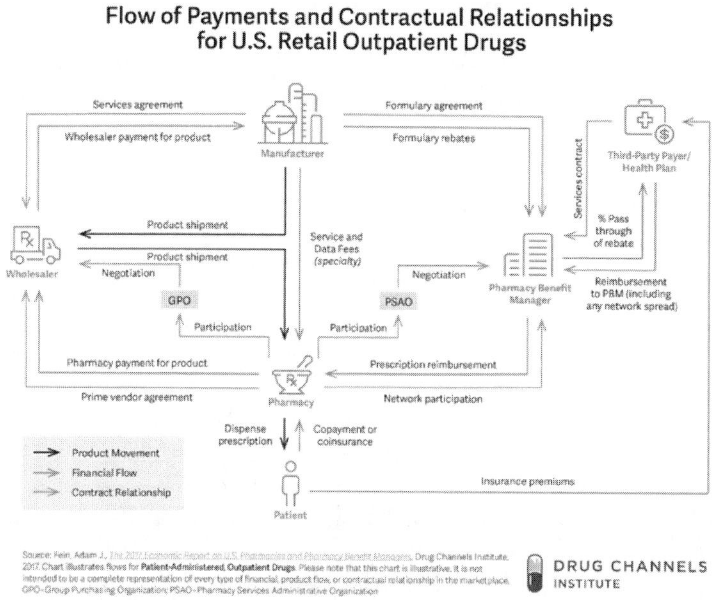

Source: Drugchannels.net, available at: http://www.drugchannels.net/p/about-blog.html.

Figure 1.

Source: https://www.drugchannels.net/2022/04/the-top-pharmacy-benefit-managers-of.html.

Figure 2.

Figure 3.

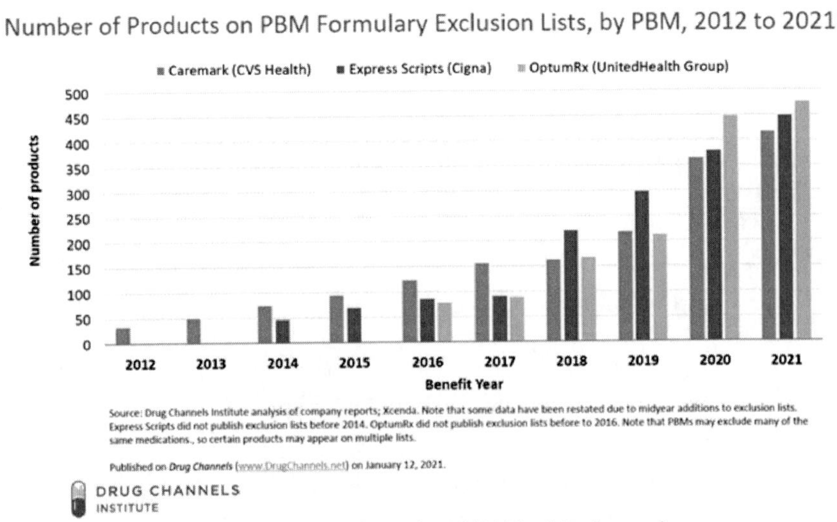

Source: https://www.drugchannels.net/2021/01/the-big-three-pbms-ramp-up-specialty.html.

Figure 4.

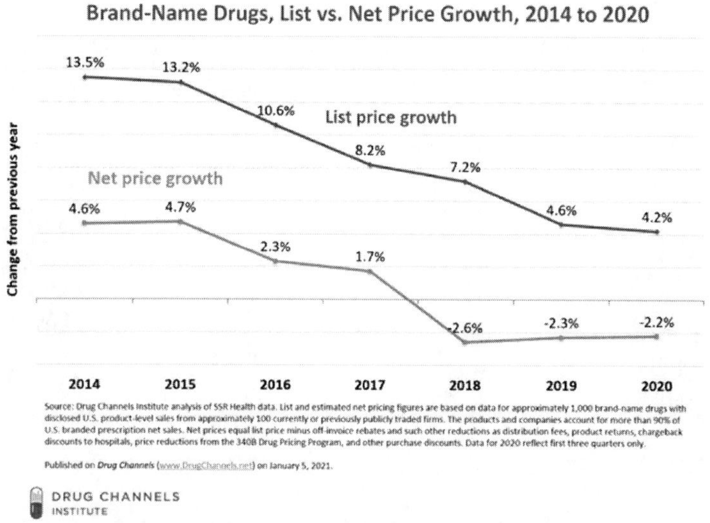

Source: https://www.drugchannels.net/2021/01/surprise-brand-name-drug-prices-fell.html.

Figure 5.

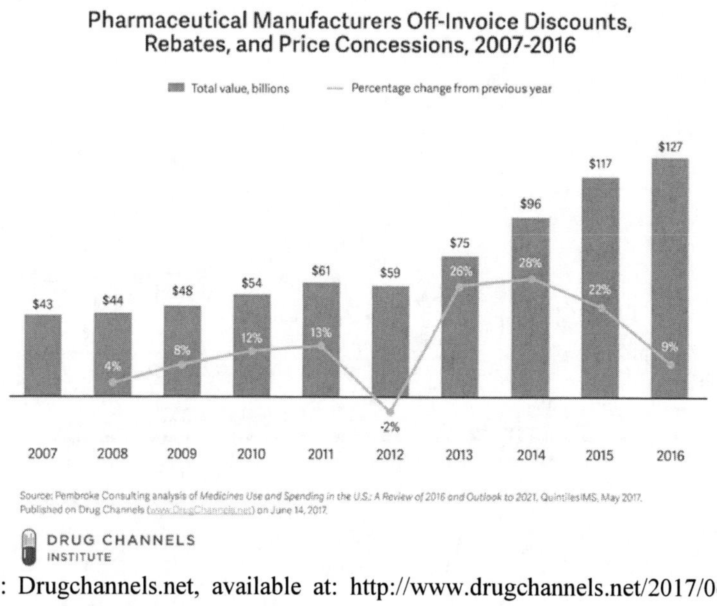

Source: Drugchannels.net, available at: http://www.drugchannels.net/2017/06/new-data- show-gross-to-net-rebate.html.

Figure 6.

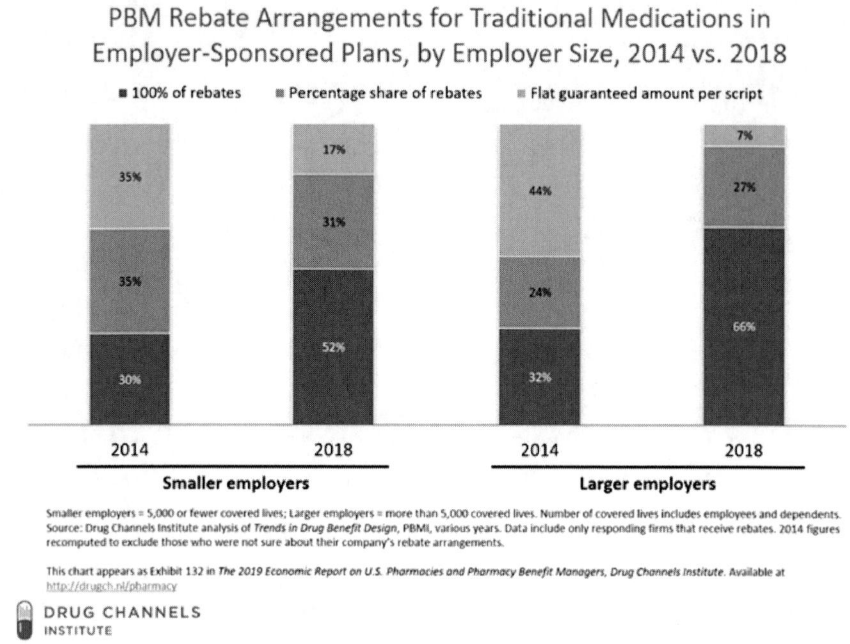

Figure 7.

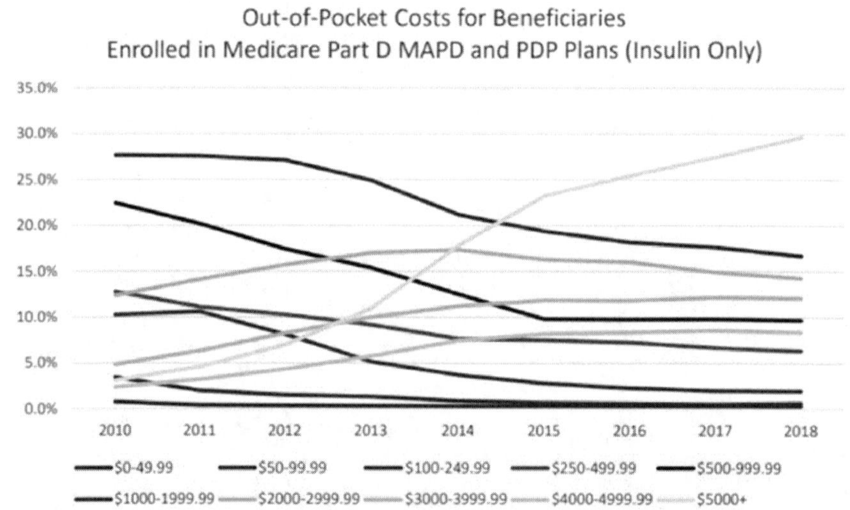

Source: https://www.finance.senate.gov/imo/media/doc/Grassley-Wyden%20Insulin%20Report%20(FINAL%201).pdf.

Figure 8.

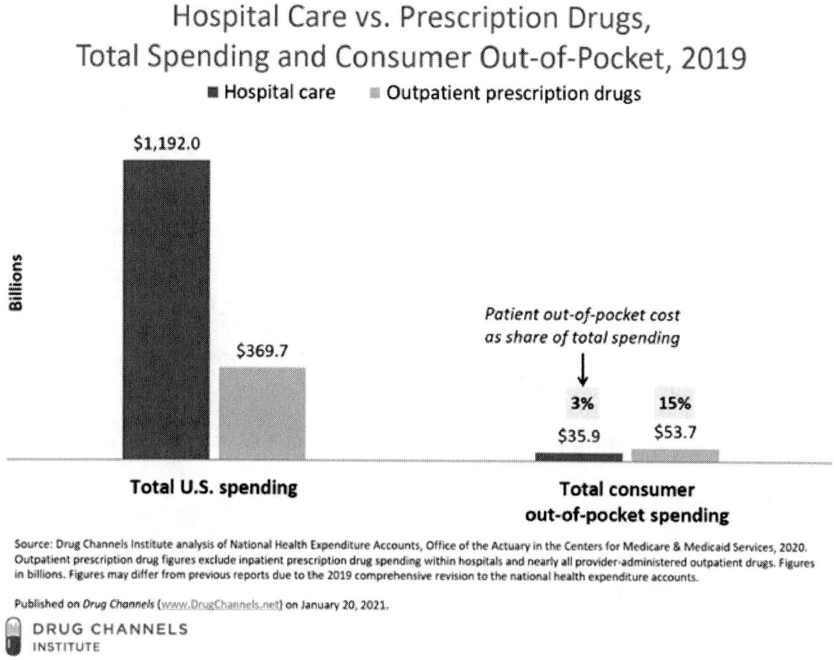

Source: https://www.drugchannels.net/2021/01/latest-cms-data-reveal-truth-about-us.html.

Figure 9.

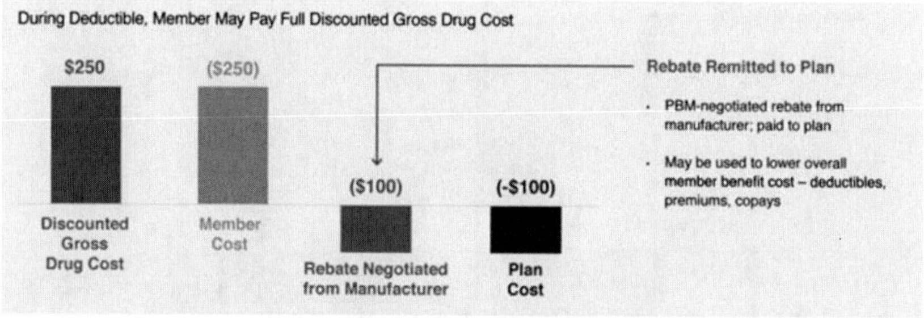

Source: https://payorsolutions.cvshealth.com/insights/consumer-transparency.

Figure 10.

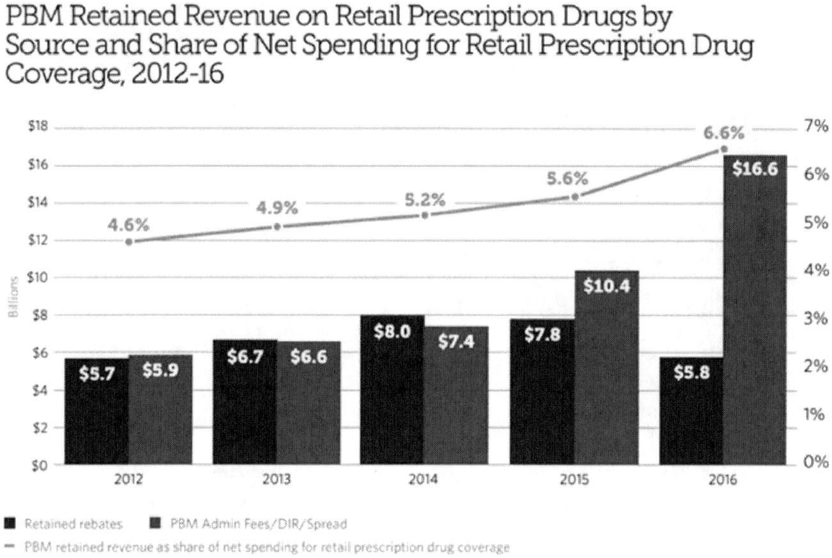

Source: https://www.pewtrusts.org/-/media/assets/2019/03/the_prescription_drug_land scape-explored.pdf.

Figure 11.

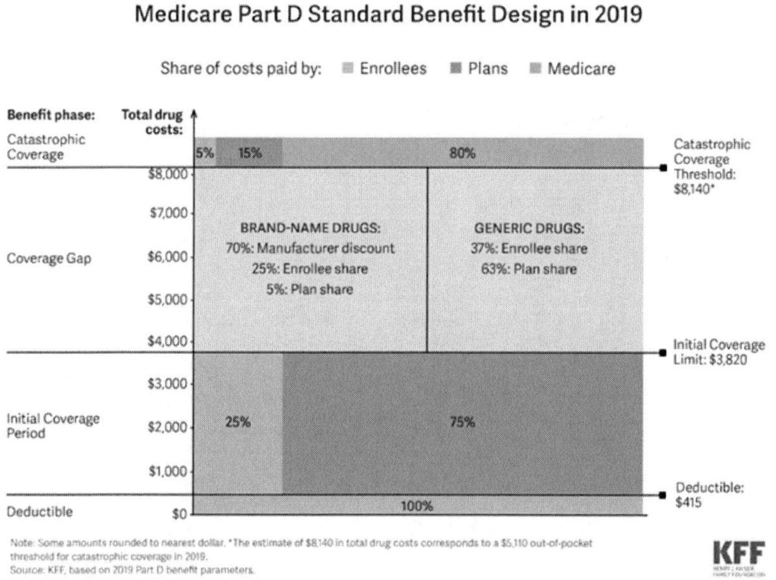

Figure 12.

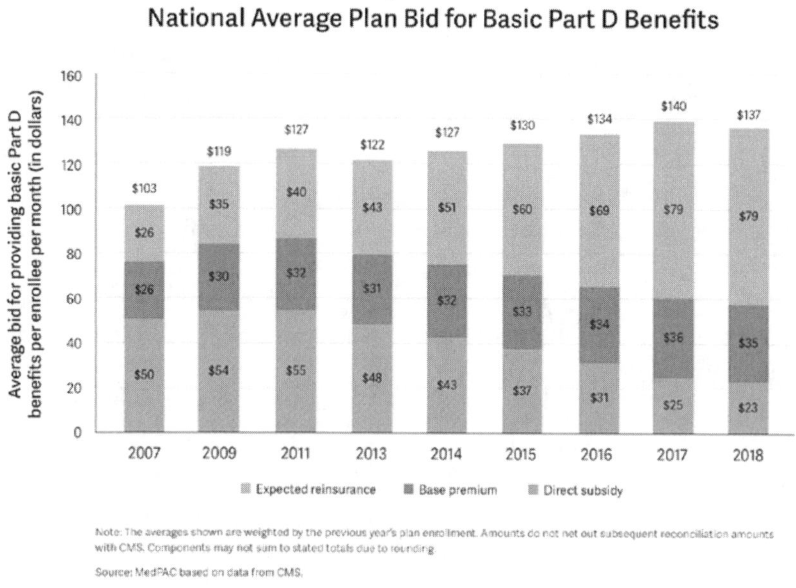

Figure 13.

Senator BLUMENTHAL. Thank you very much, Professor. We will now go to Professor Feldman.

Statement of Professor Robin Feldman, Arthur J. Goldberg Distinguished Professor of Law, Albert Abramson '54 Distinguished Professor of Law Chair, Director of the Center for Innovation, University of California Hastings Law

Ms. FELDMAN. Thank you, Mr. Chairman, and esteemed members of the Subcommittee. Open and vigorous competition is the backbone of U.S. markets. But we are not seeing that with pharmaceuticals. Instead, we are seeing troubling and persistently rising prices on everyday medications.

Now, there are many contributors to rising prices, but a critical place to start is with the industry that sits at the center of everything. Specifically at the heart of the drug pricing system lies the industry known as pharmacy benefit managers or PBMs. And historically, PBMs operated mostly as claims processors, just handling the paperwork flow.

However, 15 years ago, when Medicare expanded to include prescription drugs, PBMs took on an expanded role as well. They began serving as a health plans representative for negotiating better prices from drug companies. There are many contributing factors, but the price increases that followed have been dramatic. For example, the prices of 65 common medicines have almost tripled just during those 15 years.

So how did this happen? How did PBMs, which were supposed to help control prices, end up helping inflate prices instead? Well, the problem has emerged because rather than act fully as honest brokers for the health plans, PBMs, perhaps unsurprisingly, act in their own interests. And it turns out that their interests are not aligned with keeping prices low. So, to set the stage for how this works, consider a store that raises the price of a jacket before putting the jacket on sale at the old price.

When you walk in the store, the markdown looks like a great bargain, but it is not. For PBMs, their best interests are served when drug companies increase the starting price of the drug. That price is known as the list price. If the list price goes up and the PBM negotiates a rebate back down, the PBM looks more successful. It gets paid more by the health plan because the PBMs pay depends on the size of the rebate.

In addition, because PBMs generally get to keep a portion of the rebate, they get to pocket even more. All this might not be so bad if no one actually paid that high list price, but many plans are set up so that people do pay that list price out of pocket in various ways, and many Americans don't have coverage for prescription drugs. I talked before about raising the price of a jacket so you can put it on sale at the old price, but it gets worse.

Imagine if the price jump is higher than the sale discount. That is what is happening with medicine. Prices are rising faster than the rebates. Between 2010 and 2017 in Medicare, prices for drugs after rebates still rose 313 percent on average. We are buying the same jacket, but it is costing us more and more. And a significant portion of that increase is going to the PBMs.

And despite the fact that PBMs should be serving as honest brokers for health plans, PBMs also take side payments from drug companies for providing services to the drug companies themselves.

And what can PBMs offer drug companies to continue this payment stream of rebates and side income? Well, PBMs stand at the center of the system. As well as negotiating prices, they help decide if patients will be reimbursed for a particular medicine, how much they will be reimbursed.

So PBMs can agree with the drug company that they will exclude the competitor's product and they can also make it harder for patients to get the competitor's medicine. That is of great value to a drug company. Finally,

PBMs and drug companies claim that those rebate details are trade secrets and can't be disclosed even to the health plan. Now, markets thrive on information.

And when heavily concentrated industries tightly control the flow of information, the end result is rarely in the interests of consumers. Most important, from an intellectual property perspective, simple price and price terms shouldn't be considered trade secrets at all. Thank you, and I look forward to your questions.

[The prepared statement of Ms. Feldman follows:]

Prepared Statement of Professor Robin Feldman, Arthur J. Goldberg Distinguished Professor of Law, Albert Abramson '54 Distinguished Professor of Law Chair, Director of the Center for Innovation, University of California Hastings Law

Mr. Chairman and esteemed members of the Subcommittee, I am honored to be here today to address an issue that is causing real pain for consumers and for those trying to help them.

Open and vigorous competition is the backbone of U.S. markets, but we are not seeing that in the pharmaceutical industry. Instead, we see persistently rising prices on the medications people depend on, day after day, to treat widespread problems such as diabetes, high blood pressure, high cholesterol, and opioid addiction.[62] There are many contributors to the rising prices, but a critical place to start is with the industry that sits at the center of everything.

Specifically, at the heart of the drug pricing system lies the industry known as pharmacy benefit managers or PBMs.[63] Historically, PBMs operated

---

[62]See CTR. FOR MEDICARE & MEDICAID SERV., FACT SHEET, DRUG SPENDING INFORMATION PRODUCTS (2018), *https://www.cms.gov/newsroom/fact-sheets/drug-spending-information-prod-ucts-fact-sheet* (listing the ten drugs with highest annual price increases from 2012 to 2016 covered by Medicare); CAL. OFFICE OF STATEWIDE HEALTH PLANNING AND DEVELOPMENT, PRESCRIPTION DRUG WHOLESALE ACQUISITION COST (WAC) INCREASES (2019) (detailing wholesale price increases of more than 16 percent for hundreds of drugs between 2017 and Q2 of 2019); Feldman, Devil, supra note 1, at 2.

[63] For additional information on pharmacy benefit managers, see ROBIN FELDMAN, DRUGS, MONEY, AND SECRET HANDSHAKES: THE UNSTOPPABLE GROWTH OF PRESCRIPTION DRUG PRICES (2019) (discussing the role of PBMs in the pharmaceutical market); Robin Feldman, *Perverse Incentives: Why Everyone Prefers High Drug Prices—Except for Those Who Pay the Bills,* 57 HARV.J. ON LEG. 303 (2020) (describing the incentive structures that lead PBMs to contribute to rising drug prices); Robin Feldman, *The*

mostly as claims processors, just handling the paperwork flow.[64] However, when Medicare expanded in 2006 to include prescription drugs, PBMs took on an expanded role, as well. They began serving as the health plan's representative for negotiating better prices from drug companies.

Although there are many contributing factors, the rise in prices that followed that shift fifteen years ago has been dramatic. Looking, for example, at sixty-five common medicines that need to be taken over a long period of time, prices have almost tripled during those fifteen years.[65]

So how did this happen? How did PBMs—which were supposed to make healthcare more efficient—end up helping to inflate drug prices instead? The problem has emerged because rather than act as honest brokers for health plans, PBMs, unsurprisingly, act in their own interests. And it turns out that their own interests are not aligned with keeping prices low. To set the stage for how this works, consider a store that raises the price of a dress before putting the dress on sale at the old price. When you walk in the store, the sale price looks like a great bargain; but it's not.

PBMs, similarly, have discovered that their best interests are served when drug companies increase the starting price of the drug. That price is known as the list price. If the list price goes up, and the PBM negotiates a rebate back down, the PBM looks more successful. It gets paid more by the health plan, and—because PBMs generally keep part of the rebate—it gets to pocket more.

All of this might not be so bad if no one actually paid that high list price. But people do. Many consumers have what are called high-deductible plans, in which they pay that high list price out of their pocket until they reach a

---

Devil in the Tiers, 8 J.L. & BIOSCI. 1 (2021) (analyzing the role PBMs play in distorting the organization of drug formularies); Robin Feldman, Why Prescription Drug Prices Have Skyrocketed, WASH. POST (Nov. 26, 2018), *https://www.washington post.com/outlook/2018/11/26/why-prescription-drug-prices-have-skyrocketed/* (discussing the role PBMs play in the pharmaceutical market). For a discussion of potential solutions, see Feld- man, Devil, at 31–41 (suggesting that drugs should be located on formulary tiers based on list, rather than net, price to remove the incentive for anticompetitive formulary manipulation); FELDMAN, SECRET HANDSHAKES, at 95–102 (describing the significance of transparency and potential state and Federal level responses). For an explanation of why prices and price terms negotiated between PBMs and drug companies do not constitute trade secrets, see Robin Feldman & Charles Tait Graves, *Naked Price & Pharmaceutical Trade Secret Overreach,* 22 YALE J.L. & TECH 61 (2020) (defining trade secrets and discussing PBM efforts to assert that pricing arrangements should be considered trade secrets).

[64] Feldman, WASH. POST, supra note 1.

[65] STEPHEN W. SCHONDELMEYER & LEIGH PURVIS, AARP PUBLIC POLICY INSTITUTE, TRENDS IN RETAIL PRICES OF BRAND NAME PRESCRIPTION DRUGS WIDELY USED BY OLDER AMERICANS, 2006 TO 2020 1–2 (2021).

certain threshhold[66]; other plans require that patients pay a percentage of the high list price as what is known as co-insurance.[67] And many Americans still do not have coverage for prescription drugs, even if they have health insurance. Thus, people are often forced to pay the high list price.

I talked before about raising the price of a dress so you can put it on sale at the old price. It gets worse. Imagine if the price jump is higher than the sale discount. That's what is happening in the case of medicine. Prices are rising faster than the rebates are rising. For example, between 2010 and 2017 in Medicare, prices for drugs after rebate still rose 313 percent on average.[68] We are buying the same dress, but it is costing us more and more. And a significant portion of that increase is going to PBMs.

In addition, despite the fact that PBMs should be serving as honest brokers for health plans, PBMs also take side payments from drug companies for providing services to the drug companies.

And what do the PBMs have in their pocket to offer drug companies to continue this payment stream of rebates and side income? PBMs stand at the center of the system. As well as negotiating prices, they help decide whether a patient will be reimbursed for a particular medicine and how much they will be reimbursed. Therefore, PBMs can agree with a drug company that they will exclude the company's cheaper competitors or make it harder for patients to get the competitor's medicine.[69] That is of great value to a drug company.

PBMs and drug companies refuse to disclose the precise size of rebates or the details of the terms given, asserting that the information is a trade secret. Even auditors and regulators are not given full access. Trying to reform the system—or even talk about it—is like shadow boxing.

---

[66] For an example of a plan requiring that the patient pay 100 percent of the costs of drugs up to a certain limit, see the Anthem insurance plan described at First Am. Consolidated Class Action Compl., at para. 13, In re Express Scripts/Anthem ERISA Litigation, 2018 U.S. Dist. LEXIS 3081 (S.D.N.Y. 2016) (No. 16–3399).

[67] See Medicare Payment Advisory Comm'n, Report to the Congress: Medicare Payment Policy 408–09 (2017).

[68] Feldman, Devil, supra note 1, at 19, 21–22.

[69] *See, e.g., Charles Ornstein & Katie Thomas, Take the Generic, Patients Are Told. Until They Are Not.,*)N.Y. TIMES (Aug. 6, 2017) (describing health plans forcing patients to pay more for the generic version of a drug or declining to reimburse for the generic at all;, *https:// www.nytimes.com/2017/08/06/health/prescription-drugs-brand-name-generic.html?mtrref=unde fined* [*https://perma.cc/U4JU–4P3X*]; *see also* Complaint, Shire U.S., Inc. v. Allergan, Inc., No. 17–7716 (D.N.J. 2017) (alleging bundled rebates for the eye medication Restasis deterred health plan formularies from including competitors); Complaint, Pfizer, Inc., v. Johnson & Johnson and Janssen Biotech, Inc., 2018 U.S. Dist. LEXIS 31690 (E.D. Pa. 2018) (No. 17–4180) (bundled re- bates for the rheumatoid arthritis drug Remicade resulted in hospitals and health plan formularies essentially excluding the lower-priced biosimilar).

Finally, the PBM industry is highly concentrated. Just three PBMs control 80 percent–85 percent of the market.[70] They tend to offer the same terms to health plans. Thus, if health plans want something different, they are out of luck.

Markets thrive on information, and when heavily concentrated industries control the flow of information, the end result is rarely in the interests of consumers. Most important, from an intellectual property perspective, simple price and price terms shouldn't be considered trade secrets at all.[71]

One cannot overemphasize the major life improvements over the past century that flow from innovation in prescription medications, including new lifesaving antibiotics, treatments for pain, psychopharmacological treatments and cancer drugs. However, if we don't get a handle on the perverse incentives operating in various parts of the drug supply chain, the burden on consumers and taxpayers will continue to be crushing.

Thank you, and I look forward to your questions.

Senator BLUMENTHAL. Thanks so much, Professor Feldman. And now, Mr. Scott.

Statement of Juan Carlos ''JC'' Scott, President and CEO, Pharmaceutical Care Management Association

Mr. SCOTT. Good morning, Chairman Blumenthal, Ranking Member Blackburn, and members of the Subcommittee. My name is J.C. Scott. I am the President and CEO of the Pharmaceutical Care Management Association, the national trade association representing pharmacy benefit managers. On

---

[70] Neeraj Sood, Dana P. Goldman, & Karen Van Nuys, Follow the Money to Understand How Drug Profits Flow, STAT (Dec. 15, 2017), *https://www.statnews.com/2017/12/15/prescription-drug-profits-pbm/* (''The top three pharmacy benefit managers, which negotiate drug prices on behalf of insurers and self-insured employers, dominate 85 percent of their market.''). See also Neeraj Sood, Transcript of Understanding Competition in Prescription Drug Markets: Entry & Supply Chain Dynamics Workshop (Nov. 8, 2017), *https://www.ftc.gov/system/files/documents/videos/understanding-competition-prescription-drug-markets-panel-2/ftc_understanding_competition_in_prescription_drug_markets_-_transcript_segment_3.pdf.*

[71] Robin Feldman & Charles Tait Graves, *Naked Price & Pharmaceutical Trade Secret Overreach,* 22 Yale J.L. & Tech 61 (2020) (discussing PBM efforts to assert that price and price terms should be considered trade secrets).

behalf of PCMA's member companies, I appreciate the invitation to testify today.

Mr. Chairman, we agree drug pricing and affordability is a challenge for too many patients in America. We can and should talk about what is driving that affordability challenge and how we solve for it, which begins with an understanding of the entirety of the prescription drug supply chain, from manufacturer to wholesaler to pharmacy to those paying the bills.

Today, the Subcommittee is focused on just one piece of that ecosystem, understanding the work done by our companies pharmacy benefit managers. I appreciate the opportunity to share our perspective that our companies are delivering value for those who pay for health care coverage for patients and for patients themselves by making sure they have seamless, safe, and affordable access to the medications they need.

I know that during your time in the Senate, you have met with many people representing the health care industry. With respect to prescription drugs, you have heard from retail pharmacies who are essential to serving patients and providing access to medications, and generally speaking, argue for higher payments.

Representatives of drug manufacturers, those responsible both for the amazing innovations that benefit patients and for setting the prices, generally seek to justify their price setting decisions and argue for higher, not lower prices. I am not trying to judge either of those arguments.

I simply want to make the point that the PBM industry is the only stakeholder in the chain dedicated to seeking lower costs, and we are proud to play that role. PBMs do that work for the employer, union, health plan, and Government clients who hire them, and most importantly, the patients for whom those plans provide coverage. PBMs return $10 in savings for every $1 spent on their services.

PBMs will lower the cost of health care by $1 trillion this year alone. And for many of us, that can be a hard number to get our head around. But it comes down to savings of about $962 per person per year.

PBMs lower prescription drug costs by encouraging competition in the market, promoting the use of generic medications, negotiating discounts and rebates, encouraging better pharmacy quality, and offering things like home delivery for those on chronic medications. Understandably, stakeholders in the supply chain want to be paid more for their services and products.

For the plan sponsors who are paying the bills, they need a balancing force to push for lower costs and better access, and that is where PBMs come in. The Medicare Part D program is a great example where seniors are able to choose among private plans to get their drug benefits. PBMs support Part D plans by negotiating rebates and discounts and promoting better pharmacy quality, passing the savings from those negotiations to the plans, who in turn use that to keep premium costs reliably low for seniors.

It is worth emphasizing, no employer, union, pension fund, or health plan has to hire or use a PBM, but virtually all do choose to use a PBM to lower the cost of providing health care and to better serve the patients they represent. PBM clients choose their PBMs through a transparent and highly competitive bidding process.

And Mr. Balto was right. I am going to tell you that with over 70 full service PBMs in the marketplace, including new entrants coming into the market regularly, plan sponsors have a tremendous diversity of opportunity to contract with the PBM that best meets their unique needs. Some may choose a PBM based on their scale and ability to negotiate deep discounts and manage the risk of price changes. Others choose to hire PBMs based on their innovative care management programs or different levels of service.

It is important that there is choice and the ability for plan sponsors to decide how to set up their drug benefits to best serve their unique populations. PCMA and the companies we represent are committed to working with the Subcommittee and all stakeholders to continue improving the affordability of prescription drugs for patients.

While I have talked a lot about the work we do for those who provide health coverage for consumers, the most important lens through which to judge these issues are not what will best benefit the plan sponsor or the PBM or the retail pharmacy or the manufacturer. It comes down to what best serves the consumer.

Through their work, PBMs are contributing to lower costs for health coverage for consumers, lower cost for medications, and bet ter access, which means more people getting the medicines they need to lead healthier lives.

I hope that this hearing is an opportunity for a continued conversation not only about the work done by PBMs, but to look at the entire supply chain so that we can identify solutions for patients and consumers. Thank you again for the opportunity to speak with you. I look forward to your questions.

[The prepared statement of Mr. Scott follows:]

Prepared Statement of Juan Carlos "JC" Scott, President and CEO, Pharmaceutical Care Management Association

Introduction

Good morning, Chairman Blumenthal, Ranking Member Blackburn, and members of the Subcommittee on Consumer Protection, Product Safety, and Data Security. My name is JC Scott. I am the President and CEO of the Pharmaceutical Care Management Association (PCMA).

PCMA is the national association that represents America's Pharmacy Benefit Managers (PBMs), which administer prescription drug plans and operate specialty and mail-order pharmacies for more than 266 million Americans who have health coverage from a variety of sponsors, including through employers, labor unions, health insurers, Medicare Part D plans, state government employee plans, Medicaid plans, the Federal Employees Health Benefits Program, TRICARE and others.

PBMs are proud of the work they do to reduce prescription drug costs, expand affordable access to medications, and improve patient outcomes. PBMs negotiate with drug companies to lower prescription drug costs. PBMs work with pharmacies to create networks of pharmacies that provide the best value. PBMs facilitate home delivery of prescription drugs to patients safely and seamlessly, and PBMs help patients stay on their prescription drugs to live healthier lives. PBMs advocate for patients in the fight to keep prescription drugs accessible and affordable.

On behalf of PCMA's member companies, I appreciate the invitation to testify before the subcommittee today as it seeks to understand better the role PBMs play in the drug supply chain and our impact on consumers, small businesses, and drug costs.

Drug pricing and affordability are a challenge for too many patients in America. We can and should talk about what is driving that affordability challenge and how we solve it, which begins with an understanding of the entirety of the prescription drug supply and payment chain, from manufacturer to wholesaler to pharmacy to those providing health coverage.

Today, the subcommittee is focused on just one piece of that ecosystem—understanding the work done by our companies, PBMs.

During your time in the Senate, you have met with many people representing the health care industry.

With respect to prescription drugs, you have heard from retail pharmacies, which are essential to serving patients and providing access to medications, and which, generally speaking, argue for higher payments, which lead to higher drug costs.

Representatives of drug manufacturers, those responsible for both the amazing innovations that benefit patients and for setting prices, generally seek to justify their price-setting decisions and argue for higher, not lower, prices.

Understandably, stakeholders in the supply chain want to be paid more for their services and products. That is the way the market functions. But those paying the bills need a balancing force to push for lower costs and better access, and that is where PBMs come in.

The PBM industry is the only stakeholder in the chain dedicated to seeking lower costs. PBMs do that work for the employer, union, health plan, and government clients who hire them, and, most importantly, the patients for whom those health plans provide coverage.

PBMs return $10 in savings for every dollar spent on their services. As a result, PBMs will lower the cost of health care by $1 trillion this year alone.[72] For many of us, that can be a hard number to get our heads around, but it comes down to saving about $962 per person per year.

PBMs are able to negotiate for lower drug costs when they can bring competition between pharmaceutical manufacturers and between pharmacies to bear. PBMs lower prescription drug costs by using these negotiations to deliver discounts and rebates, promoting the use of generic medications, encouraging better pharmacy quality, and offering things like home delivery for those on chronic medications.

Simplifying the Consumer Experience

People with insurance filled more than 6.4 billion prescriptions in retail pharmacies in 2021.[73] Every day, that amounts to nearly 15 million prescriptions, so it is critical that patients can pick up their prescriptions as quickly as possible at the pharmacy counter to establish and maintain medication adherence. PBMs perform many essential functions that combine

---

[72] Visante. The Return on Investment (ROI) on PBM Services. An analysis prepared by Visante on behalf of PCMA. February 2020. Available at *https://www.pcmanet.org/wp-content/uploads/2020/02/ROI-on-PBM-Services-FINAL_.pdf.*

[73] IQVIA. The Use of Medicines in the U.S. 2022. April 2022. Available at *https://www.iqvia.com/insights/the-iqvia-institute/reports/the-use-of-medicines-in-the-us-2022.*

disparate information and expertise, as well as advanced technology to facilitate and streamline getting a prescription filled as seamlessly as possible.[74]

To achieve optimal PBM-patient coordination, once a pharmacy enters a prescription into the system, it is sent electronically to the patient's PBM, which checks the pharmacy benefit information to confirm the patient's insurance status and costsharing amount, as well as the patient's medication history for any errors and possible harmful dangerous drug interactions. While pharmacies have records of prescriptions filled by them or a fellow chain pharmacy, they do not have records of prescriptions filled in other pharmacies. However, PBMs do, as long as the patient has used insurance. Given that information and the technology, in real-time and almost instantaneously, the PBM can determine if the prescribed drug should not be taken by that patient and can alert the pharmacist to any dangerous interactions before the patient pays any cost sharing and receives any medication. All of this happens rapidly, seamlessly, and behind the scenes to improve patient safety and care.

Reducing Health Benefit Costs for Businesses

PBMs have an established record of negotiating with drug manufacturers and pharmacies to reduce drug costs. PBMs work to bring drug prices down to the lowest net cost for employers, both large and small, and others who provide health insurance.

No employer, union, pension fund, or health plan has to hire or use a PBM. But virtually all do choose to hire a PBM to lower the cost of providing health care coverage and to better serve the patients they represent.

PBM clients choose their PBMs through a transparent and highly competitive bidding process. With more than 70 full-service PBMs in the market, including regular new entrants, unions, and employers, health plans have a tremendous diversity of opportunities to contract with the PBM that best meets their unique needs.[75]

---

[74] Pharmaceutical Care Management Association (PCMA). PBM Technology and Expertise Improves Patient Health Outcomes. June 2016. March 8, 2022. Available at *https://www.pcmanet.org/pbm-technology-and-expertise-improves-patient-health-outcomes/*.

[75] Pharmaceutical Care Management Association (PCMA). The PBM Marketplace Is Highly Competitive. April 2021. Available at *https://www.pcmanet.org/wp-content/uploads/2021/04/ PBM-Landscape-2021.pdf*.

Some may choose a PBM based on its scale, ability to negotiate deep discounts or manage the risk of price changes. Others choose to hire PBMs based on their innovative care management programs or different levels of service. For small employers, many of whom may struggle to provide health insurance to employees, PBMs lower drug costs and provide cost predictability, enabling them to stretch their benefit dollars even further.

For all those sponsoring health insurance, it is important that there is choice among PBMs and the ability to decide how to set up their drug benefits to best serve their unique populations.

PBMs typically develop a basic preferred drug list, or formulary, under the guidance of their pharmacy and therapeutics (P&T) committee. P&T committees are comprised of independent physicians, pharmacists, and other clinical experts who consider the most recent data on prescription drugs and tell the PBM what drugs it must include, must not include (for safety reasons), and may include on its formulary. The drugs it ''may'' include are typically for conditions or diseases for which there are competing therapeutically equivalent treatments, and for which the PBM may leverage competition between drug manufacturers to negotiate lower costs. Once the PBM has concluded its negotiations and devised its formulary, it then recommends it to those sponsoring health insurance, who may choose to utilize it, cus tomize it, or go with another approach.[76] PBMs create formularies of clinically appropriate drugs, preferring ones that are the most cost effective, including generic drugs, biosimilars, and lower-cost alternative brand drugs.

One method that PBMs use to lower drug costs is incentivizing the use of lowercost generic alternatives to name-brand drugs. Indeed, generic dispensing has grown over the past decade as more generics have entered the market and patients have responded to health plan designs encouraging their use, so that now roughly 90 percent of prescriptions filled in the United States are for generic drugs, at a fraction of the cost of their brand-name equivalents.[77] PBMs also sometimes, for some conditions, require patients to try generic drugs before trying more expensive brand drugs, and employ other

---

[76] Pharmaceutical Care Management Association (PCMA). The Management of Specialty Drugs. June 2016. Available at *www.spcma.org/wp-content/uploads/2016/06/sPCMA_The _Management_of_Specialty_Drugs.pdf.*

[77] U.S. Food and Drug Administration (FDA). Generic Drugs. February 5, 2021. Available at *https://www.fda.gov/drugs/buying-using-medicine-safely/generic-drugs.*

tools designed to deliver high-quality drug benefits while bringing down costs.[78]

As a result, PBMs have a pro-competitive influence on the prescription drug marketplace, and PBM services provide a significant and measurable benefit for businesses and others providing health insurance. Without PBMs in the marketplace, those organizations would be left to negotiate drug costs on their own or pay the full costs of these drugs.

Lowering Drug Costs for Consumers

As mentioned earlier, PBMs, working with those providing insurance, encourage patients through formulary design and cost-sharing incentives to use the most affordable drugs, which are usually generics. For many brand drugs, PBMs negotiate directly with drug manufacturers who compete for formulary placement by offering a type of discount called rebates.[79] For drugs on the preferred tier of a plan's formulary, consumers typically have lower cost sharing.[80] As competing products enter the market, PBMs gain the flexibility to leverage competitor products to negotiate deeper drug discounts for patients and payers.[81]

PBMs have also led the industry in creating contracts that account for the value of specialty and high-cost medications.[82] Value-based arrangements are

---

[78] Pharmacy Benefit Management Institute (PBMI). Solving America's High Drug Cost Problem: Prevent Drug Company Tactics that Increase Costs and Undermine Clinical Quality. 2020. Available at *https://www.pcmanet.org/wp-content/uploads/2021/01/ Solving-America%E2%80%99s-High-Drug-Cost-Problem_whitepaper_FINAL2. pdf.* Pharmacy Benefit Management Institute (PBMI). 2017 Trends in Specialty Drug Benefits. 2017. Available at *www.pbmi.com/research.* Pharmacy Benefit Management Institute (PBMI). 2016 Trends in Drug Benefit Design. 2016. Available at *www.pbmi.com/research.*

[79] Foley Hoag. The History of Rebates in the Drug Supply Chain and HHS' Proposed Rule to Change Safe Harbor Protection for Manufacturer Rebates. April 2, 2019. Available at *https:// foleyhoag.com/publications/ebooks-and-white-papers/2019/march/the-history-of-rebates-in-the- drug-supply-chain.*

[80] Congressional Budget Office (CBO). Prescription Drugs: Spending, Use, and Prices. January 17, 2020. Available at *https://www.cbo.gov/system/files/2022-01/57050-Rx-Spending.pdf.*

[81] Congressional Budget Office (CBO). Prescription Drugs: Spending, Use, and Prices. January 17, 2020. Available at *https://www.cbo.gov/system/files/2022-01/57050-Rx-Spending.pdf.*

[82] Pharmacy Benefit Management Institute. Solving America's High Drug Cost Problem: Prevent Drug Company Tactics that Increase Costs and Undermine Clinical Quality. January 2021. Available *https://www.pcmanet.org/wp-content/uploads/2021/01/Solving-Ameri ca%E2%80% 99s-High-Drug-Cost-Problem_whitepaper_FINAL2.pdf.*

at the forefront of new drug payment designs and will be critical to managing the costs of next-generation therapies like cell and gene therapies, orphan drugs, and ultra-expensive specialty drugs. Value-based contracts will better allow plans to manage these high costs, and health plans will need broad flexibility to craft and employ value-based contracts.

The Medicare Part D program, where older Americans and those living with disabilities can choose among private plans to get their drug benefits, is a great example of PBM value. PBMs support Part D plans by negotiating rebates and discounts and promoting better pharmacy quality, passing 99.6 percent of those savings from those negotiations to the Part D plans, which in turn use them to enhance drug benefits and keep premium costs reliably low for beneficiaries.[83]

As another cost-saving measure, PBMs offer prescription home delivery through highly efficient, virtually error-free mail-service pharmacies. As with many other products, patients can safely access prescription drugs through home delivery. Mailservice pharmacies are convenient, dependable, and affordable. Patients will often fill the first few prescriptions at a retail pharmacy if the prescription is for a chronic condition. Patients may then choose to use a mail-service pharmacy for home delivery once they are stabilized on the medication(s). On 90-day supplies of medicines, mail-service pharmacies result in lower copayments for consumers and improved medication adherence overall.[84]

Savings from PBMs benefit health plans, employers, and consumers directly. Prescriptions cost health plans and employers an average of $1,315 per person per year, with consumers paying an average of $180 for their prescriptions, or 14 percent.[85] Without PBMs and the savings they generate, drug costs could be $2,000 per person per year.[86]

---

[83] Government Accountability Office (GAO). Medicare Part D: Use of Pharmacy Benefit Managers and Efforts to Manage Drug Expenditures and Utilization. August 13, 2019. Available at *https://www.gao.gov/products/gao-19-498.*

[84] O. Kenrik Duru, Julie A. Schmittdiel, Wendy T. Dyer, Melissa M. Parker, Connie S. Uratsu, James Chan, and Andrew J. Karter. January 2010. Mail-Order Pharmacy Use and Adherence to Diabetes-Related Medications. American Journal of Managed Care. Vol. 16, No. 1: 33–40. Available at *https://www.ncbi.nlm.nih.gov/pmc/articles/PMC3015238/.*

[85] Visante. The Return on Investment (ROI) on PBM Services. February 2020. An analysis prepared by Visante on behalf of PCMA Available at *https://www.pcmanet.org/wp-content/uploads/2020/02/ROI-on-PBM-Services-FINAL_.pdf.*

[86] Visante. The Return on Investment (ROI) on PBM Services. February 2020. An analysis prepared by Visante on behalf of PCMA Available at *https://www.pcmanet.org/wp-content/uploads/2020/02/ROI-on-PBM-Services-FINAL_.pdf.*

The Value of Pharmacy Networks

PBMs lower pharmacy costs by negotiating with pharmacies to establish competitive rates at which the PBM will reimburse for each prescription that a pharmacy fills, which enables the PBM to form preferred pharmacy networks. Through these pharmacy negotiations, pharmacy networks enable PBMs to maximize accessibility, choice, and quality of service, as well as hold down costs for patients enrolled in health plans, including, among others, Medicaid, Medicare Part D, state employee plans, and employer-sponsored plans.

Pharmacies have been willing to negotiate price concessions, some based on proven volume, to ensure they have access to the plans and PBMs with the largest and fastest-growing membership bases. Often, but not always, independent pharmacies participate in preferred networks through contracts negotiated and administered by their Pharmacy Service Administration Organizations or PSAOs. As of 2019, all but one major PSAO chose to negotiate for the pharmacies they represent to participate in PBMs' preferred networks and fill prescriptions for patients served by plans utilizing those networks.[87] Some 83 percent of independent pharmacies contract with a PSAO.[88] Between 2011 and 2021, the number of independent pharmacies nationwide increased by approximately 13 percent (or by 2,645), whereas chains lost around 80 stores (0.2 percent) on average.[89] Today, there are more retail pharmacies in the U.S. than Starbucks, McDonald's, Burger Kings, and Subways combined.

By creating preferred networks, PBMs are able to negotiate savings that reduce Medicare Part D premiums by $63 per member per year. One study

---

[87] Pharmaceutical Care Management Association (PCMA). Putting the Growth of Pharmacy DIR in Context. August 2021. Available at *https://www.pcmanet.org/wp-content/uploads/2021/11/Putting-the-Growth-of-Pharmacy-DIR-in-Context-2021.pdf;* Fein, Adam. The Law of Holes: Some Independents Skip 2019 Part D Preferred Pharmacy Networks. Drug Channels. October 23, 2018. (Oct. 23, 2018), Available at *https://www.drugchannels.net/2018/10/the-law-of- holes-some-independents-skip.html/.*

[88] Pharmaceutical Care Management Association (PCMA). Pharmacy Services Administrative Organizations (PSAOs) and their Little-Known Connections to Independent Pharmacies. January 25, 2021. Available at *https://www.pcmanet.org/research-pharmacy-services-administrative-organizations-psaos-and-their-little-known-connections-to-independent-pharmacies/.*

[89] Pharmaceutical Care Management Association (PCMA). Putting the Growth of Pharmacy DIR in Context. August 2021. Available at *https://www.pcmanet.org/wp-content/uploads/2021/11/Putting-the-Growth-of-Pharmacy-DIR-in-Context-2021.pdf.*

estimated that preferred networks created by PBMs for Part D health plans save Federal taxpayers at least $870 million annually.[90]

When patients present a prescription to be filled, the pharmacies in a PBM's network dispense prescriptions for them using prescription drugs that they have purchased directly from wholesalers or manufacturers. Before dispensing a drug, the pharmacy checks with the PBM to confirm the applicable plan design for the patient to determine eligibility, coverage, and cost-sharing information.

After the prescription is filled, the PBM reimburses the pharmacy at a contractually agreed-upon rate minus any applicable cost-sharing collected by the pharmacy from the patient. The PBM then separately bills the health plan at the rate negotiated between the PBM and the health plan.

Patients recognize potential savings and, as a result, most prefer plans with preferred networks. For plan year 2021, 99 percent of Part D beneficiaries chose Part D plans with preferred pharmacy networks—an increase from 92 percent in 2020. In a survey, 85 percent of Medicare Part D beneficiaries reported satisfaction with their preferred network plan, and nearly 80 percent said they would be disappointed if their plan were eliminated.[91] These examples demonstrate that PBMs are delivering value to patients through intense competition amongst pharmacies for access to preferred networks.

PBMs are instrumental in ensuring that patients have good options for where to fill their prescriptions at reasonable prices, including at independent pharmacies. In Medicare Part D, PBMs and Part D plan sponsors use a form of value-based contracting referred to as ''pharmacy DIR'' to reward high-performing pharmacies, create high-quality pharmacy networks, promote quality access for beneficiaries, improve health outcomes, and reduce premiums. Pharmacies that help Medicare beneficiaries stay on their medications, increase generic dispensing, and improve overall patient access to care are rewarded through pharmacy DIR.

---

[90] Pharmaceutical Care Management Association (PCMA). Putting the Growth of Pharmacy DIR in Context. August 2021. Available at *https://www.pcmanet.org/wp-content/uploads/2021/11/Putting-the-Growth-of-Pharmacy-DIR-in-Context-2021.pdf.*

[91] Pharmaceutical Care Management Association (PCMA). Putting the Growth of Pharmacy DIR in Context. August 2021. Available at *https://www.pcmanet.org/wp-content/uploads/2021/11/Putting-the-Growth-of-Pharmacy-DIR-in-Context-2021.pdf.*

Meaningful, Actionable Transparency

Transparency that helps patients and payers is necessary across the entire prescription drug chain. PBMs support and practice actionable transparency that empowers patients, their physicians, those sponsoring health coverage, and policymakers, so that they can make informed decisions that can lead to lower prescription drug costs. Actionable transparency encourages consumers to shop for coverage that best fits their health needs and budgets, and once covered, use the most cost-effective, highest-value healthcare goods and services. It enables prescribers and patients to avoid pharmacy-counter surprises and helps ensure that physicians can prescribe drugs that are affordable for patients. To that end, PBMs provide consumers and prescribers with real-time benefit tools (RTBTs), which provide realtime information on exactly where the patient is with respect to progressing through a deductible or another benefit phase, what drugs are on the patient's formulary, and exactly what cost-sharing to expect for a given drug at the pharmacy. PBMs also provide consumers with information on in-network pharmacies, premiums, general cost-sharing, and benefits for their prescription drug coverage.

PBMs provide health plans, employer plan sponsors, and consumers with a broad array of accurate, actionable information on price and quality to make efficient purchasing decisions. PBMs' customers are able to set the terms of the transparency and information they want to receive, as well as their audit rights, as part of their contracts.

In recent years, Congress has added more requirements for PBMs to report to Federal agencies, as well as public reporting in more aggregated form, in both cases with appropriate protections for confidential data to avoid encouraging tacit collusion, efforts that we support. As the Federal Trade Commission has noted, there are limits to the benefits of transparency and unintended consequences that can result.[92] PBMs encourage Congress to focus its efforts on actionable transparency that reduces drug costs versus transparency that raises them.

---

[92] See FTC Staff Comment to the Honorable James L. Seward Concerning New York Senate Bill 58 on Pharmacy Benefit Managers (PBMs), FED. TRADE COMM'N. March 2009. Available at *https://www.ftc.gov/sites/default/files/documents/advocacy documents/ftc-staff-comment-honorable-james-l.seward-concerning-new-york-senate-bill-58-pharmacy-benefit-managers-pbms/ v090006newyorkpbm.pdf.*

Promising Policy Solutions

PCMA supports efforts to increase competition in the pharmaceutical market and increase patient access to needed medications. Generally, we support bills by several of the committee's members and others that would:

- Increase competition in the pharmaceutical market and eliminate patent system abuses that stifle competition.
- Prevent pay-for-delay patent settlements for patent infringement claims between brand and generic manufacturers.
- Put an end to abuses of the citizen petition process that may slow new competition by slowing applications seeking market approval.
- Improve Medicare's online pricing tools, allowing beneficiaries to compare costs across healthcare settings.
- Prohibit product hopping that would allow drug manufacturers to switch from an expiring patent on a reference drug to a later-expiring patent on a follow- on product.
- Reimagine and modernize Medicare Part D to allow for comprehensive benefit redesign and increased transparency while protecting sensitive proprietary pricing information and avoiding inadvertent price increases for patients and the Federal government.

I want to thank Chairman Blumenthal and Ranking Member Blackburn and Senators Klobuchar, Cruz, Peters, and others for their work on these efforts. The PBM industry looks forward to working with the committee's members on these policy concepts.

Conclusion

PCMA and the companies we represent are committed to working with the subcommittee and all stakeholders to continue improving the affordability of prescription drugs for patients. While I have spoken a lot about the work we do for those who provide health coverage for consumers, the most important lens through which to judge these issues is not what will best benefit the plan sponsor, the PBM, the retail pharmacy, or the manufacturer; it should come down to what best serves the consumer—the affordability of their health care, the ease of their access, and ultimately their health care outcomes.

Through their work, PBMs are contributing to lower costs for health coverage, lower costs for medications, and better and more affordable access for patients, which means more people getting the medications they need to lead healthier lives. I hope that this hearing is an opportunity for a continued conversation not only about the work done by PBMs but a look at the entire supply chain so that we can identify solutions for patients and consumers.

Thank you again for the opportunity to speak with you. I look forward to answering your questions.

Senator BLUMENTHAL. Thanks, Mr. Scott. And this hearing will be indeed an opportunity to continue the conversation about all the segments of this industry. PBMs, as I indicated, right at the start, are far from the only source of increased costs. But they are, in fact, bedeviling many of the consumers we represent. Whatever the abstractions and the generalities we here in this committee room, are real life experience in Connecticut or Tennessee or elsewhere in the country show that PBMs can have a detrimental impact. And I will give you just one example.

The 47-year-old woman in Norwich, Connecticut who told my office about PBMs getting in the way of her treatment and her access to cancer drugs that she was prescribed, an oral cancer drug that was denied twice by the PBM before there was approval for the generic. The problem with the generic is that it added larger out-of- pocket costs for the patient than the brand name drugs she was denied.

I want to reiterate, she was prohibited from using the brand name drug that was prescribed, even though it would have been more affordable to her, and that is because of how the PBM set up her drug plan. Instead, she had to find assistance, literally from a charity. This 47 year old woman in Norwich had to go to a charity for help.

The PBMs who are responsible for creating these formularies, the formularies are for the health care plan. It is a core part of how the PBMs operate, but the net effect is to deny certain drugs for patients. So if the purpose of PBMs is to lower costs for patients, how is it possible that she was denied access to a drug that would have cost her less out-of-pocket?

Mr. SCOTT. Thank you, Mr. Chairman. I think that question is for me, so I will jump in. And I think you are right to focus on the real life experience. I will share briefly, if I could, my PBM story when my dad suffered from cancer as well and Alzheimer's disease, and at the end of his life as many people who have family members who suffered through dementia and Alzheimer's know, there was a constant switching of medications that was necessary that the doctor was recommending in order to control that process.

And the plan, the Medicare plan that he was on was affordable. The drugs were covered. He was able to get the access he needed, which meant thanks to that work done by the PBM to make the system work, my mom and I were able to focus on spending time with my dad rather than focusing on those issues of medication access. So I am grateful for the work that was done.

In regards to the example you raised, Mr. Chairman, about a patient with cancer drugs and having troubles navigating the formulary system, I will just level—say if I could, that first of all, PBMs develop and recommend formularies, those lists of what drugs are covered at what cost sharing amount for the patient for the plan sponsors that hire them.

Ultimately the plan sponsors making the decision to go with the PBM recommended formulary, make alterations to it, do something else altogether. Those formulary recommendations are developed with two important lenses. The very first one is always the clinical consideration, what drugs are necessary to cover in order to meet patients' therapeutic needs.

We employ teams of physician—of outside physicians and clinicians to help make those determinations. And then in those areas where there are competing therapies available that are going to work equally well for the patient, then the lens is the economic one where the PBM is recommending the preferred formulary status to the lowest net cost drug.

So that, the intention is to address the clinical, address the lowest net cost drug, which in theory should keep the health coverage more affordable for the plan offering it and for the patient who is getting access through that plan.

Senator BLUMENTHAL. In theory, but in practice, what we see in the real world is that patients don't have access to drugs at affordable prices. And the kinds of legislation that have been introduced, and I want to give credit to our chairman, Senator Cantwell, for her work in this area and her interest in this hearing, shows that all of us on both sides of the aisle are responding to a felt need that we see in the real world.

And I might just tell you, the woman I mentioned eventually got the drugs she needed, but it took 4 months. It is a woman with advanced breast cancer waiting 4 months to get the treatment she needed. Time is not on the side of a patient. It is not a neutral factor. It is not like waiting in line for your ticket at the movies. I have heard multiple stories of patients being denied coverage of cancer drugs, and the problem is only seemingly getting worse.

While there were two cancer drugs excluded from formularies in 2017, the number now or as of 2021 is 60 cancer drugs. Professor Garthwaite provided a graph that shows the number of rapidly— that that number is rapidly increasing, especially in the last 4 years. So what assurance can you give us that this increase in exclusions isn't leading to more disturbing stories like the one that I just gave you from Connecticut?

Mr. SCOTT. Mr. Chairman, first, I completely understand the urgency of the scenario that you presented, and for any patient. As I have heard others say, every family has a lot of problems until someone gets sick and then you just have one problem.

And we probably all been through that experience of feeling that urgency. When you have a sick loved one, when you are sick yourself, you simply want to get access to the medications that you need. There are steps in the process that the PBM provides to make that in theory, again, work seamlessly so that if a doctor is recommending a different drug, if they need to go through that step therapy process, that should work in real time. There are times, as you pointed out, where there is that abrasion for the patient.

I think the entire health care system could do better making use of electronic tools and certainly in the PBM industry's case, continuing to dive into that technology, which we have started down that path, to make sure that that can happen in a more real time ways, so these questions are resolved quickly when patients need to switch their medications.

Senator BLUMENTHAL. Well, I am going to yield to the Ranking Member and then come back for some additional questions. But I just want to show you this graph. It is figure 4 in Professor Garthwaite's testimony. It is pretty—pretty graphic, pretty dramatic. And I am going to be asking some additional questions about the FTC and why it hasn't taken some action to investigate. Let me yield to the ranking member.

Senator BLACKBURN. And thank you, Mr. Chairman. Mr. Garthwaite, we hear from seniors all the time that are looking for lower cost alternatives. And so talk to me about list price erosion, what you see there, and Medicare patient out of pocket cost, and how are they going to be—when you look at these things, how are you going to be able to get to lower cost, especially as you look at biosimilars that are coming into the marketplace in 2023, and maybe they are not on the formulary, maybe there is another rebate. So, just in the nugget, let's touch that impact on the market.

Mr. GARTHWAITE. I will do my best as an academic. To speak in a nugget, it is not really what we are good at——

[Laughter.]

Mr. GARTHWAITE.—but I think one thing is you want to think about what—we say cost, what we mean, right, and there is sort of clearly, there is out-of-pocket cost and then sort of the cost of the plan. I think what we have seen, particularly in Medicare Part D, is surging out-of-pocket costs for seniors. And I encourage Congress, in my testimony, to do something to address that.

There is no reason why we should see patients spending thousands of dollars out of costs to get access to medication other than using that to try and return money back to the insurer to decrease the price of the insurance plan overall. It is not serving anything good——

Senator BLACKBURN. OK, then let me ask you this. When you look at the PBMs, is the costs the PBM inserts in the marketplace worth the benefit to the patient?

Mr. GARTHWAITE. I don't think I can answer that. I am not trying to evade your question. I think it gets back to your point and why I think your bill is very important. We just don't know enough about where the money is going as it flows through the system to figure out exactly, you know, whether the PBM is, ''worth it or not.''

What I will say, and I think the Senate Finance committee report on insulin pricing you talked about is very instructive on this, that so much of the demand for high list prices appears to be coming from the plan sponsor. As I quote in my testimony, the head of diabetes for Lily, right, saying like, listen, we can't lower our list price because our plan sponsor wants the rebate so that they can maintain competition in the market.

And I think that is not the goal of insurance and certainly not of insurance that doesn't include medical underwriting and is supposed to be community rated. That we are taking money from healthy—or from sick patients and transferring it to healthy patients in the form of lower premiums. But the politics, as I understand it, when we look sort of at the debate to get rid of rebates are such that anything that increases the premiums for seniors is a nonstarter. The part of the conversation we are going to have to have here is there is going to be a tradeoff.

If you would like to get list prices lower, if you would like to remove rebates from the system, if you like to get drug prices lower, access is going to be impinged somewhere, right. It is either going to be because the PBM puts an exclusion list, or it is going to be because prices get pushed down and we get fewer drugs in the future.

We have to make a choice somewhere about where we want to have reduced access if we want lower prices.

Senator BLACKBURN. That is true. You have got to make choices within the system. But what Medicare enrollees tell us is there are fewer choices for them, and the prices are higher, and restrictions seem to increase every single enrollment period. And we know there will be an additional impact on the marketplace in 2023. Ms. Feldman, let me come to you.

Ms. FELDMAN. Yes, ma'am.

Senator BLACKBURN. Mr. Scott wrote an op-ed recently, and he is with PCMA. He is here as one of our witnesses. He argues in this that drug makers alone are responsible for setting and raising the prices. So do you agree with this, yes or no?

Ms. FELDMAN. No. I think there is plenty of blame to go around in this system. The prices are negotiated terms. That is what the PBMs are supposed to be doing, negotiating price with the drug companies. If there is no negotiation going on, why are they there?

Senator BLACKBURN. OK. So this current rebate system that we have, is it working to effectively lower the prices? Kind of the same question to you that I had to, Mr. Garthwaite, is the cost delivering the expected benefit?

Ms. FELDMAN. Let me just try to put it in very simple terms. If my job is to bring prices down, however you define price, and if we look across 15 years and we see that prices after rebates are rising dramatically, I am not doing my job somehow. I do want to be clear that rebates aren't the only problem.

There are all kinds of other flows of payments from drug companies to the PBMs. So we can call things a rebate or a flat fee or an elephant, it is still a flow of lucrative dollars and the influence that brings.

Senator BLACKBURN. OK, thank you. I would like to hear a little bit more, but I am going to ask for it in writing. Mr. Garthwaite to you, and Professor Feldman to you, I would like to know what you would see a competitive marketplace be. We know there has been consolidation.

Mr. Scott says there are 70 PBMs, but we know we have very few players in this area. So in a perfect world, how would you structure a competitive PBM marketplace that would indeed yield our Medicare enrollees a lower cost? Thank you. Thanks, Mr. Chairman.

Senator BLUMENTHAL. Thank you. Thanks for that assignment to the professors and other witnesses here.

[Laughter.]

Senator BLUMENTHAL. And by the way, I would invite all of the panelists to respond to that question in writing. It is a big question and at the heart of what we are doing here. We have been joined by the Chairwoman of the Committee. I mentioned earlier her leadership in this area, and we are grateful to her for coming today. And I recognize Senator Cantwell for her remarks and questions.

Statement Of Hon. Maria Cantwell, U.S. Senator from Washington

The CHAIR. Thank you, Chair Blumenthal and Ranking Member Blackburn, for holding this important hearing. We know that the lack of transparency in the marketplace is a concern to all of us, and let's understand where we are today. Since 2014, prescription drug prices have increased much faster than the rate of inflation. Drug prices have gone up 35 percent, while the cost of all goods and services have jumped just 19 percent. So price increases for prescription drugs have outpaced wages, gas, telephone, Internet services, food, tuition, transportation, and personal care.

So there is a consistent issue here. We have found the prescription drug prices have increased for 30 percent of Americans who take prescription drugs medications, many of whom have experienced increased annual cost of more than $100. The worst news, however, is that many who saw such spikes in their out-of-pocket costs were almost twice as likely not to fill a prescription or skip their medication.

So this is of concern. We know that the average list price for insulin has doubled over the past 10 years, even though insulin has been available for patients for over 100 years, and significant hike prices have become a matter of life or death for many Americans with diabetes. In my state, Molly Stenson, a Washington resident, used to travel from Mason County to Canada just to purchase insulin.

That is because at the time the average price of insulin was $450 a month. It wasn't until Washington State passed a law and put a cap on insulin at $100 a month that she was able to finally stop making these trips. Unfortunately, only 18 states have this cap on insulin co-payments. So there are drug insulin prices increasing faster than most goods and services.

According to Senate Finance Committee staff report released by Senators Grassley and Wyden, the price increases are due in part to the business practices of pharmacy benefit managers. That is the subject of today's hearing. They are—PBMs are contracted by Government programs, insurance companies, self-insured employers to negotiate on behalf of the pharmaceutical firms.

And the way the system works, they also make a lot of money driving up the price on consumers. Today, fewer than five PBMs control more than 80 percent of the drug benefit for over 260 million Americans. These companies, who most Americans know nothing about, set drug costs, decide what drugs will be included in your plan, and determine how drugs are dispensed. And these companies have abused their responsibility to protect Americans from these drug pricing crises—continued an opacity on the drug supply chain.

So we want to shine a bright light here. We want PBMs, the effective drug price for consumer—we want to understand how PBMs affect drug prices for consumers. First, PBMs develop what is known as formularies, which are a list of covered drugs on behalf of insurers or payers. To get their drugs placed on the formulary, manufacturers provide rebates to PBMs, some of which are passed on to consumers, but they keep some for themselves.

And because PBMs retain a share of that rebate, they have an incentive to keep those list price high. And who bears the brunt of that? Consumers, particularly if their cost sharing is based on a percentage of the list price or if they are among the 25 percent of Americans who have a high deductible health plan. The second way PBMs are affecting drug prices is something called spread pricing. Spread pricing occurs when a PBM charges an insurer a higher price for the drug than the amount it is reimbursed by the pharmacy, with the PBMs keeping the difference. According to an investigative report, PBMs skimmed off $1.3 billion of the $4.25 billion that Medicaid insurers spent on drugs in 2017.

There are examples of that. In 2015, PBMs charged Indiana's Medicaid program $204 for a drug and reimbursed the pharmacies only $197, with the PBMs pocketing the $7. Three years later, in 2017, PBMs charged the Medicaid program $147, but reimbursed the pharmacy $17, with PBMs pocketing $130.

That is right, PBMs profits increased by $123 for a single 30 day supply of a heartburn medication, all at the expense of the American consumer. And what makes spread pricing possible? The lack of transparency in the PBM market. PBMs affect drug pricing for consumers by enforcing a number of post-sale fees on pharmacies, effectively limiting the pharmacy's profits.

PBMs keep these fees—and just let me be clear, I am a big fan of the pharmacies. There is a guy across or a woman across the counter, when you go in to get your prescription, who tells you some things about that medication. Oh, be careful of this, what about this, are you taking this? So they are part of our health care delivery system. So the notion that some people want to have mega conglomerates control pharmacy drugs by mail and control the market and have a continued concentration, mark me down as not a fan.

PBMs keep these fees and really pass them on to consumers, thereby raising the costs for pharmacy—pharmaceutical market as a whole. Now, believe me, I am from an innovation State, and I also worked in software for

5 years. It is easy to raise capital if you are going to produce a product in 6 months and ship it. It is a lot harder to raise money for a product you have to have for 18 years. So no one is saying that it isn't hard to get capital to invest in new groundbreaking drugs. But the issue is, do we have enough transparency in this market? In 2019, the Washington legislature passed a law prohibiting PBMs from charging phantom fees that raised the costs of dispensing medications.

Several states have enacted laws requiring PBMs to obtain a license to operate in their state, and some have gone further prohibiting or regulating spread pricing and requiring PBMs to report pricing and rebate information to promote transparency. And they have brought enforcement actions. For example, April 13, 2022, the Louisiana Attorney General sued Optum Rx—Optum Rx, I believe that is the pronunciation, for inflating the price of prescription drug charges in their State's Medicaid program, included by spread pricing and claw back money from pharmacies without passing it back—without passing it back to the state.

But we in Congress must do more to ensure that all Americans and all American consumers are protected. That is why I am so appreciative of Chairman Blumenthal holding this hearing this morning and using your experience as a former AG to help us work through these issues at today's hearing.

We know that we have a system where patients get—if our system is where patients get inferior treatment and still pay more, this is setting us back. So it is time for us to take action on this. Mr. Chairman, I will put the rest of my statement in the record, but I would like to turn to our witness, Mr. Balto.

I understand that you are an attorney at the FTC for several years and were involved in many FTC's earliest enforcement actions involving pharmaceutical and health care companies. Could you explain why the FTC action against PBMs under a current authority of unfair and deceptive practices, and what more authority could help us in moving the market to a more transparent market? Mr. BALTO. Thank you, Senator. I think the FTC has made some major errors in terms of enforcement in this area, and part of it is relying a lot on economic theory and not looking at the reality of what is going on, and also not properly defining who the consumer is. You and I and everybody else in the room know that the ultimate consumer is, you know, real people. The FTC focuses almost exclusively on the question of the first buyer, the plan sponsor, and whether the plan sponsor is harmed, and in that way misses a lot of the anti-competitive effects.

Just to give you one example that sort of hits the point you are making about the service in the community pharmacist. Assume that you are a person who needs a complex specialty drug in which you really need the services of your community pharmacist. The PBM engages in various tactics to drive that community specialty pharmacist out of business or make it very hard for them to compete.

You are forced, perhaps into an exclusive PBM owned specialty pharmacy. And by the way, the FTC has permitted the PBMs to acquire all these specialty pharmacies. You move then from having—being able to see your community pharmacist, having them monitor your health care, having them give you advice, to all of a sudden having a pharmacist at a 1–800 number. And there is terrific testimony about HIV patients that I testify—that I cite in my testimony, that suggest how this is a problem.

The FTC Act is broad. And one thing that could be very helpful besides the efforts by Senator Blackburn and other members to compel the FTC to do well, to have the GAO do a comprehensive study of this market, and I know Senator Grassley and others have suggested the FTC to do a study, would be for Congress to specify what are unfair methods of competition that the FTC should scrutinize.

And the FTC Act is broad. It prohibits unfair methods of competition and unfair trade practices. And Congress can specify what some of those practices are. And when you look at things like the gag clauses, you know, preventing pharmacies from telling consumers where the lowest priced drug is, I mean, that is blatantly an unfair method of competition. It blatantly is something that harms consumers.

Consumers are in no fashion better off when a pharmacist can't tell them where the—you know, what is the lowest price without means of getting the drug at the lowest price. And there is no reason for that other than for PBMs to protect their PBM rebates. And so, you know, that is the kind of practice that could be specified. Also, some of the practices that prevent generics or biosimilars from getting on the formularies because, again, PBMs are preferring drugs with a high rebate to these lower cost biosimilars or generics, which offer a lot of promise for ultimately lowering drug costs.

In my testimony, I specify about five or six practices that could be outlined in legislation to attack these unfair methods of competition that ultimately harm consumers.

The CHAIR. Could you remind me, Mr. Balto, because I feel like we had this hearing a decade ago or maybe longer, and I thought we took action as a Congress to outlaw PBMs being owned by drug companies, and so that some of these same practices wouldn't be continued. What did we do before and why are we here again?

Mr. BALTO. In the Clinton Administration, we recognized that pharmaceutical manufacturers owning PBMs was like the fox guarding the henhouse. Unfortunately, in the past several Administrations, we forgot that basic principle of economic policy, you don't want foxes looking after chickens.

And so they have permitted the PBMs to acquire all of, you know, all these major pharmacies. They all have their own mail order pharmacies, which they prefer. They go and aggressively audit independent pharmacies. They reduce their reimbursement to ultimately force them to dispense below cost. They capture these retroactive DIR fees. Do you think they do those things with their own pharmacies? I don't think so.

And so that kind of fox owning the henhouse operation is just a poor recipe for competition. And by the way, Senators, you know, there is a lot of legislation going on right now to address this problem in high tech industries where we are very concerned about the major tech firms having their own—preferring their own businesses.

I don't know why we should let this happen with PBMs. As important, PBMs being able to secure part of the rebates distorts their incentives and turns competition on its head so that PBMs prefer higher, not lower drug prices.

And by the way, you have identified, many of you have identified the key issue here, which is ultimately non-uninsured consumers lose. And that is, even Professor Garthwaite identifies that problem. And that is why consumer groups, if you will note in footnote five of my testimony, consumer groups supported the past Administration's proposal to eliminate the anti-kickback safe harbor for PBM rebates.

Aggressive—and PBM rebates are just screwing up health care decisions right now and leading to a rapid escalation in drug prices, as demonstrated by the Grassley, Wyden report.

The CHAIR. Thank you. I wanted to ask you about the FTC brought a case against ABV, I think it is. If you recall, this was a court awarded the FTC $448 million in consumer redress, which had been—had to be invalidated as a result of the AMG decision. So how does the absence of 13(b) redress affect the FTC's ability in this space?

Mr. BALTO. It should be a significant priority of everybody in Congress to pass legislation to return the FTC's power to secure our financial redress. I know as being the former policy director, how crucial that is to being able to effectively enforce the antitrust laws. If bad actors, including major corporations, know that they can engage in conduct and basically get a slap on the hand, just stop now.

That is not going to deter them much from engaging in bad conduct. It is only when you can stick a significant monetary penalty on them that they know that they are going to have to pay the piper. So I think that you absolutely have to—that this is a major priority to strengthen the FTC's enforcement powers here.

And certainly if the FTC had that restored, it could look at these egregious practices that PBMs engage in and possibly bring actions under Section 13(b) to provide redress to payers and consumers for these egregious actions.

The CHAIR. So what exactly does the Committee need to do to give the FTC the authority to properly police this market?

Mr. BALTO. I think the FTC need—the Committee needs to strengthen the FTC's powers under—well, let me start off. First, I think the importance of a study is crucial, and I agree with the professor that study and more information is really vital. However, the Committee needs to instruct the FTC. It needs to identify the right consumer.

The FTC's past studies like their mail order study two decades ago just looked at the impact of the plan sponsor. You know, and a plan sponsor may or may not care, you know, if the consumers are harmed in the fashion that Senator Blumenthal and Senator— and Ranking Member Blackburn describe. They are not necessarily going to care. They need to do a study and actually focus on the real consumer.

Then, I think it is vital for the Committee to consider identifying specific practices by PBMs that are unfair methods of competition that harm consumers. For example, the DIR—you know, and to me the patient—the gag clauses is a very straightforward example.

But also the DIR fees, especially DIR fees imposed by a rival, seem relatively—seem like the kinds of things that you could consider to be an unfair method of competition, and that the Committee—the Commission needs its powers strengthened by identifying some of those practices that they should look at as unfair methods of competition or unfair trade practices.

The CHAIR. And you—but you think that those—in your testimony you outline, I think it is on page 13 here, legislative action to prevent PBM abuses. So you think there are known practices now? Is that correct?

Mr. BALTO. Absolutely, absolutely. And the fact, I mean, the FTC has brought no actions—I mean, they have received hundreds upon hundreds of complaints by pharmacies about some of these actions, about PBMs going and taking information from its PBM affiliate and sending it to its pharmacy affiliate so that pharmacy could target and try to steal those customers, or PBMs imposing, you know, egregious audit practices to try to drive those independent pharmacies out of market.

Again, you know, you are going to—you know, in other industries when you see those kind of practices occur, five alarms go off, and they should certainly go off in these industries because consumers really care tremendously about their ability to access community pharmacies.

The CHAIR. Thank you. Thank you, Mr. Chairman.

Senator BLUMENTHAL. Thanks very much, Chairman Cantwell, for the excellent remarks and questions. And I want to follow up on some of them. I think there is no question that there ought to be a study by the FTC under 6(b) into the PBM market.

As a number of our witnesses have said, there is a lack of transparency, there is a lack of current data. The 2005 study is woefully out of date. That is the reason that I and others, including Senator Grassley, six Republicans, two Democrats, have sponsored the Prescription Pricing for the People Act of 2021, S. 1388.

There are a number of other legislative proposals in this area that would produce more data and more authority for the FTC to take action. You know, one of the areas that has been mentioned is rebates. The fact of the matter is patients should know that they have to pay co-pays and deductibles based on the list price, not the actual price after rebates. That is a glaring injustice here.

This arrangement is actually costing them money. So two questions for you, Mr. Scott. How does a consumer know what this list price is, what the basis is for that payment of deductibles, what the rebates are to the PBMs, which is benefiting from the higher list price, how do they know? And did they see any direct benefit from the rebates?

Mr. SCOTT. Thank you for the question, Mr. Chairman. The short answer is, yes. The individual patient, the individual consumer does see benefit from the rebates. Again, the rebate is simply a discount that is negotiated by the PBM from the manufacturer to try and get to the lowest net cost for the drug. What typically happens in the Medicare program——

Senator BLUMENTHAL. The co-pays and deductibles are based on the list price, correct?

Mr. SCOTT. Yes, sir. And I will get there very quickly. So the Medicare example, that net—those rebates are negotiated, fully pass through to the plan sponsor, and then the plan sponsor makes the determination, even in the commercial market, how to use those savings. Are they going to go to defray premiums—?

Senator BLUMENTHAL. So you are saying that the plan sponsor has a kind of throttle or hand on whether or not consumers benefit, and if out of the goodness of their heart they decide consumers should share in the benefit, which is key to their profits, then they will do it, but there is no automatic benefit.

Mr. SCOTT. So the consumer is benefiting. The cost of the drug itself is too expensive. That is sort of a fundamental starting point that I think we can all agree on. What the plan is trying to determine is where they are going to squeeze the balloon. Is it going to be to try and bring the consumers premium cost down? Is it going to try and bring their out-of-pocket costs down?

We have to address the underlying cost of the drug that is set by the manufacturer, because otherwise it is a series of tradeoffs, and one way or the other, the consumer pays whether—depending on the plan sponsor's design.

Senator BLUMENTHAL. I think you have just summarized the problem here, one way or the other, the consumer pays.

Mr. SCOTT. Until we address the cost of the drug—— Senator BLUMENTHAL. Let's talk about——

Mr. SCOTT.—underlying drug, that is correct. Yes, sir.

Senator BLUMENTHAL. And the incentives for higher costs of the underlying drug, those incentives are increased by PBMs that profit from discounts on that higher list price. Is that true, Professor Feldman? I think that is the point you were making.

Ms. FELDMAN. Yes. The interests of PBMs are aligned with the drug companies in those moments for higher prices because their pay is based on the difference and because they get, in some cases, to keep some of those rebates.

Senator BLUMENTHAL. You agree, Professor Garthwaite?

Mr. GARTHWAITE. There are certainly contracts where that is true, but over half of employers now are in contracts where 100 percent rebates are going back to the plan sponsor. And so, again, at times—we can point to negative parts of the system we don't like and say PBMs are at fault. But I also think we need to look at insurance companies and those plan sponsors and we start talking about the consumer that is harmed.

There is the person buying the drug and then there is actually the vast majority of the insurance pool that is paying the premium but not paying for expensive medications. And they are benefiting because they are taking money from those sick patients and getting lower premiums.

Senator BLUMENTHAL. So it is a lose, lose for consumers. In fact——

Mr. GARTHWAITE. Well, it is a win for the consumer with a lower premium.

Senator BLUMENTHAL. Well, let me—let me recite to you from Professor Feldman's journal article. ''In short, it is the perfect lose, lose for patients. Manufacturers raise the price, the consumer pays the higher price, the extra goes to the PBM, and in exchange, the PBM creates competition free zones for the drug company's drug. In the short term, the patient pays more in the form of higher prices. In the long term, the patient pays more in the form of fewer competitors to offer lower priced drugs.'' Professor Feldman, that is roughly the current situation, correct?

Ms. FELDMAN. I believe that is a clear summary of what is happening for the consumer and the patient on all ends. Everyone is benefiting other than the consumer, the drug companies, the PBMs, and the plans themselves that may decide to pass through some of those rebates to some of the consumers that sometimes or may not. That could go into many other places, including their own pay. So everybody makes off well, except for the patient, the consumer.

Senator BLUMENTHAL. Mr. Scott, in your prepared remarks, you say that employers and unions, ''have a tremendous diversity of opportunities'' to select a PBM power. As evidence you offer that there are 70 full service PBMs in the market, but the Council of Economic Advisers pretty recently under the Trump Administration found, ''three PBMs account for 85 percent of the market, which allows them to exercise undue market power against manufacturers and against health plans and beneficiaries they are supposed to be representing.''

All the witnesses so far have raised the issue of consolidation, lack of competition. Among PBMs, three companies clearly controlled the market for PBMs. How can you claim there is tremendous diversity of opportunity?

Mr. SCOTT. Thank you for the question, Mr. Chairman. I think the first point to understand is that no entity, no plan sponsor, no employer, pension fund union is required to hire a PBM. This is all a voluntary decision to hire companies that they believe are going to add value in helping them to manage the cost of their drug benefit for the patients that they represent.

Senator BLUMENTHAL. But let me just interrupt to say——

Mr. SCOTT. Yes, sir.

Senator BLUMENTHAL. There is no principle of competition policy that says antitrust law and requirements for competitive conduct apply only when a consumer or some other entity is required or mandated to buy a product, right.

Mr. SCOTT. So if I could address your question about the consolidation in the market, you are correct. My testimony cites 70 PBMs actively in the marketplace today. That is actually about a 10 percent increase in new entrants into the market over just the last 3 years. So we are seeing new iterations of PBMs, new players see an opportunity to come into the market because they believe it is competitive.

You have probably read in the headlines, Amazon is looking to get into the space. Mark Cuban is looking to get into space. These are sophisticated players who see opportunity in a competitive marketplace to pick up business from employers, pension funds, and others. Some, you know, employers who choose to hire a PBM are doing it because they just simply want to get the deepest discounts possible to really focus in on that ability to negotiate.

That requires scale in the marketplace in order to be the most effective at those negotiations. Others may be looking for different services from their PBMs that are better offered by a smaller, standalone company.

Senator BLUMENTHAL. Well, let me just, again, Professor Garthwaite, this is your graph, another graph.

Mr. GARTHWAITE. It is not my graph, but yes.

Senator BLUMENTHAL. Well, I apologize. It is from Drug Channels Institute based on 2021 data. This shows CVS Health, Caremark 33 percent, Cigna, Evernorth Express Scripts 26 percent, United Health, Optum Rx 21 percent, and then way down there, there is Humana Pharmacy Solutions 8 percent, and all the others, there are only two others at 4 percent. All other PBMs, cash pay, all of them, all those 70, or let's say 64 at 4 percent. That is not what I would call a competitive market with a diversity of opportunities.

Mr. SCOTT. What we experienced in the marketplace, Mr. Chairman, is that employers have choice. They exercise that choice. So within those competitors that you see out there, whether it is those with the larger market share or the smaller ones, there is—active changes are made to over time as they look for different types of service. And they have the ability to do that because there is enough competition in that market.

Senator BLUMENTHAL. Mr. Balto, I suspect you may have something to remark.

Mr. BALTO. Yes, I just wanted to point out, the question isn't the number of competitors, the question is, can they constrain anticompetitive conduct? And obviously they haven't been—if you see— especially if you see their profits increasing so dramatically. By the way, I represent union plan sponsors and those union plan sponsors do not believe they have many alternatives. They think it is basically these three.

I wanted to also go back to a point, just so we really get this down about, you know, this question about rebates benefiting all of the subscribers, and maybe there is a small subset that are hurt. As the chairman noted, there are lots of uninsured people. There are lots of people on high deductible plans. Those people are all harmed.

And as a matter of just general competition policy, we don't say that firms can engage in anti-competitive conduct because it benefits one segment of consumers, but other segments of consumers are harmed. If there is anti-competitive conduct harming any consumers, that is a violation of the antitrust laws.

Senator BLUMENTHAL. And let me just point out a stunning fact about this health care market and the relationships involved here. Each of these three dominant PBMs are owned by or own their health insurers and have financial relationships with pharmacies and medical providers. This is a vertical integration in a consolidated industry. It is concentrated power through the industry, and it creates a high risk of conflict of interest, and in effect, a take it or leave it approach toward competitive pharmacies.

And as the Chairman rightly remarked, the pharmacies often try to offer choices and advice and pro-consumer conduct. Mr. Balto, in his testimony said, ''because of their market power and vertical integration, these middlemen increasingly stifle competition from this country's most accessible and trusted health care professionals, community pharmacies.''

The AIDS Health Care Foundation wrote in February that PBMs, ''steadily squeeze specialty pharmacies, preventing patients insured by their parent companies from using specialized pharmacies like AHF's.'' I am going to stop there. I have a couple more questions, but I want to yield to Senator Cantwell if she has any additional questions.

The CHAIR. Well, thank you, Mr. Chairman. I think I just wanted to drill down on this a little bit more, given some of the—your questions and the response, and certainly our witnesses which we appreciate them being here. But, Ms. Feldman, I saw in her testimony where she said, you know, trying to get to the bottom of this is like shadow boxing. And that is the point.

The point is PBMs negotiate on behalf of some consumers, but they pocket a lot of the discount. And that is what we are trying to get at. Like what is—we believe in buying in bulk that, yes, you get a discount. But who is getting the discount? And the question is they are pocketing that. And when we want to understand what this is about, this issue of spread pricing, there is no transparency. So the consumer doesn't have the information to make the choice or the plan that someone is representing who wants to say, why should

I let somebody go negotiate a deal for me and say that they are going to give me a 30 percent discount and then basically only give me a third of that discount and then pocket the rest, and then when I go to the pharmacy, I end up having to pay more because the out-of-pocket expense is different.

So this lack of transparency is not giving us choice. So do I have that right, Mr. Balto and Ms. Feldman on the spread pricing, is this—do I have this correct?

Ms. FELDMAN. The spread pricing and the all the price in the price terms are held as deep secrets. Both the pharmaceutical companies and the PBMs assert that they are trade secrets, and they are deeply hidden, even from the plans themselves. Auditors aren't given full access to the terms.

Regulators aren't given full access to the terms. Certainly consumers and those who might disrupt the industry don't have access to any of these things. Markets in general thrive on information, and you have got a throttle on information here.

Mr. BALTO. I totally agree. Information is essential for consumer sovereignty. And look, the PBMs won't even allow your pharmacists to tell you, don't use that card, just pay cash, you will pay less. Obviously, they are doing a lot to throttle information so that they can protect their stream of rebates.

The CHAIR. I think we had a similar situation with what was it Ticketmaster where people were going and buying all these tickets up in bulk and then charging extra pricing and then saying to people, here is what—you know, I am doing you a favor because I got these tickets. But in reality, they were just—had supply and gamed the market and then charged up, increasing pricing.

And so I think that the issue here is where is the transparency so that consumers can understand, or a plan who is making a purchase, can understand because there may be other avenues. Not saying that every PBM isn't doing something, but at what cost, at what price should be PBMs just because they got to go to negotiate a deal, how much should they be pocketing instead of passing that on to the consumer?

So, Mr. Chairman, I think that is my question and it has always been my concern, because I do think buying in bulk should get you a discount. I just believe that most of the money should go to the consumer. And the fact that we can't get answers, or the consumer can't get an answer about this is very frustrating because then they can't make decisions about these plans, or they certainly can't make judgments as it relates to what kind of savings that their plan is entitled to.

I do really, though, have a concern about this—where this keeps going. And so not surprising that more people want to jump in. Well, why not, if you can make this much money in a dark, transparent situation, why not jump in? So that doesn't mean anything. And the key thing, though, is by undermining the system and undermining that line of delivery that I think pharmacists represent as part of our health care delivery system, then I think you really do take away part of the system.

And there are people who are—who definitely would love nothing other than to just have major control over a mail in pharmacy market, and thereby have less, even less kind of delivery system for us. So, Mr. Balto, at your time at the FTC, did they deal with spread pricing and other areas?

Mr. BALTO. No. These problems have become phenomenally worse. And again, because you create an environment that is sort of a petri dish for all of this anticompetitive conduct, lack of competition, lack of transparency, and conflicts of interests, they just have gotten phenomenally worse because you—and then you don't regulate. And, you know, this is just—it is a real fertile environment for this kind of anti-competitive conduct. And——

The CHAIR. And what is the conflict of interest?

Mr. BALTO. The conflict of interest is that they make more money by securing higher rebates when they are supposed—and which results in higher list prices when they are supposed to be seeking lower list prices. That is the conflict of interest. And if you are a payor—again, I do represent some payors. If you are a payor and you want that rebate information, no way. Absolutely not.

Then you want to bring your auditor in and have your auditor check. They limit who can audit. They limit the kind of information you can audit. This isn't like other markets, you know—I mean, they just come out, and, you know, and they just come up with new and novel ways of preventing the market from working effectively. And by the way, when you think about State regulation and PBMs trying to require State regulation akin to the transparency provisions that you included in the Medicare Modernization Act, the PBMs fight those tooth and nail. They know darkness is the best environment for them to engage in anti-competitive conduct. The CHAIR. Well, why can't we do something right now about that, about making sure that there is a transparent market as it relates to these rebates?

Mr. BALTO. We can. You know, there are transparency provisions that, you know, that Congress can consider enacting so that at the very least the plan sponsors have the information so they can properly audit and make sure that they are getting the benefit of the rebates that are being secured.

The CHAIR. Thank you. Thank you, Mr. Chairman.

Senator BLUMENTHAL. Thanks, Senator Cantwell. I have just a few more questions and we have a vote that we will be beginning. I am not sure of the exact time. I want to talk about 340(b) health programs. This is a Federal law, there is a Federal law that provides for discounted drugs to health care providers who serve a high number of low income individuals, community health centers. Some of them are federally qualified community health centers. They are safety net providers who serve some of the lowest income patients. They are one type of provider that benefits from 340(b) drug discounts. I have talked to a number of them in Connecticut and have heard that PBMs are inappropriately siphoning off these discounts and pocketing them.

Rather than allowing the discounted savings to go to the community health center and the patients they serve, the PBMs force them into contracts with lower reimbursement rates, denying the community health center and its patients the benefit of the discount and instead keeping it. Mr. Scott, have you heard about such practices?

Mr. SCOTT. Senator, at the association, we don't have a position around these 340(b) questions. Our companies have different business models and deal with 340(b) pharmacies in different ways. I will say, what is important for the processing, from the processing standpoint is having those claims modifiers as they do in the Medicaid program, to be able to understand which drugs are 340(b) drugs and which are not so that we can make that distinction.

Senator BLUMENTHAL. Well, will you commit to work with the Committee in making sure that the community health centers, and the patients get the benefit of the discounts?

Mr. SCOTT. I will be happy to continue to work with you on that and other issues. And Mr. Chairman, if I could just take one more minute. I am sorry that Senator Cantwell had to leave. A number of her thematic questions were around this question of transparency. And I just want to make sure that there is a sort of complete understanding of how that transparency exists in the marketplace today.

And taking it in a bit of a reverse order, important to understand that our companies, in Part D plans already report a lot of this information to CMS when it comes to the Medicare program, and we have supported legislation to make that information available to you in Congress through MedPAC, your Congressional advisors.

Congress actually enacted new transparency requirements recently that will kick in at the end of this year. So a lot a whole lot of additional commercial market reporting to HHS, Department of Labor, the Treasury Department on rebates, fees, impact on out- of-pocket costs, premiums, and the like.

Most importantly, when it comes to the clients, the customers who hire us, and the consumers that they serve, for the client base, it is essential that they are informed, able to shape their contracts, get the information that they want. We want informed choice and so that they can best manage cost and manage risk.

And for the consumer and the physician who is prescribing their drug, it is essential that they understand what is covered, how expensive it is going to be, what the out-of-pocket is going to be. So that information is available right on hand through tools that our companies provide, electronic tools, real time benefit tools, so that that information is on hand and the prescribing decision can factor in those costs questions specific to the consumer.

So we are happy to continue to work with you to make sure you have the information you need.

Senator BLUMENTHAL. Thank you. I assume, then, that you would support the Prescription Pricing for the People Act of 2021?

Mr. SCOTT. And can you refresh that? That is calling for further FTC examinations——

Senator BLUMENTHAL. Would require an FTC study.

Mr. SCOTT. You know, we have actually engaged, and I think that the scope of the study that is contemplated there makes sense because it looks not only at PBMs, but other parts of the supply chain as well, which to me is really important for getting under the hood and understanding these questions.

Senator BLUMENTHAL. I take that as a yes?

Mr. SCOTT. We would not be opposed to that study, Senator.

Senator BLUMENTHAL. OK. That is not exactly the answer that I was looking for. I would like your endorsement of a study. You said you are for more transparency.

Mr. SCOTT. If that legislation is enacted as move forward, we would not oppose it. If that study is commenced, we would engage in making sure we provided information. We—as I articulated before, there is a lot of reporting that already happens in the marketplace. If more is required for better understanding here at the Committee or——

Senator BLUMENTHAL. Here we are. What is really required is more facts, more transparency, more sunlight on a process that is invisible to a lot of consumers. And to go back to where we began, most consumers have no idea what a PBM is. They don't know what a pharmacy benefit manager is, which is the reason why currently we have absence of competition, potential conflicts of interest, and excessive profits, and prices higher than they should be in prescription drug.

PBMs are not the only cause of drug price inflation and excessive pricing. But they are integral to this system. In fact, they are part of an increasingly integrated, uncompetitive system involving PBMs owned or owning insurers and constraining pharmacies in the amount of information they give to consumers.

That is just one slice of a broken system. And the effort to repair the system often runs into armies of lawyers and lobbyists hired by those actors that currently profit from it. So I am seeking to enlist the PBMs.

If they are blameless they should cooperate fully in uncovering every aspect of this system, full transparency, and endorsing full throatily a study into the entire system, including PBMs. I hope for the cooperation of PBMs in the work that we have ongoing. I will be submitting additional questions for the record. We are at the end of the time we have for this hearing.

And the hearing record will remain open for two weeks. Any Senators that would like to submit questions for the record should do so by May 19. We ask that your responses be returned to the Committee as quickly as possible, and in no case later than two weeks after you receive them. I apologize that we are going to have to end this hearing.

There is a lot more to discuss here, and I hope that we will continue this conversation. I appreciate all the witnesses, Mr. Balto, Professor Feldman, Professor Garthwaite, and Mr. Scott, thank you so much. This has been a very valuable session and I hope to continue it. Thank you. This hearing is concluded.

[Whereupon, at 11:50 a.m., the hearing was adjourned.]

Appendix

Prepared Statement of FMI—the Food Industry Association

On behalf of the food industry and the many thousands of supermarket pharmacies operated by our member companies, we at FMI—the Food Industry Association thank Chairman Blumenthal, Ranking Member Blackburn and the Senate Commerce Subcommittee on Consumer Protection, Product Safety, and Data Security for holding this hearing to further discussion around this important topic. FMI strongly agrees with the Subcommittee that pharmacy benefit managers (PBMs)— from how they operate to the lack of transparency surrounding their operations— have contributed to higher drug prices for consumers. For years, PBMs have leveraged their concentrated market power and lack of oversight to the detriment of supermarket pharmacies and other providers, health plans and consumers. With that in mind, FMI strongly supports the Federal Trade Commission (FTC) moving forward with a 6(b) study of the PBM industry, including the relationship between large PBMs and pharmacies and the impact of PBM anticompetitive practices on both drug prices and pharmacies, and we ask the Subcommittee to help ensure this is a major priority for the FTC. We wish to highlight for the Subcommittee the following information, which reflects not only FMI's insight, but also the expertise of FMI's Pharmacy Operations Task Force.

As the food industry association, FMI works with and on behalf of the entire industry—from retailers who sell to consumers, including supermarket pharmacies, to producers who supply the food and other products sold in grocery venues—to advance safer and more efficient consumer supply chains for both food and pharmaceuticals. In total, FMI member companies, which range from independent operators to the largest national and international players, operate roughly 33,000 grocery stores and 12,000 pharmacies, ultimately touching the lives of more than 100 million U.S. households on a weekly basis and representing an $800 billion industry with nearly 6 million employees. Throughout the ongoing COVID–19 health emergency, our members have been and continue to be a critical component of ensuring the availability of food, pharmacy and health care services in communities across this Nation. Moreover, supermarket pharmacies have played an outsized role in the COVID–19 vaccination effort while also serving as a bridge between our communities and other providers, offering patients immediate care that is close and convenient to home. www.fmi.org.

Background

PBMs were originally formed in the late 1960s, initially to assist with processing claims. Insurance plans were offering prescription drug benefits and PBMs filled out the paperwork, ensuring that reimbursements were passed along to pharmacies. Over time, PBMs portrayed themselves as cost-reducers who could form large patient networks, negotiate discounts from drug companies and pharmacies, and pass savings through to health plans and consumers. They claimed to be simple intermediaries between the health care entities. However, today's reality is very different as the PBM industry has grown and consolidated rapidly in recent decades. For perspective, in 1989, roughly 60 million prescription drug customers had their coverage administered by PBMs. Currently, however, PBMs control nearly 80 percent of the market share for prescription drug access and around 180 million prescription drug customers. Additionally, these PBMs are also vertically integrated with health insurance companies, rebate aggregators and retail, specialty and mail-order pharmacies, giving them unprecedented power.

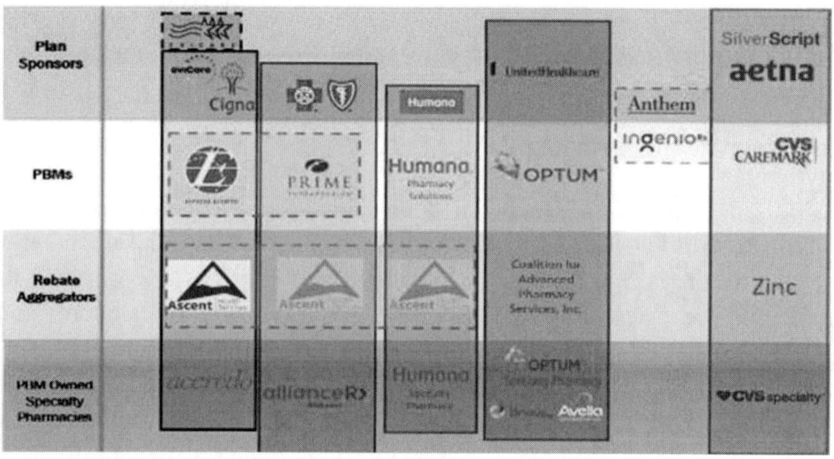

This situation, coupled with a lack of transparency, enables PBMs to enjoy multiple hidden revenue streams from other stakeholders throughout the health care system. The hidden revenue streams include, but are not limited to, the difference between the amount a pharmacy is reimbursed and the amount the PBM bills to the health plan (spread pricing), post-adjudication fees that are charged to pharmacies and often referred to as Direct or Indirect Remuneration Fees (DIR fees), and manufacturer rebates that pharmaceutical companies pay to have their drugs placed on preferred formularies. The post-adjudication DIR fees are described by the PBMs as ''performance-based pharmacy incentive'' fees designed to incentivize pharmacies to perform better, yet there is typically no transparency to the process and pharmacies are not told what metrics are being used.

Importantly, this market concentration empowers the PBMs to offer supermarket pharmacies of all sizes take-it-or-leave-it contracts. The pharmacy must either accept the PBM's mandated contract terms (including, among other things, allowing the PBM to set prices for certain drugs unilaterally and then later impose retroactive DIR fees based on an opaque methodology), or give up the ability to serve the many customers whose health plans contract with the PBM; importantly, this would include existing customers who have longstanding relationships with their pharmacists. Furthermore, given PBMs also operate their own pharmacies, FMI pharmacy members are effectively forced to accept contractual terms from their direct competitors—a clear conflict of interest.

PBMs Leverage Concentrated Market Power to Force Pharmacies to Accept Below-Cost Pricing and Other Financially Oppressive Practices

PBMs' profit model is dependent upon their ability to dictate prices and impose upon pharmacies arbitrary and often below-cost reimbursement terms for generic drugs through maximum allowable cost (''MAC'') price lists. Unlike with on-patent drugs, where PBM reimbursements typically are based on the actual prices paid by drug wholesalers to manufacturers, PBM reimbursements to pharmacies for generic drugs are based on PBMs' ''proprietary'' MAC lists, which bear no necessary relation to pharmacies' acquisition costs. Additionally, one of the many ways PBMs profit is by maximizing the difference between what they pay pharmacies for a drug and the inflated amount they charge a health care plan for that same transaction. To take just one reported example, an Iowa county was billed by its PBM $198.22 for a drug that the PBM reimbursed the dispensing pharmacy just $5.73—a markup of more than 3,400 percent.[93]

PBMs frequently assert that below-cost reimbursement is a problem only for poorly run pharmacies, and that low PBM reimbursement rates create an incentive for such poorly run pharmacies to improve their purchasing practices. However, the PBM industry has resisted attempts to force price transparency that would reveal the basis for these claims. Furthermore, pharmacies of all sizes—not just ''poorly run'' ones—are suffering as a result of PBMs' below-cost MAC pricing. Even FMI's largest members—Fortune 500 companies with efficiencies, expertise in supply chain logistics, and economies of scale—struggle to operate financially viable pharmacies.

[93] Robert Langreth et al., The Secret Drug Pricing System Middlemen Use to Rake in Millions, Bloomberg, Sept. 11, 2018.

Below-cost pricing is just one way that PBMs systematically leverage their market power. They also impose on pharmacies unfair and exorbitant retroactive DIR fees. PBMs charge these fees to pharmacies without warning or market justification weeks or months after the pharmacy dispenses a drug to a beneficiary. The Centers for Medicare & Medicaid Services (''CMS'') tracks DIR fees and recently reported an increase in such post-sale fees charged to pharmacies by PBMs of more than 107,000 percent from 2010 to 2020.[94] There is no competitive market justification for such an exponential growth in these fees. As with MAC pricing, PBMs tout these post-sale fees as disincentives to ''poor performance'' by pharmacies. In reality, however, they are just another example of PBMs leveraging their market power to maximize their profits. Charges for ''poor performance'' far exceed incentive payments to pharmacies intended to reward ''high performance.'' As a result, beneficiaries pay higher costs and drug prices become even less transparent. Additionally, FMI members cite these retroactive fees as a key reason for their pharmacies' financial struggles, forcing some to close their pharmacies altogether.

Moreover, with DIR fee reform proposals being considered by policymakers, PBMs have started including contingencies in their pharmacy contracts that would allow them to impose upon pharmacies even more aggressive rates and less favorable reimbursement terms if retroactive DIR fees become prohibited. Case in point, the following clause was recently included by a PBM in a take-it-or-leave-it contract that was offered to an FMI member. Although it cleverly does not reference ''DIR fees,'' that is clearly the focus:

> Change in Law. In the event [guidance is released] that prohibits or materially alters the economics of a Participating Sponsor's Program (the ''Change in Law''), the parties agree to promptly renegotiate the effected provisions of this Schedule, to the extent feasible, in order to preserve the relative economics of the Members, the Participating Sponsor, and Provider to that which existed immediately prior to such Change in Law.

Although PBMs claim the purpose of DIR fees is to encourage better health outcomes by incentivizing pharmacies to perform better, this clause clearly demonstrates that DIR fees are being used as a profit stream.

---

[94] *Medicare Program; Contract Year 2023 Policy and Technical Changes to the Medicare Advantage and Medicare Prescription Drug Benefit Programs.*

PBM contracts often require the pharmacy to relinquish ownership to all data and information sent from the pharmacy to the PBM. The data and information transmitted represents essentially the entire record of the dispensing event and claim(s) for coverage and reimbursement. This not only gives PBMs access to a pharmacy's competitively sensitive information, it also enables the PBMs to utilize the information to manipulate reimbursements and fees while steering patients to PBM-affiliated pharmacies.

In addition, PBMs typically include broad confidentiality language in their contracts to prohibit pharmacists from discussing their own drug costs, services, business practices, or the undefined term ''other information'' contained in the contract or provider manuals with third parties.

PBM Practices Are Driving Food Retailers Out of the Pharmacy Business

Unlike independent pharmacies, FMI members that operate supermarket pharmacies are not dependent solely on their pharmacy operations for survival. Therefore, PBM abuses may not threaten to force integrated food retailers to close their doors. Instead, PBM practices make it likely that food retailers will be forced to continue leaving the pharmacy business—either by outsourcing their pharmacy operations to the biggest players in the market, or worse, by abandoning pharmacy operations altogether.

Neither of these scenarios is merely hypothetical as several FMI members have already sold their pharmacy operations to PBM-operated chains. The number of pharmacies in supermarkets decreased by more than seven percent between 2007 and 2017[95], while food and mass-market retailers accounted for more than 45 percent of the pharmacy closures during the year from July 2018 to July 2019.[96] Supermarket pharmacy closures, and abandoned expansions, thus contribute to the overall trend of decreased access to pharmacies and ''pharmacy deserts.'' The effect of such closures is particularly acute in some rural communities, where closures are more prevalent and more detrimental to a community's access to health care. The closure of pharmacies in recent years

---

[95] Sharon Terlep & Jaewon Kang, *The Pharmacist Is Out: Supermarkets Close Pharmacy Counters,* Wall St. J., Jan. 27, 2020.

[96] Xil Consulting, *Payers and PBMs Profit from Obscure Pharmacy Fees, While Seniors See No Relief in Prescription Costs* (Feb. 11, 2020).

has created ''pharmacy deserts'' in some underserved urban communities as well.

PBMs' Concentrated Market Power Harms Health Care Plans and Beneficiaries

As employers that sponsor plans to provide health care coverage to their employees, FMI members also see how PBM practices exploit inherent conflicts of interest to the detriment of health care plans and beneficiaries. For example, PBMs are often responsible for developing health care plan formularies, or lists of drugs that a plan will cover, and drug companies compete to have their drugs listed on those formularies by offering compensation to PBMs in the form of rebates. PBMs may be incentivized to obtain more expensive drugs, to the extent their rebates correlate with the cost of the drugs they include on formularies. FMI members' health plans typically have little visibility into these rebates, making it difficult for them to monitor whether their contracted PBMs are choosing drugs to reduce plan costs or to increase the PBMs' own compensation.

Additionally, since PBMs own and have financial interests in pharmacies, they frequently steer patients to those outlets as the sole source for pharmaceuticals. By steering patients to their own pharmacies, PBMs reduce competition and have additional incentive to provide patients with more expensive drugs. As CMS has recognized, ''[m]arket competition is best achieved when a wide variety of pharmacies are able to compete in the market for selective contracting with plan sponsors and PBMs,'' not when PBMs can simply direct patients to themselves.[97]

Conclusion

PBMs have been allowed to operate without oversight, shrouded in secrecy. Increased regulation and transparency are necessary to help curb existing and prevent future abusive practices, while controlling consumers' drug costs and preserving their access to supermarket pharmacies. Moreover, the Supreme Court's *unanimous decision* in the case of *Rutledge v. Pharmaceutical Care Management Association*— which reaffirmed the states' rights to regulate

[97] 83 Fed. Reg. 62,176 (Nov. 30, 2018).

PBMs—provides a strong vote of confidence to achieve greater oversight of PBMs.[98]

Again, FMI thanks the Subcommittee for the opportunity to provide input on this critically important topic. If you have questions about these comments or would like additional information, please feel free to contact me at *pmatz@fmi.org* or (202) 452– 8444.

Sincerely,

Peter Matz,
Director, Food and Health Policy.

[98] Brief for FMI as Amicus Curiae, p. 9–17, Leslie Rutledge v. Pharmaceutical Care Management Association, available at *https://www.supremecourt.gov/DocketPDF/18/18-540/134582/ 20200302123959805_18-540%20tsac%20FMI.pdf.*

PATIENTS FOR AFFORDABLE DRUGS NOW

Statement for the Record by Patients For Affordable Drugs Now

U.S. Senate Committee on Commerce, Science, and Transportation
Subcommittee on Consumer Protection, Product Safety, and Data Security

Hearing on "Ensuring Fairness and Transparency in the Market for Prescription Drugs"

May 5, 2022

Patients For Affordable Drugs Now is the only national patient organization focused exclusively on policies to lower drug prices. We are bipartisan and independent. We don't accept funding from any organizations that profit from the development or distribution of prescription drugs.

Prescription drug prices are set by pharmaceutical companies, and our organization is dedicated to passing comprehensive reforms that will hold drug companies accountable by giving the federal government leverage over prices through negotiation and by implementing penalties on companies that price gouge. The comprehensive set of solutions passed by the House of Representatives last year and now before the Senate would finally authorize Medicare to negotiate prices directly for some of the most expensive prescription medicines, including insulin; institute a hard cap on out-of-pocket drug costs for Medicare beneficiaries and limit copays on insulin for millions of Americans to $35 each month; and limit annual price increases to no more than the rate of inflation. The Senate should advance and pass these provisions immediately.

But drug companies are not the only actors in the drug pricing supply chain, and there is ample evidence that pharmacy benefit managers (PBMs) do not always act to minimize prices and costs for patients as intended under U.S. policy. Our concern about the impact of PBMs — and the need for more oversight and accountability — is why we submitted the following comments in response to the Federal Trade Commission's solicitation for public input on the business practices of PBMs. Our comments urge the FTC to investigate PBMs in order to highlight specific areas needing reform and potential solutions. But, even while the FTC pursues its work to examine PBM practices, Congress can act now to increase accountability for PBMs by requiring transparency into the secret actions of PBMs, giving the FTC the necessary tools to regulate PBMs, and passing legislation to ensure that PBMs are accountable first to their beneficiaries, rather than their shareholders.

We're grateful for the Subcommittee's attention to lower drug prices, and we submit the following comments for the record in the hope that they will elucidate the patient perspective on PBMs and their impact on drug access and affordability.

Patients For Affordable Drugs Now Comments In Response to the Federal Trade Commission's "Solicitation for Public Comments on the Business Practices of Pharmacy Benefit Managers and Their Impact on Independent Pharmacies and Consumers"

Introduction

Patients For Affordable Drugs Now is pleased to offer these comments in response to the Federal Trade Commission's "Solicitation for Public Comments on the Business Practices of Pharmacy Benefit Managers and Their Impact on Independent Pharmacies and Consumers."

Patients For Affordable Drugs Now is the only national patient organization focused exclusively on policies to lower drug prices. We are bipartisan and independent. We don't accept funding from any organizations that profit from the development or distribution of prescription drugs.

Today, pharmacy benefit managers (PBMs) administer prescription drug benefits for more than 266 million Americans, or 80% of the population. While drug prices are set by manufacturers, there is ample evidence that indicates the profit-driven and secretive practices of PBMs play a major role in the cost of and access to drugs for our patient community. In order to better understand PBMs' impact on patients — and to guide future government and industry reforms — we urge the Federal Trade Commission to conduct a study of PBMs.

PBMs Are Shrouded In Secrecy

PBMs are supposed to act as intermediaries, leveraging the buying power of insurers, employers, and government purchasers in order to capture savings, which at the end of the day are supposed to accrue to the benefit of patients and consumers. But because the business practices of PBMs are shrouded in secrecy, policymakers and the public are left in the dark about the amount of savings actually passed on to payers and patients through lower premiums and out-of-pocket costs. While PBMs claim to be utilizing their bargaining power on behalf of patients, they are simultaneously fighting to ensure their rebate practices stay hidden from view. As a result, a patient cannot know if the preferred drug on the formulary is placed there because it is the best, most cost-effective option or because it is the one for which the PBM received a substantial rebate. Without further transparency and accountability, PBM decision-making and its impact on patients will remain a mystery.

Are Patients Actually Paying More For Some Drugs Because Of Rebate Practices?

Because larger rebates can be exchanged for more favorable formulary placement, PBM rebate practices may in fact incentivize drug companies to raise list prices in order to be able to provide deep enough rebates to gain and maintain placement. This ongoing cycle demonstrates how rebate practices can contribute to ever-increasing list prices.

Pay-for-position rebate practices also lead to higher costs for patients. A PBM may receive a substantial rebate from a brand-name drug company in exchange for placing that brand-name drug — instead of a less expensive generic option — in a preferred tier. Because patient cost-sharing is most often based on the full, non-discounted price of the drug, this structure exposes insured patients to higher costs even though an equally effective, more affordable option may exist. The impact on uninsured patients is even more severe because they must pay the entire, rebate-inflated list price without the benefit of insurance coverage to absorb some of the costs. The relationship between rebates and higher out-of-pocket costs has been substantiated in academic research.

PBM Practices May Be Used To Block Competition

Our drug pricing system is designed around the expectation that the market entry of generic and biosimilar drugs will generate competition and promote affordability. Unfortunately, PBM practices may make it difficult or impossible for generic and biosimilar drugs to gain uptake in the market. Current incentives in the negotiations between drugmakers and PBMs leave contracts vulnerable to gaming.

For example, as part of drug manufacturer Teva's effort to delay generic competition for its blockbuster multiple sclerosis drug Copaxone, the company developed a higher concentration version of the drug and began efforts to switch patients to this dosage before the existing dosage faced generic competition. The House Committee on Oversight and Reform uncovered documents that show that Teva pressured PBMs "by tying contractual rebates on [the previously marketed concentration] to adding [the newly developed concentration] to their formularies." The participating PBM conceded, seeking the sizable rebates in question. Teva's efforts to impede generic competition resulted in considerable costs to our health system and kept affordable alternatives out of reach for patients. In addition, in 2017, Pfizer filed a lawsuit accusing Johnson & Johnson of offering PBMs larger rebates to incentivize them to place its blockbuster rheumatoid arthritis drug Remicade in a favorable formulary position instead of Pfizer's new biosimilar competitor, Inflectra. Both examples illustrate instances in which drug companies worked in tandem with PBMs to hinder market penetration of more affordable generic and biosimilar medications.

PBMs Put Shareholders First, Not Patients

PBMs have become some of the most profitable players in the health care sector. In 2021, PBMs handled more than $422 billion of gross drug revenues in the United States. The profitability of PBMs has risen in recent years as a result of vertical mergers between PBMs, insurance companies, and pharmacies. Almost 90% of those gross revenues in 2021 moved through the "Big Three" alone — CVS, Express Scripts, and OptumRx. The gross profit of PBMs grew 12% between 2017 and 2019, increasing from $25 billion to $28 billion. Because they are profit-driven entities with a duty to shareholders but without a fiduciary responsibility to beneficiaries, additional transparency could clarify whether their practices best serve patients or shareholders. We believe U.S. law and policy should be amended to give PBMs a fiduciary responsibility to beneficiaries, requiring them to put beneficiary health and financial interests first.

Lack Of Competition Leads To Profits Over Patients

Concentration in the PBM industry is yet another factor that appears to contribute to a drug pricing system where profits come before patients. Because three large PBMs have a stranglehold on the market, these companies have a disproportionate impact on what medications patients have access to. For example, at the end of last year, CVS Caremark announced that it would no longer cover the blockbuster anticoagulant Eliquis in 2022 and would instead cover only warfarin and Xarelto. This decision had enormous implications for patients since CVS Caremark has the largest market share (34%) of any PBM. As a result, many patients were forced to switch products in order to remain on a covered drug. For some medications — especially biologics — a forced switch can carry with it significant health and safety implications for the patient. Patient choice can be further limited by PBMs, like CVS Caremark, that own retail pharmacies and may be directing or requiring beneficiaries to fill prescriptions with their retail affiliates.

Recent mergers have also made the lines between PBMs and insurance companies increasingly difficult to distinguish. This trend creates conflicting incentives stemming from the fact that PBMs are typically more profitable than insurance companies. Insurers, which are typically motivated by cost-containment, may pivot to direct patients to treatments with higher rebates instead of acting in the best health and financial interests of their beneficiaries. This dynamic could exacerbate all the aforementioned effects that PBMs have on patients and their costs.

Conclusion

PBMs were created with the stated purpose of negotiating on behalf of patients. Today, PBMs handle more than $420 billion and cover more than 266 million lives. Nevertheless, their work is shrouded in secrecy, so their practices remain unclear and their effects on patients are at best uncertain — and at worst deleterious. The Federal Trade Commission should investigate PBMs in order to reveal the practices and effects of these large and growing entities. Such an investigation could be critical for identifying problem areas and an important step in building a foundation for policymakers to utilize as they seek to develop appropriate legislative solutions to ensure PBMs can best serve consumers.

Commissioner NOAH PHILLIPS,
Commissioner CHRISTINE WILSON,
Federal Trade Commission, Washington, DC.

May 5, 2022

Dear FTC Commissioners Noah Phillips and Christine Wilson,

Pharmacy Benefit Managers (PBMs) work to jack up the price of life-saving drugs like insulin, steal from community pharmacies until they go bankrupt, and turn pharmacy care—one of the most important (and often only) sources of health care for rural patients—into a living nightmare.

FTC Commissioner Noah Phillips and Commissioner Christine Wilson, please stop blocking efforts to open an investigation into PBMs.

Signed,
2,406 of your constituents, including:

Katelyn, C (20002)
Paula, B (99517)
Kimberly, D (17981)
Ron, P (97402)
James, F (97520)
Russell, N (53705)
Norm, S (92399)
Jennifer, I (18704)
Mary, C (6516)
Katherine, B (93711)
Sandy, D (19958)
Christine, A (28374)
Debra, C (85044)
Carol, K (19317)
Shelley, S (23693)
Frank, B (90630)
Sherry, M (92056)
Stephanie, F (6002)
Mary, K (21044)
Nancy, S (50229)
Steve, T (8518)
Tiffany, R (80031)
Elizabeth, G (33647)
Lindsey, B (53110)
Vicki, F (20912)
Julia, E (32257)
Helen, L (17408)

Charles, F (30033)
Mimi, B (60031)
Clayton, M (98133)
Querido, G (95445)
Mary, I (30814)
Brad, W (80214)
Kamona, J (78744)
William, R (60148)
Jonathan, H (60622)
Subrina, W (23321)
Richard, Y (90066)
Heidi, W (80631)
Allan, H (95445)
Mary, R (21227)
Kaci, A (99354)
Mark, N (94960)
B., E (91361)
Layne, T (39120)
Donald, J (66762)
Dion, E (62040)
Elizabeth, S (53211)
Kevin, D (66604)
Steven, L (96789)
Candace, W (72701)
Kristin, R (89523)
Shai, W (98465)
Ellen, M (27102)
Charity, G (66215)
Erin, C (19930)
William, M (22042)
William, D (34613)
Steven, C (33594)
Jeremy, L (46052)
Jim, S (22152)
James, H (89149)
Patti, W (85254)
Christina, K (2130)
Michael, B (78705)
Jorge, C (90015)

David, G (85024)
Leslie, S (63105)
Rosa, L (92260)
Kristine, Z (32084)
Shirley, S (93030)
Deborah, E (85704)
Cynthia, S (60649)
Shawn, M (45439)
Eleanor, C (22192)
John, B (84111)
William, W (2478)
Rebecca, W (87108)
Henry, S (30344)
Angela, R (23185)
Ron, K (58481)
Teri, C (87112)
Brenda, T (37040)
Marie, M (90403)
Andrew, A (60534)
Frances, G (32963)
Leslie, O (79106)
James, J (20602)
Patrick, T (96706)
Ra'id, K (98105)
Barbara, P (11553)
Francine, L (11930)
Cynthia, S (2445)
Miranda, B (98115)
Ronald, B (54313)
Matthew, B (41014)
Raymond, K (32162)
Diana, P (12204)
Sophia, K (98146)
Mary, C (33707)
B j, P (87715) Joy, G (11208)
Kathy, G (63126)
Rodney, S (47129)
Thomas, H (93933)
Susan, N (98328)

John, K (92024)
Sarah, V (1801)
Elizabeth, M (27526)
Janet, A (90210)
C, K (60442)
Rebecca, L (55122)
Demetra, T (12603)
Taylor, B (37912)
Dawn, D (36832)
Philip, C (63141)
Brad, S (92127)
Linda, M (16669)
Keith, V (98368)
Doris, K (66701)
Jeff, B (73106)
Anne, C (95667)
Heidi, N (80516)
Carolyn, T (87557)
Pam, W (98229)
Ketty, L (33018)
Barbara, S (60089)
Darrell, N (10027)
Wanda, M (78749)
Jeannine, M (5403)
Jacqueline, C (19363)
Alice, A (8055)
Steven, W (1069)
Steve, W (6902)
Luis, P (94606)
Stacey, G (20852)
Philip, S (85281)
Dan, S (19565)
Stefani, J (95355)
Mahasen, K (8502)
Marcello, I (11747)
Khuld, H (68130)
George, M (3908)
Steve, M (45255)
Kyle, C (97302)

Ollie, J (77034)
Eugene, B (2169)
Linda, S (87025)
Teressa, B (32401)
Marilyn, M (87144)
Aaron, H (60565)
Dorita, G (73553)
Meredith, M (68763)
Margaret, R (11215)
Kathleen, G (80634)
Milt, K (33305)
Karen, A (55057)
Lisa, B (94549)
Irna, G (10010)
Mike, A (95062)
Laura, H (34982)
Alexander, M (60625)
Michael, R (60190)
Jennifer, H (33876)
Karen, P (85020)
Rebecca, I (85302)
Cynthia, L (91711)
Pam, V (87104)
Teresa, N (68106)
P.d., J (78602)
Judith, F (33021)
Patty, N (87571)
Claire, F (43756)
Melissa, S (81001)
Dee, D (48843)
Karyl, G (10028)
Paul, S (6710)
Kathy, B (78759)
Barry, M (85142)
Lois ann, G (17109) Christine, R (33872)
Jimmie, R (32505)
Margaret, M (2131)
John, K (90048)
William, G (77251)

Jim, B (33612)
Debra, H (48322)
Darnell, G (33647)
Alana, H (63135)
Ruth, A (93105)
Glenn, M (94080)
Teresa, L (80021)
Lynda, C (60185)
Judith, B (44685)
Diane, G (40601)
Klaus, W (801)
Carole, D (95492)
Edward, B (95060)
William, G (34689)
Nancy, G (91335)
Lindsay, C (5495)
Twyla, M (91767)
William, M (12020)
Lilly, T (37221)
Carolyn, M (48910)
Stephanie, L (63146)
Michelle, S (20602)
Rita, R (88435)
Sebastian, V (91770)
Pamela, A (64133)
Elise, B (8690)
Joyce, W (97403)
Carol, G (90027)
Martha, M (78209)
Lynn, B (4107)
Judith, M (53050)
Greg, S (60473)
Aimee, F (80016)
Mari, M (15218)
D, J (95688)
Debra, H (33455)
Tomdog, K (98611)
Bob, R (44120)
Jeanette, D (45120)

Raymond, M (7005)
Nancy, T (54482)
Allison, K (46250)
Carolyn, D (20854)
Cole, J (55364)
Art, S (11572)
Michael, H (92108)
Robert, S (52245)
Carol, V (68137)
Linda, M (12603)
Charles, B (99835)
Alexander, H (52001)
Thomas, T (98102)
Alia, F (91106)
Linda, H (10044)
Douglas, K (13820)
Paula, K (91302)
Sara, Q (95492)
Shelly, M (12491)
Carina, A (33175)
Tad, S (92625)
Ted, F (95123)
Francesca, W (95835)
Judy, P (98855)
Katherine, K (43227)
Jillian, S (33065)
Jackie, S (98005)
Linda, E (95407)
John, B (32725)
Patti, F (94954)
Mary, N (94118)
Amy, M (8069) L a, T (76102)
Elizabeth, B (7960)
Michael, S (95207)
Heather, R (90804)
Kate, J (15218)
Mercy, A (48314)
Marshall, T (27526)
Gail, W (73071)

Gary, R (85635)
Tami, B (33706)
Amber, S (97527)
Edward, S (24382)
Camille, B (60613)
Estey, G (7110)
Cynthia, E (48103)
Dorothy, B (60010)
Holly, G (98501)
Carol, A (90277)
Candice, S (93012)
Victoria, P (28311)
Susan, H (27511)
Martha jane, R (22066)
Loretta, G (78411)
Elihu, C (13212)
Betty, H (97402)
Carol, C (97068)
Lori, S (98597)
Maria, A (11375)
Shaeda, M (91335)
David, P (90046)
Jennifer, P (44113)
Rebecca, X (12345)
William, S (28403)
Mark, L (54822)
Joy, R (53719)
Debbie, M (6902)
Alicia, G (2148)
Jan, D (98682)
Terri, W (32259)
Brook, W (74108)
Marje, J (32259)
Jennie, C (91104)
Jim, F (21045)
Jennifer, K (14047)
Charles, F (90804)
Maria c., R (91724)
Donald, C (55411)

Madelyn, B (19067)
Vashti, S (22473)
Constance, V (47905)
Rick, C (77069)
Stacy, C (72404)
Laura, L (49405)
Paula, H (98033)
Katherine, J (85353)
James, J (67601)
Stacy, S (96790)
Kathryn, C (34420)
F, Y (6812)
Nancy, P (87740)
Deborrah, N (1420)
Eric, M (37331)
Debbie, H (60026)
Roger, L (25213)
Riley, L (45801)
Rick, L (94928)
Barbara, J (33418)
F. jay, P (6498)
Phyllis, M (13408)
Theodore, V (53704)
Susan, L (33971)
Nancy, H (98520)
Tim, V (12205)
Douglas, C (2645)
Miriam, S (10011)
Joe, D (7430)
Melanie, S (60477)
Mary, G (47250)
Cynthia, P (18951)
Tim, W (2895)
Bernadette, L (12205)
Arnold, R (97321)
Somer, R (8753)
Marianne, G (60083)
Lynn, T (98108)
James, M (94538)

Wendy, N (92507)
Nick, T (95135)
Zach, F (20015)
Alan, L (95437)
Rina, D (80538)
Justin, K (87123)
Mike, B (64772)
Rachel, G (53703)
C., V (8831)
Karen, N (98327)
Rose, G (94115)
Gina, J (35756)
Tiffany, B (62441)
Leslie, C (94618)
Howard, J (98001)
Dan, S (1756)
Stephanie, H (80207)
Cynthia, M (95415)
Yohanna, J (87544)
Edward, H (60657)
Mary n., S (86001)
Jonathan, B (8055)
Felix, L (19381)
Jim, S (2132)
Roberta, C (19147)
John, S (72120)
Jacki, R (55403)
Selena, A (34747)
Faith, B (53213)
Ken, F (20855)
Rosemary, C (31088)
Rick and sharon, N (95938)
Anne, D (15717)
Lisa, M (93428)
Nancy, H (97478)
Raina, M (41091)
Cynthia, E (55025)
Karen, L (91711)
Barry, E (85383)

Sharon, B (46526)
Graham, S (45431)
Alice, G (98236)
David, B (30339)
William, F (11207)
Claudia, J (96080)
Jennifer, H (17112)
Edward, D (19355)
Daniel, C (44240)
Anne, L (53115)
Dorothea, V (77079)
Mary, T (48219)
Barbara, P (95073)
Tony, F (90061)
Scott, P (77005)
Faith, M (96720)
Thom, W (78745)
Sarah, B (29205)
Nora, L (94122)
Doris, B (6472)
Rich, H (98310)
John, L (63026)
Ann, L (13662)
Peter, T (18420)
Ann, R (94706)
Vinodkumar, G (89108)
Joanne, T (92026)
Tyra, P (70122)
Sharon, G (78703)
Ed, F (21044)
Larry, P (97504)
Sofia, E (97202)
Marian, B (93221)
Eilish, F (60455)
Donald, L (32810)
Lara, L (98117)
Diane, S (17406)
Hashi, H (85634)
Tawny, M (95432)

J. troy, C (95953)
Eileen, A (11756)
Gail, F (98387)
Teresa, Z (93704)
Leigh, Y (80021)
Pierre, V (90034)
Dawn, K (89061)
Mary, F (55416)
Kathy, S (75706)
Carol, C (19904)
Susan, B (19107)
Diane, W (34112)
Monique, M (95971)
Veronica, S (10520)
Judith, E (55408)
Georgette, W (32065)
Michael, B (93728)
Charles, S (19709)
Paige, S (21060)
Alexandra, S (11106)
Roberta, W (8086)
Robert, B (54022)
Carol, B (19095)
Jeffrey, S (15237)
Elka, T (20016)
Gerald, G (62040)
Dave, W (93950)
H, G (48026)
April, O (94960)
Edward, G (4937)
Dale, R (78264)
Lou, P (60459)
Julia, F (80210)
Kathy, G (43152)
Diane, B (45140)
M, T (23225)
Jordan, H (94306)
Brenda, L (90712)
Jennifer, S (44024)

Erika, K (7470)
Filomena, D (11365)
Marc, S (90068)
Lynne, K (18347)
Allan, W (33024)
Janet, C (19403)
Izabella, D (78758)
Tom, C (60502)
Marlen, C (97211)
Enid, A (80212)
Marilyn, P (92376)
Frances, R (66206)
George, H (7090)
Tl, M (19106)
Brenda, G (91602)
Marybeth, F (23038)
Patricia, D (14085)
Jl, A (95672)
Helen, A (10522)
Elizabeth, E (5495)
John, C (91354)
Geness, L (93101)
John, H (63116)
Douglas, L (43221)
Erma, L (37043)
Jo, H (98047)
Hal, P (10573)
Scott, G (90042)
Olga, H (78045)
A.f., S (90036)
Michael, S (68310)
Sharon, G (33040)
Curt, Y (44903)
Melinda, A (1930)
Tithi, D (2180)
Penny, W (85375)
Sandra, S (11218)
Kevin, S (7010)
Beverly, K (93306)

Marge, S (4102)
Kimberly, S (8873)
Ellen, F (11215)
Marge, F (8830)
Bonnie, A (16066)
Hal, P (10573)
Tammy, C (54751)
Dave, F (50023)
Jeffery, B (54636)
Jonathan, H (98607)
Diane, G (11725)
Richard, J (98227)
Mary, S (45243)
Susan, M (60075)
Patricia, S (87301)
Susan, K (44145)
Connie, S (43229)
Terrie, P (53189)
Ken, R (90212)
Sydney, S (85029)
Olga, C (34990)
Charles & pat, S (80524)
Simuel, B (73507)
Scott, B (15206)
Katharine, S (11238)
Zenda, B (98226)
Renee, Z (30141)
David, C (85750)
Janet, W (98155)
Julia, B (28711)
Jana, G (40513)
Ralph, W (80521)
Barbara, N (94115)
Andi, P (60411)
Susan j, M (87326)
Karen, M (97405)
Joe, G (94558)
Ron, S (34990)
Josephine, H (90026)

Regina, E (27527)
Tara, K (24592)
Avery, J (30650)
Marge, H (5033)
David, M (50323)
Mary, S (54701)
Alison, Z (48307)
Nisa, W (92507)
Barbara, H (60707)
Ron, F (87112)
Kerri, C (36066)
Michael, C (60010)
Gerald, W (56601)
Rachel, M (19901)
Fran, M (11374)
Sara, S (61822)
Kathryn, V (98107)
Allen, C (44622)
Lauren, G (48205)
Jan, E (10032)
George, L (95667)
Kathleen, R (19465)
Carla, C (85143)
Kara, S (14586)
Victoria, S (90025)
Stephen, G (47130)
Gail, S (1701)
Joan, P (65203)
Scott, B (94087)
Allan, A (85716)
Judith and robert, P (98506)
Beth, D (50707)
Chester richey, M (36830)
Kathy, K (93003)
David, S (23701)
Jacob, H (92026)
Nancy, P (98597)
Bryan, G (98146)
Joshua, A (73501)

Carolyn, E (75181)
Holly, D (94947)
Michael, S (27408)
Terence, H (43302)
Matthew, V (27560)
Tina, M (90024)
Larry, R (6840)
Janet, H (92058)
Bruce, S (90065)
Andrea, C (76248)
Joseph, M (89031)
Bruce, S (62069)
Stephen and robin, N (6053)
Nancy, C (6753)
Naida, L (97211)
Gemma, P (91030)
Philip, B (75019)
Carole, H (80524)
Tamas, F (34238)
Nazir, M (70769)
Tom, B (78737)
Peter, E (35630)
Sally, B (98404)
R, I (95050)
Sherry, W (97367)
Sandra, J (97239)
Ilona, K (21208)
Lois, M (83864)
Mark, J (12303)
Chris, O (54871)
Deborah, T (10128)
Barbara, K (32605)
Jamie, F (75217)
Donaldson, S (33063)
Bob, O (54871)
Paula, B (93065)
Barbara, H (95012)
Jordyn, M (80831)
Cathy, P (94582)

Catherine, E (32803)
Ryan, F (44090)
Phillip, P (60471)
Matthew, S (68521)
Ghaziyah, H (17701)
Yova, M (80227)
Stephen, W (98548)
Michael, F (45409)
A.l., S (12418)
Terry, H (98584)
Pan, W (1062)
Deborah, S (28730)
Barbara, S (5767)
Carrie, S (19608)
Dmitra, T (22892)
Benjamin, M (6492)
Judi, W (1902)
Barbara, R (28734)
Patrick, F (98223)
Chuck, T (96753)
Del, P (28803)
Peter, B (96145)
Josephine, L (5602)
Richard, N (94928)
Js, I (12206)
Al, B (72958)
Sandra, B (32773)
Jonathan, P (10036)
Steve, H (60605)
Marc, N (98178)
Phyllis, R (94708)
Barbara, V (33076)
Guna, S (27514)
Mary, V (60421)
Susan, C (4105)
Jo, J (61701)
Linda, D (92079)
Sharan, G (92027)
Gail, G (87008)

Peter, R (80517)
Mary, S (55431)
Pat, M (14610)
Hollis, M (12866)
John, B (72205)
Jason, F (95340)
Christina, C (19904)
Victoria, B (10019)
Eileen, M (27312)
Sharon, A (20191)
Isabel, P (32839)
Steve, G (1886)
Leeallen, M (2152)
Nicholas, P (11932)
Dayna, C (97068)
William, T (6058)
Linda, R (68901)
Andrew, J (77047)
David, K (18104)
Eric, R (97386)
Kathleen, S (19087)
Trae, S (2816)
Kellen, L (84066)
Christopher d., R (76541)
Kevin, Q (87043)
Jacqueline, B (91302)
Kara, H (11230)
Jennifer, K (66865)
Byron, B (94530)
Anna, R (10128)
Lawrence, E (28540)
Judith, Z (70118)
Cynthia, F (97914)
C, M (55360)
Brian, E (44512)
Carl, P (3820)
Brigitte, G (92109)
Jennifer, B (55037)
Bridget, W (97209)

Mari, M (33062)
Joseph, S (28078)
Evan, K (27358)
Caley, R (97306)
Patricia, C (49230)
Gary, M (62625)
Timothy, R (98513)
Liz and larry, H (97501)
James, S (86441)
Mary ann, P (60609)
Conni, V (92691)
Grace, W (33023)
Laura, M (83843)
Peter8, D (2825)
Jon, L (34605)
Marsha, K (78130)
Joy, Z (90807)
Donna, S (94112)
Christy, V (94960)
Mary, D (34212)
Yevette, L (11003)
Steve, F (90292)
Susan, H (8759)
Steve, H (98223)
Lloyd, S (23456)
Amy, D (32824)
William, B (91401)
Judith, L (55082)
Catherine, C (55107)
John, C (85603)
Brenda, P (27534)
John, A (92057)
Janet, G (80863)
Ronn, K (42102)
Karen, M (45135)
Susan, S (35761)
Kari, B (1950)
Beverly, M (83709)
Marilyn, B (6880)

Michele, K (89108)
David, L (90008)
Joan, C (13413)
Maria, T (46217)
Matthew, F (28376)
Suzie, O (46311)
Kyle, R (97451)
Michael, O (46311)
Diana, W (3819)
Marie, P (94705)
J, M (6759)
Jan, S (95062)
Charlotte, P (95356)
Catherine, G (20912)
Ian, D (95959)
Josh, E (10025)
Norman, B (33180)
Melissa, H (63131)
India, H (21222)
Sara, M (27504)
Megan, A (15216)
Judith dawn, S (60625)
Julie, K (95819)
Richard, O (49045)
Ethelyn, B (30337)
David, W (48203)
Pamela, M (90505)
Sandra, D (92308)
Maureen, C (3872)
Pat, L (94022)
Eugene, K (96826)
Veroune, C (97538)
Leslie, M (98026)
Jean, C (65101)
Christine, D (95542)
Renata, W (55407)
Andrea, W (97405)
John, V (47112)
Justin, M (2466)

Melinda, M (4106)
Lillian, L (20902)
Kimberlee, K (48837)
Lauren, W (35749)
Melissa, A (36801)
Claudette, B (48108)
Paul, M (48624)
Keith, J (27344)
Jacqueline, K (94965)
Gavi, S (33771)
Mary, D (46228)
William, F (7712)
Gail, F (98233)
Bill, S (55345)
Jewel, R (7017)
Rachel, W (95060)
William c., R (16066)
Ljubica, S (10033)
Carolina, G (91401)
Dierdre, O (2155)
Mariame, K (19022)
Thea and steve, M (94022)
Rita, P (19144)
Sherita, W (14228)
Vicky, O (88310)
Diana, B (6850)
Bill, L (93611)
Nancy, M (98501)
Bonita, H (68828)
Richard, F (98908)
Sbs, C (80238)
Robert, L (91342)
Janice, E (10003)
Mari, C (38671)
Linda, H (89123)
J. r., B (84084)
Rebekah, M (97232)
Thomas, M (78613)
John, B (95139)

Ostrum, L (95901)
Lorraine, J (98125)
Dawn, L (60645)
Gerri, G (92610)
Irwin, S (33021)
C p, S (10025)
Thomas, F (19380)
Jeffrey, J (23703)
Susan, S (85286)
Maureen, W (43235)
Karen, B (91020)
Naomi, K (10011)
Jim, L (95412)
Dana, L (34714)
Robert, B (27501)
Penelope, G (28401)
Marianne, R (27260)
Audrey, P (98203)
Patrick, D (32162)
Alma, V (78043)
Paul, J (97267)
Anne-kristine, B (6042)
Joy, H (34491)
Dorothea, K (95128)
R, D (28226)
Nora, W (48371)
Cheryl, B (33948)
Wendy, M (77378)
Judith, B (95301)
Christian, H (94612)
Larry, M (90401)
Kim, D (80301)
Judy, A (99003)
Kib, R (80045)
Ervin, K (27410)
Chow-chi, H (45069)
Steven, C (95445)
Zachary, L (59802)
Janet, H (10923)

Noel, B (63379)
Dixie, P (87552)
J, L (85023)
Jackie, U (63670)
Robert, S (1072)
Cara, M (14215)
William, G (60022)
Chris, R (6511)
Laurie, S (10974)
Corey, S (7711)
Karen, V (93426)
Daniel, G (13904)
Christopher, C (2184)
Judy, S (55422)
Haseeb, H (10022)
Tamra, C (90031)
Sue, K (94588)
Michelle, G (89512)
Paul, A (75773)
Phil and catherine, S (2446)
Mike, A (97501)
Terri, M (63144)
Howard, S (34606)
Daniel, C (92397)
Michael, C (95032)
J, Y (90409)
Bonnie, G (48309)
Gail, T (93117)
Ellen, M (29940)
Elizabeth, P (94401)
Rick, D (97303)
Jimmy, S (3894)
Susan, D (80302)
Natalie, S (60601)
Richard, K (28269)
Tammy, L (33066)
Prisca, G (90066)
Sandra, S (46224)
Miranda, H (94612)

Felicia, H (39503)
Christopher, J (2746)
Ryan, S (85224)
David, R (76160)
Sonja, B (1510)
Mitch, M (92262)
Marianne, B (94028)
Pattie, N (98661)
Daniel, D (94306)
Russell, D (1778)
Bill, J (50313)
Sandra, S (75042)
Robert, A (43551)
Gina, H (73075)
Mel, M (90808)
Judy, C (92646)
Darlene, W (91945)
John, F (29526)
Cate, W (95336)
Sandi, R (60077)
H., U (99803)
Mary, L (98072)
Clyde, S (71055)
Frank, T (81007)
Michael, L (19054)
Relda, H (33884)
Monica, S (63385)
Jonathan, K (94028)
Jonathan, M (21702)
Barbara, L (30606)
Wendy, D (94707)
Dave, X (80122)
Karen, J (95811)
James, S (92570)
Rosiland, R (78704)
Sand, S (80204)
Kimberly, B (46804)
Russell, K (54467)
Wayne, A (60458)

Jolynn, J (80222)
Mike, D (35040)
Annette, H (60647)
Victoria, S (17545)
David, S (83274)
Andrea, D (55045)
Ronald, R (60430)
Ronald, Z (49858)
Kevin, R (78737)
Cynthia, B (60102)
Dalia, S (90017)
Cami, L (95405)
Miriam, P (7306)
Carol, M (34112)
Lina, P (33331)
Tinika, M (21229)
June, C (85719)
Gayle, S (11572)
Steven, V (22046)
David, T (75230)
Lamont, G (89123)
William, S (46725)
Betsy, S (13045)
Susanne, D (32615)
Nicholas, M (90069)
Anne, J (95403)
Cornelia, R (80487)
Tim, B (95112)
Kathy, E (61109)
Kelvin, E (15061)
Diane, M (1876)
Katharine, S (2889)
Nancy, C (60090)
Bonnie, M (1741)
Sherryl, K (27517)
Hector, B (38075)
Irene, B (14485)
Judy, B (87106)
Schuyler, K (90020)

Mark, A (27214)
Renee, M (60548)
Dorothy, K (12304)
William, H (27609)
Judith, H (98026)
Carolyn, S (34990)
Donna, B (33598)
Kim, F (16666)
Sally, S (46219)
Ronald, S (89509)
Charlie, O (16877)
Jerrika, S (89815)
Teresa, D (97103)
Chris, B (17522)
Jane, K (75013)
Casonya, C (38701)
Richard, L (87544)
Tana, B (55104)
Caroline, K (10023)
James, B (97477)
Karen, B (94707)
Dan, P (20018)
George, B (15146)
Stan, K (19014)
Kristine, W (5143)
Brad, B (55104)
Elaine, M (36106)
Cynthia, W (90057)
Connie, C (22903)
Timothy, S (85016)
Laurie, S (98584)
Attilio, P (84030)
Robert, M (85718)
Sarah, L (6074)
Szefong, N (11720)
Diane, F (1719)
Jarrett, C (7950)
Letitia, D (66502)
Suzan, L (99645)

Thomas, N (10023)
Roger, R (85234)
Robin, L (83607)
Robert, O (33319)
Wendi, M (34613)
Lacey, K (94536)
Helen, L (77365)
Sandy, W (91723)
Edna, M (55972)
Elizabeth, O (1824)
Mike, C (18202)
Alison, C (33967)
Pamela, C (12491)
Patricia, M (80012)
Jim, W (33406)
Janelle, M (94560)
David, H (92105)
Linda, S (95409)
Pavel, L (44134)
France, M (98908)
Delphia, F (86324)
Reed, W (80237)
Mary, E (55426)
Janice, S (64485)
Al, D (28546)
Victor, C (34219)
S, V (8054)
Corrina, O (85741)
Ben, S (94087)
Carol, G (19711)
Terri, C (21158)
Susan, C (10021)
Kellie, M (13851)
Linda, H (33708)
John, T (98229)
Colleen, C (33625)
Patty, S (11021)
Loren, S (80303)
Richard, C (94518)

Jacqueline, F (72301)
Jean, S (12721)
Michele, F (11417)
Nancy, L (1945)
Charles, M (7753)
Ira, K (60202)
Maggie, H (90723)
Michael, F (94803)
William, M (27909)
Debra, T (27705)
Edward, N (97404)
Bernard, G (60608)
Barbara, W (97015)
Barbara, H (81631)
Jin adams, P (28739)
Todd, S (94115)
Paul, H (80302)
Joan, A (54475)
John, H (1002)
Melissa, G (2148)
Robert, R (48207)
Jan, B (80020)
Thomas, W (82049)
Blair, W (91950)
Lindsay, B (10017)
Perish, B (21224)
David, W (92115)
Gail, F (55417)
Debra, W (18428)
Richard, S (10023)
Robert, G (87106)
Kai, L (52001)
Girel, S (91362)
Nadia, D (79701)
Jasmine, G (7111)
Bob, W (5465)
Mark, G (94044)
Sylvia, D (85321)
Carol, C (8823)

Kathleen, L (43220)
Francisco, S (79901)
Ned, C (84049)
Annette, M (22150)
Loretta, D (32751)
Louanne, M (97215)
Judith, H (75056)
Mary, S (28571)
Eddie l. and yvette, S (90043)
Peggy, L (12208)
Pedro, H (39211)
Linda, L (21403)
Jeffrey, M (44077)
Scott, M (98503)
Tara k, F (1075)
Mary, Z (2543)
William, R (60645)
Robert, S (32539)
C, E (53217)
Francis, F (19144)
Judith, W (82201)
Sonja, D (34787)
Penny, H (95476)
George, E (15065)
Adolfo, G (30518)
Richard, H (62703)
Denise, B (48326)
Ella, G (3108)
Cynthia, S (49816)
Cynthia, K (60610)
Crystal, A (63379)
Dorothy, V (32084)
Katharina, L (90032)
William, G (19023)
Rob, K (85713)
Deborah, C (17602)
Rachel, R (89431)
Thomas, T (91335)
A, W (27828)

Mark, R (16830)
Thomas, B (7642)
Annabelle, H (97219)
Debby, G (5262)
Carl, O (98366)
Mary, D (91711)
Bernadette, B (11001)
Michael, H (84037)
Lilly, K (11530)
Silvia, H (33431)
David, G (45322)
Marilyn, M (97538)
Kim, C (66062)
Thomas, C (55706)
Betty, Y (15210)
Shel, K (49009)
Kate, S (35243)
Joseph, R (95121)
Henry, K (6511)
Sharon, N (2536)
Debra, P (7460)
Martha, V (33612)
Jonathan, D (10025)
Elliot, B (91321)
Nancy, W (95460)
Amy, D (86286)
Curt, D (19002)
Diane, R (90501)
Stefanie, W (1748)
Frank, D (60660)
Donald, F (43506)
Marlow, J (53546)
Jon, S (94028)
Lisa, Z (80108)
James, D (2118)
Amy, B (15234)
Gail, F (33134)
Doug & mary, W (80004)
Deborah, S (80907)

Daniel, B (30339)
Sue and john, M (5658)
Michael, H (29605)
G, C (89166)
Paul, C (92128)
Lori, B (63031)
Elizabeth, L (98221)
Mary, M (63132)
Charlotte, S (2664)
Sharon, B (94611)
Susan, F (99516)
Rob, S (90265)
Leslie, C (23229)
Ramona, C (91106)
Richard, V (63139)
Kim, P (4609)
Jeszica, G (95061)
Mary, M (90028)
Michele, M (78731)
Stephen, S (85224)
Barbara, S (94002)
Barb, R (60178)
Rich, N (13862)
Mary, S (98117)
Brigit, H (54548)
Sheryl, A (92083)
Rebecca, R (8057)
Arlene, K (95762)
Thomas, C (93611)
Wade, J (55407)
Michelle, S (63069)
John, O (63304)
Jean, H (55057)
Ana, H (12401)
Chris, C (97206)
Melissa, H (97230)
Latisha, W (11236)
Julius, A (19713)
Roger, O (92545)

Marvin, W (24503)
Ashley, P (16508)
Kicab, C (27312)
Bruce, K (11209)
Rachael, H (45241)
Benjamin, K (48846)
Ruth, R (60201)
Veronica, B (94303)
Christopher, W (91303)
Michael, P (94109)
Greg, S (67206)
Sam, M (98661)
Robin, D (21113)
Sylvia, W (34601)
Judith, L (97225)
Pandora, H (32210)
Michael, R (92084)
Pat, J (88030)
B, D (95436)
Kathy, R (98057)
Denise, L (7095)
Brian, D (76248)
Marilyn, B (80230)
Marilyn, M (92399)
Angie, G (55016)
Carolyn, S (60639)
Shiela, C (94002)
Kent, M (59601)
Steve, S (22802)
Kathy, K (48097)
Kathleen, K (48135)
Della, H (64804)
Rhonda, M (46131)
Loraine, F (2184)
Chris, L (2189)
Sheila, M (32811)
Danna, G (92075)
Dolores, P (98230)
Fran, B (32819)

Lisa, F (48154)
Judi, C (34691)
Sandra, M (53211)
Doris, A (39206)
P, P (95467)
Sara, F (90034)
Jess, S (48198)
Chris, F (48154)
Kathleen, B (7876)
Claire, O (4062)
Glenn, G (19075)
Amen, W (60628)
Richard, G (20854)
Daniel, B (98116)
Frank, D (7107)
Steven, V (91320)
Penny, W (21060)
Esther, M (98059)
Paula, S (85603)
Mark, D (11572)
Jeanette, P (95472)
Kay, R (56560)
Helen, B (4011)
Rhea, Z (95409)
Trent, G (94619)
Elizabeth, L (93003)
Mayra, D (11572)
Sue, H (75040)
Kay, G (54401)
Diana, C (34209)
Fernando, G (91744)
Ronald, S (19150)
Peter, C (85257)
Renee, P (88012)
Emily, B (76001)
Fred, M (59068)
Kim, M (4112)
Saad, S (76002)
George, C (2910)

Karen, D (48734)
Bruce, B (94028)
Daniel, E (10026)
Alan, G (68601)
Margaret, R (95821)
Linda, B (97034)
Sue, V (54311)
Sally, W (85209)
Patti, R (60540)
Raymond, D (44137)
Sara, D (64052)
Margaret, D (6417)
Ruth, S (94005)
Kristine, W (80020)
Linda, C (62703)
Bill, R (11374)
Sara, C (89005)
Deanna, H (66215)
Samuel, K (23875)
Jean, T (30135)
Brenda, N (45701)
Jeremy, L (90046)
Suzanne, T (28031)
Alex, C (48327)
Linda, R (96701)
Jeffrey, B (94070)
Keith, E (46219)
Roberta, W (83713)
Elliot, C (44313)
Nicole, E (55122)
Sandra, S (11561)
Norma, P (92692)
Ann, G (18651)
Andrew and kathleen, W (10570)
Helen, H (49643)
Elle, F (98081)
Karen, R (42743)
Cheryl, N (19440)
Peg, B (49855)

Ingrid, B (1923)
George, M (4901)
Johannes, D (98272)
Marjorie, S (80033)
Katlyn, S (98125)
Samuel, B (97132)
Sandra, M (85018)
Paul, H (78745)
Murray, B (96134)
Deborah, M (47130)
Joan, S (18037)
Donna, D (77087)
Peter, D (6896)
Carol, O (35739)
Jose, D (32822)
Michael, D (13045)
William, C (28752)
Terry, B (14623)
Elizabeth, K (61455)
Karol, G (30002)
James, F (45840)
Anna, S (30016)
Marvin, K (54466)
Freda, K (7753)
Ruth, F (48183)
Deidre, B (30080)
Jerry, B (48381)
Kris, S (84629)
Diana, H (6110)
Igor, T (11375)
Crystal, S (55110)
Debra, M (60563)
Tracy, H (92393)
Malini, B (22102)
Eric, S (2840)
Shameem, K (55443)
Nancy and craig, C (97239)
Barbara, S (22304)
Nancy, P (5055)

Elizabeth, Z (94062)
Alena, J (91780)
Sharon, M (43050)
Diane, S (14607)
Robert, L (32244)
Diana, A (94024)
Tania, M (85719)
Judy, J (34420)
Robert, F (10512)
William, R (18504)
A, R (7902)
Roberta, M (80120)
Jennifer, F (92040)
Peter, B (90042)
Abigail, G (50613)
Marjorie, C (1721)
Merilyn, D (10536)
Patricia, R (91423)
Annie, M (86324)
Christine, M (12701)
Cristy, M (97045)
Kendra, K (53405)
Joy, L (59718)
Marie, W (94602)
Mike, S (89005)
Judi, T (33446)
Kiel, V (98597)
Christine, P (12206)
Kevin, B (80026)
Victor, P (33467)
Nolan, W (37774)
Raymond, M (40216)
Theresa, T (8873)
Hugh, M (46383)
Richard, K (62656)
Mary, L (42134)
Jan, H (95492)
Wayne, P (6067)
Ted, J (6385)

Joseph, M (14609)
Rita, M (53704)
Elvira, J (6385)
Jan, M (88062)
Dominick, D (80123)
Ed, C (62040)
Karen, L (94402)
John, R (80401)
Barbara, I (55345)
Esther, D (85033)
Glenn, M (98208)
Edward, H (40241)
June, D (1541)
Clyde alan, L (97221)
Jackson, J (42303)
Susan, S (80022)
Janae, D (83864)
Marla, F (50315)
Dennis, U (98404)
Maria, M (91301)
Jeff, K (5045)
Chilton, G (87106)
Beth, B (37062)
Richard, M (20155)
Jean, K (37763)
Alexander, O (32909)
Sharon, R (32119)
Rosa, H (30364)
Diane, V (14428)
Ron, Z (63123)
Nancy, O (32080)
Linda, J (66210)
William, C (19335)
Leah, F (93441)
Richard, O (94108)
Julie, J (91325)
Jan, K (15137)
Anne, B (6068)
Marc, I (20616)

Catharina, H (94577)
James, T (98020)
Patricia, V (46767)
Randy, L (77573)
Diana, W (90277)
Christine, T (32110)
Tina, S (80817)
Virginia, J (1060)
Gary, W (34109)
Debra, B (49004)
Jacki, B (12302)
Mary, A (80923)
Sheila, F (85374)
Joy, A (7083)
Potter, P (12581)
Mary, B (30033)
Johnny, M (27516)
Madeline, S (15232)
Althea, H (80504)
David, L (18519)
Rita, R (83835)
John, P (7016)
Jose, C (33073)
Javier, R (11249)
Dona, V (90405)
Lorraine, S (10710)
Bernie, G (93609)
Mark, F (93013)
Kelly, C (19131)
Scott, K (11005)
Dara, G (91406)
Tracey, S (32312)
Stamatina, P (19020)
Rick, M (25705)
Maragale, R (8619)
John, S (99824)
Jennifer, B (8816)
Josef, K (95490)
Athene, G (34243)

Betty, A (42103)
Pam, P (45245)
Mary ellen, L (6441)
Scott, S (37917)
Greg, L (77511)
David, A (6333)
Heidi, W (99216)
Jan, W (80503)
Wanda, L (80044)
Katie, B (55124)
William, L (52403)
Howard, R (96761)
Craig, M (97730)
Kathy, D (33070)
Myron, F (99835)
Marilyn, R (10010)
S., R (33484)
Elizabeth, N (7030)
Tom, S (64152)
Kerin, M (98366)
April, F (85250)
Daniel j., D (50315)
Philip, S (95422)
Kim, H (94945)
Bruce, C (60169)
Michael, M (65401)
Leslie, K (90027)
Stanley, B (95966)
Tina, G (25302)
Rick, S (32801)
Jeffrey, E (30096)
Dedric, G (37341)
Sandra, J (4401)
Carey, P (64133)
Kimberly, M (48180)
Jerry, H (92130)
Marilyn, T (96001)
Amanda, O (54601)
Roy, G (22207)

Robert, H (2126)
Joan, G (19805)
Katrina, D (44054)
Glen/joyce, R (17036)
Howard, S (60615)
J justin, K (76021)
Steven, N (10956)
Birgit, V (90404)
Anne, D (1581)
Stephen, D (40207)
Stephanie, P (32608)
Jose, A (80905)
Terry, L (98660)
Brian, O (88011)
Mary ellen, R (2035)
Carla, D (95437)
Jean, G (92007)
Zander, M (48111)
Evelyn, G (8534)
Terri, D (96001)
Laurel, U (13021)
Vinton, G (23605)
Jim, S (29418)
James, S (98685)
Sam, F (80631)
Robert, S (17042)
David, N (33852)
Scott, S (98101)
Amy, S (55336)
Sandra, W (78212)
Lise, G (98225)
Joyce, R (10002)
Rehana, H (14850)
Robert, P (97317)
Nicole, T (89131)
Gloria, M (98274)
Drew, H (41005)
Alfred, H (98801)
Share, J (98110)

Donna, F (2360)
Bailey, S (1463)
L, K (7093)
Steven, S (95136)
Maggie, K (53212)
Willie, F (32310)
Joan, G (5401)
Jerry, B (52404)
Anne, H (60614)
Steven, C (94945)
Pamela, B (49431)
Eva, R (47906)
Lauren, O (95691)
Mary, K (87901)
Larry, F (92557)
Debbie, S (73527)
Susan, C (10538)
Justine, H (98103)
Clarence, J (56296)
Eugene, W (98335)
Patrick, R (33141)
Helen, A (21244)
Ruth, B (8088)
Jim, C (60004)
Lorraine, H (95949)
Pamela, L (75965)
Christine, M (93110)
Steven, C (60643)
R., P (2054)
Ryan, R (27513)
Joan, D (19038)
Britton, S (53208)
Barbara, L (30064)
Helen, L (7946)
Carol, T (93023)
Robert, M (11740)
Mary, F (97230)
Marc, K (10003)
Janice, B (80110)

Teri, S (94061)
Rita, W (7712)
Anne, S (95008)
Richard, B (30311)
Marion, J (20877)
Renee, G (60633)
Roann, G (8827)
Kay, T (80304)
Crawford, J (19106)
Dawn, B (93442)
Rey, V (98362)
Edmund, C (47401)
Wendi, Q (2155)
Robert, H (98844)
John, V (56560)
Jeanine, C (48105)
Jeverna, H (22405)
Louis, M (76006)
Beverly, H (78660)
Heidi, B (91977)
Phebe, S (98225)
Carol, M (11357)
Joyce, O (96744)
Gary, B (92646)
Gini, T (11782)
Dorothea, L (16914)
Glenda, P (91335)
Randy, A (80234)
Sammy, C (40107)
Chris, B (75002)
Martha, W (60613)
Karin, T (85614)
Cynthia, M (95465)
Richard, G (99301)
Ruth, F (55408)
Arthur, E (34288)
Scott, O (98408)
Sharon, S (80249)
Melba, R (30080)

T, M (84741)
Patricia, S (19968)
Marcus, H (92707)
Mildred, C (47715)
Ann, M (60625)
Marga, B (98408)
Julie, S (93402)
Cathy, C (12345)
Norman, D (4092)
Greg, S (78741)
George, B (99163)
Daniel, W (13207)
Deb, M (63005)
Brad, H (84065)
Frances, L (94005)
Carol, D (67037)
Mary, M (19031)
Deserie, L (95815)
Patrick, S (78704)
Andrea, R (98362)
Myriam, R (91941)
Debbie, T (89406)
Timothy, B (14425)
Margaret, S (27534)
Tracy, F (27713)
C., C (95453)
Jackie, G (1098)
Scott, B (86001)
Dayle, S (24538)
Kathy, Y (93001)
Catherine, W (85719)
Nicholas, B (61821)
Jaen, L (75240)
Leon, L (8080)
Gerry, W (46617)
George, S (19436)
Elaine, P (94708)
Earl, B (28092)
Gita, J (86327)

Thomas, K (49307)
Amelia, C (91941)
Carmen, P (78154)
Robert, S (1226)
Marlene, W (66212)
C.jean, B (50310)
Kathleen, W (3038)
P, B (80015)
Dustin, D (81321)
Greg, P (90808)
D., C (1702)
Mary, H (98109)
Bonnie, W (17361)
Bernice, R (11554)
Lori, D (92232)
Sean, S (2136)
Lauren, U (29466)
Celeste, R (96707)
Dogan, O (99701)
Janis, M (16323)
Rebecca, T (29609)
Lorraine, G (87508)
Paul, F (99362)
Liz, M (36527)
Tyler, C (29154)
Carol, C (94402)
Tameryn, D (15845)
Dennis, A (55113)
Dian, L (56308)
Mindi, W (90046)
Mercedes, L (74017)
Emmah, D (4037)
Peter, K (1831)
Julie, M (86303)
Charlie, B (93285)
Charlene, D (8060)
Eric, M (91304)
Monique, T (6300)
John, H (98665)

Alison, S (85257)
Mark, B (43123)
Mike, M (77573)
Dennis, N (89156)
Ronald, G (92882)
L., A (93004)
Dan, V (15241)
Louise, F (34653)
Dan, V (15241)
Macushla, R (2048)
Lynne, M (45231)
Carlotta, H (30281)
T, H (98362)
Linda, K (90245)
Robert, J (90245)
Susan, H (32571)
Craig, B (80104)
Renny, R (98117)
Christine, M (98032)
Guy, W (62024)
Wanda, B (28210)
Bruce, H (51270)
Kristy, B (48327)
Wanda, B (27610)
Seth, P (2139)
Nicole, W (17055)
Frankie, H (32533)
Tracy, M (98626)
J, W (32837)
Susan, C (59727)
Norman, H (23112)
Charlotte, H (97058)
Dianne, D (85042)
Ray, F (22601)
Marilee, M (98362)
Sandi, A (68521)
Richard, B (97007)
Lesley, P (21093)
Susan, L (32907)

Theodore, K (98121)
Sandra, D (4210)
Mark, K (44095)
Robyn, M (94110)
Rosemary, S (38116)
Cynthia, P (20175)
Sheryl, G (96789)
Tom, K (92084)
Cynthia, H (97306)
Joan, G (1201)
Thel, F (47304)
Charles, E (24179)
Frances, S (95407)
Carissa, F (68407)
Mark, P (98106)
Margaret, G (98105)
Steven, B (60466)
Elyce m, B (97217)
Jaye, D (81147)
Susan, H (85704)
Margaret, S (60643)
Lorna, F (4430)
Estelle, V (97501)
F, F (85008)
Brenda, C (89122)
Kathi, H (54303)
Stacey, T (97212)
Patricia, P (93105)
Michael, K (48169)
Ruth ann, O (1062)
Martha, Y (10024)
Anoel, R (97330)
Robert, M (42445)
Barbara, H (10025)
Kristin, C (43220)
Sally, M (94025)
Lance, L (46142)
Sean, S (75070)
Nick, B (98087)

Susan, C (90278)
Erin, A (85203)
S, Z (97477)
Steve, W (95928)
Betty, M (89108)
Robert, L (75206)
Warren, G (94143)
R, U (96789)
Mary jane, D (14526)
Alice, N (95136)
Marti, J (93021)
Iris, A (97209)
Mili, B (10023)
Michael, O (98036)
Shabbir, B (98296)
Joel, S (94595)
David, C (14610)
Owen, D (10013)
Cynthia, H (94510)
Lia, B (97527)
Elizabeth, G (94559)
Matt, C (81303)
Rosemary, D (15005)
Raquel, M (95350)
Meryl, M (93546)
Leslie ann, R (94597)
Anita, W (94611)
Mark, B (63116)
Emil, M (10029)
William, B (90254)
Steven, T (86504)
Nancy, B (94596)
Timothy, M (93307)
Sophie, F (52223)
Evette, A (95945)
Cheryl, V (97223)
Carrie, W (75002)
Gary, G (54301)
Helen, G (98512)

Jon, B (90026)
Karen, L (60625)
Cami, L (85016)
Michael, G (95301)
Roberto, D (15010)
Fabiola, M (79912)
Pamela, C (81001)
Yvonne, F (90293)
Mark, S (48638)
Bernadine, T (32669)
Michael, A (47714)
Kathleen, A (48430)
Md, B (92037)
Chris, N (98087)
Ros, G (7254)
Peter, S (18017)
Christine, A (19103)
Erica, H (30022)
Marga, W (97229)
Christine, F (34759)
Ml, E (62321)
Catherine, L (87901)
J, K (48361)
Angela, C (48133)
Aileen, T (34217)
Angelia, F (27028)
Paul, G (5477)
Martin, W (97215)
Barbara, L (32967)
Nancy, B (65265)
Cara, S (85719)
Oliver, B (18072)
Dina, P (27607)
Carol, S (60403)
Jalissa, I (34759)
Susanna, M (23451)
Mildred, M (38133)
Patrick, F (52807)
Alice, V (97128)

Richard, B (96744)
Marilyn, R (49621)
Cindy, H (37028)
Gretchen, H (14850)
Jenafur, M (27604)
Janet, S (8848)
Lisa, H (11354)
Deborah, P (30501)
Kellyann, M (34613)
Amy, S (7470)
Du, N (95123)
Melanie, D (34695)
Katherine, C (37214)
Paul, W (8757)
Lenore, S (4260)
Carole, M (15126)
Leanne, M (96734)
Mary, O (47909)
Gail, S (33437)
Connie, T (18104)
Yasenta, N (19320)
Bonnie, O (18353)
James, S (49855)
Polonia, M (10463)
Jim, B (37029)
Teri, D (32812)
Milton, D (24084)
Susan, L (60614)
Robert, S (75143)
Anahata, I (30230)
Kathryn, L (48350)
Barbra, M (10024)
Bill, W (41042)
Elizabeth, D (48183)
Manny, M (5143)
Lynn, L (7640)
Jessie, A (37221)
Thomas, B (83607)
Desiree, G (44710)

Joan, P (94619)
Ralph, H (48189)
Tom, S (34109)
M, A (43205)
Shirley, M (27705)
Thomas, L (5072)
Anna, T (19148)
Kelly, K (85014)
Michael, M (92649)
Santi, B (2186)
Rob, B (96048)
Salvatrice, L (14043)
Bill, R (11374)
Lloyd, H (21015)
Charles, B (17078)
Tom, B (18938)
J, N (10025)
Dorothy, D (19966)
Catalina, Z (70816)
Loretta, M (27609)
Sally, R (28765)
Iherman, H (15221)
Ross, C (89108)
Sheldon, D (31605)
Bob, R (54406)
Alan, M (30080)
Bryon, K (48069)
Ariana, N (2791)
Karen, N (28124)
Pat, G (80219)
Mindy, K (52402)
Michael, T (44084)
Larry, W (62236)
Julie, S (75080)
Fran, D (32256)
James, J (46131)
Emily, H (87111)
Marianne, M (19020)
Lori, G (2892)

Curtis, C (60004)
Cathy, R (1852)
Summer, S (17821)
Tom, N (90505)
Herman, K (80233)
Barbara, T (6002)
Devon, J (27405)
Sharon, K (64029)
Chris, B (11576)
Steven, P (46201)
Patricia, D (44231)
Sarah, A (48076)
Elizabeth, F (95124)
Lynn, D (1562)
Jerry, W (55406)
Brandie, D (98021)
Christine, P (12449)
Matt, W (43430)
Stacey, C (78664)
David, S (76201)
Wendy, C (93602)
Doug, M (3253)
Jesse, G (33484)
Amy, A (40741)
Geo, P (33033)
Margot, M (78414)
Denise, S (60156)
Susan, R (2132)
Jeff, P (85303)
Diane, M (10014)
Roberta, K (60403)
Grzeskowiak, R (48130)
Sara, M (97103)
Cathleen, C (92026)
James, S (54235)
Lynda, H (43015)
Ron, S (55405)
Richard, H (90291)
Lawrence, G (22193)

Lena, O (10075)
Agnes, R (90403)
Sharon, R (61604)
Sylvia, B (30087)
Joann, D (65233)
Kevin, P (47150)
Don, V (49546)
Marilyn, S (36022)
Vera, J (10128)
John, H (94930)
Christine, K (1073)
Christina, C (48026)
Cathy, S (8003)
Lori, O (3054)
Corey, C (98034)
Tina, F (70130)
Harvey, B (55939)
Barbara, S (19966)
Mary, M (1803)
Susan, S (97302)
Stephan, F (93023)
Libby, C (78232)
Terrance, H (55418)
Renae, B (28147)
Claudia, D (14530)
Joyce, E (85013)
Kim, H (2675)
Vic, B (91001)
Mitzi, M (79311)
Shannon, R (22802)
Jerry, M (48073)
Mary, K (54162)
Ritchie, S (94501)
Linda, B (48911)
Rev. maurice, H (55906)
Ron, M (54915)
Steve, M (94954)
Joan, B (1033)
Helen, D (94619)

Cynthia, H (98685)
Vicki, H (92648)
Leroy, J (36605)
William, G (95070)
Arlene, B (99037)
Patricia, K (94945)
Jessica, V (80228)
Mitchell, R (33322)
Karen, L (92126)
Pamela, M (55407)
Bill, P (10960)
Catherine, L (92024)
Phil, C (93035)
Bartley, L (45011)
Phil, G (87507)
Linda, P (19007)
Marie, M (21701)
Amy, W (78704)
Arlene, B (94952)
Kari, D (98021)
Gail, M (97103)
Gregory, M (31750)
Brian, A (32714)
Michael, P (13668)
Jean, C (56601)
Lynne, C (83860)
Matthew, P (83705)
Vicky, E (99208)
Kellee, A (97030)
M s, D (33133)
Ron, G (10312)
A., G (11238)
Stefanie, W (56304)
Heidi, S (21209)
Revel, P (94116)
Haydee, R (33162)
A, M (75044)
Claire, L (92122)
Nancy, H (55118)

Carol, F (48103)
Linda, M (92661)
Cindy, A (97031)
Richard, H (95973)
Pam, T (92405)
Laura, S (95120)
Roberta, A (47338)
Timothy, L (32605)
Marilyn, D (60202)
S, C (36925)
J, A (36601)
Diane, N (94601)
Eric, W (92780)
Robert, U (46808)
Ed, H (0)
Cindy, J (37862)
Sally, B (45441)
Sandra, C (44022)
Karen, I (53202)
Carl, B (81252)
Rachel, S (93101)
Robert, V (7480)
Kathryn, A (97225)
S, Y (27262)
Donna, K (29902)
Robert, A (76086)
Sydney, K (1720)
Erica, M (11782)
Sabine, O (4103)
Cecile, A (53150)
Martha, G (95018)
Jenny, N (12446)
Betty, C (28054)
Lily, M (92543)
Mohammed, A (94583)
Don, I (36608)
Susan, L (48104)
Sally, R (32615)
Laura, R (76133)

Adrianne, M (95687)
Steve, S (49097)
Nazrul, C (10462)
Matthew, B (98052)
Patricia, J (20744)
Nelson, S (48198)
Lj, R (76133)
Mark, G (47711)
Lindsay, D (7059)
Louise, H (98115)
Prashant, K (92122)
Dane, B (28227)
Karen, B (54703)
Eugene, D (94115)
Will, S (80302)
Damaris, T (10037)
David, T (21234)
Brian, T (11432)
Marceau, J (62704)
Shena, K (97420)
Marilyn, R (1604)
James, G (78245)
Thomas, C (24440)
Richard, B (92530)
Karen, F (91505)
Helga, B (98672)
Mario, G (95608)
Kristen, S (33315)
Meghan, O (78504)
Dennis, M (85259)
Linda, H (7747)
Elizabeth, L (10522)
Gary, S (11978)
Elisabeth, L (91007)
Rachel, M (29455)
Sharon, B (85024)
Roth, W (48103)
Karrin, H (15001)
Wood, L (94559)

Roger, B (43324)
Brian, S (54303)
Stephen, P (63040)
L, N (95038)
Jennifer, R (97702)
Sammy, L (98292)
Jeffrey, B (65203)
Melissa, S (41017)
Diana, B (67205)
Anne, H (80401)
Bobbie, M (97537)
Kathryn, R (80205)
Laura, C (29609)
Marcy, P (95037)
Robert, D (60610)
Babs, W (49801)
Melvin, S (76001)
Jane h, A (33549)
Babs, C (37211)
Catherine, F (11790)
Jim, B (44111)
Constance, L (87513)
Jesse, F (80005)
Zakaria, A (75048)
Stephen, R (94301)
David, V (93117)
Adina, P (98292)
Robert, W (43065)
Susan, T (95503)
Noemi, R (11385)
Brenda, W (62067)
Luv, F (11722)
Robert, M (21015)
Philip, L (91101)
Donna, U (36605)
Shannon, N (74301)
Jerrie, K (12601)
Diana, T (14850)
Heather, W (32825)

Joyce, F (10021)
Micaela, E (46514)
Pearl, H (2886)
Samone, J (7001)
Chris, B (74346)
James, L (45335)
Wendy, G (97217)
Fred, E (98391)
Blair, A (60110)
Cj, J (48135)
Jennifer, S (80916)
David, P (85712)
Jason, S (84601)
Emily, M (60645)
Margot, B (77098)
Kanika u. f., A (29201)
Dmitry, L (11421)
Patricia, C (33705)
J.m, E (97210)
David, K (80005)
Judith, L (1469)
Elisabeta, R (94131)
Shelli, C (78734)
Trina, H (48236)
L scott, K (60061)
Matthew, L (87567)
Kimberly, B (13669)
Dennis, K (7603)
Amanda, C (5452)
Scott, V (85301)
Renee, B (85338)
S, B (54481)
Carolyn, E (98110)
Timothy, G (6043)
Mary, H (95812)
Barbara, S (85742)
Cori, B (8215)
Noah, S (45239)
Lawrence, J (91770)

Artineh, H (91501)
Randall, H (98516)
Joanne, Z (75074)
Jane, S (53717)
Laurie, M (0)
Duane, V (92346)
Karen, D (6255)
Sage, G (90066)
John, G (98198)
Jeanne, K (66046)
Morgan, P (60626)
Pam, S (96782)
James, G (78754)
Gracie, C (97206)
Joseph, H (81503)
Bev, P (50228)
Tina, A (94924)
Eric, M (22043)
Lillian, K (80215)
Bill, V (94952)
Emily, S (94062)
Kuo, Y (94703)
Mary, F (89147)
Sherry, K (56601)
Barbara, W (21012)
Bruce, B (95060)
Jordan, S (12561)
Judith, J (92028)
Joseph, G (44313)
Richard, K (10606)
Kevin, W (98104)
Donald, S (21209)
Anjarew, E (10706)
Karen, O (86303)
Scott, H (53147)
Wiliam, D (55112)
Walter, P (85206)
Nancy, D (11718)
Tia, T (90066)

John, M (30025)
David, F (78759)
Cynthia, N (80918)
Jacen, L (75088)
Ervin, Z (46324)
Tim, H (33708)
Mojubaolu, O (11230)
Jess, Z (91601)
Cheryl, L (7869)
Helen, K (44044)
Jody, B (5769)
D, C (29414)
Judith, C (18938)
Jole, L (48042)
Cathryn, C (30281)
Adam, F (54720)
Sharon, W (80233)
Lee, S (97499)
Theresa, K (45215)
Matt, M (33604)
Marilyn, F (54956)
Lisa m, R (72076)
Logan, B (10001)
Joan, E (90266)
Linda, K (85118)
Janie, M (36609)
Carol, C (76180)
Terry, S (11963)
David, M (22152)
Stefan, W (27703)
Heather, B (98532)
Renee, R (85258)
Kathy, M (48759)
Catherine, L (97477)
William, V (8830)
Nora, E (92807)
Leanne, J (56601)
Joan, A (10913)
Regina, F (97071)

Arthur j, A (81301)
Lois, U (30016)
Christopher, W (94539)
John, R (10304)
Oscar, A (91042)
Dopeusera, A (47203)
Mary, M (55406)
Stacy, C (92651)
Sarah, E (20015)
Evelyn, F (10960)
Nicole, J (11222)
Gregory, H (81082)
Cara, M (45874)
Rochelle, G (59019)
Garrick, B (60177)
Courtney, S (76504)
Russell, T (63109)
Tanya, M (95472)
Cindy, W (61802)
Craig, R (7416)
Mark, W (97038)
Thomas, J (33708)
Lezlie, P (98012)
Albert, G (81082)
Araya, H (28806)
Dalia, G (94601)
Singgih, T (95123)
Rita, H (64127)
Juliet, P (6424)
Brad, H (66549)
Joel, Q (77340)
Hans, P (11177)
Shalkta, B (33510)
Anne, H (32244)
John, U (60586)
Crump, D (63031)
Walter, E (7438)
Courtney, B (23185)
Jillian, M (11418)

Annamarie, B (60445)
Jeff, M (43606)
Carol, L (32708)
S., A (10031)
Jolinda, C (60707)
Linda, D (48178)
Daphne, J (33708)
Henry, D (6518)
Sherridina, B (44135)
Lucy, P (90731)
Thang, D (90504)
Tim, C (94401)
Roberta, W (14850)
David, N (2481)
Ryan, K (1752)
William, K (50702)
Amy, W (27513)
Twila, L (33711)
Benny, Q (78225)
Susan, K (77006)
Lauren, V (17853)
Jared, C (37318)
Faith, S (95971)
Clarissa, M (92506)
Miranda, B (47725)
Sarah, B (5356)
Elizabeth, B (33617)
Sean, M (1754)
Amelia, J (90405)
Ronald, M (34481)
Brad, N (93035)
Kay, G (90012)
Jeremy, D (15358)
Betty, H (92345)
Michele, A (94619)
Shaylene, A (60914)
Radia, H (94070)
Dennis, S (75141)
Shari, A (90815)

Melinda, F (20902)
Teri, A (44149)
M, D (19009)
Sylvia, B (90808)
Peggy, M (6473)
Amelia, D (27607)
Celina, E (85716)
Catherine, B (91702)
Sharon, O (47713)
Shawn, T (6040)
Kristin, M (55720)
Charles, B (72701)
Doc, B (99507)
Deborah, B (98570)
Jayne, N (45011)
Elena, R (98052)
David, F (80128)
Kristin, F (10920)
Alayna, B (98406)
Terri, C (78247)
Pamela, M (30096)
Scott, E (68124)
Denise, S (1342)
Jason, C (11102)
Mrs. mary, F (80211)
Elaine, E (91362)
Clint, K (13839)
Robert, J (84084)
Heather, H (60610)
Sandra, D (2809)
Aaron jaocb, L (83704)
Xtian, G (98102)
David, F (80128)
Brinna, C (25526)
Brandon, C (19713)

Federal Trade Commission
Washington, DC, May 5, 2022

Hon. MARIA CANTWELL,
Chair,
Committee on Commerce, Science, and Transportation,
United States Senate,
Washington, DC.

Hon. RICHARD BLUMENTHAL,
Chairman,
Subcommittee on Consumer Protection, Product Safety, and Data Security, Committee on Commerce, Science, and Transportation,
United States Senate,
Washington, DC.

Hon. ROGER WICKER,
Ranking Member,
Committee on Commerce, Science, and Transportation,
United States Senate,
Washington, DC.

Hon. MARSHA BLACKBURN,
Ranking Member,
Subcommittee on Consumer Protection, Product Safety, and Data Security, Committee on Commerce, Science, and Transportation,
United States Senate,
Washington, DC.

Dear Chair Cantwell, Ranking Member Wicker, Chairman Blumenthal, and Ranking Member Blackburn:

I write to express my strong support for the Senate's ongoing work and upcoming hearing on pharmacy benefit managers (PBMs) entitled, ''Ensuring Fairness and Transparency in the Market for Prescription Drugs.'[99]

[99] Ensuring Fairness and Transparency in the Market for Prescription Drugs: Hearing Before the Subcomm. on Consumer Protection, Product Safety, and Data Security of the S. Comm. on Commerce, Sci., and Trans., 117th Cong. (May 5, 2022), https://www.commerce.senate.gov/2022/5/ensuring-fairness-and-transparency-in-the-market-for-prescription-drugs.

I believe that PBMs play a critical and under-examined role in determining the price and availability of prescription drugs to patients at the pharmacy counter and clinic, and I am concerned that certain incentives and the surrounding lack of transparency means that PBMs' interests may not always align with patients and others who pay for prescription drugs. I am also concerned that PBMs' vertical integration and dominant market position may allow them to under-reimburse independent pharmacies and steer business to PBM-owned mail-order and specialty pharmacies, which may threaten the long-term viability of independent pharmacies in both urban and rural communities.

Addressing dominant intermediaries such as PBMs has been a top priority during my tenure at the FTC.[100] In line with this priority, FTC staff has been working since last year to use the FTC's 6(b) authority to conduct an inquiry into PBMs, and I am hoping that the Commission will vote to initiate a study as soon as possible.[101] Given the life-and-death stakes of this work, I believe the FTC has a moral imperative to act swiftly.

As part of this effort, the FTC has issued and recently extended a Request for Information seeking public comments on PBM business practices.[102] Hundreds of unique comments have been submitted to date on how PBMs are impacting patients, doctors, and pharmacists. The comments touch on a range of issues, including Direct and Indirect Remuneration (DIR) fees, inadequate pharmacy reimbursements, unnecessary prior authorizations and step therapy requirements, detrimental formulary exclusions, and the steering of patients to PBM-owned pharmacies.[103]

While the FTC will continue its work in this important area, I also welcome legislative action on PBMs, including efforts to ensure that these intermediaries are serving the interests of American patients and contributing to a fair and accountable prescription drug system.

---

100 Memorandum from FTC Chair Lina M. Khan to Commission Staff and Commissioners Regarding Vision and Priorities for the FTC, at 3 (Sept. 22, 2021), https://www.ftc.gov/system/files/documents/public_statements/1596664/agency_priorities_memo_from_chair_lina_m_khan_9-22-21.pdf (''The second area I'd like us to prioritize addressing is dominant intermediaries and extractive business models.'').

101 Remarks of Chair Lina M. Khan Regarding the 6(b) Study on Pharmacy Benefit Managers (Feb. 17, 2022), https://www.ftc.gov/news-events/news/speeches/remarks-chair-lina-m-khan-rearding-6b-study-pharmacy-benefit-managers.

102 Solicitation for Public Comments on the Impact of Prescription Benefit Managers' Business Practices, FTC–2022-0015, *https://www.regulations.gov/docket/FTC-2022-0015/comments* (last visited May 5, 2022).

103 *Id.*

Sincerely,
Lina M. Khan,
Chair,
Federal Trade Commission.

COMMUNITY ONCOLOGY ALLIANCE
Innovating and Advocating for Community Cancer Care
1225 New York Avenue, NW, Suite 600
Washington, D.C. 20005
(202) 729-8147 | communityoncology.org

May 11, 2022

The Honorable Richard Blumenthal
Chair, Senate Commerce, Science & Transportation Subcommittee on Consumer Protection, Product Safety, and Data Security
SH-706
120 Constitution Avenue NE
Washington, DC 20002

The Honorable Marsha Blackburn
Ranking Member, Senate Commerce, Science & Transportation Subcommittee on Consumer Protection, Product Safety, and Data Security
SD-357
50 Constitution Avenue NE
Washington, DC 20002

Re: *Submission for the record: Ensuring Fairness and Transparency in the Market for Prescription Drugs*

Dear Chair Blumenthal and Ranking Member Blackburn:

On behalf of the Board of Directors of the Community Oncology Alliance (COA), I want to express our thanks for the hearing you held last week on *Ensuring Fairness and Transparency in the Market for Prescription Drugs*. Senator Blumenthal cited one example of a cancer patient from Connecticut who was unable to get her drugs on a timely basis. Unfortunately, this is not a one-off event. Cancer patients and their oncologists are in a constant, daily fight with pharmacy benefit managers (PBMs) to get their critical drugs on a timely basis, especially when PBMs mandate that the drugs be delivered by their own mail-order pharmacies.

I could go on and on about the abuses cancer patients face at the hands of PBMs but will let the attached five volumes of "horror stories" speak to real-life Americans battling with PBMs.

I submit this letter with attachments to the record of the hearing *Ensuring Fairness and Transparency in the Market for Prescription Drugs.*

Thank you.

Sincerely,

Ted Okon
Executive Director

April 2017

Delay, Waste, and Cancer Treatment Obstacles:

The Real-Life Patient Impact of Pharmacy Benefit Managers

COA COMMUNITY ONCOLOGY ALLIANCE
Over 15 Years of Making a Difference in Cancer Care

There is growing awareness of the problems and pitfalls with Pharmacy Benefit Managers (PBMs) in the United States health care system. Contracted by insurance carriers to negotiate on their behalf with pharmaceutical companies, these 'middle men' corporations have quietly become an unavoidable part of our nation's health care system. Controlling at least 80 percent of drug benefits for over 260 million Americans, PBMs have the power to negotiate drug costs, what drugs will be included on plan formularies, and how those drugs are dispensed. Oftentimes, patients are required to receive drugs through PBM-owned specialty pharmacies.

However, while the role PBMs play in the U.S. health care system is complex and under scrutiny by policymakers and the public, with much of the debate focusing on economics, little discussion takes place of the impact PBMs have on patients.

This paper is the first in a series that will focus on the serious, sometimes dangerous, impact PBMs are having on cancer patients today. These are real patient stories but names have been changed to protect privacy.

AN AVOIDABLE DEATH?

Derek, a young husband, was diagnosed with advanced melanoma with brain metastases. Prognosis was grim, yet a ray of light appeared in the form of a new drug prescribed by his doctor. Proven to have the potential of significantly extending life, the drug offered Derek and his wife real hope. Located in his doctor's office was the clinic's pharmacy, where this potentially life-prolonging medication was simply waiting on the pharmacy shelf— but not for Derek. Derek's PBM mandated that Derek purchase his meds from one of their own mail-order specialty pharmacies. The clinic immediately faxed to the PBM all the necessary information for receiving prior authorization, and for the next ten days, Derek and his wife waited to hear that the prescription had been approved. Upon receiving the go-ahead, they then faxed the prescription to the PBM's specialty pharmacy, and sat back to wait again.

One week later, the drug still had not appeared; instead, the couple was notified that they first had to remit the drug's $1,000 co-pay, an amount they were unable to afford. Derek's wife now began arranging co-pay assistance, but she had to deal with the matter on her own at this point, because Derek had been admitted to the ICU. Several days later, she received approval for co-pay assistance, and forwarded the information to the PBM's pharmacy, which then FedExed the drug to Derek. The medication finally arrived— only there was no one to take them. By this time, Derek could no longer swallow pills, and sadly, shortly after, he died.

The most common and devastating issue that cancer patients face with PBMs is the fact that they must wait, for weeks or even months, to obtain medication that they could have received within 24 hours, had they been permitted to get it at the point of care from their oncologist. Beyond the stress and aggravation incurred, delays in receiving medication often translate into delayed treatment and worsening of the patient's condition, and in the most tragic of cases, possibly contributing to the patient's death.

The Real-Life Patient Impact of Pharmacy Benefit ManagersDate

TREATMENT DELAYED DUE TO PHARMACY RESTRICTIONS

Bill was prescribed an oral medication that works to prevent his cancer cells from replicating, thus reducing the growth and spread of the disease. His oncologist faxed the prescription to the specialty pharmacy indicated by Bill's PBM. Unfortunately, this particular pharmacy does not carry the medication prescribed, and so they forwarded the script to another specialty pharmacy that does carry it. However, that pharmacy does not accept Bill's insurance.

So, the prescription was forwarded again to yet another specialty pharmacy, which is the preferred pharmacy of Bill's insurance company. However, they don't carry the medication either. By this time, ten days have passed since the medication was first prescribed. Bill's physician, attempting to expedite things, now sends the prescription to a fourth specialty pharmacy that does carry the meds, and personally calls the insurance provider to explain the situation and ask for immediate approval. Five days later, and more than two weeks since the initial prescription was made, Bill receives his medication.

Agreements between insurance carriers and PBMs, which may be part of the same corporation, grant them full authority to determine where patients may or may not purchase their medication. This is carried out regardless of the detrimental effect it often has on patient health and wellbeing. In such a system, one must wonder whether the objective of curing patients from terminal disease has been usurped by that of achieving financial gain.

MEDICATION DELAYED 6 WEEKS DUE TO PBM SPECIALTY PHARMACY INDIFFERENCE

Carol was battling metastatic colon cancer. Unable to receive the same chemotherapy Carol had been treated with initially, her oncologist prescribed a medication to help stop the cancer from spreading any further. Her physician sent all documentation necessary to the specialty pharmacy mandated by Carol's PBM.

One week later, when Carol's oncologist phoned the PBM-mandated pharmacy to check on status of the prescription, again, they were told that nothing had been done— they refused to process the prescription without knowing Carol's current weight. Rather than calling Carol or the doctor to ascertain the necessary information, they had simply done nothing.

Another week went by, and the doctor called in again to check on the prescription. This time she was told that there was a form the doctor needed to fill out, in order to request Prior Authorization from the PBM. The doctor couldn't understand why they hadn't simply sent the form to her— or told her about it a week ago, when she had called. Eventually the doctor received the form, filled it out and submitted it, as Carol continued to wait and her cancer continued its lethal advance. Ultimately Carol received the medication— a full six weeks after it was initially prescribed, the most terrible irony being that had she been allowed to receive the pills at the site of care, she would have had them within a day.

Another serious issue patients and doctors face with PBMs and specialty pharmacies is their passive attitude towards patient care. Time and again, patients and doctors wait for medication that will never arrive. One small detail missing in the documentation is enough to delay its delivery, and the specialty pharmacy staff, who do not see themselves as partners to patient care, also do not see it as their responsibility to take any action to hasten the process.

LIFE-SAVING TREATMENT POSTPONED

Barbara, who was battling brain cancer, was prescribed two drugs: one a form of chemotherapy and the other an antiemetic that would alleviate the symptoms of nausea caused by the chemo. Both were to be taken in conjunction with the radiation treatments scheduled to begin six days later.

At Barbara's clinic, well aware of the urgency of the situation, the nurse on call faxed Barbara's prescriptions over to her PBM-mandated specialty pharmacy, and at the same time, applied for prior authorization from Barbara's PBM. Five days later the nurse called over to the pharmacy, asking for an update, since neither she nor Barbara had heard anything. The pharmacy worker informed the nurse that the prescriptions had indeed arrived and they were now about to enter them into their system to see if prior authorization was necessary.

The nurse was nonplussed— why had the prescriptions not been entered five days earlier, when they were sent and received by fax? And what if the nurse had not called to follow up; how much longer would it have taken? Most importantly, how is it that the PBM-mandated pharmacy staff, who are dispensing medication aimed to keep people alive, do not see it as their duty to provide customers with the very best and fastest service possible? Barbara's radiation treatments, scheduled to begin the next day and already delayed nearly a week, now had to be postponed until the medication could be received.

Multiple cases are reported in which doctors must reach out to PBM-mandated specialty pharmacies to enquire about the status of medication— only to find that while the pharmacy has received the patient's prescription, it's been just sitting on someone's desk, untouched, with no concern for the person on the other end, who is being treated for a life-threatening condition.

PBM Horror Stories Series | 2

The Real-Life Patient Impact of Pharmacy Benefit ManagersDate

PATIENT DENIED MEDS DUE TO TECHNICAL GLITCH

Carl, battling prostate cancer, was prescribed an oral chemotherapy drug to help control his disease. Under his insurance plan, however, the co-pay costs for the medication came to over $4,000 per order. Carl simply could not afford to pay such an exorbitant amount. Fortunately, the pharmaceutical company that manufactures the drug has a co-pay program of its own, for eligible patients, making the drug affordable. Furthermore, the in-house pharmacy at the clinic where Carl receives his treatment benefits from this arrangement, and is able to acquire these and other cancer drugs for the low patient co-pay of $20.

The clinic phoned Carl's PBM on his behalf, explained the situation and asked them to accept the pharmaceutical company's co-pay as a 'secondary insurance.' Their request was promptly denied, as the PBM explained that their system did not have the capability to add in a secondary insurance. When asked if they could then simply authorize the clinic to fill the prescription instead, as they had it right there, this was also refused. Unwilling to believe that his patient was not going to receive this medication because it could not be entered into the PBM's computer system, Carl's physician made repeated calls to the PBM, speaking to one supervisor after another. Ultimately, he was forced to admit defeat, and Carl was denied a treatment that might have extended his life.

Patients who receive medication at their treating physician's in-house pharmacy benefit from the fullest in personal care and attention, and have access to a team that will strongly advocate on their behalf. Patients who are forced to deal with PBMs and specialty pharmacies, on the other hand, are often relegated to numbers and statistics, and if their case requires special attention or extra effort, their needs are likely to go unmet.

BUSY SIGNALS AND PBM SPECIALTY PHARMACY PROTOCOLS DELAY DRUG DELIVERY

PBM specialty pharmacies require patients to schedule delivery of their medications by phone, which seems, on the surface, a simple enough task. John, who was undergoing chemo for bone cancer, tried for an entire week to get through to his specialty pharmacy and schedule the next delivery of his medication, but no matter what time of day he called, the line was always busy. Finally, one day before he was supposed to start a new chemo cycle, and with no medication left, John called the clinic in frustration, and asked if they could intervene in some way.

Calling the specialty pharmacy, John's clinic was able to speak with a representative. "You are lucky you got through! " she was told by the rep. "Our lines are so busy, we cannot make outbound calls because all of our lines are used up. " Their luck ran out fairly quickly however; as the clinic staff member was not on John's list of 'approved' contacts at the pharmacy, she was unable to speak on John's behalf and schedule delivery of the medication. And with the lines tied up throughout the day, the specialty pharmacy rep was unable to call John to verify. The clinic staff hung up, and had to call John back to tell him his only recourse was to continue trying to call in and hope that he will eventually reach someone— before it becomes too late to matter.

Another reason for delays in receiving medication from a PBM specialty pharmacy is the difficulty in adhering to their complex bureaucratic protocols. Pharmacies insist on speaking to the sick patient firsthand, hearing them name the drug, and confirming their shipping details before they will send the medication. However, patients often miss these calls, which are most often automated, and which stop after three missed attempts. In many cases, even when the patient answers the phone, they cannot confirm the name of the drug, causing another cycle of delay to begin.

SPECIALTY PHARMACY TRIES TO STEAL A PATIENT

For two days, a PBM specialty pharmacy had been calling and faxing a doctor's clinic, which offers a pharmacy to provide integrated care to the patients it treats. The specialty pharmacy was claiming that one of the clinic's patients, William, had requested that his lung cancer medication be transferred to their pharmacy, and was demanding the clinic's immediate compliance in the matter.

Surprised by the news, the physician contacted William to enquire about his decision, only to discover that this was the first time William had heard of the matter. "Please do not transfer it anywhere else! "William asked. " I want to get it filled through the dispensary. I did not ask for this. I love being able to get this right away and with no hassles. I was on an oral chemo before and it was filled by a specialty pharmacy and I always was getting it late, missed a few days of medication sometimes and had numerous phone calls from them. They never seemed to know what was going on with my medication."

At first it may seem surprising to hear of a specialty pharmacy resorting to lies in order to steal business from an in-house dispensary. On deeper examination, however, it would seem just the next step in a long line of unethical behaviors resulting from the industrialization of the pharmacy system and the dehumanization of patients seeking medical care.

The Real-Life Patient Impact of Pharmacy Benefit ManagersDate

PATIENT AND CARE PROVIDERS GET THE RUNAROUND

Diana, a patient with metastatic breast cancer living in Ventura County, California, needed to refill her oral medication. On a Thursday, the clinic staff called in to the PBM specialty pharmacy to refill it on her behalf. The specialty pharmacy representative promised to expedite the process and overnight the medication, at no additional cost.

On Monday morning, the staff member walked into her office to find several faxes, e-mails and voicemails from Diana's family, friends and assisted living staff. Apparently, they had received a phone call from the specialty pharmacy on late Friday afternoon, saying that the drug was out of stock in their pharmacy, and suggesting that she call around to local pharmacies to try and find some. Over the weekend, Diana's family and friends called every pharmacy in the county, before starting on those in Los Angeles and Santa Barbara, all with no success.

Hearing the news, the clinic staff immediately contacted the drug manufacturer, who gave her the name of another specialty pharmacy to try. She faxed over the prescription, and then followed up over the next few days, each time being told that the script was being processed. Near the end of the week, the new specialty pharmacy called her to say that they were unable to fill the prescription for at least another month, as it had already been filled by the initial specialty pharmacy— the one that had said they were out of stock. The staff member now called back the first specialty pharmacy, asking that they reverse their claim; however, they reported that the medication had already been shipped out via UPS. Tracking it down, the staff member discovered that indeed the medication was on the truck, ready for delivery.

The cost in hours wasted per patient, per medicine, multiplied by the millions of people living with cancer today in the US, is astronomical. This is in addition to the high toll that the resultant stress takes on patients and their caregivers, as they race through bureaucratic hoops and set off on what often prove to be wild goose chases.

THOUSANDS OF DOLLARS IN WASTED MEDICINE

Laura was prescribed a regimen of drugs to treat her multiple myeloma. She was supposed to take it for three weeks, and then take a break for a week. After two weeks on the medication, Laura began exhibiting symptoms of toxicity, so her oncologist lowered her dosage. However, her specialty pharmacy had already sent her another bottle of the medication in its initial, stronger dosage, to be used the following month. Unable to be returned, the $12,000 worth of medication had to be taken into the clinic and destroyed.

Numerous instances are reported in which patients' therapies have changed, but the specialty pharmacy continues to send the medicine anyway. For expensive anti-cancer drugs and therapies each wasted delivery can be worth tens of thousands of dollars. Each time, the medicine must be brought in and destroyed— a shameless waste of money, time and medicine.

About the Community Oncology Alliance

The Community Oncology Alliance (COA) is the only non-profit organization dedicated solely to preserving and protecting access to community cancer care, where the majority of Americans with cancer are treated. COA helps the nation's community cancer clinics navigate a challenging practice environment, improve the quality and value of cancer care, lead patient advocacy, and offer proactive solutions to policymakers. To learn more, visit www.CommunityOncology.org

Real Horror Stories of How PBMs Hurt Patient Care

NEARLY A MONTH OF DELAYS

James, a 73-year old husband, father and grandfather, had been battling metastatic non–small cell lung cancer (NSCLC) for a while, when his oncologist prescribed a new medication that was FDA approved for cases like James', in which the cancer was "locally advanced or metastatic."

On November 13th, James' doctor submitted a request for prior authorization to the PBM. The first sign that things were not as they should be was when the request was denied—in a way that made absolutely no sense; they were demanding the results of his blood tests for jaundice. His doctor was incensed. How could the PBM deny someone an FDA-approved medication that was indicated for their illness and prescribed by an oncologist? They resubmitted the request, and for the next three weeks, waited in vain for the determination, with the doctor occasionally calling for status, only to be disconnected or told to call back.

On December 4th, as the doctor waited on hold with James' insurance company, James' family called to say that James had died. They would never get a chance to see if the medicine would have prolonged his life.

PBMs, by giving decision-making power to administrative workers with no medical background and little to no patient contact, have created a system that often results in treatment delays and, in worst-case scenarios, the patient's untimely death. In contrast to this, when patients are permitted to purchase their medication from a physician-owned pharmacy, they are spared the crippling bureaucracy of the PBM system.

REFILLING MEDICATION TO TREAT THE DECEASED

A practice in California began receiving request after request from a particular PBM for prior authorization to initiate a refill—what was unusual was that they were for a variety of expired prescriptions. What was going on? None of the practice's patients had been prescribed these drugs recently. In fact, some were for drugs that patients had stopped taking months earlier, while others were for patients who had died.

The practice was puzzled at first, but then came to the following conclusion: "It seems they [the PBM] are just going through their files, and when a prior authorization expiration date pops up for prescriptions filled through their pharmacy at one time, they are automatically sending out prior auth requests."

An amusing anecdote on the surface, stories such as this reveal the wholesale approach taken by the PBMs, in which patients are viewed not as individuals in need of medical care, but rather as a potential market of consumers. Spread across the entire health care system with drug benefits managed by PBMs for millions of patients, this scenario also potentially means millions, if not billions, of dollars of wasted costs in cancer medications.

THE BUREAUCRACY KNOWS BETTER THAN DOCTORS' ORDERS?

George, a patient with multiple myeloma, was prescribed two specific medications that work in conjunction with each other. It was thus a great surprise when the specialty pharmacy refused to send his medication, saying that they wanted to discuss with his oncologist the drug interaction between the two medicines. His oncologist was also perplexed; it was common knowledge that these two drugs are always prescribed together, as the second medicine provides a key part of the maintenance for the first drug, a fact that was not only clinically known but actually spelled out clearly on the manufacturer's website. George had also been on the medication combination for nearly 18 months at that point without problems.

After over a month of delays, the oncologist and PBM finally got this sorted out, but George's fiasco wasn't over. The specialty pharmacy then caused further delay, as they insisted upon speaking again to the doctor, this time to ascertain how many refills were needed. The irony of this was that this particular medication cannot be refilled, so it was simply additional time wasted, while George's treatment cycle was again delayed.

PBM specialty pharmacies have a long list of complex bureaucratic protocols. While they may be designed to prevent mistakes and ensure patient safety, the result is just as often unnecessary, time-consuming delays that in fact endanger the patients they are trying to protect.

MANY PATIENTS… ONE PBM SPECIALTY PHARMACY FULL OF PROBLEMS—A PRACTICE DOCUMENTS CHRONIC DELAYS

A community oncology clinic became so fed up with the problems and delays their patients faced in dealing with a PBM specialty pharmacy that they opened a dedicated file to document each case.

Real Horror Stories of How PBMs Hurt Patient Care

Michelle, a patient at a Florida community oncology practice, had arranged for the PBM specialty pharmacy to ship her medication to one of their local branches, for easy pickup. However, when Michelle arrived at the store, she discovered that they had thrown away her prescription. She now had to request a new prescription from her doctor, get a new prior authorization from her insurance carrier, and then have the medication shipped again—all of which resulted in a two-week delay of treatment.

Diane, another patient at the clinic, had her prescription faxed to the same PBM specialty pharmacy. The pharmacy confirmed it had received the prescription. However, 50 days later, the medication had still not arrived. Clinic staff called the pharmacy, who then claimed they had never received the prescription. By the time it was all sorted out, Diane had been left two months behind in treatment.

The following month, another patient of theirs, Juan, came home to find that his medication had been delivered and left in the middle of the road. Exposed to the Florida heat and rain, the drugs were ruined and had to be reordered—subjecting him to another round of authorizations, delay of his life-saving treatment, and unnecessary cost for the health care system.

No system is perfect. But when a PBM specific pharmacy is repeatedly documented making life-threatening mistakes with no accountability, and cancer patients are forced to remain with them, unable to choose another pharmacy, it would seem that something needs to change.

NEARLY THREE WEEKS OF BROKEN PROMISES AND SHIPPING DELAYS

On January 12th, the clinic treating Liane, a cancer patient, submitted a prescription to her PBM's preferred specialty pharmacy. On January 19th, the day Liane was scheduled to begin treatment, her insurance company notified the clinic that even though they already had prior authorization, they were now requiring a new prior authorization.

Liane was understandably upset by the news; why had the insurance company not contacted them a week ago, when the prescription was first sent? This would now delay her treatment unnecessarily. Later that day, the clinic's pharmacist ascertained that the additional approval required was related to the medication's cost, which had been put under a separate review. Over the next five days, the clinic's authorization specialist, Barbara, was in constant contact with the PBM, who assured her that the medication would be going out at any moment.

A week later, Barbara discovered that this was not true, for when she finally reached a PBM supervisor, Barbara learned that authorization was still pending. She was told that it could take another seven business days or more, before a decision was made.

Barbara's call must have made a difference however, because later that day the PBM faxed over a form to the clinic, to be filled out and returned to them. The following day approval was granted, albeit for the mail order specialty pharmacy. It took another two days for the specialty pharmacy to receive the prescription, another day to process it, and then the pharmacy contacted the patient to arrange for shipping. All together it took nearly three weeks from the original prescription being submitted to the PBM for the patient to receive it.

"Approval of your medication is pending" may well join the list of phrases that savvy consumers have long-since stopped believing, such as "Your call is important to us" and "The check is in the mail." Too many patients and physicians have been promised things too many times by PBM and specialty pharmacy reps, only to find those promises unfulfilled or completely contradicted.

DATA MIGRATION OR PATIENT NEGLECT?

Cathy was one of the fortunate ones; after seven and a half years, she was among the 22% of patients diagnosed with Stage IV cancer who had made it past five years. Unfortunately, Cathy's survival was dependent upon the specialty pharmacy her PBM had mandated she use—despite the fact that her oncologist had an in-house pharmacy that she would prefer to use. The problem was that every month, Cathy had to engage in a battle with the PBM pharmacy just to obtain her oral chemo medication.

As an example, on October 12th, Cathy called the PBM specialty pharmacy to verify that they were planning to over-night the oral chemo medication to her, so she could stay on schedule. The PBM specialty pharmacy told her that her oncologist had not sent in the renewal subscription. Cathy then called the pharmacy manager at her oncologist's office, who assured her that the prescription had indeed been faxed over one week earlier.

Trying to help Cathy out, the practice pharmacy manager then called up the PBM specialty pharmacy, who placed her on hold until they eventually located the script, which indeed had arrived a week before. "Why was the medicine not shipped? " the pharmacy manager asked. "Data migration," she was told; this meant that the PBM specialty pharmacy was in the middle of reorganizing its filing system, and had failed to take proper precautions to ensure that no patient care information was lost or misplaced along the way.

May 2017

COA Community Oncology Alliance — Over 15 Years of Making a Difference in Cancer Care

Unaccountable Benefit Managers:

Real Horror Stories of How PBMs Hurt Patient Care

There is no shortage of horror stories associated with the increasingly large role that Pharmacy Benefit Managers (PBMs) play in the United States' health care system. With their numerous offshoots and service lines, PBMs have managed to take on an oligopolistic presence that adversely impacts patients receiving treatments, their health care providers, and everyone else in between.

Originally created to lower prescription drug costs, it has become clear that these multibillion dollar PBM corporations have transformed into gargantuan and almost completely unaccountable arbiters of the care that cancer patients receive. As this story series demonstrates, the dangerous combination of PBM unaccountability, opacity, and lack of oversight have resulted in benefit managers that are focused on their profits and not patient care.

This paper is the second in a series from the Community Oncology Alliance (COA) that focuses on the serious, sometimes dangerous, impact PBMs are having on cancer patients today. These are real patient stories but names have been changed to protect privacy.

PBM KNOWS BETTER THAN THE DOCTOR?

A community oncology and hematology clinic in Pennsylvania was being forced to use a specific PBM specialty pharmacy for their patients' oral chemo prescriptions, despite the practice having its own in-office dispensary. They had actually applied to the PBM two years earlier for the right to dispense drugs; however, approval was still "pending."

Frank was one of the clinic's patients battling rectal cancer. His oncologist prescribed an appropriate medication and submitted it to the PBM specialty pharmacy for filling. Soon after, the PBM called the clinic and announced that approval was denied for the submitted diagnosis, however if the oncologist were to change the diagnosis to one of several other cancers, they would then approve it. The clinic responded by noting that this would be a fraudulent change, that they refused to comply with it, and would be reporting it to the State of Pennsylvania. Within ten minutes of that call, Frank's medication was approved without any changes.

Edward was another of the clinic's patients, also battling rectal cancer. He had been prescribed the same drug, with a specific dosage, to be taken twice daily, seven days a week, for five weeks. However, when the medicine arrived, the PBM specialty pharmacy had changed the dosage and instructions. This was done despite the fact that a pharmacy is forbidden to change prescription instructions without the approval of the prescribing physician. To make matters even worse, the quantities sent to Edward were incorrect, even for the adjusted regimen.

Chris was another patient at the practice battling with rectal cancer and prescribed the same medication with the same dosage. He too found that his prescription had been changed by the PBM specialty pharmacy—from seven days per week to five days per week. When the PBM specialty pharmacy called Chris to schedule shipment he refused because the instructions were different from those he'd been given at the doctor's office. At this point, the PBM specialty pharmacy called the patient's physician, who had to reinstate the original prescription.

Because of the constant, unauthorized changes to the details of prescriptions made by oncologists, this practice worries that patients' care is in danger. And these changes are not isolated to just this PBM or practice—specialty pharmacies seem to be playing it fast and loose with the oncologists' directed treatment plans. Details, such as number of dosages and their size, are crucial life-and-death matters, and PBMs and their specialty pharmacies should not be changing them.

Real Horror Stories of How PBMs Hurt Patient Care

Had Cathy not called up the specialty pharmacy, she would never have received her medicine in time. Furthermore, the pharmacy manager at her oncologist's office informed Cathy that while she had been talking with the PBM specialty pharmacy, another patient had called her with the exact same issue. Every month, without exception, Cathy has had difficulty getting the medicine shipped on time from the PBM specialty pharmacy. No matter what, whenever her oncologist calls it in, the PBM specialty pharmacy manages to misplace the order.

Customer satisfaction, integrity, and commitment are important qualities for any profession or field. Yet, they are even more crucial in those professions that deal directly with people's lives. As PBM specialty pharmacies deal in products that have the potential to lengthen the time another person has on Earth, there must be a different standard to which their employees are held, and clearly indifference, apathy and carelessness should have no place.

PATIENT AND CARE PROVIDERS GET THE RUNAROUND

One serious complication that often results from chemotherapy and radiation treatments is a condition called neutropenia, in which there is a significant reduction of the white blood cells that provide essential first line of defense against infections. Neutropenia can lead to sepsis, organ failure, and death; however, it need not progress this far, if properly treated in time.

Marvin, a cancer patient being treated by a community oncology clinic, had developed neutropenia, and his oncologist prescribed a medication that helps the body to produce more white blood cells. His PBM indicated that, in order for Marvin to receive this particular medication, it had to be mail ordered from a specific PBM specialty pharmacy.

The clinic where Marvin was being treated faxed the prescription over to the specialty pharmacy on February 27th. Three days later, they called to check on status, and were told that the prescription was in the 'benefits verification stage,' in which the PBM pharmacy confirms that the patient's insurance provider will indeed cover the medication's costs. The clinic asked if prior authorization was required, but the PBM specialty pharmacy representative was unable to say; she promised to call back with that information. Two days later, having heard nothing, the clinic called again, and a PBM specialty pharmacy representative told them that indeed prior authorization was required. That same day, the clinic arranged for prior authorization, called the PBM specialty pharmacy back, told them the medication had been approved, and requested that they now call the patient and arrange for delivery. The PBM specialty pharmacy representative refused, however, stating that the prescription was still 'being processed.'

Having had enough, the clinic manager asked to speak with a supervisor, who under pressure, agreed to deliver Marvin's medication on March 7th. However, the date came and went, without any medicine being delivered; nor did Marvin or his clinic receive any phone calls from the PBM or specialty pharmacy, to let them know about or explain the additional delay. When the clinic called back the next day, the PBM specialty pharmacy representative told her that the medication was out of stock, but they would arrange for delivery on March 9th.

Because of the PBM delays and runaround, Marvin's neutropenia continued to go untreated for nearly two weeks, leaving him vulnerable to any number of infections and diseases that his body was unable to fight off on its own.

Dealing with PBM bureaucracy often feels like being trapped on a merry-go-round, with no way off. Every issue is handled by a different person or entity, each with its own agenda and protocols, and there is no one person who has a bird's-eye view of the patient's situation. Nor is there any accountability or certainty that the promises made will be met.

PBM SPECIALTY PHARMACY INDIFFERENCE DELAYS MEDICATION FOR TWO MONTHS

Darla had been taking a medication to treat her thyroid cancer since June. Then, in January her insurance provider changed to a new PBM, although they assured Darla that she would be able to continue filling her prescription at her doctor's in-house pharmacy. However, when it came time for her January refill, the PBM denied the clinic authorization to fill the script, saying it had to be filled at their own specialty pharmacy.

Despite being a federal government-supported plan under Obamacare, which mandated that the PBM consent to any "willing provider," Darla never received her January refill. By the time the PBM contacted her for benefits verification, an entire month had gone by. Another week passed, and then another, without Darla ever receiving her medication.

Six weeks later, on March 7th, the PBM called Darla to schedule delivery, but there was more to come. Now her case was passed on to the PBM clinical department, where they needed to verify the dose, diagnosis, allergies, and drug interactions, despite the fact that Darla had been on the medication already for nearly ten months.

Once everything was verified, someone at the PBM realized that the medication was being used off-label. They called up Darla's oncologist, who confirmed that the patient had received prior authorization back in June to use the drug for thyroid cancer. He also asked the PBM specialty pharmacy representative for an explanation as to why it had taken so long to get Darla her medicine, and why there had been so many lags in communication, but the PBM representative had none to offer. As the call came to an end, the physician asked if Darla could now finally get her medicine. "No," the specialty pharmacy representative said. "Now we forward to the payment verification center. Once complete, it will be forwarded to the dispensing center. Then we can ship it out."

If Darla had been allowed to purchase her meds from the in-office pharmacy at her oncologists practice, she would have had them within 48 hours at the most. With the PBM specialty pharmacy, it took closer to two months.

Even when PBM specialty pharmacies are unable to provide a patient with the necessary medicine, they still will not release that patient so he or she can purchase it where it is available. The greed is so deep that they would rather risk a patient's life than allow another pharmacy to profit in their stead.

About the Community Oncology Alliance

The Community Oncology Alliance (COA) is the only non-profit organization dedicated solely to preserving and protecting access to community cancer care, where the majority of Americans with cancer are treated. COA helps the nation's community cancer clinics navigate a challenging practice environment, improve the quality and value of cancer care, lead patient advocacy, and offer proactive solutions to policymakers. To learn more, visit www.CommunityOncology.org

September 2017

Bureaucracy, Deadly Delays, and Apathy:

Pharmacy Benefit Manager Horror Stories — Part III

Over 15 Years of Making a Difference in Cancer Care

The dire consequences of having Pharmacy Benefit Managers (PBMs) within the United States' health care system continue to be seen, especially by the millions of cancer patients across the nation who must interact with them to access life-saving drugs.

Initially established as a way for insurance companies to outsource the management of drug benefits, PBMs have slowly morphed from simply handling prescription transactions to managing pharmacy benefit plans, negotiating with drug manufactures for discounts, and determining which drugs a patient will receive and from whom they will receive them. It's even reached the point where PBMs have become so bold as to usurp physicians' treatment decisions without consulting or notifying them of their actions.

This paper is the third in a series from the Community Oncology Alliance (COA) that focuses on the severe impact PBMs are having on cancer patients today. The stories are all real and provided by community oncology practices; only the patient names have been changed, to protect their privacy.

The vast number of horror stories from PBM abuses that are being reported by COA and others, shows the devastating result these institutions are having on patient care. From medication never sent or never received and mistaken dosages, to insurmountable red tape erected between the patient and their treatment, the problems are numerous and lead to one incontrovertible conclusion: action must be taken to stop PBM abuses.

PBM-PHARMACY ERROR NEARLY KILLS PATIENT

Carla, a colorectal cancer patient, was prescribed a common oral medication that has been on the market for nearly 20 years. Carla's PBM mandated that she fill the prescription at a large, well-known specialty pharmacy. Each time, the pharmacy had the medicine auto-shipped to Carla, with no patient contact or instructions.

Carla's oncologist prescribed the medication to be taken in rounds with the following specific instructions: 'two weeks on, one week off.' The PBM mail-order pharmacy, unfortunately, neglected to include the 'one week off' part of the instructions on the label. After her third refill, Carla ended up in a hospital's intensive care unit, fighting for her life.

Carla's experience was the straw that finally broke the camel's back, and the practice established its own oncology pharmacy with a pharmacist-managed program. However, many of their patients are still required to purchase their drugs from PBM-mandated, mail-order specialty pharmacies.

PBM pharmacies have been repeatedly documented making life-threatening mistakes; yet patients are forced to remain with them, unable to receive their medication at their physician-managed pharmacy, where they would receive the close, personalized care and monitoring that would easily prevent such potentially fatal occurrences from happening.

A PBM BUREAUCRACY FAILS TO HELP PATIENTS

Dylan had been on a specific medication for several years to manage his chronic cancer. Each time, he would simply fax the refill script to his pharmacy and the prescription would be filled with no glitches. Dylan's new insurance policy, however, required him to now fill his prescriptions at a specific PBM specialty pharmacy.

As usual, the clinic treating him faxed his refill prescription over to the new pharmacy in mid-May and Dylan waited for his medication to arrive. He waited and waited. In fact, over

PBM Horror Stories Series | 1

the next few weeks, Dylan's wife began calling the pharmacy on a daily basis, asking them when the medication would arrive. Each time, she was told there was some issue delaying delivery, but that it would be resolved in just a day or two, not to worry. Every few days, she would call back to say it had still not arrived, only to have the same conversation with a different person.

Finally, after over a month of waiting, Dylan's wife asked his oncology clinic to intervene and one call from them determined the actual problem. Apparently, the prior authorization for the medication had expired, something no one at the specialty pharmacy had bothered to inform Dylan, and no one his wife had spoken to had bothered to check what the real issue was holding up delivery. The clinic handled the situation, arranging for authorization and for the medicine to finally be shipped.

Patients and practices often find their efforts to be futile in trying to overcome the massive bureaucracy morass they face with PBM-mandated specialty pharmacies. This creates a costly burden on the physician offices throughout the country, who must now take up the task of contacting pharmacies, resubmitting medication approval, locating missing prescriptions, questioning holdups, and more. But what of the thousands of patients out there with no one in their corner, who are forced to fight these battles on their own?

ONE-SIZE FITS ALL IS NO WAY TO TREAT A CANCER PATIENT

About a year ago, Darlene was diagnosed with multiple myeloma and prescribed a particular medication. Single and living alone, Darlene decided she would continue to work full-time while being treated for the disease.

The first hurdle Darlene met was getting her 21-day supply of medication filled by the mail-order pharmacy mandated by the PBM. The pharmacy called her while she was in a meeting at work and insisted that she listen to the mandatory recital of the "Patient Understanding." They promised it would take no longer than five minutes, yet forty-five minutes later, having been transferred to four different representatives as part of the process, Darlene finally hung up the phone.

While confused and upset, Darlene also felt relieved that the PBM ordeal was over, and all she had to do now was to wait for the medication to arrive. She could not have been more wrong. Although Darlene had made it very clear that she arrives home every day from work at 4:30pm, two days later Darlene arrived home to find a note on her door that UPS had tried to deliver her medicine at 2pm. She spent the rest of the day trying to locate the medicine.

After a great deal of effort, Darlene managed to schedule future deliveries of her medication for Saturdays before 1pm. Darlene is hard of hearing, so that Saturday, she sat in her front room from 8am to 1pm, afraid to even go to the bathroom lest she miss the knock on the door. At 2pm, she opened her front door and found a note from the UPS driver that he had attempted to make the delivery but found no one at home. Again, she had to chase down the package and finally ended up retrieving her drugs from a drop center twenty-five miles away from home.

As time went on, Darlene's situation only worsened, becoming more and more time-consuming for this elderly woman who was already contending with a fatal cancer. Each time she attempted to speak to a PBM representative to resolve the issue, she was passed to a new person who refused to listen to what Darlene had to say, but rather droned on repetitively that Darlene must "follow procedures" or she would not receive her medication.

Not every cancer patient has a vast network of family and friends who are there to assist them in their time of need. Often the elderly, or those living alone without close friends nearby, are forced to handle everything by themselves. While a physician-managed pharmacy would be able to adjust to such a patient's needs and assist them in easily accessing their medication, PBM mail-order pharmacies are not set up to handle the requirements of individuals. Patients must comply with their procedures and regulations, regardless of the personal cost.

POTENTIALLY FATAL DELAY IN DELIVERY

Bertrand was diagnosed with renal cell carcinoma and prescribed a specific oral medication by his doctor. The oncology clinic sent out his prescription to the PBM-mandated specialty pharmacy on February 4th. Four days later, the clinic called the pharmacy to follow up, and was told that the pharmacy was waiting for additional information from Bertrand. Ten days later, they called again to see where things stood, and were told that while the pharmacy had tried to call the patient and schedule delivery, they had been unsuccessful in reaching him. The

Pharmacy Benefit Manager Horror Stories — Part III

patient's clinic asked why the pharmacy had not tried to call the patient's doctor; were they not aware that Bertrand was suffering from renal cell carcinoma, and that it was quickly progressing without medication?

Another eleven days passed — nearly one month from the initial prescription — and Bertrand informed the clinic that the medication had still not arrived. The clinic once again called the pharmacy and were told that the pharmacy had closed the patient's account there, having been unable to reach him and verify his information in order to schedule shipment. The clinic then called Bertrand and asked him to contact the pharmacy in order to re-open his account and immediately schedule delivery.

Nearly forty days since being prescribed the medication, Bertrand had still not received it. The oncology clinic ultimately filed a formal complaint with the insurance company and is waiting for a resolution. Meanwhile, Bertrand continued to wait, though his cancer did not; in fact, between Stage I and Stage IV of renal cell carcinoma, five-year survival rates go from 90% down to 10%.

Time and again, patients wait for medication from PBMs that will never arrive — because of a small detail missing in the documentation, or a situation that requires the specialty pharmacy worker to take some proactive measure. These workers, with their passive attitude towards patient care, unfortunately, do not see themselves as partners to the process, nor do they see it as their responsibility to shorten the time needed to deliver patients' medication.

COMPLETE INDIFFERENCE TO A SITUATION'S URGENCY

Lorraine, a multiple myeloma patient, was being denied by her insurance company the medication prescribed by her doctor. A worker at the clinic where she was being treated called Lorraine's PBM to sort the matter out. She got through to a company representative and began reviewing the situation until, at some point, the call was disconnected. Upon calling back, the worker had to start all over from the beginning with a different customer service representative.

A few days later, she called the PBM a third time, reaching yet another representative, who seemed unable to understand the situation. The clinic worker asked to speak to a supervisor, yet she turned out to be even more abysmal than the prior three representatives, both in terms of her attitude and her inability to understand the situation. The supervisor transferred the matter over to someone in appeals.

Now, the clinic worker found herself speaking to a fifth employee of the PBM who became even more aggressive, and questioned the worker's role in the doctor's office and her right to be making the call. When the worker began to conference the doctor in, so he could participate in the phone call, the PBM representative hung up on them.

As a last resort, the worker tried reaching someone in the PBM investor relations department, and had the call transferred over to the executive escalation team. She began by emphasizing the urgency of the matter; the longer it took to get Lorraine her medication, the worse her prognosis. She added that their office would be contacting both Medicare and the Insurance Commissioner's office in Maryland, to complain about the unprofessional handling of the matter with a patient's life on the line. Within twenty-four hours, there was a case worker assigned to Lorraine's case, yet no knowledge yet of how long it would be before — or even if — Lorraine would receive authorization for the lifesaving treatment she needed.

Dealing with PBM bureaucracy often feels like being trapped on a merry-go-round with no way off. Every issue is handled by a different person or entity, each with its own agenda and protocols. Patients must wait for weeks or even months, to obtain medication that they could have received within twenty-four hours, had they been permitted to get it at the point of care from their oncologist. These delays often translate into delayed treatment and worsening of the patient's condition, and in the most tragic of cases, possibly contribute to the patient's death.

BUREAUCRACY LEAVES A PATIENT IN LIMBO

Janine, a 22-year-old woman with Hodgkin's lymphoma, was prescribed a specific medication for fertility preservation. Her clinic's representative contacted the PBM specialty pharmacy to determine if prior authorization was required for the drug, and what Janine's co-pay would be.

The PBM pharmacy representative rudely responded that Janine's doctor needed to follow the proper procedures: send in the prescription and wait the necessary two days before obtaining the benefits information. The clinic representative explained that they only wanted the benefit information in order to make a treatment decision; that without knowing the co-pay they didn't know if Janine could afford the medication, and therefore didn't know whether or not to prescribe it.

The response was that the PBM specialty pharmacy could in no way help in this, nor could they refer them anywhere for more information. As a result, the clinic's hands were tied; they had no idea if the insurance company would authorize the medication, and if not, if Janine would be able to afford them on her own.

PBM specialty pharmacies have a long list of complex bureaucratic protocols, but shouldn't they be able to help patients and practices make cost saving decisions? Unfortunately, PBM bureaucratic protocols are often harmful to the very patients they are meant to help.

ONE DANGEROUS MISTAKE AVERTED… HOW MANY AREN'T?

Maria was a colon cancer patient prescribed several rounds of chemotherapy. For her first round of treatment, all went smoothly; she was permitted to fill the drug prescription right there at her clinic's physician-run pharmacy. However, for the second round of treatment, her insurance company mandated that she use one of the large, well-known PBM specialty pharmacies.

The problems began when the specialty pharmacy delivered Maria's medicine late, which delayed the beginning of her second treatment round. The following month, things worsened. Maria had suffered profound side effects from the medication, causing her oncologist to lower the dose for her third round of treatment. When Maria called the pharmacy, however, they said they had no record of the new prescription on file — though it had been sent and received.

Confusingly, shortly after the call, the PBM pharmacy called Maria back and said the medicine was about to be shipped. Upon her inquiry, the pharmacy informed her of the dosage; it was the same dosage and instructions as the previous two rounds, which had caused the intolerable side effects. Maria proceeded to spend the next several hours on the phone with the pharmacy to correct the situation. In addition, her physician's office called and spent time clarifying the matter with them. Had Maria been any less vigilant, her health could have been severely compromised by such sloppy drug administration.

With PBM specialty pharmacies being run completely separately from the point of care and physicians, patients must be extremely vigilant at all times to ensure they receive the correct medication. For cancer patients who are already dealing with a life-threatening disease and a range of debilitating side effects of the toxic medications they are on, this additional burden can be very costly — and for some, simply not feasible.

TOTAL INDIFFERENCE TO PATIENT'S PROGNOSIS

James was a patient in his late 50s, suffering from advanced renal cell carcinoma. On May 18th, his oncologist prescribed a particular medication, and they began a two-week wait for his insurance company to approve usage. Upon receiving approval, the doctor's office sent the prescription over to James' PBM-mandated pharmacy, with a request that it be handled ASAP, as the patient's situation was dire.

One week after making the urgent request and having heard nothing, the practice followed up to ascertain the status of his prescription. A few days later, a response came back from the pharmacy that they had attempted to contact James twice, but had not succeeded to reach him. They asked the doctor's office to have the patient call the pharmacy himself. The office asked the pharmacy if and when they had been planning to contact them, to notify them that there was an issue with delivering James' medication. The pharmacy responded that their policy is to try phoning the patient three times, and then they either contact the prescribing doctor's office or simply mail the prescription back to the patient.

While the PBM bureaucracy failed to try to remedy the situation, James' cancer continued to spread, untreated, leaving him no closer to receiving his medication than he had been three weeks earlier. As for the PBM pharmacy, they seemed completely unconcerned, despite the fact that the five-year survival rate for advanced renal cell carcinoma goes from 53% down to 8%, if it passes from Stage III to Stage IV.

Time and again, doctors reach out to PBM-mandated specialty pharmacies to enquire about the status of medication— only to discover that the process is stuck, and no one at the pharmacy feels any sense of urgency, despite the fact that the patient in question is being treated for a life-threatening condition in which time is of the absolute essence.

Pharmacy Benefit Manager Horror Stories — Part III

THE HORROR IS NOT LIMITED TO CANCER DRUGS

Carl was prescribed regular injections of anticoagulant medication. The initial prescription was sent off to the local branch of a major pharmacy and filled without issue. Three weeks later, however, when Carl tried to refill his medication, the pharmacy charged him a $700 co-pay. They explained that they could not offer refills; they must go through his PBM-mandated specialty pharmacy. Now there was an emergent situation because Carl needed those syringes immediately.

Carl paid the high price to obtain four syringes, which was all he could afford, while his doctor contacted the insurance company, who said that if the local pharmacy would call them, they could offer an override. The doctor called the pharmacy with the terrific news, only to hear them refuse the request, outright. "We don't have time for this," they said. "If the customer wants an override, he needs to make the call himself."

Several hours later, Carl received a call from the local pharmacy, saying that they had spoken with his insurance company, and that the mail-order pharmacy will need a new prescription. No word about the override — they hadn't even bothered to enquire about it while on the phone with the insurance company. Three hours later, the mail-order pharmacy sent Carl's doctor a request… only it was for a refill on medication used to prevent side effects caused by chemo and radiation — not for the anticoagulant meds that Carl actually needed.

At this point, Carl was twenty-four hours away from being out of medication. Adding to the absurd irony of the situation, Carl's doctor actually had an in-house pharmacy that stocked the necessary medicine. However, while the pharmacy was once part of the network of Carl's insurance company, in 2011 their contract had been cancelled, as they presented competition to the PBM's specialty pharmacy.

Even when PBM specialty pharmacies are unable to provide a patient with the necessary medicine, and even when the situation is urgent to the point of life and death, they still will not release that patient so he or she can purchase it where it is available. The greed is so deep that they would rather risk a patient's life than allow another pharmacy to profit in their stead.

About the Community Oncology Alliance

The Community Oncology Alliance (COA) is the only non-profit organization dedicated solely to preserving and protecting access to community cancer care, where the majority of Americans with cancer are treated. COA helps the nation's community cancer clinics navigate a challenging practice environment, improve the quality and value of cancer care, lead patient advocacy, and offer proactive solutions to policymakers. To learn more, visit www.CommunityOncology.org

August 2018

Danger, Delay, Denial:

Pharmacy Benefit Manager Horror Stories — Part IV

The cautionary tale of the Pharmacy Benefit Manager (PBM) system is a lesson not yet learned. The United States' health care system continues to be strangled by the dark presence of these ever-growing corporate middlemen, siphoning off billions of dollars in profits while leaving behind pain, suffering, anxiety, and despair for the millions of cancer patients.

This is the fourth paper in a series from the Community Oncology Alliance (COA) that focuses on the very real and negative impact PBMs continue to have on cancer patients today. This impact threatens to grow even stronger under recent proposals put forth by the Centers for Medicare & Medicaid Services and in President Trump's Blueprint. Rather than heed warnings about abusive PBMs and limit their influence, the current administration has proposed to do the exact opposite and increase the role PBMs play in our health care.

Today, while PBMs are contracted to handle Medicare Part D, which includes self-administered medications such as pills, they are not involved in Medicare Part B, which covers all doctor- administered drugs, such as infused chemotherapy. The government is now proposing a slew of changes, including that some, or all, of Part B medications be shifted to fall into Part D. It has also dictated that insurance middlemen, some of which own PBMs, can require step therapy for Part B medications in Medicare Advantage.

These proposals have been put forth to lower drug prices. Unfortunately, they ignore the vast evidence that the incompetence and greed of middlemen has not only failed to reduce drug prices but has ironically caused them to increase thanks to the network of shadowy rebates and discounts siphoned off by these middlemen. And, as these horror stories clearly demonstrate, this has all been done at the expense of cancer patients.

The following PBM horror stories have been provided to COA by community oncology practices. While patient names have been changed to protect privacy, the terrifying stories and details are unfortunately very real.

BUREAUCRATIC MADNESS AND A GAME OF TELEPHONE

Donald, an electrical engineer, husband and father of two college students, had been diagnosed with colorectal cancer and was scheduled for radiation treatments. His doctor prescribed an oral chemotherapy to be taken alongside the radiation and faxed the prescription off to Donald's PBM-mandated specialty pharmacy. Three days later, the pharmacy contacted Doreen at the clinic treating Donald, to clarify his prescription. Doreen handled the matter without delay, and then, four days later, called to ask when the medicine had shipped... only to discover that due to 'issues' it had not yet gone out.

The pharmacy transferred Doreen to the Medicare department, and after a lengthy wait, a representative came on, to whom Doreen explained that Donald was in fact not a Medicare patient. After another lengthy wait, the silence was broken only by the occasional interjection of "One moment," the representative explained that regardless of the patient's coverage, this particular medication ordered for him needed to be 'released' from the Medicare Part B department.

Pharmacy Benefit Manager Horror Stories — Part IV

The representative informed Doreen that the next step was for her to call Donald and ask him to call them – the pharmacy – to schedule delivery, as the pharmacy was not able to make outbound calls. However, she said, another option was for Doreen to bring Donald in on a third-party call and then wait on the line while the pharmacy verified the entire shipping process with him.

A very frustrated Doreen hung up and called Donald to explain the situation. By now it was Friday afternoon, and Donald was scheduled to begin radiation treatments on Monday, accompanied by the oral medication. It was looking more and more unlikely that Donald would have his medication in time. Adding to the absurdity of the situation was the fact that Doreen had plenty of the medication Donald needed – right there in the in-house pharmacy, and could easily have filled Donald's prescription herself, had the PBM allowed her to do so.

Countless times, bureaucratic PBM delays mean that patients must postpone treatment – or begin, but without the right combination of medicine – that will give them their best chance at battling this devastating disease. Yet, even when the situation has become a matter of life and death, patients have no recourse other than to wait it out, as the bureaucratic machinery of the PBM is not programmed to make any kind of exception.

SHAMELESS BLAME GAME WHILE THE PATIENT SUFFERS

James, a third-grade teacher in his early 40s, has lived with leukemia for many years, keeping it in remission with a daily oral medication. In November, his insurance provider notified James' doctor that a new prior authorization was required to continue receiving his medication. There was no time to lose; James had just finished his last bottle and needed an immediate refill. The authorization was immediately obtained, and the clinic forwarded it on to the PBM-mandated specialty pharmacy.

Four weeks went by, yet no medication arrived. Brenda, a clinic worker, contacted the specialty pharmacy, and a voice on the other end stated that a new prior authorization was needed. Confused, Brenda again faxed the approval letter to the pharmacy, while continuing to wait on hold. After a considerable wait, the pharmacy worker came back on the line and told Brenda that this letter was already in the patient's file, but that a new prior authorization was needed.

What on earth for? Brenda wondered to herself, as she hung up the phone. They were in February, so perhaps it was because the previous prior authorization had been sent in 2017? Yet, according to the insurance company, the old prior authorization was still in effect. She called the specialty pharmacy back, and this time a different representative answered. He looked up James' case and stated that all was well; in fact, the medication should arrive in just a few days.

Brenda hung up and called James to let him know he should expect his medication any day now. Answering the phone, James told Brenda that for the past four weeks, going without medication, he'd been frantically calling the pharmacy on a regular basis, trying to order it. They had told him each time that they'd been unable to contact Brenda, despite many attempts, and that his being without medication was due to the clinic's negligence.

Meanwhile, during those same four weeks, while James' blood counts were reaching horrific levels, Brenda was able to fill five prescriptions of the same drug for other patients, whose PBM allowed them to receive their medications in-house.

Dealing with PBM bureaucracy can be frustrating to say the least. Getting the runaround… being told one thing by a representative, only to have that information contradicted the next moment by someone else… having the person on the other end of the phone lie to you… these are the things patients and clinic workers meet time and again. And, as if lying about the status of a drug's delivery wasn't bad enough, to add insult to that situation by implying the delay is the fault of the very people treating the patient, is unconscionable.

TROLLING FOR BUSINESS

The pharmacist of an in-house clinic at a community oncology practice was going over patient files one day when the phone rang.

The caller politely introduced herself as an employee of a well-known PBM specialty pharmacy, and then abandoned all niceties as she proceeded to ask why the pharmacist was filling a prescription for a patient that by all rights belonged to them. The in-house pharmacist pulled up the file for the patient in question, who was battling advanced stage ovarian cancer. Not seeing any conflict of interest, he requested further details.

In clipped tones, the caller explained that his filling of this script was "outside of the manufacturer's contract, and illegal." Unfazed, the pharmacist responded by saying that there was no law preventing them from filling it. At this point, realizing that her strong-arm tactics were getting her nowhere with the pharmacist, she changed tactics; perhaps the doctor would be an easier target. "Did the patient's physician intentionally send the script to you?" she asked, to which the pharmacist replied, "Of course he did. Our pharmacy is located inside of the practice."

With no wiggle room left, the caller said that she would be informing the patient of all this, and abruptly ended the call. The pharmacist was left to marvel at the audacity of trying to intimidate him into handing over a patient – and the corporation that clearly couldn't care less about what was best for her.

When that corporation's income is derived from 'trolling' the system to collect more profit-generating patients receiving treatment for life-threatening ailments, we realize things have gone way too far. At some point, something must be done to rectify the perverse profit-motives and incentives behind the corporate PBM approach patient care.

CAN'T BE BOTHERED TO GET THE PRESCRIPTION RIGHT

Annabelle, a retired cosmetician and widow, had been diagnosed with Philadelphia chromosome-positive + chronic myeloid leukemia. Her community oncologist tried her out on 180mg of a particular medication, and Annabelle's response was highly positive. Her blood work showed immediate improvement, and she showed no significant side effects.

The doctor wrote out a prescription for the medication, which according to Annabelle's PBM had to come from their mandated mail order specialty pharmacy. As the medicine does not come in pills of 180 mg, the prescription clearly stated: one 100 mg tablet and one 80 mg tablet. Nevertheless, over the following months, each time Annabelle had her prescription renewed, she was given either 100 mg or 80 mg – never both. This meant that she was not only taking the wrong dosage, but also her dosage was changing each month, according to the whim of the pharmacy and whoever happened to be filling her prescription.

Annabelle did not do well with the incorrect dosing; her laboratory results showed dangerous levels in her blood work, again.

Despite the clinic's repeated attempts to get the PBM to deliver the right medication, the PBM specialty pharmacy refused to take the necessary measures to ensure that Annabelle received the proper dosage. When the doctor tried to have the script filled in the in-house pharmacy at his clinic, it was denied. Meanwhile, Annabelle continues to be improperly dosed, impacting her opportunity for remission.

This story exemplifies the constant dangers patients are in at the hands of incompetent, faceless PBM pharmacy workers. Removed several times from the patients they are meant to serve, their inattention to crucial detail is not what we should expect from a company in the business of caring for patient lives.

PBMs STANDING IN THE WAY OF TIMELY STANDARD OF CARE TREATMENT

Rhonda, a 55-year-old wife, mother, grandmother, nurse, world traveler and self-described Disney expert had been diagnosed with Her2-negative breast cancer. She was receiving treatment at a local community oncology center. Her physician prescribed treatment and attempted to fill it on the same day at the in-house pharmacy; however, the co-pay was too high for Rhonda's limited means.

The clinic's financial assistance coordinator went to bat and, six days later, had secured a co-pay card from the drug manufacturer. Two days later, however, when the practice tried to fill Rhonda's script, her PBM rejected the use of the co-pay card at the practice pharmacy. Instead, the PBM required the script to go out to its own specialty pharmacy. Not wanting to delay her treatment, the practice quickly faxed the prescription over.

Another six days passed before the specialty pharmacy notified the clinic that the prescription must first go

Pharmacy Benefit Manager Horror Stories — Part IV

through the specialty pharmacy connected with the patient's PBM, regardless of who would ultimately fill it. The clinic staff filled in all the additional forms and handled all new bureaucratic measures, and then proceeded to wait. Three days later, a clinic RN called the specialty pharmacy to ask for an update. The representative who answered told her that all was well, and that no prior authorization would be needed. She then placed her on hold. Ten minutes later, the representative returned, only to say that actually prior authorization was needed. With the greatest of patience, the nurse filled out all the new forms and faxed all relevant records necessary for the prior authorization, over to the specialty pharmacy.

Later that day, the pharmacy contacted the RN to inform her that the prescription had been denied, based on the patient's Her-2 positive status. The RN again sent the patient's records to the pharmacy, highlighting the fact that she was, and had always been, since she was first diagnosed Her-2 negative. Two days later, the medicine finally arrived.

All-together, Rhonda's therapy was delayed 19 days, which, had she been permitted to fill her prescription in-house, would never have happened. In total, the clinic staff spent five hours dealing with red tape.

Worst of all, Rhonda never had the opportunity to take the first pill. The night before the medication arrived at her home, she was hospitalized for complications of her metastatic disease. After a lengthy hospital stay she was discharged home to hospice.

While the physicians caring for Rhonda were busy trying to "march to the beat of the PBM's drum", this sweet, young, vibrant woman's window of opportunity closed. How many other scenarios involving pointless deterioration, hospitalization, and death from PBM incompetence are there? When reflecting on the life and care of the patients, PBMs should not be part of the conversation.

WOULD IT KILL YOU TO WAIT?

In 2012, a 45-year-old salesman named Bill was diagnosed with colorectal cancer. Bill had a good job working for a large office supply manufacturer based in the Midwest, a loving wife and two small children, and he decided to fight with everything he had. Following surgery, Bill was treated with IV chemotherapy, but with negligible results. The cancer progressed over the next year, and his doctor changed to a different IV chemotherapy. This time his response was very good, and for the next four years things were fairly quiet.

In 2017, tests showed that Bill's cancer was back, and this time he was treated with yet a third kind of IV chemotherapy. His response seemed good at first, but by the following year, the cancer had progressed to Stage IV and metastasized to his liver. At this point, Bill's oncologist ordered an oral medication specially prescribed for relapsed or metastatic colon and rectal cancers.

Bill's physician at the community oncology practice sent the prescription over to the in-house pharmacy to fill. Unfortunately, according to Bill's new insurance plan, his prescription could only be filled by a PBM-mandated pharmacy. Despite the facts that Bill's Stage IV cancer was aggressive, that his doctor wanted to get him started on the medication that very same day, and that the medication was sitting on the shelf of the in-house pharmacy, Bill had to wait. Even the option sometimes given to have a 'one-time fill' that would let him get started while waiting for the PBM pharmacy to mail him his medication was denied. Thus, with the drug's prohibitive list price (over $10,000/month), Bill had no option but to wait.

The doctor sent his prescription on to the new pharmacy, along with Bill's contact details, so that they could arrange for delivery. Meanwhile, Bill went to his clinic and received detailed in-person counseling on how to take the drug, since it was a somewhat complicated regimen. There were specific directions on how to take the medication, what side effects to expect, and how to ensure the proper dosing. The latter could be confusing, since the drug is taken in multiple tablets twice daily on days 1-5 and 8-12 of a 28-day cycle.

After seven full days of waiting to start his therapy regimen, Bill finally received his medication in the mail. Opening the box, he began to read the label, and found to his great surprise, that it stated: "take once a day." Picking up the phone, Bill checked in with his oncologist to report the change in instructions. The clinic pharmacist confirmed that the instructions were wrong, and reached out to the PBM pharmacy, which promised to contact Bill about clearing up the matter.

Bill received a call from the PBM-mandated pharmacy representative, who apologized for having sent the wrong prescription with the wrong amount of medication. They assured Bill he would receive an additional supply of medication. First, however, they asked Bill to please return the medication he had been sent, so it could be properly labeled. Now Bill, with Stage IV metastatic cancer and his treatment already having been delayed a week, was being asked that rather than take his life-saving medicine, he ship it back to the warehouse for proper labeling and reshipping.

This was not the last time the PBM pharmacy impacted and delayed Bill's care. Later, when it came time to refill his medication, Bill's treatment was again delayed. The PBM pharmacy, it seemed, decided that before filling his prescription, it had to first clarify the dosage. It then claimed to have had difficulties in contacting Bill's community oncology clinic, despite having been provided with all the correct contact details. Ultimately, Bill had to call his local clinic and ask for the in-house pharmacist to call the PBM to confirm dosage, before they would ship it out. And while he waited, his cancer was allowed to progress, unchecked.

One of the most dangerous parts of PBM-mandated pharmacies is the distance between the pharmacy and patient. In this, we are speaking not only of geographical distance, but also of when patients are forced to wait for medicine to be shipped, rather than walk across a hallway to purchase it. More to the point, however, is the situation in which the patient becomes a name or number on a call sheet, rather than an actual human being facing a life-threatening illness; rather than a patient for whom there is care and endearment. That distance is at the core of many PBM mistakes and apathy.

About the Community Oncology Alliance

The majority of Americans battling cancer receive treatment in the community oncology setting. Keeping patients close to their homes, families, and support networks lessens the impact of this devastating disease. Community oncology practices do this while delivering high-quality, cutting-edge cancer care at a fraction of the cost of the hospital setting.

The Community Oncology Alliance (COA) advocates for community oncology and on policy issues that affect patient care. Our members include patients in active treatment, cancer survivors, caregivers, family members, medical and oncology professionals, and members of the general community. For more than 15 years our members have advocated for smart public policy that ensures the community cancer care system remains healthy and able to provide all patients with access to local, quality, affordable cancer care. Learn more at www.CommunityOncology.org

April 2019

Dangerous Health Care Middlemen & Bureaucracies:

Pharmacy Benefit Manager Horror Stories — Part V

The Pharmacy Benefit Manager (PBM) industry lobby claims that it successfully achieves drastic price reductions on medications. They say this comes from PBMs negotiating with competing drug companies and by "encouraging consumers to use the most cost-effective drugs."

Setting aside clear evidence that secretive PBM rebates and fees are actually driving drug prices higher, the last claim should give all Americans pause. How exactly does a PBM "encourage" a treating physician to use cost-effective but life-saving drugs? How do they know what is right for each individual patient and disease? What tactics or methods do PBMs use to do this? And are the changes in the patients' best interests, or simply to save money for PBM profit margins?

Unfortunately, time after time, PBMs have been exposed for abusing their position to do this, getting between the patient with cancer and their physician to dictate care. All too often, the PBM bureaucracy does this by simply and heartlessly delaying or denying make patients' access to needed medications. Perhaps most egregiously for patients facing a ticking clock of cancer, PBMs deny prescribed treatments and demand that patients first fail on a list of 'approved' drugs before receiving the medication that their physician prescribed in the first place.

For patients with cancer, this intrusion into their care plans is painful, potentially life-threatening, and unnecessarily stressful. For oncologists it is yet another bureaucratic burden placed between them and caring for a patient, wasteful of scarce health care resources, and insulting to the doctors that went to medical school and prescribe treatment plans.

These and other monstrous by-products of the PBM system are further exposed here, as the Community Oncology Alliance (COA) presents the fifth in a series that focuses on the very real and negative impact PBMs continue to have on patients with cancer today. The infuriating stories presented here are real but made anonymous with personal details changed to protect the privacy of the patients.

A NARROW WINDOW FOR TREATMENT

Brian, a married social worker with two young children, was in his early 30s in February 2014, when he was diagnosed with a relatively rare form of cancer in his appendix. Brian underwent surgery and chemo at a large hospital system, and for the next few years, his life went back to normal.

In late 2017, however, Brian suffered a relapse. He underwent surgery to remove all traces of the cancer, and his oncologist followed up with a round of chemotherapy. Despite the metastasis, Brian's doctors thought he had a good chance at survival, and recommended that he immediately begin a six-month regimen of oral medication to help keep the cancer at bay. He was young, strong, and had everything to live for; they were optimistic the cancer might never return.

On February 8th, Brian's oncologist sent a prescription for the pills to the local pharmacy his clinic worked with. They informed him that while they had the medicine in stock, Brian's insurance and PBM prohibited them from filling the prescription. Instead, they forwarded the prescription to a PBM-mandated specialty pharmacy to receive prior authorization.

Pharmacy Benefit Manager Horror Stories — Part V

The PBM-mandated specialty pharmacy granted the prior authorization, but was also unable to fill the prescription, so it was forwarded to yet another PBM specialty pharmacy. By this point, 11 days had passed. After another few days of silence, the second PBM pharmacy sent a message that they were unable to fill the prescription; it had to be done by the first PBM specialty pharmacy. It seemed that no one really knew who was responsible or able to fill the script.

On February 23rd, the same day that Brian finally received his oral anti-cancer medications, he was rushed to the emergency room for severe pains in his abdomen. There they discovered he had contracted an infection that necessitated surgery to repair his abdominal wall. The pills in his hand were no longer relevant.

Today, Brian must remain on chronic antimicrobial therapy pills to ward away abdominal infection; should he stop, they might easily return. Unfortunately, this precludes any further chemotherapy, and Brian's once promising prognosis has been replaced by one far direr. In effect, Brian missed his very narrow window and it is likely that he will never get well again.

Oncologists are on the front lines treating patients with cancer who have complex needs – they know the exact state of their patients, and how very precious even a day can be. PBMs and their mandated specialty pharmacies are several times removed from the exam room, and as a result, their lack of urgency and inability to cut through bureaucratic red tape can easily become an indirect – or even direct – cause of patient suffering.

NOT A HEALTH CARE PROFESSIONAL? YOU DON'T STAND A CHANCE

After having survived her battle with thymus cancer in 2015, Rachel was surviving with several autoimmune disorders, including myasthenia gravis, a condition in which the body attacks its own neuromuscular connections. After utilizing several immunosuppressants, Rachel has managed to keep the illness in remission for the past two years, by taking a wonder drug that works as an immunosuppressant, maintaining a low volume of antibodies in her system.

An advanced oncology certified nurse at a community oncology clinic, Rachel knows her condition well and how to stay healthy. For two years she has been taking her medication faithfully every day, working to care for her patients, and living life as normally as could be.

Then, at the beginning of 2019, her employer changed insurance carriers. When it came time one Friday for Rachel to refill her meds, she went to the local pharmacy to pick them up, only to be told that there were 'issues.' The pharmacist was confused and said he would look into it.

Two hours later, the pharmacist called to say that from now on, Rachel must obtain her medication through the PBM's specialty pharmacy. She immediately called the new pharmacy's number, where she waited a long time until she was connected. After trying fruitlessly to locate Rachel in the system, he put her on hold for ten minutes. When someone else finally came back online, Rachel had to tell her entire story from the beginning. This happened several times, with Rachel's blood pressure rising exponentially. It was Friday afternoon, and she had six pills left – enough for two days.

Rachel hung up the phone; this had been a dead end. Falling back on a trick she had learned after dealing with countless PBM bureaucracies on behalf of patients, Rachel called the member services number on the back of her insurance card. After being passed around from representative to representative, she reached "Brian," who promised to establish a new member's account for her. However, as to her refills, he insisted he first needed to call her doctor to get prior auth.

Rachel began to see red. It was Friday afternoon, and her neurologist's office was closed. Trying to remain calm, Rachel explained to Brian that she still had several refills left. Brian promised he would contact her pharmacy and have the refills transferred over. "Call me in the morning," he said. Saturday morning, at 7:30 am, she called the specialty pharmacy, where she was told that no one named Brian had been in touch, and there was nothing in the computer about her issues. However, this new representative was the real deal. She handled everything over the next few hours, and arranged for the meds to arrive by Monday – which they finally did – just as Rachel's pills had run out.

Infinite patience coupled with buckets of determination and self control seem to be de rigueur when it comes to dealing with PBM Specialty Pharmacy bureaucracies holding one's life-saving medicine hostage. If it was this difficult for a seasoned, tough-as-nails advanced oncology nurse to get her own meds, what is going to happen to the other 99.9% of the population?

Pharmacy Benefit Manager Horror Stories — Part V

CLERICAL ERRORS MARRIED WITH INCOMPETENCE

Paula was a very intelligent company executive battling breast cancer. Her oncologist prescribed a particular medication and she faced no issues in having it filled or refilled the first time. When it came time for the second refill, however, she met a PBM roadblock. Despite several calls to the PBM, and speaking with several different people, all the patient could get them to explain was that there were insurmountable "insurance issues." Not knowing what else to do, she came into the oncologist's office so they could call the PBM together to resolve the matter.

After a long wait on hold, the doctor and his patient finally reached a representative who informed them that they were unable to fill the prescription because it could have a negative interaction with another medicine she was currently taking. The doctor and the woman looked at each other for a moment, before asking the rep, "What medicine?" The patient was not taking any other medication. This was, however, not what the PBM had in their records. It took quite a bit of additional convincing by the patient and her doctor before the PBM would believe them, and agree to provide authorization.

By this point, due to clerical error and the absence of anyone to take responsibility, the patient had already gone 10 days off of her regimen, something which never should have happened.

Practices report that they spend an absolutely 'ridiculous' amount of time trying to obtain prior authorizations from PBMs – well beyond any reasonable expectancy. Even getting to the point where there is another human being on the other end of the phone to talk to is an achievement in and of itself. This, of course, is only the beginning of the PBM process that is fraught with errors and poor record keeping, all of which can add up to dozens of hours of staff time wasted dealing with bureaucracy, and drag on over days, weeks, even months. In the meantime, patients with cancer are left waiting without the treatment that they need.

PBMs SERVING THEIR OWN BOTTOM LINE

Gordon, a retired FBI agent with a distinguished record of security service on behalf of the United States, was diagnosed with an aggressive form of lung cancer. Proving resistant to the drug regimen his oncologist initially prescribed, the cancer metastasized to his brain, and he was immediately started on radiation therapy. It was at that point that his doctors made an important discovery: Gordon's cancer had the EGFR mutation, which indicated he would do better with oral medication than infusion chemotherapy. More importantly, there was a new drug that had just been approved by the FDA as the first-line treatment for EGFR-mutated non-small cell lung cancer. This gave Gordon and his cancer care team a window of hope.

Gordon's oncologist prescribed the new medication, but the PBM denied authorization, providing the name of an alternative drug they wanted him to try first. His doctor argued that his original prescription would be better for the patient: It had been shown to have far higher efficacy for patients whose cancer had metastasized to the brain. The PBM argued back that it had been initially approved for a different EGFR mutation than the one Gordon had. His doctor argued back that this was irrelevant, as it was effective for Gordon's mutation as well, and was now FDA approved.

Back and forth, the fight went on for an entire month, with the doctor providing data and rationale to support his clinical decision making. Meanwhile the cancer grew inside Gordon, unchecked. He began to feel increasingly fatigued, and a man who had remained very active throughout his cancer battle began to deteriorate.

Ultimately, after more than 30 days of wasted time, the PBM approved the doctor's original prescription. Upon beginning the regimen, Gordon's condition began to slowly improve, but it never should have been allowed to reach such a low state.

Again and again, we see PBMs playing doctor, choosing to authorize one medication and not another, for reasons that have nothing to do with patient care. From pushing the drugs from pharmaceutical companies with which they have made sweetheart deals, to demanding patients be prescribed lower-cost medication, their actions are profit-driven and often in complete contradiction to what the patient actually needs to get well.

PBM APATHY LEAVES BOY IN DANGER OF BLEEDING TO DEATH

Diagnosed with hemophilia, 15-year old Jason had to simultaneously contend with his blood's inability to form clots and the danger of bleeding uncontrollably. Jason's oncologist had him on a once-daily oral medication that can slow the spread of his cancer by blocking a specific protein the disease needs to thrive.

One day, Jason missed his footing on the stairs at home. Falling, he hit his thigh and developed a significant hematoma, common with hemophiliacs. He now urgently needed a specific recombinant factor injection to help his blood clot, and quickly.

Jason's oncologist quickly prescribed the necessary self-injected medication to be taken at home. Prior authorization was received, however the PBM handling Jason's case refused to allow the practice's pharmacy to fill the script, so they forwarded it to the PBM-mandated pharmacy. Unfortunately, they could not fill the prescription, and without informing Jason or his doctor, they outsourced the prescription to yet another pharmacy.

Recognizing the urgency of the situation, Jason's mother, a full-time nurse, stepped in to see how things could be expedited. She made numerous phone calls, verifying that the pharmacy she used to work with before her insurance changed had the medication in stock and, due to a contract with the PBM, was able and willing to ship it out the next day. Not wanting to lose out on the business, the original PBM-mandated pharmacy stepped in and vetoed the plan, stating that as it had already been ordered from them, there could be no cancellations.

Adding another layer of unnecessary problems to the mix, the PBM suddenly claimed that there had been no prior authorization filed for the prescription. Undeterred, the practice pharmacist spent hours trying to get it all done as soon as possible, so that Jason could get the medicine he needed.

Finally, just when it felt like the situation was starting to be resolved, the PBM pharmacy representative on the phone belatedly realized that the medication in question was for injection and stopped the process. Prescriptions for injections, she said, had to go through a different department. Unfortunately, it was now 5 pm on a Friday and the PBM offices were closed for the weekend, so they would have to wait to submit the prescription until Monday. Because of his hemophilia, young Jason was now in danger of developing a dangerous complication that could require emergency surgery and a long hospital stay if not treated immediately.

With no alternative, the doctor sent Jason to the hospital emergency department to receive the necessary injection. While this prevented any life-threatening occurrences, it incurred an enormous expense for his family and insurer, one that could easily have been avoided. Due to the astonishing bureaucracy, a patient fell through the cracks, with no one outside his personal doctor standing up to take responsibility or showing the slightest concern.

Patients do not walk off the pages of a textbook or an encyclopedia of illnesses and their recommended treatment. Each case is individual and ought to be treated as such, in a thoughtful, intelligent, holistic manner. Additionally, patients do not stop treatment just because it is the weekend or after the phone lines shut down. The more control PBMs are given over patient care, the more sweeping and infuriating their bureaucracies become, and, ultimately, the more dangerous their decisions and actions prove to be.

WOULD YOU LIKE SOME KIDNEY FAILURE WITH YOUR CANCER?

In the Fall of 2012, Trisha, a medical software instructor in her early 60s, suffered renal failure and was rushed to the hospital. Diagnosed with Multiple Myeloma, she underwent dialysis and was referred, by her community oncologist, to a Myeloma specialist at the nearby hospital system. The specialist recommended a particular regimen of chemotherapy to keep the disease in check, and Trisha was released.

A few months later, tests revealed that the cancer was progressing. Her chemo was clearly not working; a new medication had to be tried. This would not be simple, for following Trisha's renal failure, her kidneys had never returned to normal. This meant her doctors had to be extremely careful about what drugs they prescribed, as certain medications for Myeloma are known to take a heavy toll on the kidneys.

Trisha's oncologist, in consultation with the hospital specialist, decided to prescribe a particular drug that could slow the progression of her disease, without having any adverse effects on her already stressed kidneys. Her oncologist sent in the prescription to the PBM mandated specialty pharmacy, which promptly sent back a notice denying the request.

At first, the pharmacy said that prior authorization was needed. Her doctor said, "No problem," and instructed the in-house clinic to fill out all the necessary forms and fax them over. This was followed by a second denial, which stated that the patient did not meet "the proper requirements" to receive the requested drug. What were those requirements? Trisha had to first have tried two other drugs, one after the other, and to prove that either her body had been unable to tolerate them, or that they had failed to slow the cancer's advancement.

Of those two drugs that the PBM demanded Trisha try - and fail - first, one was the very same drug she had been prescribed the previous year that had already failed to slow the cancer's progression. The second was a medication that, had she taken it, would have seriously damaged her kidneys and likely put her back into renal failure.

Over the next two months, Trisha's oncologist appealed the PBM's decision, and a long series of communications ensued between the oncologist, the Multiple Myeloma specialist, and the PBM specialty pharmacy. Trisha, meanwhile, watched with increasing anxiety as her myeloma protein markers quadrupled, indicating that the cancer was gaining ground. The appeal turned into a letter of medical necessity, and ultimately, after more than two months of delay, the correct medicine was finally approved by the PBM.

PBMs have been given enormous amounts of control over what doctors may and may not prescribe. They try to strong-arm doctors into prescribing the medicine that the PBMs choose, even though they have never met the patient, and often have no medical background to support the decisions they are making.

PBM DELAY TACTICS VICTIMIZE PATIENTS

Belinda, a kindergarten teacher and mother of two, was fighting thyroid cancer. Her oncologist had her on a particular medication that was approved for off-label use on thyroid cancer; she'd been taking the medication for seven months and was doing well.

In January, Belinda's insurance carrier moved to a new PBM, which required her to fill her prescriptions at their mandated specialty pharmacy. They assured Belinda that it would be no trouble for them to continue filling her medication. So, that same month, when it came time for Belinda's refill, her oncologist sent the e-prescription directly to the new pharmacy, and called Belinda to confirm.

When Belinda tried to pick up the prescription, however, the PBM-mandated pharmacy said they were unable to process it "at that time." She waited an entire month before being contacted by the PBM pharmacy to verify benefits and schedule delivery. After another week went by with no medication, a very frustrated Belinda called her oncologist to see if they could dispense the medication directly to her. Unfortunately, according to Belinda's insurance policy, they were not allowed to do that.

Another week passed, and, after six weeks of delays, the PBM-mandated pharmacy contacted Belinda. They wanted now to schedule delivery – again. The prescription was then sent to PBM's Clinical department to verify dose, diagnosis, allergies, and drug interactions.

At this stage, someone at the PBM finally noticed that the drug was being prescribed for an off-label usage, and called her oncologist to verify the diagnosis. The oncologist spoke to the PBM pharmacist, explaining that the drug had been approved for nearly a year, with the patient taking it all that time, to very beneficial results. It had always been for off-label usage, and the insurance company had always agreed to it. What was the matter?

The PBM pharmacist had no explanation for the time lag, nor was there any documentation to explain why more than two months had passed. At the end of the conversation, the doctor asked if Belinda could finally expect to receive her medication now. "No," the pharmacist replied. "Now, we forward the matter to the payment verification center. After that stage, it will be forwarded to the dispensing center. Then we can ship it out."

Had Belinda been authorized to purchase her medicine from the in-house pharmacy at her doctor's office, the entire process would have taken a single day.

The larger an organization, the more complex the bureaucratic procedures. This is often done under the guise of ensuring safety. However, how far do things need to go before it can be said that the harm to patients has greatly surpassed any intended good? At what point do the PBMs themselves become accountable to a certain standard of care – even in terms of something as simple as response time?

IT IS TIME TO STOP PBM ABUSES!

While much of the debate over PBMs focuses on economics, there is often not enough discussion about the impact PBMs have on patients. The sad fact is that PBMs make more money by delaying or denying patients access to necessary medications. Every pill they stop from being dispensed is money they can pocket. COA has documented real-life patient horror stories from practices and physicians about patients battling cancer who have suffered at the hands of PBMs due to delayed coverage decisions, denial of coverage, arguments with physicians over proper treatment, and failure to receive medications in a timely manner.

Read our other PBM Horror Stories papers at https://www.communityoncology.org/category/horror-stories/

About the Community Oncology Alliance

The majority of Americans battling cancer receive treatment in the community oncology setting. Keeping patients close to their homes, families, and support networks lessens the impact of this devastating disease. Community oncology practices do this while delivering high-quality, cutting-edge cancer care at a fraction of the cost of the hospital setting. The Community Oncology Alliance (COA) advocates for community oncology and smart public policy that ensures the community cancer care system remains healthy and able to provide all Americans with access to local, quality, affordable cancer care. Learn more at www.CommunityOncology.org

Response to Written Questions Submitted by Hon. Marsha Blackburn to Robin Feldman

Question 1. Can you elaborate on how PBMs' consolidation within the pharmaceutical supply chain has been able to go unchecked?

Answer. Markets should be fair, open, and efficient. Unfortunately, the PBM market lacks these essential qualities. The level of concentration within the market is concerning, with just three PBMs controlling 80 percent–85 percent of the market.[104]

Competition issues also arise regarding consolidation between PBMs and other players in the pharmaceutical supply chain, such as PBMs merging with pharmacy chains and specialty pharmacies. A discussion of a variety of competition concerns when PBMs merge with pharmacies can be found in my most recent book,[105] but as one example, PBMs can drive patients towards their own pharmacies. Specifically, some health plan formularies restrict patients from purchasing a 90-day supply of medicine from any pharmacy other than the one owned by a particular PBM—and, of course, it's the PBM that helped write the formulary. Activities such as these can dampen competition at other parts of the pharmaceutical supply chain, as well as reducing patient choice and harming access to medicine.

The negative impact of concentration at many levels of the supply chain for medicine has various causes, but governmental gaps and failures have certainly allowed concentration to go unchecked. These include: 1) the need for regulatory enforcers to take a "second look" post-merger to determine if their competitive predictions proved accurate, take appropriate measures, if not, and to adjust future merger and acquisition protocols accordingly; 2) the failure of insurance regulators and legislators to protest that PBMs have breached their duty to act in the best interest of health plans and, by extension, plan enrollees; and 3) the failure of insurance plans, regulators, and courts to push back against PBMs' baseless reliance on trade secret law to shield their pricing data from public and regulatory scrutiny.[106]

---

[104] Neeraj Sood, Dana P. Goldman, & Karen Van Nuys, Follow the Money to Understand How Drug Profits Flow, STAT (Dec. 15, 2017), *https://www.statnews.com/2017/12/15/prescription-drug-profits-pbm/* ("The top three pharmacy benefit managers, which negotiate drug prices on behalf of insurers and self-insured employers, dominate 85 percent of their market."). See also Neeraj Sood, Transcript of Understanding Competition in Prescription Drug Markets: Entry & Supply Chain Dynamics Workshop (Nov. 8, 2017), *https://www.ftc.gov/ system/files/documents/videos/understanding-competition-prescription-drug-markets-panel-2/ftc_understanding_competition_in_prescription_drug_markets__transcript_segment_3.pdf.*

[105] *See* ROBIN FELDMAN, DRUGS, MONEY, & SECRET HANDSHAKES: THE UNSTOPPABLE GROWTH OF PRESCRIPTION DRUG PRICES 46–50 (Cambridge 2019).

[106] *See* Robin Feldman & Charles Tait Graves, *Naked Price & Pharmaceutical Trade Secret Overreach,* 22 YALE J.L. & TECH. 61 (2020) (examining PBM efforts to assert that pricing ar- rangements should be considered trade secrets).

- Is the consolidation in the PBM market ultimately working to lower drug prices for patients?

Answer. A heavily consolidated market is rarely in the interests of consumers. In the PBM market, the Big Three tend to offer the same terms, preventing the customers of those three from having meaningful options and avoiding the challenge of true competition. None of this has been helpful for lowering drug prices for patients.

- What would a competitive PBM market do for the consumer at the counter? Answer. A PBM's job is to negotiate better prices for the benefit of patients. However, the perverse incentives operating in the PBM market have helped to inflate profits for PBMs instead of appropriately driving down prices for consumers. Although there are many contributors to rising prices, true competition in the PBM market could help drive down the prices that consumers pay at the pharmacy counter, as well as the dollars they pay for insurance plan premiums.
- What are some ways we can spur innovation within the PBM market?

Answer. As noted above, markets should be fair, open, and efficient. To spur competition and innovation in the PBM market, I would recommend four key approaches related to Fiduciary Duty, Transparency, and Concentration:

1) First, clarify that PBMs have a fiduciary duty, certainly to the health plan if not the patients, themselves.
2) Second, clarify that price and price terms in this context are not trade secrets.
3) Third, ensure that competition agencies have the proper tools to reduce concentration in the PBM and related industries. We won't see price improvements until we improve competition.
4) Fourth, encourage regulators to adopt a robust "Second-Look" policy. Rather than relying on crystal-ball predictions of what will happen after a merger or acquisition, competition agencies should establish a system of post-merger review to ensure past decisions had the intended results and to improve future evaluations.

Question 2. What is your view of copay accumulators that prevent patient support from counting toward a patient's deductible or maximum out-of-pocket costs. Do you know where these revenues are going?

Sometimes, a gift is a Trojan horse. It seems like a wonderful offering—even a blessing—but, beware of what lies within. That can be the case with patient assistance programs. And, as I will describe below, the patient is always the one who loses out.

For patients who are struggling to afford tremendously expensive medication, providing a coupon seems heaven-sent. Even more so if the coupon pays for a life-saving drug. But the costs to the patient, not to mention the health care system, are carefully camouflaged.

With a coupon, or other form of patient assistance program, the brand-name company agrees to pay all, or a significant portion, of the patient's out-of-pocket costs. Thus, the patient sees tremendous relief in the form of out-of-pocket costs. But it can be an illusion. The health insurance plan pays for the more expensive, brand-name drug, rather than a less expensive competitor. The extra amount that the plan pays for the drug is then reflected in the cost of the annual premium patients pay. If this happens enough, premiums can rise for everyone in the plan, including the specific patient.

In 2020, a U.S. House Oversight Committee report provided an inside view of how pharma companies themselves think about patient assistance programs. The report examined reams of documents from Novartis, relating to its blockbuster oncology drug Gleevec. The company's documents showed that co-pay assistance programs were a crucial piece of its strategy to encourage patients to stay with the brand-name drug after generics entered the market. The company even calculated that beefing up the strategy 6 months before generics entered the market would be the timing that provided the greatest return on investment by keeping the maximum number of patients attached to the drug before the generics made it to market.

The return on the company's investment was impressive. Company documents showed that the company's patient assistance on the drug provided a return on investment of $8.90 for every dollar spent on the program. When a company is making nine additional dollars for every dollar it hands out with a coupon, the company is not acting out of the goodness of its heart.

In response, health plans have created policies that prevent such programs from counting towards a patient's deductible or out-of-pocket maximum. Their theory is that the patient did not pay that amount out-of-pocket; the pharma company did. These health plan limitations are being called co-pay accumulators or co-pay maximizers. They are intended to save money for the plan which, in the best of circumstances, would flow through to keep the premiums lower for patients. I have not studied, however, whether that actually happens. Nor am I aware of academic studies concluding that these savings do, indeed, flow through to create lower premiums for patients.

In the process of handing out patient assistance, of course, brand companies purchase brand loyalty.[107] The patient—who is now wedded to an expensive brand-name drug, rather than a generic, biosimilar, or less expensive alternative—may be reluctant to change. When the maximum value of the company's coupon is reached, the patient is socked with the extremely high out-of-pocket cost of the drug. That is, yet again, another hidden price that patients must pay.

As always, the patient is caught in the middle of the struggle, and no matter what, the patient seems to lose out.

Question 3. I am concerned that copay accumulators may negatively impact prescription drug access for vulnerable patients. How can we best address this issue to help patients and caregivers?

Answer. As noted in my response to the prior question, the patient is always the one who loses in these struggles. In particular, brand companies can begin handing out copay coupons before the generic or biosimilar has arrived on the market—an effective method for ensuring that patients have continued loyalty when the generic or biosimilar does arrive.[108]

If the health plan and the brand company truly wanted to help a vulnerable patient, the drug could be provided to the patient's health plan at a severely reduced cost with the agreement that the particular patient would enjoy a low out-of-pocket cost. Congress could help by clearing any regulatory hurdles in the way. Moreover, programs such as these should be designed so that they provide a long-term benefit

for a vulnerable patient, rather than as a limited-time offering of free samples that reel in a patient, who will then be stuck paying large sums for a long time.

---

107 Studies show that these patient assistance programs increase brand-name drug sales by 60 percent, mostly by reducing sales to generic competitors. See Leemore Dafny, Christopher Ody & Matt Schmitt, When Discounts Raise Costs: The Effect of Copay Coupons on Generic Utiliza- tion, 9 Am. Econ. Jl.: Econ. Policy 91, 93 (2017).

108 See U.S. HOUSE OF REPRESENTATIVES, STAFF REPORT: COMMITTEE ON OVERSIGHT AND REFORM, DRUG PRICING INVESTIGATION: NOVARTIS—GLEEVEC SELECTED INVESTIGATION DOCUMENTS (2020) (finding that Novartis made significant changes to its copay assistance program for the blockbuster oncology drug Gleevec six months before generics entered the market, offer- ing patients the allure of steep reductions in out-of-pocket payments, a strategy that convinced patients to stick with Gleevec once generics were on the market).

And, of course, the best help for vulnerable patients—as well as access to medicine for all patients—would be to inject transparency and competition into the PBM system. I am heartened to see the Subcommittee's work on these important issues.

Response to Written Question Submitted by Hon. Richard Blumenthal to Juan Carlos "JC" Scott

Question. As you know, the dynamics of the 340B program are always complicated. There has been a lot going on over the last couple of years with respect to contract pharmacy, and I am hearing often from South Dakotans with concerns about actions taken by both PBMs and manufacturers. At the end of the day, these actions are harmful to the program that is meant to help our hospitals support their communities. Resolving these issues will take some time, so I just ask for your commitment to be willing to be part of the conversation.

Answer. Thank you for taking the time to share your concerns about the 340B program. I appreciate the opportunity to respond, and I am always willing to contribute to the discussion. While PCMA is neutral on the 340B program, we are aligned fully with the program's goal of helping safety-net entities provide better care to vulnerable populations. Our members process claims in support of the program, but PBMs cannot always determine when a claim is related to a 340B transaction, which causes complications for PBMs, pharmacies, manufacturers, and individuals paying for health insurance. To maintain eligibility to sell drugs to state Medicaid programs, manufacturers must agree to participate in 340B. While Medicaid eligibility and 340B participation are linked, the programs are separate, and Federal law prohibits duplicate discounts—mandated Medicaid rebates do not apply to drugs obtained at 340B pricing. To support efforts to avoid duplicate discounts for 340B pharmaceuticals, claims modifiers, like those used in the Medicaid program, are needed to better understand which drugs are 340B and which are not. PCMA welcomes the opportunity to continue working on this and other issues in the 340B program to ensure fairness and transparency in the prescription drug marketplace.

Response to Written Questions Submitted by Hon. Marsha Blackburn to Juan Carlos "JC" Scott

Question. (Blackburn) I would like to know what you would see a competitive marketplace be. We know there have been consolidations. Mr. Scott says there are 70 PBMs, but we know we have very few players in this area. So, in a perfect world, how would you structure a competitive PBM marketplace that would, indeed, yield our Medicare enrollees a lower cost? (Blumenthal) I would invite each panelist to respond to that question in writing. It is a big question and at the heart of what we are doing here today.

Answer. To foster a more competitive market for prescription drugs, Congress should focus on increasing competition to promote consumer accessibility and affordability and enhance the value of dollars spent on health care. Last year, PCMA announced a three-part policy platform focused on lowering prescription drug costs by updating Medicare Part D, increasing competition, and moving consumers toward a more value-driven health care system.[109] Our policy platform outlines concrete policy steps to make prescription drugs more affordable for all consumers, and the PBM industry's vision for a health care system that delivers more value to all Americans. If fully implemented, PCMA's policy platform would reduce prescription drug costs, make pharmaceutical care more accessible to all Americans, and save tax- payers $257.5 billion to $398.7 billion over ten years.[110]

The first set of policies propose modernizing Medicare Part D. PCMA suggests specific policy options to make Medicare Part D more affordable, including capping out-of-pocket costs, eliminating misaligned incentives that keep drug prices artificially high, building on Part D's record of choice and competition, allowing plan sponsors access to additional tools for managing costs, repealing the rebate rule to protect seniors by preventing significant premium increases, and preventing tax-payers from paying substantially more for Part D. Additionally, we support enhancing manufacturer liability throughout all phases of the benefit to ensure that manufacturers bear a fair share of the responsibility to provide American seniors with high-quality coverage.

---

[109] PCMA. The Critical Path Forward: Rx Policies to Reduce Patient Costs, Improve Access. June 2021. Available at *https://www.pcmanet.org/pbms-solutions-to-lower-patient-rx-costs-im- prove-access/.*

[110] PCMA. PCMA's The Critical Path Forward Will Save Taxpayers $255.5 Billion Over 10 Years. July 2021. Available at *https://www.pcmanet.org/wp-content/uploads/ 2021/07/ pcma_criticalpathforward_7-6-21.pdf.*

The second set of policies would prevent patent abuses like patent thickets, evergreening, product hopping, and misuse of citizen petitions that drug manufacturers use to prevent fair competition from generic and biosimilar drugs. As we work together to bring greater savings to Medicare beneficiaries, we must also focus on real solutions to lower drug costs for everyone. Consequently, PCMA supports policies aimed at reducing market distortions, like those aimed at limiting patent and exclusivity abuses that stifle competition and keep drug prices high. We also need solutions to ensure drugs compete fairly, including the production of more cost- effective generics and biosimilars.

The third and final set of policies would foster broader adoption of value-based purchasing and the acceleration of consumer-focused pharmacy care. More health care spending does not automatically result in better outcomes. To promote the use of high-value treatments and reduce the use of those which do not provide the necessary or expected benefit to patients, PCMA proposes policies to accelerate value-based and consumer-centered care. We also support bringing the same value-driven tools used by employers to Medicare and Medicaid and promote the production and use of rigorous evidence of drug performance in the real world. Improving health outcomes requires the treatment of patients based on their individual needs. Therefore, PCMA supports driving a concerted effort to reduce health care disparities and inequities. Value-based care arrangements for consumers would be made possible by granting Part D drug plans access to Medicare Parts A and B claims data, establishing safe harbors for value-based contracting, and allowing Part D and state Medicaid plans greater flexibility to adopt private-sector formulary management techniques.

Question. I have been hearing about new PBM programs called copay accumulators that impact certain patients in high-deductible health plans. These programs prevent patient support from counting toward a patient's deductible or maximum out-of-pocket costs. As a result, patients face sudden and often unexpected higher out-of-pocket costs when their patient assistance runs out, and they discover their deductible has not been met. Can you please explain to me how these programs impact patients?

Answer. Copay accumulator programs are health-plan programs designed to prevent drug manufacturers from using copay coupons to steer or coerce employers, unions, and government programs to pay for expensive, unnecessary brand medications. Under Federal law, the use of copay coupons to obtain healthcare services under Medicare and Medicaid is prohibited as marketing tools to induce a consumer to purchase a particular brand they might not otherwise purchase. Similarly, copay coupons for prescription drugs are an inducement to obtain a particular drug even when a lower-cost therapeutic alternative is available. Therefore, legislation seeking to stop payers from managing their costs by prohibiting the use of accumulator programs would eliminate a crucial tool in their fight against rising drug costs. If drug companies are concerned about patients accessing medications, they should simply lower their prices; this is the simplest, most effective way to reduce patient costs for drugs.

Chapter 3

Competition in Prescription Drug Markets, 2017-2022*

U.S. Department of Health and Human Services

Executive Summary

The cornerstone of a well-functioning market is competition. President Biden's Executive Order 14036, "Promoting Competition in the American Economy" identified a lack of competition as a key driver for problems across economic sectors. By incentivizing competition, it is possible to foster innovation and improve the stability of a market, in turn increasing access and affordability of products. The U.S. prescription drug market is the largest drug market in the world; however, drug prices in the U.S. are much higher than in most of the world. High drug prices mean that people often cannot afford prescription drugs, even when those drugs are otherwise available. We used IQVIA data from 2017 through 2022 to identify the level of competition in different prescription drug markets. We focus on competition in the prescription drug market, because the number of competitors for a particular drug is associated with pricing power – drugs with fewer or only one manufacturer, on average, have higher prices than drugs with multiple manufacturers, holding all else constant. Understanding the baseline level of competition in drug markets will allow us an opportunity to further incentivize innovation and competition.

* This is an edited, reformatted and augmented version of ASPE Report Prepared by The Office of the Assistant Secretary for Planning and Evaluation (ASPE) At the U.S. Department of Health and Human Services, dated December 2023.

In: The Price of Prescription Medicine
Editor: Cornelius Lowery
ISBN: 979-8-90134-014-1

Key Findings

- In 2022, average cost of a biological product, $174 per prescription, was 3.7 times greater than average cost of a small molecule drug, $48 per prescription.
- Among the 1,838 small molecule drugs in 2022, 43 percent (796 drugs) had only one manufacturer, 16 percent (298 drugs) had 2-3 manufacturers, 9 percent (156 drugs) had 4-5 manufacturers, and 32 percent (588 drugs) had 6+ manufacturers. Drugs with a single manufacturer accounted for a disproportionate share of drug spending; the 43 percent of drugs with one manufacturer accounted for 65 percent of small molecule drug expenditures.
- Among the 268 biological products on the market in 2022, 81 percent (216 products) had only one manufacturer, 13 percent (34 products) had 2-3 manufacturers, 4 percent (12 products) had 4-5 manufacturers, and 2 percent (6 products) had 6+ manufacturers. The 81 percent of biological products with only one manufacturer accounted for 74 percent of total biological product expenditures. The pattern of biological products with one manufacturer accounting for a smaller share of the total spending is different than the pattern seen for small molecule drugs.
- Between 2017 and 2022, for small molecule drugs, the proportion of drugs with 6+ manufacturers rose while those with a single manufacturer declined over time. In contrast, biological products predominantly had one manufacturer, and the proportion of products with one manufacturer continued to increase over time.
- We then focused on high-cost drugs. Among specialty drugs, in 2022, 63 percent of small molecule drugs (273 drugs) and 87 percent of biological products (164 products) had only one manufacturer. Focusing on the top 10 percent of drugs based on price, i.e., the highest priced drugs, 89 percent of small molecule drugs (136 drugs) and 100 percent of biological products (59 products) had only one manufacturer.
- Among the highest priced drugs, the most common therapeutic classes were enzyme inhibitors (68 drugs), immunomodulators (21 drugs), antineoplastic monoclonal antibodies (20 drugs), miscellaneous antineoplastics (9 drugs), and other neurological/

neuromuscular (9 drugs). Ninety-two percent had only a single manufacturer.

Report

Introduction

The cornerstone of a well-functioning market is competition. President Biden's Executive Order 14036, "Promoting Competition in the American Economy" identified a lack of competition as a key driver for problems across economic sectors. By incentivizing competition, it is possible to foster innovation and improve the stability of a market, in turn increasing access and affordability of products. The U.S. prescription drug market is the largest drug market in the world; however, drug prices in the U.S. are much higher than in most of the world. High drug prices mean that people often cannot afford prescription drugs, even when those drugs are otherwise available. Enhancing competition in drug markets is a key priority of this administration. By increasing competition, standard economic theory suggests that the price of drugs will decrease, and more Americans will have access to affordable prescription drugs.

The goal of this report is to examine the level of competition in the U.S. prescription drug market, defined as the number of manufacturers that are currently selling a given active ingredient. We examine different drug characteristics, including small molecule drugs versus biological products, specialty drugs, and the highest priced drugs between 2017 and 2022. We focus on competition in the prescription drug market, because the number of competitors for a particular drug is associated with pricing power – drugs with fewer or only one manufacturer, on average, have higher prices than drugs with multiple manufacturers, holding all else constant. Understanding the baseline level of competition in drug markets helps us identify tailored policy solutions to further incentivize innovation and competition, and it will be important to continue examining competition in prescription drug markets as they evolve over time.

Data and Methods

The primary dataset for this analysis was IQVIA National Sales Perspective (NSP) from 2017 through 2022.[1] IQVIA data are derived from a panel of wholesalers, distributors, and pharmaceutical manufacturers that represent 90 percent of the pharmaceutical market and are weighted to be nationally representative.[1] The IQVIA data include whether a drug was a small molecule drug or a biological product, the setting to which a drug was sold (i.e., retail, mail, or non-retail setting), and the total expenditure associated with the transaction (i.e., sales from manufacturers and wholesalers to pharmacies, hospitals, and other health care settings). While the data do not include payer information, the data include drugs that are eventually used by Americans of all ages and covered by commercial insurance, and public insurance programs, including Medicare, as well as self-pay. Drug spending was measured in inflation adjusted dollars.[2] The IQVIA dataset reports gross drug spending, meaning it does not include rebates.[3] The number of prescriptions was calculated as a measure of the number of units of a drug a manufacturer sold to a wholesaler or pharmacy.[4]

Competition was measured by the number of unique pharmaceutical manufacturers that sold a drug. To assess the level of competition in prescription drug markets, we identified drugs based on their active ingredient. For each drug, we counted the number of unique corporations (i.e., manufacturers) with sales in the data for each year and stratified the results into brackets of competitive intensity measured as the count of active manufacturers, regardless of their market share. For example, if a single manufacturer marketed a given molecule,[5] then we categorized this as a single

---

[1] Source of the data: IQVIA. U.S. National Data. <https://www.iqvia.com/insights/the-iqvia-institute/available-iqvia-data>.

[2] The spending data includes an adjustment for inflation, thereby representing a "real" dollar. The data represent the value of a real dollar as of quarter 1 of 2022. Source: U.S. Bureau of Economic Analysis, Gross Domestic Product: Implicit Price Deflator [GDPDEF], retrieved from FRED, Federal Reserve Bank of St. Louis; https://fred.stlouisfed.org/series/GDPDEF, January 30, 2023.

[3] Retail drugs can be subject to rebates while non-retail drugs do not have rebates. As a result, retail drug spending may be overestimated relative to non-retail spending.

[4] The variable in the IQVIA data that is used to measure the number of prescriptions, "eaches", is defined as "the number of single items (such as vials, syringes, bottles, or packet of pills) contained in a unit or shipping package and purchased by pharmacies in a specific time period. In this report, the term "prescription" does not refer to units that are sold directly to patients. Additional information can be found in the appendix.

[5] We count the unique number of manufacturers that are marketing a drug. In most cases, a single manufacturer would be the brand manufacturer of the originator drug, but in select cases a

manufacturer on the market. These are also known as "single source" drugs. The same process was used to identify whether there were 2-3 manufacturers, 4-5 manufacturers, or 6+ manufacturers.

This report has two primary outcomes of interest: the number of manufacturers for a given molecule and the percent of total revenue that was associated with each level of competition (e.g., what percent of a market had 2-3 manufacturers based on revenue). The goal of assessing the number of manufacturers for a given molecule is to examine how many drugs do not have competition. The goal of assessing the percent of total revenue associated with each level of competition is to understand the monetary value of the prescription drug market that is associated with monopolistic practices. Importantly, we relied on the drugs that appear in the IQVIA database, meaning that a drug had to have been marketed by the manufacturer.[6]

In this analysis, we separately assess small molecule drugs and biological products. In addition, we examine a subset of "specialty" drugs (as opposed to "traditional" or "non-specialty" drugs) and then focus on the top 10 percent of drugs based on price, i.e., "highest priced drugs", most, but not all, of which are specialty drugs. The highest priced drugs were defined on an annual basis, meaning the drugs change for each year of the sample. Table 1 defines the types of drugs examined in this report.

Table 1. Drug categories and corresponding definitions

Drug Category	Definition
Small Molecule Drugs	Small molecule drugs are made using chemical processes with low molecular weight
Biological Products[7]	Biologics are generally large, complex molecules that may be produced through biotechnology in a living system, such as a microorganism, plant cell, or animal cell. Examples include therapeutic proteins (such as filgrastim), monoclonal antibodies (such as adalimumab), and vaccines (such as those for influenza and tetanus)

single manufacturer could be a generic or biosimilar manufacturer if the brand name manufacturer is no longer marketing their product.

[6] There is a subset of drugs that are approved by FDA but not sold by the manufacturer. Examples include: 1) an approved drug in shortage may not have an adequate supply to be utilized in large enough quantities to appear in claims data; 2) in some cases, settlement of patent litigation between brand and generic companies may result in agreements that delay marketing of approved generic drugs; or 3) a drug product has been discontinued from marketing.

[7] U.S. Food and Drug Administration. Biological Product Definitions. https://www.fda.gov/files/drugs/published/Biological-Product- Definitions.pdf.

Table 1. (Continued)

Drug Category	Definition
Specialty Drugs[8]	Typically cost more than $6,000 per year and require administration by a health care provider
Highest Priced Drugs	The top 10 percent of drugs in IQVIA based on price per prescription

Results

Small Molecule Drugs Versus Biological Products

Table 2 shows drug expenditures and the total number of prescriptions from 2017 to 2022 for small molecule drugs and biological products. Total inflation-adjusted expenditures on prescription drugs grew from $522 billion in 2017 to $618 billion in 2022, an 18.4 percent increase. Total prescriptions had a similar percentage point increase, from 8.019 billion in 2017 to 9.315 billion in 2022 (a 16.2 percent increase). The increase in total expenditures was driven by a 54.6 percent increase in expenditures on biological products, from $163 billion in 2017 to $252 billion in 2022. This was despite only a 1.9 percent increase in the number of prescriptions, which suggests that spending per prescription, rather than changes in utilization (i.e., a greater number of prescriptions being filled) was the primary driver of increased biological product spending. This pattern is similar to that for the broader prescription drug market.[9] In contrast, spending on small molecule drugs remained almost flat during this period, at approximately $360 billion per year, while the number of prescriptions increased 19.2 percent. This indicates that the price per small molecule drug was dropping during this time period. Overall, the share of total expenditures on small molecule drugs decreased from 69 percent in 2017 to 59 percent in 2022, with a corresponding increase in the share of expenditures on biological products.

[8] Specialty drugs are defined by IQVIA as products used to treat chronic, rare, or complex diseases that also meet certain additional criteria. More details on the definition of a specialty drug can be found in the appendix. The IQVIA definition of specialty drug is different than the definition of a "specialty tier" in Part D.

[9] Parasrampuria, S. and Murphy, S. (2022). Trends in Prescription Drug Spending, 2016-2021. https://aspe.hhs.gov/reports/trends- prescription-drug-spending.

Table 2. Drug expenditures (in inflation adjusted dollars) and number of prescriptions for small molecule drugs and biological products, 2017-2022

	Small Molecule Drugs		*Biological Products*		*All Drugs*	
	Expenditures Billions, $	Number of Prescriptions Millions	Expenditures Billions, $	Number of Prescriptions Millions	Expenditures Billions, $	Number of Prescriptions Millions
2017	359	6.60	163	1.42	522	8.02
2018	357	6.59	185	1.74	542	8.33
2019	355	6.91	210	1.73	565	8.64
2020	360	6.80	223	1.52	584	8.32
2021	366	7.18	239	1.46	604	8.64
2022	366	7.87	252	1.45	618	9.31
% Change 2017-2022	1.9%	19.2%	55.0%	1.9%	18.5%	16.2%

Source: ASPE analysis of IQVIA National Sales Perspective (NSP) Data. Number of prescriptions refers to the number of units of a drug sold by manufacturers and wholesalers to pharmacies, hospitals and other health care settings. All dollar amounts include an adjustment for inflation meaning they represent a "real dollar" as of quarter 1 of 2022.

Competition Among Small Molecule Drugs and Biological Products

Figure 1 shows the level of competition in small molecule drug and biological product markets. The number of manufacturers can fluctuate from year to year, because it includes both new market entrants, but also market exits. That means that the number of small molecule drugs and biological products reported for each year is the *net* number of drugs on the market, after accounting for both discontinued drugs and new drugs introduced on the market. In total, there were 1,808 unique small molecule drugs in 2017, which increased to 1,838 by 2022. Throughout this six-year period, approximately 800 small molecule drugs (43 percent in 2022) had only one manufacturer, about 300 small molecule drugs (16 percent in 2022) had 2-3 manufacturers, about 150 small molecule drugs (8 percent in 2022) had 4-5 manufacturers, and 500-600 small molecule drugs had 6+ manufacturers (32 percent in 2022). The number of drugs with 6+ manufacturers rose while those with a single manufacturer declined over time. Overall, between 2017 and 2022, for small molecule drugs, the number of drugs with 6+ manufacturers rose while those with a single manufacturer declined over time.

The biological product market was smaller than the small molecule market based on the number of products and total spending. There were 209 biological products on the market in 2017, which increased to 268 in 2022 (28 percent increase). On net (after accounting for discontinued products and new products introduced on the market), there were fifty-nine new biological products on the market in this five-year time span, which was approximately twice the number of new small molecule drugs on the market, 30, during the same time period.

The level of competition among biological products was significantly lower than for small molecule drugs. In 2017, there were 166 biological products with only 1 manufacturer (79 percent of biological products), and this increased steadily over time to 216 biological products in 2022 (81 percent of biological products, 30 percent increase). However, the level of competition for 2+ manufacturers remained relatively flat over time (the one caveat is that the level of competition for 4-5 manufacturers doubled during this time period, however there are so few drugs that fall into this category that it is not discernible in the graph). Of the 268 biological products on the market in 2022, 34 biological products (13 percent) had 2-3 manufacturers, 12 biological products (4 percent) had 4-5 manufacturers, and 6 biological products (2 percent) had 6+ manufacturers. The takeaway from this figure is that the percentage of single manufacturers for biological products has seen a slight increase, despite a growth in the number of biological products on the market.

Overall, Figure 1 indicates that there was significantly more competition in the small molecule drug market relative to the biological products market. This is in large part because there are a lot of generics approved by FDA, but only a few biosimilars. There are many reasons that are more generic drugs than there are biosimilar products. Importantly, the generic approval pathway was established in 1984 under the Hatch-Waxman Act, while the biosimilar pathway was established by the Biologics Price Competition and Innovation Act in 2010 as part of the Affordable Care Act.[10] While the biosimilar pathway was modeled off the generic drug approval pathway, the pathways are not the same. For example, while generic drugs are automatically substitutable with the brand name drug by pharmacists, biosimilars require a determination of interchangeability to be considered substitutable by a pharmacist. Another difference is that the first generic drug applicant to submit a substantially complete application and challenge one or more patents listed for the brand drug can receive 180- days of market exclusivity, but there is no such exclusivity for biosimilar products (although the first interchangeable

---

[10] U.S. Food and Drug Administration. (2016). Implementation of the Biologics Price Competition and Innovation Act of 2009. https://www.fda.gov/drugs/guidance-compliance-regulatory-information/implementation-biologics-price-competition-and-innovation-act-2009.

biosimilar receives a period of exclusivity). And a third difference is that Hatch-Waxman links FDA approval of follow-on applications to brand name drugs with the patents listed in the Orange Book covering those products, but there is no equivalent linkage for biologic reference product manufacturers. In addition to the differences in the approval pathways, there are other reasons for differences in competition between generic drugs and biosimilars. For example, generic drugs are significantly easier to manufacture than biological products. Generic drugs are usually synthesized from chemicals meaning each lot of manufactured drugs is the same. In contrast, biological products, including biosimilars, are typically manufactured from living systems (e.g., microorganisms, like yeast and bacteria, and animal cells), resulting in inherent variation (i.e., small changes to the molecule) as a natural part of the manufacturing process.[11] The complexity and variability of these large molecule products usually means that manufacturers conduct significantly more testing, which is both time consuming and costly, to get biosimilar products to market. In addition, reimbursement practices for generics and biosimilars tend to be different, especially for public programs, and there are often differences in formulary placement and exclusive contracting for products. Taken together, we see that competition overall has been declining in the more expensive biological product market, while it has been gradually increasing in the small molecule market.

Figure 2 breaks down the number of manufacturers in 2022 among small molecule drugs and biological products based on two criteria 1) the relative percent of total revenues that are attributable to each level of competition (e.g., what percent of market sales are for drugs with only one manufacturer), and 2) the relative percent of unique molecules associated with each level of competition (e.g., what percent of all molecules sold have only one manufacturer). By comparing the respective percentages for each criterion, we can examine whether sales and units sold are equivalent for each level of competition or whether there are systematic differences.

[11] U.S. Food and Drug Administration. Biosimilars Info Sheet. https://www.fda.gov/media/154912/download.

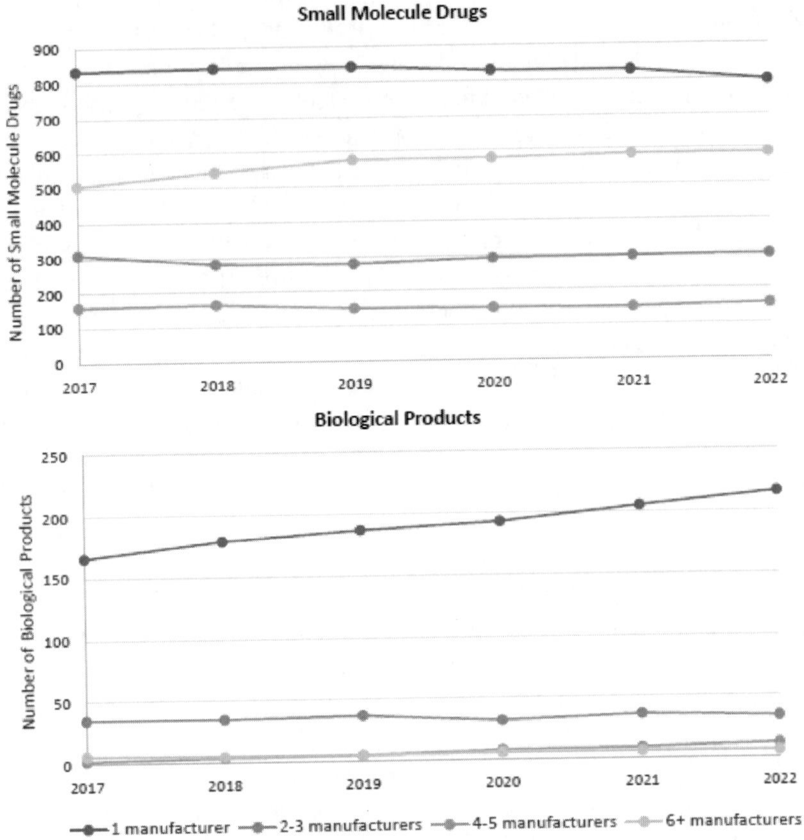

Source: ASPE analysis of IQVIA National Sales Perspective Data.

Figure 1. Number of Manufacturers of Small Molecule Drugs and Biological Products, 2017-2022.

Overall, in the small molecule drug market, in 2022, the 43 percent of small molecule drugs with a single manufacturer accounted for 65 percent of small molecule drug expenditures – indicating that single source drugs are responsible for an outsized share of total spending. Among the other competition categories, the relative percent of total expenditures was lower than the relative percent of drugs represented.

In the biological product market, the vast majority of products, 81 percent, had only one manufacturer and these products accounted for 74 percent of total revenues. In the remainder of the market, 13 percent of products had 2-3 manufacturers, which accounted for 13 percent of total revenues, 4 percent of products had 4- 5 manufacturers, which accounted for 9 percent of revenues, and 2 percent of products had 6+ manufacturers, which accounted for 4 percent of revenues. It is important to note that there are a relatively small number of products in these latter categories, so a single biological product can have a large impact on this pattern.

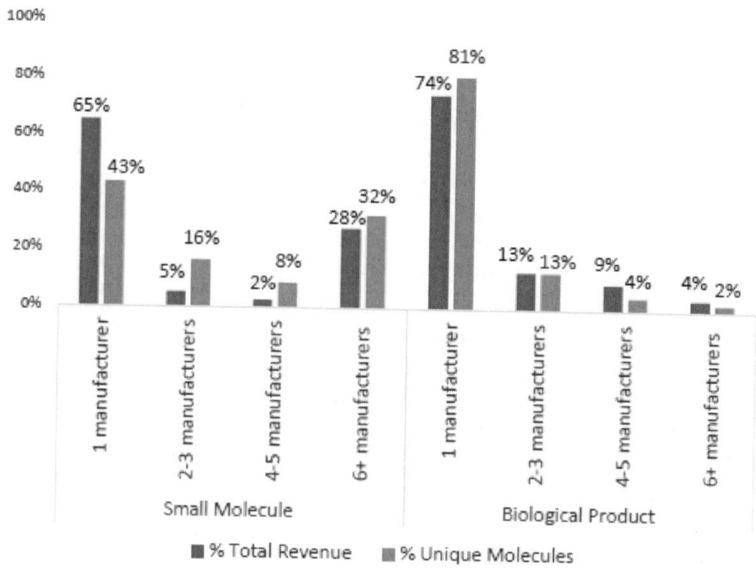

Source: ASPE analysis of IQVIA National Sales Perspective Data.

Figure 2. Percent of Total Revenue and Unique Molecules Based on the Level of Competition for Small Molecule Drugs and Biological Products, 2022.

Specialty Drugs

Table 3 shows drug expenditures and the total number of prescriptions for specialty drugs from 2017 to 2022 and also breaks out these statistics for small molecule drugs and biological products. Total inflation-adjusted expenditures on specialty drugs grew from $226 billion in 2017 to $316 billion in 2022, a 39.9 percent increase. However, the number of specialty prescriptions decreased from 1.16 billion in 2017 to 1.09 billion in 2022, a 6.2 percent decrease. This means that spending per specialty prescription increased 49.2 percent between 2017 and 2022, from $195 in 2017 to $291 in 2022.

The distribution of small molecule drugs versus biological products also changed during this time frame. Between 2017 and 2022, the percentage of specialty drug spending on small molecule drugs decrea*sed* from 50 percent to 40 percent, while the percentage of specialty drug prescriptions for small molecule drugs *increased* from 19 percent to 23 percent. The inverse translates to the percent of specialty spending on biological products: there was a 10-percentage-point *increase* in spending share, while there was a 4 percentage-point *decrease* in prescription share. Biological products represent a disproportionate and growing share of specialty drug spending over time.

Table 3. Specialty drug expenditures (in inflation adjusted dollars), 2017-2022

	Total Specialty Spending Billions, $	Number of Specialty Prescriptions, Billions	Spending Per Specialty Prescription, $	% of Specialty Spending on Biological Products[12]	% of Specialty Prescriptions on Biological Products
2017	226	1.16	195	50	81
2018	246	1.44	171	53	84
2019	270	1.41	191	56	83
2020	288	1.16	248	56	80
2021	302	1.12	271	58	78
2022	316	1.09	291	60	77
% Change 2017-2022	39.9%	-6.2%	49.2%	19.2%	-4.5%

Source: ASPE analysis of IQVIA data. Number of prescriptions refers to the number of units of a drug sold by manufacturers and wholesalers to pharmacies, hospitals, and other health care settings. All dollar amounts include an adjustment for inflation, meaning they represent a "real dollar" as of quarter 1 of 2022.

Figure 3 shows the level of competition among specialty drugs in small molecule drug and biological product markets, and both curves show an increase in the share of single-manufacturer products. In total, there were 347 specialty small molecule drugs in 2017 (19 percent of all small molecule drugs), which increased to 434 by 2022 (24 percent of all small molecule drugs). In 2022, 273 specialty small molecule drugs (63 percent) had only one manufacturer, 51 specialty small molecule drugs had 2-3 manufacturers (12 percent), and 26 specialty small molecule drugs (6 percent) had 4-5 manufacturers. The only competition category that changed noticeably, as a percentage share of the total, over the sample period was the number of

[12] The amount of specialty spending on small molecule drugs is the inverse of the numbers presented for biological products (e.g., 81 percent of specialty prescription on biological products translates into 19 percent of specialty prescriptions for small molecule drugs).

specialty small molecule drugs with 6+ manufacturers, which increased from 49 drugs in 2017 to 84 drugs in 2022, an increase of 71.4 percent.

In the biological product market, there was an increase in the number of products with only 1 manufacturer from 114 biological products (55 percent of all biological products) in 2017 to 164 biological products (61 percent of all biological products) in 2022. This translates to a 44 percent increase. Among all the other competition categories there were also substantial changes: a 25 percent decrease in manufacturers for drugs with 2-3 manufacturers, a 300 percent increase in manufacturers for drugs with 4-5 manufacturers, and a 25 percent increase in drugs with 6+ manufacturers, but these percent changes were driven by small numbers that likely cannot establish a trend.

Similar to the overall small molecule drug and biological product markets, we saw that in the specialty market, there was more competition among small molecule drugs than among biological products. We also observed a greater percentage increase in biological products with a single manufacturer over time, 44 percent, relative to a 19 percent increase among small molecule drugs. However, the total number of new specialty molecules with only one manufacturer was similar, 50 and 43 for biological products and small molecule drugs, respectively.

Figure 4 breaks down the level of competition by total revenue and total molecules in 2022 among specialty drugs. Overall, in both markets, more than three quarters of total revenue and unique molecules were associated with only 1 manufacturer. However, the directional relationship between the percent of revenue and the percent of molecules was different between small molecule drug and biological product markets. In small molecule drug markets, the 63 percent of molecules with only one manufacturer accounted for 79 percent of total revenue, while for biological products, the 87 percent of molecules with only one manufacturer accounted for 84 percent of total revenue. The remaining categories of competition had a smaller share of the total revenue and molecules, although there was more competition among specialty small molecule drugs than there was competition among specialty biological products.

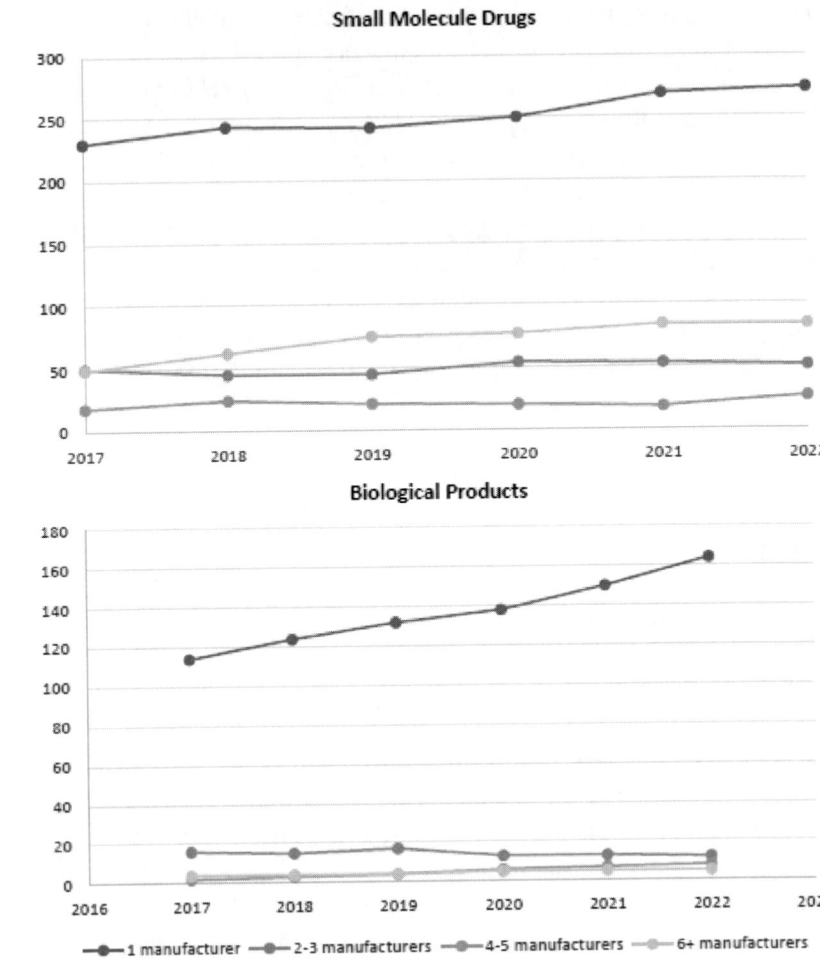

Source: ASPE analysis of IQVIA National Sales Perspective Data.

Figure 3. Number of Manufacturers of Specialty Drugs, 2017-2022.

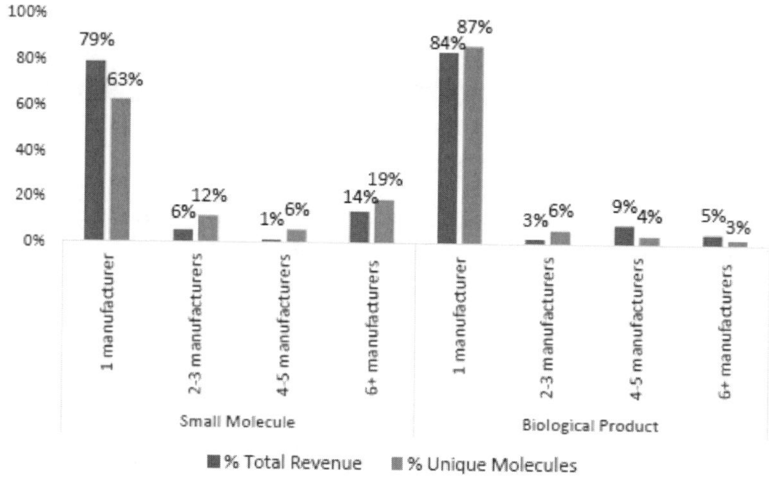

Source: ASPE analysis of IQVIA National Sales Perspective Data.

Figure 4. Percent of Total Revenue and Unique Molecules Based on the Level of Competition for Specialty Drugs, 2022.

Highest Priced Drugs

Table 4 shows drug expenditures and total prescriptions for the top 10 percent of drugs based on price per prescription ("highest priced drugs") from 2017 to 2022. It breaks out expenditures and prescriptions separately for small molecule drugs and biologic products. Total inflation-adjusted expenditures on the highest priced drugs grew from $87 billion in 2017 (17 percent of total spending) to $108 billion in 2022 (17 percent of total spending), a 25 percent increase. However, the number of prescriptions for the highest priced drugs *decreased* from 13.2 million in 2017 to 11.4 million in 2022, a 14 percent decrease. This means that spending per prescription among the highest priced drugs increased by 45 percent $6,561 in 2017 to $9,505 in 2022.

From 2017 through 2022, an increasing share of spending and prescriptions on the highest priced drugs were for biological products, with a corresponding decrease for small molecule drugs. In 2017, biological products comprised 30 percent of spending and 34 percent of prescriptions among these highest priced drugs, but by 2022, both of these rates had increased to 49 percent. Accordingly, the share of drug spending and utilization of small molecule drugs among the highest priced drugs dropped from 70 percent to 51 percent and from 66 percent to 51 percent respectively.

Table 4. Highest-priced drug expenditures (in inflation adjusted dollars), 2017-2022

	Total Spending on the Highest Priced Drugs (Billions), $	Prescriptions for the Highest Priced Drugs (Millions)	Spending Per Highest Priced Prescription, $	% of Highest Priced Drug Spending on Biological Products	% of Highest Priced Drug Prescriptions on Biological Products
2017	87	13.2	6,561	30	34
2018	89	12.3	7,224	42	53
2019	95	11.9	7,991	43	49
2020	100	11.9	8,473	50	58
2021	96	10.0	9,618	46	48
2022	108	11.4	9,505	49	49
% Change 2017-2022	24.5%	-14.0%	44.9%	66.9%	43.6%

Source: ASPE analysis of IQVIA data. Number of prescriptions refers to the number of units of a drug by manufacturers and wholesalers to pharmacies, hospitals, and health care settings. All dollar amounts include an adjustment for inflation, meaning they represent a "real dollar" as of quarter 1 of 2022.

Figure 5 shows the level of competition among the highest priced drugs in small molecule drug and biological product markets. We found that the vast majority of the highest priced drugs had only one manufacturer. This may be because the highest priced drugs are also usually those that still have market exclusivity and thus competitors are not yet allowed on the market. In 2022, among the 211 highest priced drugs, 152 (72 percent) were small molecule drugs and the remaining 59 drugs (28 percent) were biological products. In both 2017 and 2022, the vast majority of small molecule, highest priced drugs had only 1 manufacturer: 127 of 145 products in 2017 (88 percent) and 136 of 152 products in 2022 (89 percent). The other categories had so few drugs that trends were not reliable.

We found even less competition in the biological product market – there was no competition at all as each product was manufactured by a single corporation. This striking finding was robust across the sample period with the only exception being one molecule that had 2 manufacturers in 2018, which then disappeared in the subsequent years of analysis. The number of biological products that ranked among the highest priced drugs also remained mostly flat, 57 molecules in 2017 and 59 in 2022.

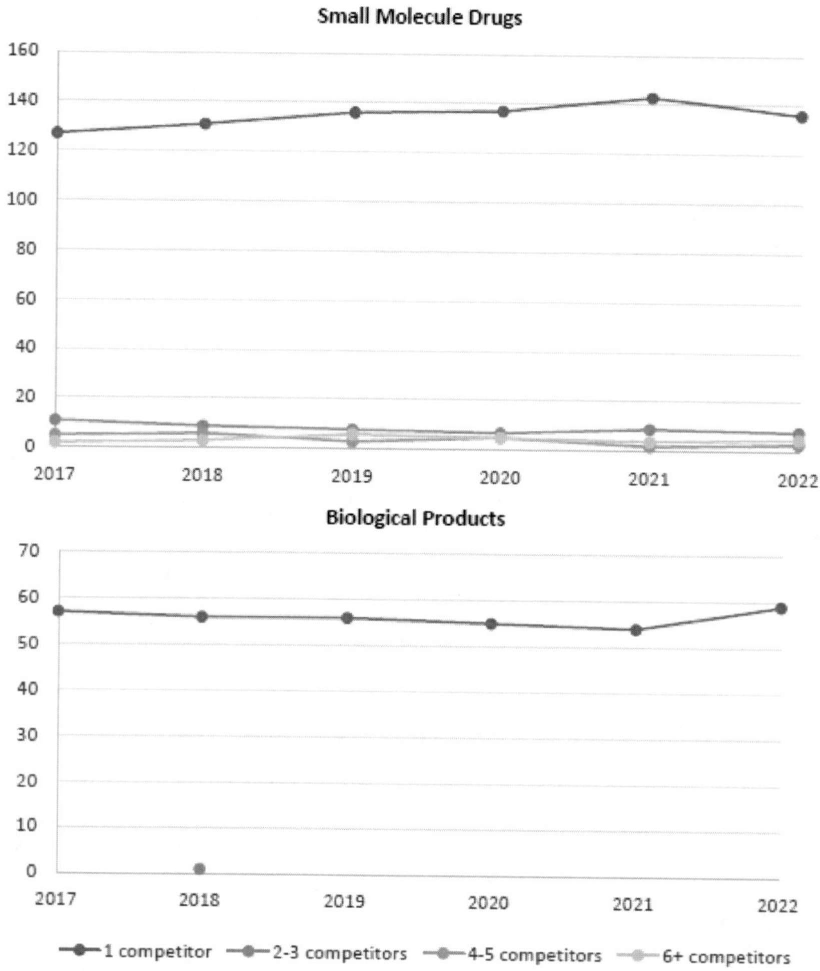

Source: ASPE analysis of IQVIA National Sales Perspective Data.

Figure 5. Number of Manufacturers of the Highest Priced Drugs, 2017-2022.

Figure 6 breaks down the level of competition by total revenue and total molecules in 2022 among the highest priced, small molecule drugs (we did not examine biological products, since there was no competition). We observed that the 89 percent of small molecule drugs with only one manufacturer accounted for 86 percent of revenues. The other competition categories each accounted for fewer than 9 percent of revenues and molecules.

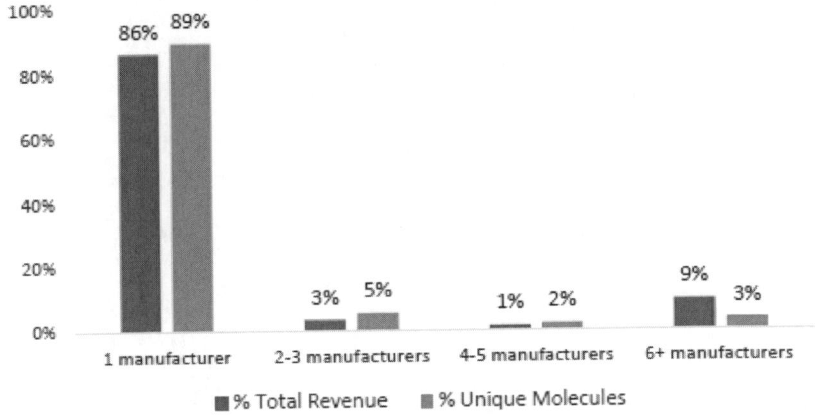

Source: ASPE analysis of IQVIA National Sales Perspective Data.

Figure 6. Percent of Total Revenue and Unique Molecules Based on the Level of Competition for the Highest Priced Drugs, 2022.

Therapeutic Classes

Our final analysis was to characterize the types of drugs that have the highest spending. Figure 7 shows the therapeutic classes associated with the highest priced drugs. The therapeutic classes that are most common were enzyme inhibitors (68 drugs), immunomodulators (21 drugs), antineoplastic monoclonal antibodies (20 drugs), miscellaneous class (14 drugs), miscellaneous antineoplastics (9 drugs), and other neurological/ neuromuscular (9 drugs). Enzyme inhibitors suppress a chemical reaction from occurring in the body. Common examples include methotrexate (used in chemotherapy and to treat rheumatic arthritis) and protease inhibitors that are used to treat HIV/AIDS. Immunomodulators and antineoplastic monoclonal antibodies are typically used to treat cancer. Immunomodulators are most commonly used to treat multiple myeloma. Some examples are thalidomide (Thalomid), lenalidomide (Revlimid), and pomalidomide (Pomalyst). Antineoplastic monoclonal antibodies treat a variety of cancers, including breast, gastric, kidney, cervical, endometrial, colon, lung, head and neck, and brain cancer, multiple myeloma, acute myeloid leukemia, and melanoma, and osteoporosis.

Examples include Bevacizumab (Avastin), daratumumab (Darzalex), trastuzumab (Herceptin), and nivolumab (Opdivo). The "miscellaneous" and "other" categories include a wide swath of drugs used within a general class.

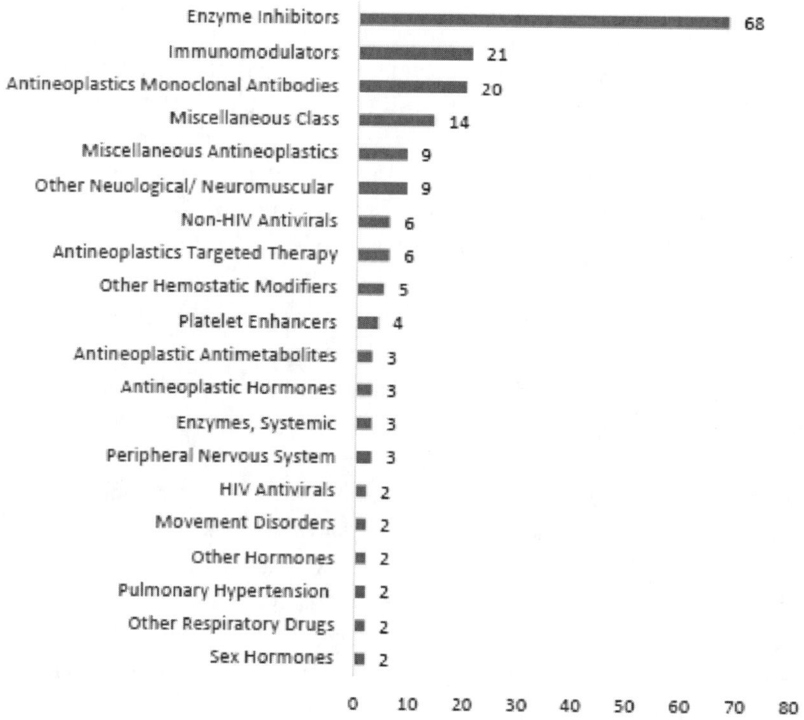

Source: ASPE analysis of IQVIA National Sales Perspective Data.

Notes: Among the top 10 percent of drugs based on price, the following classes had 1 drug each which are not represented in the figure: Systemic Antiarthritics, Gout Specified Antiarthritic, Anticoagulants, Coagulants, Other Systemic Anti-infectives, Antimalarials, Other Gastrointestinal, Other Genitourinary, Bile Therapy, Other Cardiac Agents, Alkylating Agents, Antimitotic/ Antimicrotubule, Other Vascular Agents, Cholesterol Red, Other Antihyperlipidemic Agent, Antineoplastic Radiopharmaceuticals, Dermatological Prep, Other, Diabetes, Non-Insulin, Therapeutic Enzyme Stabilizers, Hematinics, Hematopoietic Stem Cell Age, Other Ophthalmic Preps, Antidepressants, Tuberculosis Therapy, and Specific Antagonists.

Figure 7. Therapeutic Classes Represented by the Highest Priced Drugs, 2022.

Conclusion

In this report, we examined the level of competition in small molecule drug and biological product markets. We found that, on average, there was much more competition in small molecule markets, compared to biological product markets. When examining small molecule drugs, 57 percent had at least 2 manufacturers, whereas only 19 percent of biological products had at least 2 manufacturers. However, once we narrowed the market to only specialty drugs and the highest priced drugs, then competition in both markets eroded substantially. Among specialty drugs, 63 percent of small molecule drugs and 87 percent of biological products had only a single manufacturer. Finally, when examining only the highest priced drugs (i.e., those in the top 10 percent of spending per prescription), we found that 11 percent of small molecule drugs and 0 percent of biological products had at least 2 manufacturers.

There are several limitations to our analysis. IQVIA is a national, all-payer database. The advantage of this data is that we have the broadest picture of the U.S. prescription drug market to determine levels of competition.

However, by not being able to observe payer type, we cannot examine how different plans may use their bargaining power to employ formularies or utilization management tactics. For example, it may be possible for larger insurance companies with greater volumes of prescriptions to negotiate for larger discounts in exchange for preferred placement on their formulary; however, the downside is that such tactics can restrict access to drugs. This means that patients may experience even more or less competition in the prescription drug market than we observed in our data. Relatedly, we do not know the cost sharing structure of those plans either. As a result, we cannot examine the costs borne by patients via copays or coinsurance for drugs resulting from low competition.

Another limitation relates to how we count the number of competitors - our methodology cannot adjust for the more nuanced effect of how large or aggressive a competitor may be. In our analysis, all competitors are treated equally, so further research is warranted to examine whether different types of market entrants result in a differential effect on the price and volume of drugs sold. Finally, we define competition based on an active ingredient, rather than examining therapeutic competition, which would be a more expansive definition of competition.

Appendix

The variable used to measure the number of prescriptions throughout this report is the "eaches" variable in IQVIA data, which is defined as "the number of single items (such as vials, syringes, bottles, or packet of pills) contained in a unit or shipping package and purchased by pharmacies in a specific time period. An each is not a single pill or dosage of medicine (unless one package consists of a single dose). An each may be the same as a unit if the unit does not subdivide into packages."

The variable used to identify distinct molecules in this report is "combined molecule". This variable treats combination products as distinct, meaning that it will separate combination products from their constituent parts (if those are also sold individually). For example, if there is a product that is just molecule A and a second product that is just molecule B and a third product that is the combination A+B, then there will be 3 separate line items.

We identify competitors based on the "Corporation" variable in IQVIA.

Specialty drugs are defined by IQVIA as products used to treat chronic, rare or complex diseases and that meet 4 or more of the following criteria:

- Initiated and maintained by a specialist
- Generally injectable and/or not self-administered
- Products that require an additional level of care in their chain of custody (i.e., refrigerated, frozen, chemo, biohazard, etc.)
- Expensive (USD $6K annual cost of therapy)
- Unique distribution (e.g., specialty MO, REMS)
- Requires extensive or in-depth monitoring/patient counseling
- Requires reimbursement assistance

Products that clearly meet the above criteria are defined as Specialty. Products that are borderline (e.g. meet three, rather than four criteria) will be brought before IQVIA's Specialty Governance Board for review and final decision.

Appendix Exhibits

The data that created Figure 1 "Number of Competitors for Small Molecule Drugs and Biological Products, 2017- 2022" are:

Small Molecule Drugs

	1 competitor	2-3 competitors	4-5 competitors	6+ competitors	Total
2017	834	309	159	506	1,808
2018	841	280	164	543	1,828
2019	842	278	151	576	1,847
2020	828	291	149	578	1,846
2021	827	295	148	586	1,856
2022	796	298	156	588	1,838
Growth	-4.6%	-3.6%	-1.9%	16.2%	1.7%

Biological Products

	1 competitor	2-3 competitors	4-5 competitors	6+ competitors	Total
2017	166	35	2	6	209
2018	179	35	4	5	223
2019	187	37	5	5	234
2020	193	32	8	6	239
2021	205	36	9	6	256
2022	216	34	12	6	268
Growth	30.1%	-2.9%	500.0%	0.0%	28.2%

The data that created Figure 3 "Number of Competitors for Specialty Drugs, 2017-2022" are:

Small Molecule Drugs

	1 competitor	2-3 competitors	4-5 competitors	6+ competitors	Total
2017	230	50	18	49	347
2018	243	45	24	62	374
2019	242	45	21	75	383
2020	250	54	20	77	401
2021	269	53	18	84	424
2022	273	51	26	84	434
Growth	18.7%	2.0%	44.4%	71.4%	25.1%

Biological Products

	1 competitor	2-3 competitors	4-5 competitors	6+ competitors	Total
2017	114	16	2	4	136
2018	124	15	3	4	146
2019	132	17	4	4	157
2020	138	13	6	5	162
2021	150	13	7	5	175
2022	164	12	8	5	189
Growth	43.9%	-25.0%	300.0%	25.0%	39.0%

The data that created Figure 5 "Number of Competitors for the Highest Priced Drugs, 2017-2022" are:

Small Molecule Drugs

	1 competitor	2-3 competitors	4-5 competitors	6+ competitors	Total
2017	127	11	5	2	145
2018	131	9	6	3	149
2019	136	8	3	6	153
2020	137	7	5	5	154
2021	143	9	2	4	158
2022	136	8	3	5	152
Growth	7.1%	-27.3%	-40.0%	150.0%	4.8%

Biological Products

	1 competitor	2-3 competitors	4-5 competitors	6+ competitors	Total
2017	57	-	-	-	57
2018	56	1	-	-	57
2019	56	-	-	-	56
2020	55	-	-	-	55
2021	54	-	-	-	54
2022	59	-	-	-	59
Growth	3.5%	-	-	-	3.5%

U.S. Department of Health And Human Services

Office of the Assistant Secretary for Planning and Evaluation

200 Independence Avenue SW, Mailstop 434E Washington, D.C. 20201
For more ASPE briefs and other publications, visit: aspe.hhs.gov/reports

About the Authors

Sonal Parasrampuria is a Social Science Analyst and FDA portfolio lead in the Office of Science and Data Policy in ASPE. Stephen Murphy is an Economist in the Office of Science and Data Policy in ASPE.

Suggested Citation

Parasrampuria, S. and Murphy, S. Competition in Prescription Drug Markets, 2017-2022. Washington, DC: Office of the Assistant Secretary for Planning and Evaluation, U.S. Department of Health and Human Services. December 2023.

Copyright Information

For general questions or general information about ASPE: aspe.hhs.gov/about.

Chapter 4

Litigation Continues Over Use of Contract Pharmacies in 340B Drug Discount Program*

Hannah-Alise Rogers

The 340B Drug Discount Program enables eligible hospitals and other safety net providers to purchase outpatient prescription drugs at discounted prices. The Health Resources and Services Administration (HRSA), an operating division of the U.S. Department of Health and Human Services (HHS), administers the program. In recent years, both legal and policy disagreements have arisen between HHS, drug manufacturers, eligible providers (known as "covered entities"), and other stakeholders about the size of the program, how it should function, and who should benefit from it. For example, disagreements about covered entities' use of retail pharmacies to distribute 340B drugs to patients have led to a number of lawsuits that challenge both the Secretary of HHS's and states' authority to regulate the program.

This Legal Sidebar discusses recent judicial opinions ruling on HHS's and states' ability to regulate the 340B program. The U.S. Court of Appeals for the Third Circuit (Third Circuit) (*Sanofi-Aventis U.S. LLC v. HHS*), the U.S. Court of Appeals for the D.C. Circuit (D.C. Circuit) (*Novartis Pharmaceuticals Corp. v. Johnson*), and the U.S. Court of Appeals for the Eighth Circuit (Eighth Circuit) (*Pharmaceutical Research and Manufacturers of America (PhRMA) v. McClain*) each addressed interpretations of the 340B statute, focusing on the lack of statutory language around contract pharmacy use while addressing different legal questions associated with the same. According to the Third and D.C. Circuits, the statute restricts HHS from taking certain

---

* This is an edited, reformatted and augmented version of Congressional Research Service Publication No. LSB11163, dated Updated May 23, 2024.

In: The Price of Prescription Medicine
Editor: Cornelius Lowery
ISBN: 979-8-90134-014-1

actions to address covered entities' use of contract pharmacies, which has enabled some drug manufacturers to effectively create 340B pricing restrictions for their drugs. The Eighth Circuit, assessing a different legal question, upheld an Arkansas law that prohibited such manufacturer restrictions, finding that the state prohibition was not preempted by the 340B statute.

Background

The 340B statute requires the Secretary of HHS to enter into purchase price agreements (PPAs) with drug manufacturers who participate in federal health care programs. The PPAs require manufacturers to "offer" to sell certain outpatient prescription drugs at a ceiling price, which is calculated based on a statutory formula. The statute provides a list of covered entities that may purchase drugs from manufacturers at the discounted ceiling price, including Federally Qualified Health Centers (FQHCs), Rural Referral Centers, and some hospitals, such as Disproportionate Share Hospitals and Children's Hospitals. Covered entities can generate revenue from 340B (known as "340B savings") by dispensing these lower-cost drugs to patients and receiving list price reimbursement from third-party payers (e.g., insurance companies).

Rather than distributing 340B drugs through their own in-house pharmacies, the majority of covered entities contract with retail pharmacies, known as contract pharmacies, who then sell drugs to patients. In accordance with the statute, 340B drugs may be provided only to patients of covered entities, and the statute prohibits covered entities from receiving duplicate discounts from both Medicaid and 340B. For additional information, see CRS In Focus IF12232, *Overview of the 340B Drug Discount Program*, by Hannah-Alise Rogers.

In summer 2020, some drug manufacturers began announcing restrictions on 340B covered entities that distribute 340B drugs using contract pharmacies. These restrictions vary, but they generally aim to limit covered entities to distribution to one contract pharmacy. Manufacturers say that the restrictions are necessary to prevent duplicate discounting and unlawful distribution of 340B drugs to nonpatients (also known as *diversion*), arguing that such practices have grown more prevalent in recent years and that HRSA does not adequately police them. The restrictions have financial consequences for covered entities, who argue they are now paying more for certain 340B drugs and are unable to generate 340B savings from them. Currently, there are at least 20 manufacturers with such restrictions.

HRSA responded to the restrictions in 2021 by issuing violation letters to manufacturers, informing them that their policies violated the 340B statute and threatening civil money penalties if they continued.

Several manufacturers then sued the agency, claiming it lacked the authority to issue the violation letters because the statute permitted manufacturers to enact such restrictions. Several district court decisions were appealed to the D.C. and Third Circuits as well as the U.S. Court of Appeals for the Seventh Circuit (Seventh Circuit). The Third and D.C. Circuits have issued rulings, discussed below, finding that HHS lacked authority to issue violation letters. The Seventh Circuit has not yet issued a decision. More information about the district court decisions may be found in CRS Legal Sidebar LSB10842, *Courts Evaluate the Role of Contract Pharmacies in the 340B Drug Discount Program*, by Hannah-Alise Rogers.

At the same time that manufacturers were challenging HHS's authority to regulate contract pharmacy use, several states began considering legislation to make it unlawful for drug manufacturers to restrict contract pharmacy use by covered entities within that state. For example, in May 2021, the Arkansas General Assembly enacted Act 1103, which says that manufacturers may not prohibit pharmacies "from contracting [with] or participating with any [covered] entity." PhRMA challenged the state law, arguing that it was preempted by the 340B statute and the Commerce Clause. In December 2022, the district court held that the 340B statute and the Food, Drug, and Cosmetic Act (FDCA) did not preempt the Arkansas law. The Eighth Circuit affirmed this ruling, and its decision is discussed below.

Litigation Concerning HHS's Regulation of Contract Pharmacies: The Third and D.C. Circuits' Decisions

After HHS issued violation letters to several drug manufacturers for restricting access to 340B pricing for covered entities that used contract pharmacies, some manufacturers, including Sanofi-Aventis, AstraZeneca, Novo Nordisk, Novartis, and United Therapeutics, sued the agency to challenge its authority to issue the letters. In the Sanofi-Aventis case, the District Court for the District of New Jersey upheld HHS's action, in part, finding that the drug manufacturer's 340B pricing restriction policy was unlawful; Sanofi appealed, and the government cross-appealed. The Third Circuit's decision on appeal focused on two issues: whether the 340B statute permits drug manufacturers to limit covered entity drug purchases that are distributed by contract pharmacies and whether the statute gives HHS the authority to stop such practices. Similarly, in the Novartis case, the D.C. Circuit reviewed the D.C. District Court's order setting aside HHS's violation letter. The issue on appeal was whether HHS's enforcement letter was "arbitrary, capricious, an abuse of discretion, or otherwise not in accordance with law" under the Administrative Procedure Act.

In reaching its decision in favor of manufacturers, both the Third and D.C. Circuits began by considering the language of the 340B statute. The Third Circuit reasoned that the manufacturers' policies restricting contract pharmacy use were lawful because "[n]o . . . language in Section 340B requires delivery to an unlimited number of contract pharmacies." The D.C. Circuit's opinion further pointed out that the Secretary of HHS "lacks rulemaking authority over the 340B program." Both courts analyzed the statute's specific words, including that manufacturers are required to "offer" to sell 340B drugs, which are "purchased by" covered entities at or below a "ceiling price." The courts observed that the text of the statute did not speak directly to the delivery of drugs to contract pharmacies. The Third Circuit disagreed with HHS's argument that such terms required manufacturers to "offer" to sell and deliver drugs wherever the covered entity demands, holding this argument to be "one giant leap from the text," and observing that "when Congress's words run out, covered entities may not pick up the pen." The D.C. Circuit reached the same conclusion as the Third Circuit, finding that HRSA's position would "produce absurd consequences." The D.C. Circuit reasoned that under ordinary principles of contract law, offers may include price and nonprice terms. As for the statute's silence on contract pharmacies, the D.C. Circuit found that "[s]tatutory silence implies that manufacturers may impose distribution conditions by contract," consistent with the Supreme Court's ruling in Christensen v. Harris County, in which the Court held that a federal employment statute's silence on the imposition of contractual conditions did not implicitly prohibit the conduct.

The circuit courts also looked to the legislative history and overall purpose of the 340B statute, with the Third Circuit observing that "neither calls for a different outcome." With respect to the legislative history, the Third Circuit observed that previous attempts by Congress to amend the 340B statute to reference contract pharmacy use "can support opposite inferences," that either Congress did not want contract pharmacies to be part of the program, or that their use was so widespread that they were unnecessary to mention. The D.C. Circuit similarly disagreed with HRSA that the 340B statute's legislative history, specifically Congress rejecting an amendment that would have limited drug discounts to "on-site pharmacy services," supported a different result. The court stated that even if the "on-site pharmacy" amendment was significant, it "hardly suggests that Congress opted for the opposite extreme of categorically requiring manufacturers to deal with an unlimited number of contract pharmacies."

The courts were likewise unpersuaded by the government's argument that allowing drug manufacturers to limit contract pharmacy usage would "thwart Congress's purpose in enacting Section 340B." For example, the Third Circuit acknowledged that many covered entities would be unable to access 340B discounts without contract pharmacies, as most do not have their own pharmacies in-house. It found that "Congress might have expected that a covered entity without its own in-house pharmacy could instead use one contract pharmacy" but that this was a "far cry" from HHS's position that the statute allows covered entities to use an unlimited number of contract pharmacies. The D.C. Circuit also discussed HRSA's invocation of Justice Scalia's "predicate-act canon" of statutory interpretation, under which a court should disfavor a statutory construction that would frustrate congressional purpose or otherwise render a statute ineffective. The D.C. Circuit said, however, that "wider distribution" of 340B drugs via contract pharmacies "was not necessarily better," and that the agency's prior prohibition on the use of multiple contract pharmacies, which lasted nearly 20 years, "hardly rendered the scheme [of 340B] self- defeating or ineffectual."

The Third Circuit also pointed to other structural clues in the 340B statute to support its holding, citing the subsection of the statute that allows covered entities to contract with "prime vendors" to purchase and distribute drugs. The Third Circuit reasoned that Congress could have included similar language to permit covered entities to contract with outside pharmacies to distribute drugs or could have imposed delivery- related requirements on manufacturers, but it did not do so. The court also cited other language within the Veteran's Health Care Act that enables Department of Veterans Affairs hospitals to access drug discounts that are purchased under "contracting systems." The court presumed that, because the 340B statute did not contain similar language, Congress did not intend for covered entities to contract with outside pharmacies to distribute 340B drugs.

Unlike the Third Circuit, the D.C. Circuit dedicated a portion of its opinion to analyzing the manufacturers' specific conditions on offers to sell drugs to 340B covered entities. For example, one manufacturer's condition is that it will deliver 340B drugs only to a covered entity's in-house pharmacy or a single contract pharmacy; the court observed that such a condition neither "precluded [the manufacturer] from making a bona fide 'offer'" to sell a 340B drug nor increased the requisite 340B ceiling price, in violation of the statute. The court did note, however, that a future, more "onerous" condition "might violate the statute," leaving open a window for future challenges.

Litigation Concerning State Attempts to Regulate Contract Pharmacies: The Eighth Circuit's Decision

PhRMA sued the State of Arkansas after it passed a law that prohibited drug manufacturers from restricting covered entities in the state from accessing 340B pricing when using contract pharmacies to distribute 340B drugs. The district court found that the state law was not preempted by the 340B statute, and PhRMA appealed this ruling to the Eighth Circuit. The issue on appeal concerns whether the 340B statute preempts Arkansas Act 1103, which was intended "to protect contract pharmacy arrangements in Arkansas." In addition to prohibiting manufacturers from disrupting contracts between pharmacies and covered entities, the law also prevents manufacturers from denying 340B pricing to community-based pharmacies in the state that receive 340B drugs for distribution.

The preemption doctrine stems from the Supremacy Clause, which states that federal laws made under the authority of the Constitution are the "supreme Law of the Land." Federal law preempts state law where (1) Congress expressly states its intention to prevent state regulation (express preemption), (2) state law stands as an obstacle to accomplishing the federal law's purpose (obstacle preemption), (3) Congress implicitly occupies the field (field preemption), or (4) where it is impossible to simultaneously comply with state and federal law (impossibility preemption). The Supreme Court has held that "[a] field is occupied when the federal regulatory scheme is so pervasive as to make reasonable the inference that Congress left no room for the States to supplement it." PhRMA argued that Act 1103 is unconstitutional because the 340B Program occupies the field of federal law, it presents an obstacle to drug manufacturers who are attempting to comply with the 340B statute, and it is impossible to comply with both the state law and other federal laws under the FDCA.

The Eighth Circuit ultimately concluded that the 340B statute did not preempt Act 1103. In support of its decision, the Eighth Circuit first highlighted several facts about both the federal program and the state law. It considered the structure of the 340B statute, which it broke into three essential components: (1) capping manufacturer prices; (2) restricting covered entities from engaging in duplicate discounting or diversion; and (3) creating compliance mechanisms for both manufacturers and covered entities. Citing the Third Circuit's decision in *Sanofi Aventis*, the Eighth Circuit observed that "the 340B Program is silent about delivery and distribution of pharmaceuticals to patients." The court noted, however, that "pharmacies are essential, and legally required" for the functioning of the pharmaceutical supply chain, and that they "have always been important participants in delivering 340B drugs to patients." Although retail pharmacies are vital to the functioning of 340B, the court said they are merely "agent[s] of the covered entity," which both purchases and assumes legal responsibility for the drugs. The court then looked at the specific wording of the Arkansas law, observing that its primary focus is the agreements between covered entities and contract pharmacies.

After reviewing the relevant facts, the Eighth Circuit began its analysis with field preemption, quoting a Supreme Court decision holding that field preemption occurs when Congress leaves "no room for the states to supplement" federal law. Noting that the text of the statute does not mention the delivery of drugs, the court found that "Congress's decision not to legislate the issue of pharmacy distribution indicates that Section 340B is not intended to preempt the field." The court further reasoned that Congress was aware that the regulation of pharmacies has traditionally been an issue of state law and thus "Congressional silence on pharmacies in the context of 340B indicates that Congress did not intend to preempt the field." Although the Arkansas law empowers the state to penalize drug manufacturers who refuse to distribute drugs to covered entities' contract pharmacies, the court said this does not interfere with HHS's jurisdiction over the program, which concerns disputes between manufacturers and covered entities regarding pricing of drugs, rather than the distribution of those drugs.

The court further found that the Arkansas law is not unconstitutional due to obstacle preemption, because rather than creating an obstacle to 340B compliance, the Arkansas law "assists in fulfilling the purpose of 340B" by protecting the relationship between contract pharmacies and covered entities and ensuring that covered entities can distribute their drugs to patients. The court concluded that the state law "is simply deterring … manufacturers from interfering with a covered entity's contract pharmacy arrangements," and thus manufacturers could, and indeed have, complied with both the 340B statute and state law.

Finally, the court dismissed PhRMA's impossibility preemption argument that it was impossible to comply with both the state law and the FDCA's REMS provisions, which restrict distribution of certain drugs to ensure public safety. The court observed that covered entities are responsible for meeting REMS requirements, but that "just because a medication is subject to multiple legal requirements does not make it impossible to comply" with state law.

Now that the Eighth Circuit has ruled on the Supremacy Clause and federal preemption issues, litigation will continue on PhRMA's claims that the state law is invalid under the Commerce Clause, which the district court has not yet addressed. PhRMA argues that because the state law will "inevitably regulate commerce wholly outside" of its borders, it should be invalidated under the dormant Commerce Clause doctrine.

Considerations for Congress

Taken together, the Third, D.C., and Eighth Circuit rulings seem to suggest that states may use their authority to regulate pharmacies within their state to address the use of contract pharmacies in the 340B Program, even if HHS cannot do so. According to the Third and D.C. Circuits, the federal government lacks the authority to broadly prevent manufacturers from adopting policies that attempt to restrict covered entities' use of contract pharmacies, but the Eighth Circuit ruling suggests that states may address this problem by legislating on retail pharmacies. Without clarification from Congress on the appropriate role of contract pharmacies in the 340B program, uncertainty over their use may continue. Additionally, the matter could be further complicated if the Seventh Circuit splits from the Third and D.C. Circuits' rulings and finds that the 340B statute does enable HHS to enforce the 340B statute in such a way that would prevent manufacturers from restricting contract pharmacy use. If such a contrary ruling were to occur, HHS may be able to address manufacturers' policies in some states but not in others.

Even assuming that no contradictory rulings are issued, the decisions from the circuit courts did not resolve all facets of the contract pharmacy issue, and disagreements between HHS, drug manufacturers, and 340B covered entities are likely to continue. For example, in its ruling, the Third Circuit did not explicitly resolve the question of how many contract pharmacies a 340B covered entity should be permitted to use, finding HHS's "unlimited number" argument unpersuasive while simultaneously acknowledging that contract pharmacies seem vital to the program and that without them, many covered entities would be unable to generate 340B savings. The Third Circuit reasoned, "Congress might have expected that a covered entity without its own in-house pharmacy could instead use one contract pharmacy. But this is a far cry from the government's current position that covered entities may use an unlimited number of contract pharmacies." Several manufacturers have subsequently interpreted the court's opinion to permit covered entities without a pharmacy in-house to use one contract pharmacy, and HHS has not publicly commented on whether it intends to take any action to try to expand this number. Similarly, the D.C. Circuit suggests that while the statute does not "categorically prohibit manufacturers from imposing conditions" on contract pharmacies and the specific conditions at issue did not violate 340B "on their face," this conclusion "do[es] not foreclose the possibility" that the conditions could violate the 340B statute "as applied in particular circumstances" or that "other, more onerous conditions might violate the statute."

Additionally, in light of the Eighth Circuit's ruling that the 340B statute does not preempt state laws regulating contract pharmacy use, other states may enact similar laws. A number of states considered enacting 340B legislation in 2023, and stakeholders expect a similar trend in 2024. For example, on March 27, 2024, West Virginia became the third state to enact protections for 340B covered entities' use of contract pharmacies. More changes to state law could lead to legal challenges and litigation in other federal district and circuit courts, and conflicting rulings are possible, depending on how those courts rule on the preemption question. Litigation will also continue in the Eighth Circuit, because the district court has not yet ruled on whether the Arkansas law is invalid under the dormant Commerce Clause.

Amidst this litigation, several Members of the 118th Congress have expressed interest in making changes to the 340B statute. For example, in June 2023, a group of six Senators released a letter to stakeholders and the public seeking information on how Congress could "further the original intent of the [340B] program" and strengthen its ability "to support entities serving eligible patients." In February 2024, the group released a discussion draft of a bill to reform the program, along with a supplemental request for information highlighting stakeholder concerns about contract pharmacy use, the prevention of duplicate discounts, transparency issues, and ensuring that drugs are dispensed only to eligible patients. In late 2023 and early 2024, one Senator also requested information from 340B stakeholders, including FQHCs and contract pharmacies, as a part of his investigation into how certain entities generate revenue from the 340B program. Additionally, the House is considering legislation to address contract pharmacy use, such as the PROTECT 340B Act. Further congressional action to address these or other issues could impact the outcome of the litigation and the program as a whole.

Index

Q

R

S